WRITING ABOUT POLITICS AND SOCIETY
THE ESSENTIAL GUIDE FOR STUDENTS

CHARLES EUCHNER

The New American Press

This version of the book was updated in December 2020.

For more information, visit theelementsofwriting.com, email Charles Euchner at cce@awriteratlarge.com, or call (203) 645-6112.

(Last updated January 22, 2022.)

CONTENTS

PART THREE
DEPICTING A PLACE

PART FIVE

EXPLAINING A PROCESS

PART SIX
ANALYZING AN ISSUE

FOREWORD: ABOUT THIS BOOK

When I was a freshman in college, a professor got exasperated with my wordiness and my use of expressions like "It is interesting to note" and "The fact that." Rather than providing a point-by-point critique of my first paper, she suggested that I buy *On Writing Well*, by William Zinsser.

I did and it helped. Zinsser was a proponent of a simple, clear style. Rather than dazzling the reader with a linguistic circus, Zinsser taught, writers should describe things as simple as possible. Use as few words as possible. Use the simplest words possible. Use telling details. Show action. Cut clutter. If you follow these simple dictates, your writing will improve.

Many years later, I taught a class called "Reading and Writing the Essay" at Yale. It turns out that Zinsser had developed that class back in the early 1970s. *On Writing Well* was his effort to distill the lessons of those classes.

In his Yale classes, Zinsser taught writing by teaching reading. Rather than lecturing students about his principles, he gave them essays and asked them to identify the writer's tricks and techniques. He assigned George Orwell, Mark Twain, E.B. White, Joan Didion, Gay Talese, Tom Wolfe, Joseph Mitchell and other masters of the essay and nonfiction narrative. Sometimes, Zinsser read his work aloud in class. Always, he tried to get students to identify the techniques that they could use in their own work.

When I taught at Yale, Zinsser's spirit was still much alive. Fred Strebeigh, who coordinated the program that Zinsser started, insisted that all of the course instructors *teach writing by teaching reading*. Don't lecture, he said. Don't just tell students what to do. Show them how to read critically. Get students to read like a writer, so that *they* could identify the tricks and maneuvers of the masters.

And so week after week, in English 120, my students and I reverse-engineered many of the writers that Zinsser first used in his classes, as well as other old masters (like Frederick Douglass and H.L. Mencken) and more contemporary writers (like Elizabeth Gilbert, Judith Cofer, Paul Fussell, and Shelby Steele). Week by week, we identified specific techniques the students could use to produce better prose.

Students wrote an essay every two weeks: a profile of a person, a description of a place, a description of action, an explanation of a complex process, and an analysis of a controversial issue.

THE PLAN OF ATTACK

This book opens with an explanation of the core skill for all writing: the Golden Rule of Writing. If you can apply this simple imperative, at every level of writing, you will write better and faster, right away.

Then we move into the five kinds of essays:

- **Person**: We start with creating a profile of a person. Why? Because nothing is more compelling and vivid to people as other people. We are, as Truman Capote once remarked, voyeurs. We love gossiping and delving into the character of other people.
- **Place**: Winston Churchill once remarked that first, we make the building, then the building makes us. The setting not only creates a container for a story. It also shapes the characters and everything else in the story.
- **Action**: Life is a series of actions. All day long, we act on the world and get acted upon. And so the next assignment is to describe a simple, isolated set of movements. Any movement that changes the world, in some meaningful way, can be considered an action.
- **Process**: What happens when different actions come together in a coordinated way? When we make actions part of a

process, we show how the world can be coordinated. It could be as simple as tying a shoe or sending a rocket to space.

- **Analysis**: *What causes what*—not just once but over many instances? That's the focus of the analysis. Here, we try to figure out how the world works, not just in isolated moments but on a regular basis. Acting as scientists, we seek to identify how variables interact to produce predictable results.

Most essays, of course, explore more than one of these topics. A profile of a person, for example, often requires descriptions of places and actions. A description of a process often requires profiling a person, describing action, and even analyzing an issue.

The best writers bring all of these skills to whatever they write. For the sake of learning, though, we focus on one skill at a time.

TWO SKILL SETS

Each of the five sections of the book teaches two kinds of skills.

- **Subject skills**: We start with the focus of the essay—*what* we want to explore. Each section starts with two or three chapters on the substance of the essay—people, places, actions, processes, and issues.

- **Mechanical skills**: Then, in two or three "how to" chapters, we explore the skills of composition: sentences and paragraphs, words, grammar, editing, and various matters of style.

As you move through this book, you'll learn about *what* you're writing about—and then *how* to write it.

Ready? Let's get to work.

PART ONE
THE CORE IDEA

Imagine, if you will, a world in which people follow a simple eleven-word lesson.

This lesson is almost universal. Religions and ethical systems across the world embrace this ideal. It is so simple that even small children understand it. And when followed, even imperfectly, it guides people to live well and to take care of each other.

I am talking, of course, of the Golden Rule: "Do under others as you would have them do unto you."

The power of the Golden Rule lies in its call for empathy. When trying to decide whether to commit some act, imagine how you would *feel* if someone else took the action. The Golden Rule is the ultimate lesson in empathy, in caring for others. If we all followed it, the world would be a better place, as the jazz great Louis Armstrong once explained. Critics criticized his song "What a Wonderful Life" as naive, but Armstrong disagreed:

> All I'm saying is, see, what a wonderful world it *would be* if only we'd give it a chance. *Love, baby, love.* That's the secret. Yeah! If lots more of us loved each other, we'd solve lots more problems. And then this world would be a *gasser.*

Under the Golden Rule, we don't have to *love* everyone—we only need to *respect* everyone. That should be easy enough, right?

Now imagine, if you will, another, even simpler imperative to guide writers. This one is just eight words long. It has two parts, each four words. Those two parts are really just statements of the same idea from different angles.

1. Make everything a journey.
2. Start strong, finish strong.

This imperative—which I call the Golden Rule of Writing—will not solve all your problems.

You still need to understand your topic, figure out what to say, and gather ideas and evidence. These and other writing skills take time and effort. Anders Eriksson, a famous Swiss psychologist, estimates that mastery in any skill requires 10,000 hours of deliberate practice.

The Golden Rule of Writing doesn't offer any magic. But it does offer an approach that—if you use it—provides the basic focus and ideal you need to thrive as a writer. If you consciously follow this simple little rule—as you compose and edit sentences and paragraphs, and then organize those pieces into sections and whole pieces—you can't fail.

Here's how to do it …

CHAPTER 1
THE GOLDEN RULE OF WRITING

I don't know where I am going, but I am on my way.

VOLTAIRE

TO GO SOMEPLACE, you need to know your starting point and your destination.

The first time I visited Paris, I arrived to a steady drizzle and a transit strike. I took a cab to the Left Bank but didn't know where to go; I had left my friend's contact information at home. So I schlepped around, getting soggy while carrying two bags. I studied the maps in my *Plan de Paris* and scanned street signs, hoping I would recognize the name of my friend's street. But I didn't. I was lost.

Finally, I got help in a travel agency. An agent found a hotel and told me about nearby restaurants and sights. After I called home to get my friend's contact information, the agent unfolded a map and pointed to my hotel and my friend's apartment. I was just a block and a half away.

Once I knew where I was—and where I was going—everything worked well.

Writing works like that. If you know where you start and finish a journey, you will never get lost or disoriented. Neither will your readers. But if you don't know where you begin and end, you will struggle.

Too often, writers wander without direction, like me on that first answers and evidence. Then weigh the evidence and make a judgment. Finally, you arrive at your destination, which is the answer.

For all kinds of writing, you need to know the following: What do the readers know at the beginning? What do you want them to know by the end? What steps do you need to take to get from one place to the other?

If you can answer these questions, at every level of your stories and descriptions and analysis, your job as a writer will be clear.

Part 2: Start strong, finish strong

Now we get to Part 2 of the Golden Rule: *Start strong, finish strong.* Remember how I got lost in Paris because I didn't know the beginning or ending of my journey? As it turns out, the most important elements of your writing are the starts and finishes.

Research shows that people pay the most attention to the beginnings and endings of things; they are remember the starts and finishes more than what comes in the middle. The beginning marks an interruption of what's been happening, so we notice; the end marks a completion, so we feel a sense of closure. Of course we notice and remember these two moments.

If readers pay most attention to the beginnings and endings, where should writers put their most important ideas? At the starts and finishes, of course. At every level of writing—the sentence, paragraph, –start with a bang and end with a bang. Put at the beginnings and endings.

Rule to all of your challenges, you will

———

ELEMENT 1: MAKE EVERYTHING A JOURNEY

We write in order to show readers something new. We want our readers to experience a story, make an observation, peer at an image, savor a moment, consider an idea, or assess a theory.

And so we take the reader on a journey from one place—or one understanding or experience of the world—to another, different place.

- A storyteller shows the hero's journey from ignorance to enlightenment—or from innocence to corruption.
- A critic takes the reader to insights about a movie or play.
- A scientist takes the reader from a question about a problem to a new understanding that problem's causes or effects.

Every story, every journey, involves *change*. "There ain't no journey what don't change you some," David Mitchell says in *Cloud Atlas*. Whatever the characters, setting, or issues, something changes by the end of the piece.

If everything in writing is a journey, we should be able to map that journey. Just as I can map out my journey from my home in Connecticut to a meeting in Manhattan—drive to New Haven's Union Station, jump on the 8:53 Metro North train to Grand Central Station, take a subway to Greenwich Village, walk five blocks, and so on—I should be able to map out the journey of every unit of writing.

To map a passage, simply draw pictures of the journey. Get out a clean piece of paper. Write down, on one side, the starting point for the journey. Then, on the other side of the paper, write down the ending point. Between those two places, mark the steps you need to get from the starting point to the ending point. If the journey is simple, a straight line will do. If the journey is more complex—if the journey involves detours and wrong turns and meanderings—show that with curves and other deviations from the path.

Very great story provides this kind of journey. Pick up a book or story of any of the best writers you know. Pick a story from Ernest Hemingway or Scott Fitzgerald, Virginia Woolf or V.S. Pritchett, Truman Capote or Tom Wolfe or Joan Didion, Ta-Nehisi Coates or Toni Morrison. You can map the story from beginning to end. You will see a clear journey—often with some zigs and zags, tension and struggle, along the way—from one state of being to another, different state of being.

CASE STUDY: BRENT STAPLES'S 'BLACK MEN AND PUBLIC SPACE'

Growing up in Chester, Pennsylvania, in the 1960s, Brent Staples confronted the dangers of poverty and violence first-hand. But he managed to escape the pathologies of the street. Here, he describes how:

> As a boy, I saw countless tough guys locked away; I have since buried several, too. They were babies, really—a teenage cousin, a brother of 22, a childhood friend in his mid-20s—all gone down in episodes of bravado played out in the streets. I came to doubt the virtues of intimidation early on. I chose, perhaps unconsciously, to remain a shadow—timid, but a survivor.

Let's map Staples's journey. The journey begins with Staples as a boy. Why there? Staples wants to show us an unformed person who is open to all the possibilities of life but also innocent and vulnerable. Surrounded by the dangers and temptations of the streets, anything can happen.

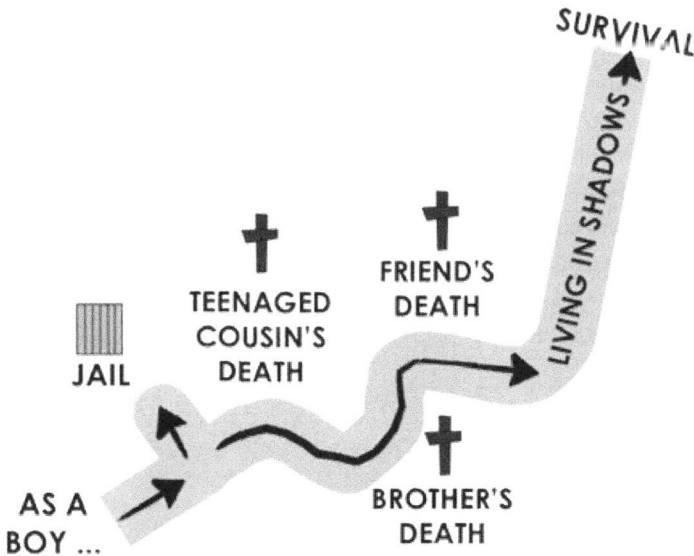

So what happened with young Brent Staples? He witnessed

day in Paris. Struggling to get their bearings, uncertain what ideas and evidence matter, they meander without purpose. If asked where they want to take the reader, they talk about a bunch of topics and ideas. But they do not state, clearly, where they want to take the reader.

Part 1: Make everything a journey

To guide writing, at every, level, I propose Part 1 of the Golden Rule: *Make everything a journey.* Make sure you know exactly where where you want to take your readers and how you want to get them there. In every sentence, paragraph, section, and whole piece, take your reader from one point to another, different point.

Be clear about this journey. What's the point of the journey? Maybe you want to tell a story. If so, what kind of characters do you want to follow? Where are they? What do they want? How do they seek it— and what kinds of barriers do they face? That's the journey.

Or maybe the point of your piece is to describe an idea or a process. Again, what's the point? Don't talk in general terms. Get specific. Who or what, specifically, is the focus? When and where does this take place? Why are they acting the way they do and how do they do it? Define your terms. Explain the context and why it matters. Describe the journey, step by step. Know where you want to begin and where you want to end. Then figure out the steps that get you there.

To get focused, label the journey. See if you can spot the stories behind these one-line descriptions: *An injured photographer suspects a neighbor of murdering his wife. A Midwestern girl joins three friends to get home, by way of a wizard's magic powers. A cynical nightclub owner must decide whether to fight the Nazis or reclaim his lover. A jaded TV weatherman must relive his least-favorite day, over and over, until he discovers his truest self.*

(These are descriptions of *Rear Window, The Wizard of Oz, Casablanca,* and *Groundhog Day.)*

Maybe you want to analyze an issue and make an argument. Start with a question or a puzzle, which takes this basic format: *What causes what?* For example: *What causes poverty in rural areas? What causes school success? What causes entrepreneurship? What causes success in Major League Baseball?* Then think of the journey you need to explore and explain your mystery. Start with questions. Then explore some possible

Think about your own experiences in life. We remember best the first and last parts of any experience. We remember the beginnings and endings of songs, books, movies, and events. What happens in the middle matters too, of course. But the beginnings and endings frame the whole experience.

Research shows that people pay the most attention to the beginnings and endings of things. Even words we apprehend by paying closest attention to the beginnings and endings. Let me give you a simple example. Read this paragraph:

> You can udnrestnad the paassge eevn touhgh I hvae srcmblaed all the mddile ltteres of the wdros. To udnrstnead even splime wrdos, we uallusy jsut need the bgnneigns and ednngis of tsohe wrdos. Azamnig!

I bet you understood that whole passage—even if you read it quickly—because the beginnings and endings of the words gave you most of the information you needed. In microseconds, you apprehended the first and last letters of the words. That was usually enough to know the word. When it wasn't, you quickly scanned the letters in the middle. Accessing your vast knowledge of vocabulary, you made sense of even the most scrambled words.

We understand all levels of writing—sentences, paragraphs, sections, and whole pieces—by glancing at the beginnings and endings. To understand why, let's explore the three parts of all journeys.

Start Strong

In the beginning, we invite the reader into our journey.

Usually, that means telling the reader, right away, *who does what*. When the reader knows the subject right away—the focus, the point of it all—she can understand whatever follows. So we might say:

- *Reagan looked out* at the crowd …
- *Macbeth expressed doubt* …

These simple passages bring the reader into the action, right away. Without delay, the reader learns exactly what's happening, who does what, without any confusion.

All too often, we writers wander before getting to the point. We provide background information, define terms, and explain possible objections before saying a word about who does what. Pick up any newspaper, magazine, or book and find a dozen random passages. How long does the writer take to get to the subject and verb? I wouldn't be surprised if some sentences wandered for a dozen or more words before getting to the point. I have seen sentences meander for 40 or even 50 words before stating who does what. Almost always, that's too much.

Of course, starting every single sentence with a subject and verb might get tedious. Also, sometimes it makes sense to provide a brief setup—some context—before stating the subject and verb. So you might "start strong" like this:

- *Before uttering his historic lines*, Reagan looked out at the crowd …
- *Appalled by the murder plans*, Macbeth resisted his wife's plans…

These openings offer important context, so we can understand the meaning of the action that follows. Still, they don't take too long. Each uses just five words before getting to the subject.

Finish Strong

Whatever we do in life, we need a sense of closure and completion. We need to know how something "turns out." So we feel great satisfaction when a writer clinches a point—and unease when a writer fails to so so. Therefore, at the end of every sentence, paragraph, section, and piece, give the reader a sense of closure. Complete your thought. Like this:

- Reagan looked out at the crowd and challenged Gorbachev to *"tear down this wall."*
- Macbeth expressed doubt about killing Duncan, prompting Lady Macbeth to *question his manhood.*

These sentences end with a bang—Reagan's challenge to Mikhail

Gorbachev and Lady Macbeth's challenge to her husband. Each comes like a thunderbolt.

You can "finish strong" by raising a question or offering an intriguing image. Questions and images activate the reader's mind—and help propel the piece forward, to the next sentence, paragraph, or section. Look at these two possible conclusions:

- Reagan looked out at the crowd at the Berlin Wall, not knowing *whether Mikhail Gorbachev would make good on his promise of reform.*
- Macbeth, troubled by the plan, *stammered and paced before his stern wife.*

Both of these endings create suspense, making the reader want to read on.

Bridges and Brackets in the Middle

If the beginnings and endings frame the journey, the middle material offers the pathway. The middles offer two kinds of information, which I call *bridges* and *brackets*.

Let's start with bridges. Bridges take the reader, step by step, from the beginning to the end of the passage. These two sentences, for example, offer a pathway for the reader's journeys:

- Reagan looked out at the Berlin crowd, *gauging the mood of the crowd and pausing for effect,* then challenged Gorbachev to "tear down this wall."
- When Macbeth *expressed doubt about killing Duncan, professed his love for the king, raised qualms about the witches, and expressed fears about a bloody civil war,* Lady Macbeth questioned his manhood.

In these passages, you can almost see the steps on the path. Reagan *looked, gauged, paused,* and *challenged.* Macbeth *expressed, professed, raised* and *expressed.*

Now, consider the other way that we fill the middles: the bracket. Think of the bracket as an aside. Sometimes we need to provide notes, extra information that helps us to understand the situation. We might want to provide the source of the information, for example. Many readers don't care about the sources, but specialists and skeptics do care because they want to assess whether the information is credible.

See how these two sentences "bracket" sources in the middle:

- Reagan looked out at the crowd feeling upbeat, *according to aides who sat near him on the podium,* and challenged Gorbachev to "tear down this wall."
- Macbeth expressed doubt about killing Duncan, in Act I, Scene 7, prompting Lady Macbeth to question his manhood.

The brackets here—"according to aides" and "in Act I, Scene 7"—provide the sources of information. For readers who want to assess the passage's credibility or simply get more detail, the middle chunks provide a place to go.

Many readers skim over the middles. Some readers don't care about the steps needed to get from the start job the finish. And even more readers don't care about source information. In fact, you could delete the middles from most well-built sentences and paragraphs and still convey the main idea. But for readers who *do* care about this information, it's there.

Strong starts and finishes are essential for every level of writing. With them, you have the bones of a good piece of writing. Without them, you are doomed.

CASE STUDY: YUVAL NOAH HARARI, *21 LESSONS FOR THE 21ST CENTURY*

Yuval Noah Harari has became a literary sensation in recent years with his trilogy on Big History. His first book, *Sapiens,* traces the history of humans from prehistory to the present. His followup work, *21 Lessons for the 21st Century*, offers insights into the challenges we face in this era. His third book, *Homo Deus,* explores how humans will develop with artificial intelligence in the coming years.

Harari's narratives distill the human experience a few pages at a time. He offers bracing views of human nature and the real-world workings of politics, economics, society, science, and religion. But even more important, his writing is spare and clear. Consider this passage:

Truth and power can travel together only so far. Sooner or later they go their separate ways. If you want power, at some point you will have to spread fictions. If you want to know the truth about the world, at some point you will have to renounce power. You will have to admit things —for example about the sources of your own power—that will anger allies, dishearten followers or undermine social harmony. Scholars throughout history faced this dilemma: do they serve power or truth? Should they aim to unite people by making sure everyone believes in the same story, or should they let people know the truth even at the price of disunity? The most powerful scholarly establishments— whether of Christian priests, Confucian mandarins or communist ideologues—placed unity above truth. That's why they were so powerful.

This passage—like just about any passage you will find in Harari's books—moves with energy and purpose. Every sentence is a shot of truth, delivered straight. Look at how each sentence starts strongly:

> *Truth and power can travel ...*
> *Sooner or later ...*
> *If you want power ...*
> *If you want to know ...*
> *You will have to admit ....*
> *Scholars throughout history faced ...*
> *Should they aim ...*
> *The most powerful ...*
> *That's why ...*

In five of these sentences, Harari starts with the action (subject and verb): *Truth and power..., You will..., Scholars... The most powerful..., That's...* In the other four, Harari quickly sets up the action: *Sooner or later..., If you want..., If you want..., Should they aim...*

Harari's sentences also end strongly:

> *... only so far.*
> *... separate ways.*
> *... spread fictions.*
> *... renounce power.*
> *... undermine social harmony.*
> *... serve power or truth?*

... at the price of disunity?
... unity above truth.
... so powerful.

Look closely and you will see that Harari describes abstract ideas with images of physical space four times (*so far, separate, spread*, and *above*), action three times (*renounce, undermine*, and *serve*), and images three times (*disunity, unity*, and *powerful*).

You cannot do any better than to imitate Yuval Noah Harari's prose style. If you want to writer longer, more complicated sentences, go ahead. But start with Harari's strong core.

––––––

ELEMENT 3: TAKE THE LANDSCAPE VIEW

To apply the Golden Rule of Writing, I have devised a simple technique that I call the Landscape View. Here's what to do:

1. Use the landscape (horizontal) format for all your documents.
2. Write one sentence per line.
3. Single-space your document.
4. Type two spaces at the end of each line.
5. Skip a space between paragraphs.

I developed the Landscape View when I was teaching writing at Yale. Over the course of one semester, my students and I explored the Golden Rule. The students understood the concept; that was no problem. Together, we parsed sentences, broke down paragraphs, and analyzed essays and books. The students vowed to "start strong, finish strong" at all levels of their writing. But just as soon as they made this vow, they slipped back into old habits. They didn't start or end strongly.

One day, desperate for a simple way to guide their writing, I came up with the Landscape View. I required students to do an assignment using this format. Their writing improved dramatically, right away. In fact, from that point on, my students never wrote a sentence that I struggled to understand. Not only that, they wrote with greater energy and creativity than before.

Why does the Landscape View work so well? We discovered five benefits:

1. Checking starts and finishes: With the Landscape View, you can easily check to see whether you start and finish strongly. Just run your finger down the left side of the page, line by line, to see if you start strongly. Run your finger down the right side to see if you end strongly. Finally, run your finger down the middle of the page to check for bridges and brackets.

If you start or end weakly, you usually know what to do right away. Sometimes you need just a minor fix, like clarifying the subject and verb. Sometimes you need to recast the whole sentence. Sometimes, you need to delete the sentence. Whatever needs fixing, it's easy to find the problems because every sentence starts on the left side of the page.

Can't we check sentences in the standard blocks of text? Sure, but we usually don't. Even if we intend to check the starts of the sentences, we usually stop trying after two or three paragraphs. It just takes too much effort when the sentences are packed into blocks of text. The brain, as researchers tell us, is *lazy*. If you ask the brain to do too many things, it will falter. The Landscape View makes it easier to find the beginnings of sentences—and, therefore, to check to see if they start strongly.

2. Controlling sentence length: The landscape format helps to monitor sentence length. Using the TimesRoman font, with 12-point type, you get about 20 to 24 words per line with the landscape format. Research shows that readers best comprehend sentences that average 17 to 19 words. It's easy to see when you exceed that length.

Oldtimers remember old-fashioned typewriters that sounded a bell at the end of every line, signaling the need to return the carriage. The end of every line should ring a bell in your head, signaling you to ask: *Should this sentence be so long? Or should I recast it or break it up?*

Inevitably, your sentences will vary in length; some will be more and some will be less than the average. If your sentence runs onto a new line, that's OK; it's fine to write sentences of 30, 40, or even more words. If a sentence runs long, just make sure you *need* all those words to make your point. Make sure that one long sentence conveys your ideas better than two or three shorter sentences would. Make sure you're writing long sentences *on purpose*.

3. Varying sentence length: The Landscape View also shows, instantly, whether you vary sentence length.

Why does this matter? Reading a piece with all short sentences creates a dreadful rat-a-tat-tat. And reading a piece with all long sentences feels endless droning. So to keep the reader engaged, make an effort to vary your sentence lengths. Write three to five short sentences, then two or three longer sentences, then swing back to short sentences, and so on.

Varying sentence length also helps to pace your writing. Short sentences create a sense of action, movement, and suspense. Longer sentences offer a more relaxed, reflective mood, where the reader can explore the different aspects of an issue without rushing. It's also demanding on your reader's time, attention, and effort.

4. Focusing on sentences, line by line: The one-sentence-per-line rule does something even more powerful. It forces you to pay attention to each sentence. It gives every sentence *integrity.*

When my students turned in their first papers using the Landscape View, a student named Jessica smiled and said: "It looks like *poetry.*" And it does. In poetry, of course, every line matters. The line-by-line system forces us to pay attention to each sentence as if it's a line of poetry. That's good, because the sentence is the most important unit of writing. As I said before, if you can write a good sentence, you can write anything—but it you can't, you're doomed.

Academic researchers actually discovered the power of the line-by-line approach more than a century ago. In a 1901 study of the rhythm and format of language, research subjects read poetry and prose. When they read prose passages with the line-by-line format, they thought they were reading poetry. When they saw those passages packed into standard paragraphs, they thought they were reading prose. Here's why it matters: They paid greater attention when they used the line-by-line approach. As writers, we need to pay close attention to every line we write.

5. Checking paragraphs: Can the Landscape View help us write better paragraphs, too? And better whole pieces? Yes and yes.

Since we can easily spot the first and last phrases of the paragraphs, we can check whether the "journey" begins in one clear place and ends in another, different place. And we can assess whether all the middle lines offer the brackets and bridges we need—sources and attribution, steps and context—to get from the beginning to the end.

The Landscape View offers a simple, effective mechanism to test the basic elements of writing. Once you write a draft, you can easily check whether you start and end strongly—not just sentence by sentence, but also paragraph by paragraph.

A Danger

When you think too much about a process, you tend to get self-conscious. It's kind of like the golf fan who asks the pro: Do you breathe in or out when you start your backswing? Thinking too much about form upsets the golfer's focus and flow.

Writers face the same problem when they are writing drafts. If we think too much when we craft a sentence, we get distracted and freeze. We fall out of our natural, creative rhythm. We lose sight of what we want to say. We lose access to the powers of our subconscious thought. As a result, we write badly.

The solution is simple: *Don't think too much about the Golden Rule as you write your first draft*. Line by line, just write one sentence after another. Don't worry about journeys or starting and ending strongly. *Just get your ideas down on paper, line by line.*

Use the Golden Rule—*later*—to make sure you start and end strongly. The Landscape View's greatest benefit comes with the editing process. The format makes it easy to check the beginnings, endings, and middles *after you have written them.* Only after you have drafted a section, check the lines.

Here's where the magic comes in. Over time, by composing one line at a time, you'll internalize the imperatives of the Golden Rule. When you edit a passage using the Golden Rule, you'll burn the skill into your brain. Writing strong sentences will become almost automatic.

How can you internalize the Golden Rule even faster? I tell students to use the Landscape View when writing emails. Most recipients of these emails won't notice anything funky about the format. But by composing your emails, line by line, you will rewire your brain to write well. You will make it second nature.

Researchers call this process "deliberate practice." When you repeat an action, intently, you rewire you brain. Actions that at first require attention become automatic. By intently practicing the Golden Rule, using the Landscape View, you will make a habit of crafting strong sentences and paragraphs.

The Landscape View will improve your writing even if you are a seasoned writer. This approach focuses your attention on what matters —on sentences, lengths, variety, beginnings and endings. It also offers a *process* for editing. By using the Landscape View, you will write with the clarity and energy that your readers deserve.

CASE STUDY: APPLYING THE LANDSCAPE VIEW

Take a look at the image, which explains and models the use of the Landscape View. See how easy it is to check whether you start strong? And whether you finish strong? And whether the material in the middle offers a bridge or bracket from beginning to end? And see how quickly you can tell whether you vary sentence length? And whether your sentences run longer than 20 words?

Finally—most important—do you see how easy it will be to fix what ails your sentences and paragraphs? When you find a clunker at the beginning of a line, you know right away. Usually, you will know how to fix it right away. That's the power of the Landscape View. Use it and you will never write a bad sentence again.

For most readers, you probably need to format your test in standard paragraph blocks. Once you have produced and edited your drafts, then you can convert your final draft from the Landscape View to the traditional block paragraph format. It's easy. Just follow three steps:

1. When you're ready to convert, go to the FIND and REPLACE functions of your Word document.
2. In the FIND area, type two spaces and then the symbol for paragraph (^p).
3. In the REPLACE area, type two spaces. Hit the RETURN key.

Voila, you have now converted from the Landscape View to the block format.

To convert the block format to the line format, do this:

1. When you're ready to convert, go to the FIND and REPLACE functions of your Word document.
2. In the FIND area, type two spaces.
3. In the REPLACE area, type two spaces and then the symbol for paragraph (^p). Hit the RETURN key.

Voila! Now you have covered from the block format to the Landscape View.

Remember: You must type two spaces at the end of every sentence for this formatting trick to work.

The Landscape View offers a tool to managing the writing process so that you can follow Ernest Hemingway's famous advice: "Write with your heart and edit with your brain." Once you get words onto the screen, you have a foolproof tool for checking them. That's important; after all, as Joyce Carol Oates notes, "all writing is editing." Only in the editing process can we turn substandard work into good work—and good work into great work. The Landscape View offers a priceless tool for that.

When you use the Golden Rule—with the help of the Landscape View—your writing will not only be clear. It will have purpose and power. Your sentences and paragraphs will be mini-dramas that move briskly. You will own the reader along, from the beginning to the end.

—————

AND ANOTHER THING ...

The Landscape View offers a whole new approach to the two core levels of writing, the sentence and paragraph. Once you use this format, everything changes. Whenever you sit down to write, you will be guided to give the reader a journey—with clear beginnings, middles, and ends—and not just spit out a bunch of facts and ideas.

A few years after developing the Golden Rule and Landscape View, I discovered *Several Short Sentences About Writing*, a book by a newspaper editor named Verlyn Klinkenborg. The book illustrates both the power and peril of the line-by-line approach.

The book is an essay on writing, written in a poetic, line-by-line format. Some lines are complete sentences; others are just fragments and phrases. By using this simple format, Klinkenborg forces the reader to pay close attention to every line. Here's how he describes his experiment:

> *Imagine it this way:*
> *One by one, each sentence takes the stage.*
> *It says the very thing that it comes into existence to say.*
> *Then it leaves the stage.*
> *It doesn't help the next one up or the previous one down.*
> *It doesn't wave to its friends in the audience*
> *Or pause to be acknowledged or applauded.*
> *It doesn't talk about what it's saying.*
> *It simply says its piece and leaves the stage.*

Klinkenborg's experiment sparks some magic. But we also lose something in this process. It's too choppy. These short lines do not offer the kind of *flow* that most readers want and need. Although writers should construct each sentence with care—as Klinkenborg does here—readers want forward movement. They want to glide, effortlessly, from sentence to sentence and from paragraph to paragraph.

Use the Landscape View as a guide, but don't fetishize the lines. Make sure you keep the reader moving. Let's leave the final word on this topic to George Saunders, one of the best stylists of our time. In his masterful work *A Swim in a Pond in the Rain*, he describes how an editor said he knows he likes a story: "Well, I read a line. And I like it … enough to read the next."

Every line matters, but so does the forward movement of one line to the next. Don't just write a set of choppy lines. Create a sense of excitement and purpose as you move through the piece, paragraph by paragraph, section by section.

MODELING THE GOLDEN RULE OF WRITING

Start Strong	Bridges or Brackets	Finish Strong

To write well, make *everything a journey*—every sentence, paragraph, section, or whole piece.
Start in one distant place and finished in another, different place.
Make sure the journey shows important change.
Make sure the steps along the way lead to the end.

How do you ensure a meaningful journey?
Start strong and finish strong.
Right just one sentence per line; when finished, hit the return key.
Then write a new sentence.
Skip a space to separate paragraphs.

So what does "start strong" mean?
Usually, as your default approach, tell the reader, right away, who does what.
Sometimes, to start strong means to provide an important setup.
Tell the reader, in other words, essential information to make sense of everything that follows.

So what does "finish strong" mean?
It means one of two things.
Whenever possible, complete your thought.
Otherwise, leave the reader with an powerful question or image.
Satisfy or intrigue the reader, line by line, as you move the piece forward

The middle of a passage connects the beginning and the end.
As a bridge, the middle shows the reader the steps needed to get from the beginning to the end.
As a bracket, the middle offers asides with important background information or attributions.

The Landscape View helps to focus on what matters—and to fix problems without too much unnecessary work.
Rather than searching dense blocks of type, you can run your finger down the left and right sides of the page to find the beginnings and endings of sentences.

The Landscape View also displays, at a glance, whether you offer a mix of longer and shorter sentences.
Since a typical word document allows 20 to 24 words per line, you can also see when your sentences might be getting too long.
Above all, the Landscape View teaches us to make writing decisions consciously.

PART TWO
PORTRAYING PEOPLE

"A wonderful fact to reflect upon," Charles Dickens once remarked, is "that every human creature is constituted to be that profound secret and mystery to every other."

And, he might have added, *to himself.*

The ancient Greeks challenged us to "know thyself." But that's not so easy. People are inscrutable. We are strangers to each other and to ourselves. We regularly misconstrue each other's motivations and abilities. If only we had a process for *understanding* people better.

Your first job as an essayist is to do just that: to understand a person and put that understanding into words.

Writing provides a wonderful discipline for studying people. When we write, we learn to observe carefully and then arrange our observations and knowledge into some kind of recognizable portrait. That portrait usually begins with outward appearances—she is tall and thin, with a birthmark on her hip and an athlete's body, and so on—and then moves inward. As we get to know someone, we explore what lurks beneath. We explore the person's experiences, knowledge, hopes and fears, strengths and biases.

Creating a portrait is a psychological excavation. To understand someone, we have to dig deep. We have to move into the past to discover a person's true character. We have to explore their deepest and darkest secrets, hidden motivations, triumphs and failures, injuries and fears, and narratives and prejudices.

Understanding people is not just essential to the essayist's art. It is also a skill that we need for our everyday lives, as parents and family members, friends and neighbors, students and teachers, professionals and customers, strangers on a train and elsewhere.

Our goal here is to get to understand what makes people "click." Who are they? Where they come from? What they want? How can we understand their history and psychology? What are their contradictions? What are their desires?

If you can describe people, with accuracy and heart, you can understand the underlying challenges of politics. That's not enough—but it's a great start.

THE PLAN OF ATTACK

In this section, we will focus first on mastering two *subject skills*. First, we'll learn everything we can about the subject of our portrait. Then we will put the character into action.

- Chapter 2: Character
- Chapter 3: Narrative

Then we will learn two *mechanical* skills of writing:

- Chapter 4: Sentences
- Chapter 5: Words

Once we master these skill sets, we will have a strong foundation for a broad range of writing challenges. We can build on this foundation, step by step.

CHAPTER 2
CHARACTERS

It begins with a character, usually, and once he stands up on his feet and begins to move, all I can do is trot along behind him with a paper and pencil trying to keep up long enough to put down what he says and does.

WILLIAM FAULKNER

IN THE SUMMER OF 1968, after graduating from Macalester College, Tim O'Brien came home to find a draft notice in his mailbox. As a college activist, O'Brien had demonstrated against the Vietnam War and worked for Eugene McCarthy's presidential campaign. He agonized over whether to report for military service or flee to Canada.

All summer O'Brien worked in a pig factory in Minnesota. He blasted grapefruit-sized clots of blood from the carcasses that passed on a moving line overhead.

As the date of his military induction approached, O'Brien got in a car and drove north, stopping just south of the Canadian border. An old man put him up in a cottage for six days. One day the two went out on a boat to fish. As they sat with their lines in the water, O'Brien realized he could leap out and swim to Canada. But at that moment, he decided to report for military duty. He started crying—not because of a fear of war, but because he realized that he was too cowardly *not to fight* a war he considered immoral.

As he tells the story in *The Things They Carried*, O'Brien journeys from a state of fear to a state of cowardly commitment. As O'Brien ponders his lack of nerve at the lake, he remembers his boyhood ideals: "Tim O'Brien: a secret hero. The Lone Ranger." He fell terribly short of his childhood ideals.

Years later, Tim O'Brien told a different story to a group of students at Brown University. "All I could tell you," O'Brien said, "was that I played golf and I worried about getting drafted."

The Tim O'Brien who wrote the book was not the same Tim O'Brien who was a character in the book. So which one was more real? On one level, O'Brien told the "true" story to the students at Brown. But to relate the larger truths of his Vietnam experience—to tell a "truer" story—O'Brien fictionalized his story. He embellished his story to reveal larger truths about youth and innocence and war.

You will do the same with every character you create, fictional or real. All characters are creations. Whether we take "real life" figures like Julius Caesar, Napoleon Bonaparte, or Tim O'Brien—or fictional characters like Huck Finn, Lisbeth Salander, or Tim O'Brien—all characters are creations of the author. The author gathers piles of information about his character, sorts it, discards most of it, and creates a character to reveal some truth about life.

Could O'Brien have told a more factually accurate tale? Of course. Even if the real Tim O'Brien was not as colorful as his novel's hero, his character still had plenty of intriguing qualities. Even if the real O'Brien falls short as a dramatic character, the author could use great stories about his fellow G.I.s or college friends. Or he could create a compelling portrait of O'Brien's hometown or Army battalion. Any person's life, as the essayist Alain de Botton says, offers a suitable subject just as soon as "they start to rattle the bars of their cages."

Extraordinary events happen in many ordinary lives. Read Studs Terkel's books and you see that even the most ordinary people lead rich, complex lives: ministers and teachers, housewives and factory workers, lawyers and accountants, cooks and janitors, scientists and artists. Or read the rash of memoirs published in recent years. On every conceivable topic—homelessness (Jeannette Walls's *The Glass Castle*), abuse (Margaux Fragoso's *Tiger, Tiger*), rags to riches (Christopher Gardner's *The Pursuit of Happyness*), mental illness (Elizabeth Wurtzel's *Prozac Nation*), dementia (Carol O'Dell's *Mothering Mother*), family life (Frank Gilbreth's *Cheaper by the Dozen*), immigrant life

(Frank McCourt's *Angela's Ashes*), teaching (Bel Kaufman's *Up the Down Staircase*), faith (Anne Lamott's *Traveling Mercies*)—ordinary people tell their stories to express timeless themes.

Whether your characters are ordinary or larger-than-life, show their complexity and drive. "Character is that which reveals moral purpose," Aristotle writes in *The Poetics*, "showing what kind of things a man chooses or avoids."

Push your characters hard to discover what they choose and avoid. Put your characters in challenging situations; make life hard on them. As soon as they begin to resolve their problems, throw new challenges their way. Kick your characters; as soon as they get up, kick 'em again. Test their capacity to learn and grow.

How do you know when you have a worthy character? "I have to be able to *defend* this character," says Aaron Sorkin, the screenwriter for *The West Wing* and *The Social Network*. "You want to write the character as if they are making their case to God why they should be allowed in heaven."

––––––

ELEMENT 4: COMPILE DOSSIERS FOR YOUR CHARACTERS

To send your hero and other characters on their journeys, you need to know who they are and what they're trying to do.

So learn everything possible about your characters' lives. Know the most intimate details of their physical, mental, and spiritual lives. Don't just discover the surface facts; explore their backstories. Don't just find your characters' names; discover how they got their names and what they mean. Don't just talk about their jobs; find out what work means to them emotionally.

Be complete. Don't dismiss any ideas as unimportant. Each detail, somehow, matters. Just as a P.I. gets his best stuff while tracking down unlikely leads, you will discover telling details when you gather information about every aspect of their lives:

Personal Background
Name
Age and birthday
Birthplace

Parents' ethnic and religious background
Parents' upbringing, hopes and fears, and careers
Place in the family's birth order
Relations with siblings and other relatives

Physical Characteristics
What others notice first
Body and build
Hair and eye color
Sound of voice
Conversational oddities
Physical peculiarities
Mannerisms while walking, talking, working, and playing

Growing With Others
Activities and hobbies as a child ... and as an adult
Sidekicks and mentors
Intellectual and emotional influences
Rivals and foes at different stages of life
Not-so-good influences—skeptics, and tempters
Political leanings—and major political influences
How the character changes over the course of life
Turning points in life

Psychology
All-consuming desires
Pathological maneuver
Most admirable qualities
Least admirable qualities
Sexual identity
Philosophy of life
Optimism or pessimism
Energy level
What the character does when alone
What the character thinks about when alone
Greatest fears at different stages of life

Gathering so much information might seem like overkill. But you need to know *everything* about your characters before you can decide what's important.

As you compile your dossier, look for tensions. Look for the qualities or experiences that make the character uncomfortable. Look for the inner conflicts, which lead to conflicts with other people. Take note of how the character manages the conflicts. Does he avoid them? Does he project them onto other people? Does he avoid certain activities and people? When he wins or loses, how does he respond? We find people's character in the choices in the most difficult moments.

People usually behave well when they win—but not always. A presidential historian named James David Barber believed that you could discover a politicians' characters by understanding their first independent political success, or FIPS. You would think that everyone would be happy and even gracious in victory. But in fact, winning reveals people's insecurities too. For some, a victory makes them even more vulnerable and insecure. It makes others more hungry for another win. It offers others a chance for retribution against enemies. So even happy results can reveal something ugly.

Losing can reveal otherwise important traits. When some people lose, their egos are crushed and they seek to compensate. They claim the other side cheated, that supporters betrayed them, or that the whole game was rigged. Others respond with grace, reaching out to their opponent and offering help and best wishes. Even if they feel wronged, they realize that larger values are at stake—that the community matters more than a single person's fortunes.

When you gather these details, you can move from *characterization* to *character*. Characterization offers the simple surface facts of a person's life; character goes deeper to the heart and soul of their life.

By defining the character, the dossier helps to tell the story. In fact, it's almost impossible to create a dossier without also beginning to tell the story.

CASE STUDY: IRIN CARMON AND SHANA KNIZHNIK'S *THE NOTORIOUS RBG*

In the 2000s, U.S. Supreme Court Justice Ruth Bader Ginsberg became a cultural phenomenon. Appointed to the Supreme Court in 1993, she first played the role of the Court's swing vote and later its most compelling dissenter. She was nicknamed "The Notorious RBG"—a pun based on a rapper known as the The Notorious BIG—and a symbol of the power of ideas to change the world.

Fiercely independent, Ginsberg was a trailblazing lawyer in the movement to gain equal rights for women in employment, education, the military, and other fields. A workaholic, she was also a devoted wife and mother. As her husband Martin battled testicular cancer when they were students at Harvard Law School, Ruth gathered notes from his classmates so he could keep up with classes; she also did her own studies and cared for their baby. She left Harvard Law to join her husband Martin during his military service in Oklahoma and again when he took a job in New York City.

Despite having served on the law reviews at both Harvard and Columbia (where she transferred to be with Martin in New York), she was denied positions with major law firms because she was a woman. So she began a long career as a professor and advocate before joining the D.C. Court of Appeals in 1980.

Personal Background
Name: *Joan Ruth Bader Ginsberg.*
Birthday: *March 15, 1933.*
Birthplace: *Flatbush section of Brooklyn, New York.*
Parents' ethnic and religious background: *Father Nathan was a Jewish emigrant from Odessa, Ukraine; mother Celia was born in New York to Austrian Jewish parents*
Parents' upbringing, hopes and fears, and careers: *From Irish, Italian, and Jewish families.*
Place in the family's birth order: *Ruth was the second of two girls.*
Relations with siblings and other relatives: *Her older sister Marilyn died of meningitis when she was eight years old. Ruth then grew up as an only child.*

Physical Characteristics
What others notice first: *She had a collection of jabots (the collars that she wore with her robes for sittings of the Supreme Court) for every occasion.*
Body and build: *Tall and thin, with some muscles as she exercised to counter her aging and illness.*
Hair and eye color: *Brown hair and brown eyes.*

Sound of voice: *An educated style, accented by traces of her old Brooklyn neighborhood. Emphatic yet reserved. Formal.*

Conversational oddities: *Deliberate in her pronouncements, she was careful to conjure and utter every word well; at the same time, she spoke with little affectation. She often spoke with a touch of humor, using brief pauses to allow the listener to grasp her points. "If I had any talent that God could give me, I would be a great diva," she said. "But sadly I have a monotone … [I sing] only in the shower and in my dreams."*

Physical peculiarities: *As she grew older, she took up exercise to maintain her strength after several bouts with cancer.*

Mannerisms while walking, talking, working, and playing: *A bemused smile with a clear sense of direction.*

Growing With Others

Activities and hobbies as a child … and as an adult: *Growing up as a bookworm, she was a regular of the local library. As an adult, she devoured briefs and other research materials.*

Sidekicks and mentors: *Throughout her adult life, her husband Martin was her constant companion. Martin's gentle, jocular approach; RBG remained serious, but also wry and ironic.*

Intellectual and emotional influences: *In her work as a professor and advocate, she became immersed in the feminist movement.*

Rivals and foes at different stages of life: *Her whole life, Ginsberg had to work twice as hard as her male counterparts because of pervasive gender discrimination. Her greatest rival on the Supreme Court, Antonin Scalia, was also a close personal friend and fellow opera and travel enthusiast.*

Not-so-good influences—skeptics, and tempters: *Some criticized her political commitments. After she expressed alarm at the prospect of Donald Trump's election in 2016, she apologized for expressing a political opinion.*

Political leanings—and major political influences: *Left of center, she sought to apply feminism not just to give women better opportunity but to also help men live their lives more fully. She said she was "really turned on" by #MeToo movement.*

How the character changes over the course of life: *From her earliest days as an advocate, Ginsberg's place on the ideological spectrum shifted to the left as the Supreme Court shifted to the right.*

Turning points in life: *Meeting Martin Ginsberg, while a student at Cornell. She and Martin embarked on legal careers together and helped each other, as circumstances demanded, at every step.*

Psychology

All-consuming desires: *Fair and tenacious application of the law.*

Pathological maneuver: *Pathological? Hard to think of her as having any pathological traits. Her kids said her cooking was awful. Does that count?*

Most admirable qualities: *Intense intelligence as well as ambition. Devoted wife and parent.*

Least admirable qualities: *Some might say she was so devoted to her work that other worthwhile pursuits suffered. She would answer that she loved the law and was fully alive when immersed in her work. Still, she also enjoyed the opera, history, art, and travel.*

Sexual identity: *Hetero. A devoted wife and mother.*

Philosophy of life: *Devote yourself to your calling, with whatever time and energy is demanded. Stay focused on core principles. Grow with the times. Sacrifice for others.*

Optimism or pessimism: *Overall, hopeful about the power of the law and people's good will to improve opportunity—but also clear-eyed about the real threats facing democracy and basic rights.*

Energy level: *High level of energy, especially about her work. Willing to work all night to master complex issues and write legal briefs.*

What the character does when alone: *She worked, read, listened to music, and microwaved meals.*

What the character thinks about when alone: *She thought*

> *constantly about the people involved in the legal cases she considered. Also: Her family, especially her late husband Martin.*

Greatest fears at different stages of life: *The erosion of civil liberties and democratic processes. She was especially disturbed by the* Citizens United *decision, which eliminated restrictions on corporate political donations. The majority in that case declared that corporations are people, entitling them to the same rights of unfettered speech.*

Late in her career, Ginsberg was determined to "plant the seeds" for a new age of inclusive, balanced jurisprudence. Most of her later opinions were dissents that called for a revival of civil rights, voting rights, electoral reform, free speech, and principled regulation.

———

ELEMENT 5: EXPLORE CHARACTERS' LIVES, ZONE BY ZONE

When you first meet someone, you begin conversations with superficial questions and answers. *Where do you go to school? What do you do? Where do you live? Where did you grow up? Are you married? Do you have kids?*

Before we can ask deeper, more personal questions, we need to build a foundation. We need to understand the superficial facts of a person's life before we can probe deeply. We need to earn trust before we can explore someone's intimate stories and feelings.

Imagine what would happen if you asked intimate questions in your first meeting. *Nice to meet you. Does your family have a history of alcoholism? Abuse? Have you ever been arrested? Do you fantasize about a neighbor or coworker? Have you ever cheated on your taxes?*

Even psychiatrists, priests and rabbis, and other confidantes must start with simple, unthreatening questions. Counselors might learn intimate information right away—"Father, my husband is cheating on me"—but they have to work hard to find the deepest truths. The opening revelation is really just the beginning of a more searching dialogue.

The same principle holds for storytelling. Start exploring your characters at their outside edges. Get to know the basic information first, then move inward.

Characters live in four zones. Let's explore them, one by one.

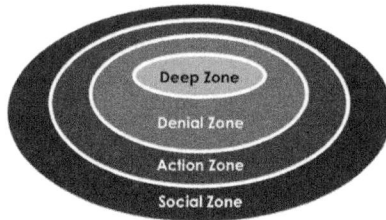

The Social Zone: Here, people play roles assigned by society. People and institutions around us—in our families, schools, work-places, and community—set powerful expectations and incentives. We make decisions, sure; but the world around us determines the range of our possibilities.

"I did not direct my life," said B.F. Skinner, the father of behaviorist theory. "I didn't design it. I never made decisions. Things always came up and made them for me. That's what life is."

To understand how people behave, Skinner observed how repeated actions shape people's habits and decisions. He started by studying rats. When a rat performed an action and got a reward (usually food), that rat was more likely to perform the same action again. In time, the rat got conditioned to respond to prompts in specific ways. Likewise, society establishes a complex matrix of rewards and punishments for people. These rewards and punishments define our roles as parents and children, boss and worker, priest and parishioner, coach and player, clerk and customer, and more.

In Skinner's world, roles and rewards rule. People act like lab rats, responding the demands and incentives in order to maximize pleasure and minimize pain.

The Action Zone: All of us all have the capacity to act with purpose. When we see the world around us, assess threats and oppor-tunities, and decide on possible courses of action, we can take *action*.

To act, we need to make decisions consciously, rather than repeating unconscious habits. We need to figure out what matters to us, assess our possible courses of action, decide to act, and then *act*.

Too often, we allow our circumstances and conditioning to

constrain our action. We get in a rut. Rather than actively deciding, we take the course of least resistance. But contrary to what Skinner says, we are always *capable* of making up our own minds and acting consciously. Even under severe constraints, we still have the capacity to decide how we want to respond to those constraints. And then we can act, however limited our choices.

Consider the case of Victor Frankl. A prisoner in Nazi concentration camps in World War II, Frankl did not know whether he would survive. But he noticed that survivors in the camps focused on what they loved and not on the brutality of the conditions. And so Frankl decided, consciously, to focus on the possibilities of his future. He thought about reuniting with his wife, even though he didn't even know if she was still alive.

Action requires responsibility. "Ultimately, man should not ask what the meaning of his life is, but rather must recognize that it is he who is asked," Frankl writes in his classic *Man's Search for Meaning*. "In a word, each man is *questioned by life*; and he can only answer to life by answering for his own life; to life he can only respond by being responsible." To act, you must be willing to accept responsibility for your own life. By taking responsibility, you make yourself a complete human.

If Skinner depicts a world that seems determined by outside forces, Frankl depicts a world open to conscious action.

The Denial Zone: When confronted with an uncomfortable truth, our first response is denial. All our lives, we carry heavy baggage: insecurities, hurts, and feelings of inadequacy. This baggage can be so harmful that we sometimes even deny our powers to act. People struggle, Albert Ellis said, because they refuse to face the truths of their lives. "You largely constructed your depression," Ellis said. "It wasn't given to you. Therefore, you can deconstruct it."

Facing deep-seated problems is hard. We usually don't understand our problems because we are so immersed in those problems; they are everywhere, like the air we breathe. Without thinking about it, we we construct a whole way of life around those problems. We struggle to notice, much less address, a lifetime of attitudes and beliefs, stories and rationalizations. Most of us would rather dwell in denial than take on the hard work of overcoming our dysfunctional ways.

What about your characters? Who in your story denies the truth about their families or their own behavior? Who struggles to acknowledge addiction, abuse, moments of meanness or cowardice—or other truths? Who lives with shame or fear? And what do they do to avoid facing these truths?

The Deep Zone: Most of our drives and desires are buried deep in our subconscious—so deep, in fact, that we don't even know they exist. But by confronting the issues in the outer zones, we can dig into the Deep Zone.

Sigmund Freud, the father of modern psychoanalysis, believes our deepest struggles occur beyond our consciousness. At the center of this struggle is the battle between Eros and Thantos, the individual's love and death instincts. Unconscious struggles bubble underneath the surface, beyond our attention, until a crisis bursts into the open. Therapy, Freud believes, can bring these unconscious drives and desires to the surface. But that requires hard work.

Carl Jung believes that Freud oversimplifies man's mind and soul. Every person's psyche, Jung teaches, is connected to mankind's "collective unconscious." Deep down, the human race shares a common heritage of stories and feelings. "This collective unconscious does not develop individually but is inherited," Jung says. "It consists of pre-existent forms, the archetypes, which can only become conscious secondarily and which give definite form to certain psychic contents."

To understand any character, then, we need to understand ideas and emotions that extend back for ages. The Deep Zone includes not only the primal urges of Eros and Thantos, but also the deepest desires for family and friendship, beauty and creativity, mythos and meaning. These desires stretch back for millennia.

As your characters wrestle with their psyches, how deep will they go? Will they play out the roles that society makes for him? Will they attempt to act consciously? Will they wrestle with their own denial and confront their own warring instincts? Or will they, possibly, go deeper still?

CASE STUDY: MILAN KUNDERA'S *UNBEARABLE LIGHTNESS OF BEING*

Tomas, the hero of Milan Kundera's *The Unbearable Lightness of Being*, lives a privileged life as a doctor in Communist Czechoslovakia. He makes good money, lives in a nice apartment in Prague, and enjoys the company of a long train of beautiful women. Tomas is likable, but also shallow and narcissistic.

Tomas would probably maintain this lifestyle forever if he did not meet Tereza at a spa in the countryside. While reading a book in the hotel restaurant, the two meet. She is a waitress aching to leave the narrow life of the country. A reader herself, she yearns for a more worldly life. The two flirt until he catches a train back to Prague.

Not long after, Tereza appears at the door of Tomas's apartment. He brings her inside, they make love, and then she gets a cold and he cares for her. Soon she is settling into a new life in Prague—first on her own, and then with Tomas. Their relationship is not easy. Tomas does not want to commit. He maintains a relationship with an artist named Sabina. But Tereza's presence and energy challenge his bachelor lifestyle. She becomes a professional photographer. Tereza is a woman of substance and Tomas must change to be part of her life.

The turning point for Tomas comes when he takes a public stand against the Communist government. He writes a letter to a newspaper mocking the Communist authorities, comparing them to Oedipus, who put out his eyes after discovering his tragic mistakes. Unlike Oedipus, the Communists felt no shame when they ruined people's lives. The Communists, outraged by the letter, punish Tomas by taking away his prestigious job and and his privileged life. Government authorities offer to restore his status if he will retract the letter. But he doesn't. He has found a truth and is unwilling to give it up.

When the Soviets invade Prague, the couple flees to Zurich. When Tereza returns to Prague, Tomas follows her, knowing he will never be able to leave Czechoslovakia again.

With Tereza, Tomas settles into a new life, first as a lowly doctor without privileges, then as a window washer, and finally as a tractor driver in the country. Shorn of privilege, he finds his true self.

After a life as a womanizer, Tomas commits wholly to Tereza. "Haven't you noticed that I'm happy here, Tereza?" he asks toward the end. Tereza reminds him that he has lost his surgery practice, his mission in life. "Missions are stupid, Tereza," he responds. "I have no mission. No one has. And it's a terrific relief to realize you're free, free of all missions."

Over the course of his journey—step by difficult step—Tomas becomes the man he was meant to be. He is a shallow Lothario no more. He is deep, courageous, caring, and willing to take risks. He sacrifices privilege for principle, moving from hedonism to *eudemonia*.

By going deep, he overcomes the emotional emptiness and moral compromises of modern life under a totalitarian system.

––––––

ELEMENT 6: FIND YOUR CHARACTERS' THROUGHLINES

To take a great journey—and to become a deeper person—your characters need a powerful desire. They must strive to achieve a vision, even if it takes a while to understand that vision. Once they find their vision, they need to be obsessive about it. As Martin Luther told Charles V: "Here I stand; I can do no other."

Stage actors and directors use the term "throughline" to describe a character's deepest ambitions and drives. A character expresses this desire simply:

I want to ...

The throughline shapes the character's every decision. Consider Shakespeare's Hamlet. What is his great desire? Is it to ascend to power? Achieve truth? Avenge his father's death? Salvage his mother's integrity? Restore the kingdom? You can make a case for each of these motivations. How you portray a character's actions depends on which throughline you embrace for the character.

The philosopher Nietzsche puts the challenge this way: "Become who you are." All of us have a destiny. Our purpose in life is to realize that destiny. What do you want to be? A great teacher? Entrepreneur? Seller? Parent? Coach? Writer? Friend? Leader? Follower? Whatever it is, be prepared to make whatever sacrifice is necessary to achieve it.

To make the character unique, express his or her desire in *specific ways*. No one strives or makes sacrifices for general and vague ideals. The ideal of "freedom," for example, may excite some patriots; but most people need to understand these ideals in much more visceral, emotional, concrete terms before they can embrace sacrifice and hardship. American rebels hated King George, Confederates hated Yankees, and Allied soldiers in World War II hated Nazis. Give your character something *specific* to love or hate.

Make the character's desire so intense that he will make great sacrifices to realize it. Give your character not just a powerful *goal,* but also a compelling *approach* to realizing that goal.

A philosopher named Harry Frankfort distinguishes first- and second-order desires. First-order desires represent your primary goals in life: to become a great writer or lawyer, to achieve fitness, to develop a deep relationship. Second-order desires express everything you must do to achieve those primary goals: work hard, make sacrifices, focus intently, surround yourself with like-minded people.

If you won't make the sacrifices necessary to realize your dream, you don't really *want to achieve* that dream. Lots of kids say they want to be professional athletes, actors, musicians, and astronauts. But to become an athlete, to take one example, you also need to *want* to work out, eat the right foods, get sleep, avoid drugs and alcohol abuse, and train your mind. You have to *want* to grind out practices on tough days, work on fundamentals when your friends are having a pool party, and make long road trips to games.

By looking hard at your character's messy life, you can figure out the answer to the ultimate question: What does the character care about so much that he will sacrifice *anything* to achieve it?

CASE STUDY: HEROES OF CIVIL RIGHTS MOVEMENT

Over the course of a century-long struggle, the civil rights movement adopted a common goal: to gain blacks their basic rights as Americans. But what other values and desires sustained that struggle? What sacrifices would blacks make to gain their rights? What other values did they need to embrace to achieve this goal?

Consider three heroic leaders of the movement: A. Philip Randolph, Bayard Rustin, and Martin Luther King, Jr. Each embraced the goal of civil rights. But to succeed, they embraced specific values. So when the civil rights struggle got tough, they were ready, willing, and able to make the necessary sacrifices.

Start with Mr. Randolph, as he was known. More than any previous black leader, he understood the power of mass action. Black people, he reasoned, could not gain their rights unless they overcame their slave mentality. To do that, they needed to break out of their isolation and passivity. They needed to assert themselves—*publicly.* They needed to march, as a mass, to demand their rights. We might state Randolph's desire, then, like this:

I want to give blacks confidence to put their bodies on the line to demand their rights.

Now consider Bayard Rustin. To fight for freedom, he believed, activists needed to act more intelligently than their opponents. They needed a strategy that not only expressed their deepest values but also gave them leverage over their opponents. And so Rustin embraced the strategy of nonviolent protest.

This approach offered more than a Christlike commitment to "turning the other cheek." It was, in fact, the strategy that could confront the racist regimes in the South. Since segregationists controlled governments, including local and state police, they would always win battles that used violence. Nonviolent conflict—peaceful protests, resistance and refusal to follow unjust laws—gave blacks a different kind of power. We might state Rustin's desire like this:

I want to equip blacks with the intelligence of nonviolent action.

Martin Luther King added his own values to the struggle. Freedom, he believed, required a willingness to suffer. "Unearned suffering is redemptive," he declared. No one voluntarily gives up power, King understood, so freedom fighters need to accept that they will suffer everyday indignities, risk their jobs and homes, and face violence and even death. So King's throughline might be:

I want to bear the necessary suffering to end segregation.

Only by embracing this willingness to suffer could blacks achieve their first-order desire of basic rights.

When brought together in the same great cause, these three throughlines expressed the highest and most intelligent approach of that cause:

To prevail in the great struggle for civil rights, we must put out bodies on the line, in ways that strengthen our resolve and exert leverage on the opposition, understanding that we will suffer in the process.

When you understand not only people's greatest goal, but also their means to achieve that goal, you will produce a compelling character.

––––––

ELEMENT 7: USE THE WHEEL OF ARCHETYPES

Inside all of us, a swirl of different psychological qualities shape the way we think and act.

People are complicated. In different measures, we are heroic and devious, loyal and impulsive, wise and foolish, brainy and emotional. Our character builds on one or two dominant qualities. One person's character revolves around heroism and wisdom, another's around strength and impulsivity, a third around love and nurturing.

Going back to ancient times, the eternal character traits have been called archetypes. "Archetypes," Jung wrote in *The Structure and Dynamics of the Psyche*, "are the living system of reactions and aptitudes that determine the individual's life in invisible ways."

Archetypes provide simple ways make sense of a complicated world. We use stereotypes all the time to make quick judgments. We not only decide who to approach and who to avoid, but also how. In an early scene of the movie *Mean Girls*, a student explains the different cliques at school:

> You got your freshmen, ROTC guys, preps, JV jocks, Asian nerds, cool Asians, varsity jocks, unfriendly black hotties, girls who eat their feelings, girls who don't eat anything, desperate wannabes, burnouts, sexually active band geeks ...

To be sure, archetypes simplify the world too much. The groups on the *Mean Girls* map are more complex than their labels. But the stereotypes offer a useful shorthand to understand motivation and behavior.

Each character type reveals something about the human condition. However strong, each character type is incomplete. Their story depends on how well they express their values, understand others' values, and interact with other types to grow and develop.

Archetype are timeless. We find all of the major character types throughout history. The qualities of a hero 3,000 years ago—intelligence, empathy and caring, daring and adventure, courage and integrity—define the modern hero as well. The same can be said for other major character types.

How many archetypes are there? Too many to count. "There are as many archetypes as there are typical situations in life," Jung said. "Endless repetition has engraved these experiences into our psychic constitution, not in the forms of images filled with content, but at first only as forms without content, representing merely the possibility of a certain type of perception and action."

Still to understand the concept in more depth, let's chart eight distinct character types. They come in four pairs of opposing values: hero and villain, mentor and tempter, sidekick and skeptic, and mind and heart.

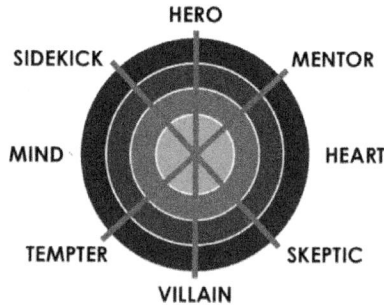

- **Hero**: The hero is the center of the story, the lead character who pursues his mission with gusto. Sometimes inspired by his own ambitions and dreams, other times forced into action by a crisis, the hero seeks something big. He might want fame or fortune, admiration or wisdom, family or friends. Whatever the hero wants, the audience wants for him.

Usually likable, the hero pursues his mission with zeal. He is willing to take almost any action to achieve his goal. He builds his life around this quest. With his charisma, he attracts others to his cause. He radiates something otherworldly as he pursues his purpose.

Still, even though he embodies ideals we all admire, he is far from perfect. He struggles to face his own flaws, often denying them to the point of endangering himself and others. Eventually he is willing to step out of his "comfort zone"—his normal way of life, which requires little effort or thought—in order to become a better person. His attraction lies not in any superpowers or perfection but in his integrity and willingness to face his most difficult flaws.

Virtually every great story has a great hero. Heroes' characters vary as much as the human race: innocent (Huck Finn) or clever (Sherlock Holmes), trapped (Rabbit Angstrom) or adventurous (Odysseus), wise (Jesus) or courageous (Ivan Denisovich), lecherous (Humbert Humbert) or upright (Atticus Finch), lazy (Oblomov) or industrious (Horatio Alger), well rounded (Jane Eyre) or shallow (Babbitt).

• **Villain**: The hero's victory does not come easily. At every turn, the villain and other characters attempt to block his way.

The villain rejects the hero's virtues. Deep down, the villain understands that the hero's best qualities often represent his own repressed or damaged qualities. The villain resents the hero's success and righteousness. So he battles the hero physically and psychologically. He conspires with others to undermine the hero. He lies and deceives. In the process, he tests the hero's mettle and morality.

Villains do not consider themselves bad, at least not completely. As their creator, you must find a way treat the them sympathetically. Blake Snyder, a screenwriter and script doctor, suggests giving every villain a "save the cat" moment—that is, a moment when he does something for humane reasons. Rather than denouncing villains, the best stories explore their complexity.

Search for what's admirable in your villains; find their struggles, vulnerabilities, wounds, even their hopes and dreams. Search for the moments that forged their character, the choices that put them to the dark side.

Like heroes, villains vary in their makeup and morality. Consider the different drives of great literary villains—political ambition (Lady Macbeth), narrow-minded authority (Javert), jealousy (Mrs. Danvers), revenge (Iago), psychological illness (Norman Bates), sadism (Nurse Ratchett), and pure evil (Satan).

No hero can test and develop his capacities—physical, intellectual, or moral—without a worthy opponent. Make your villain complex and intriguing, even worthy of some love and understanding.

• **Sidekick**: Most heroes need a sidekick or alter ego, a loyal companion who joins in their adventures. The sidekick supports the hero but also provides a contrast, revealing dimensions of the hero that we would not otherwise see.

Think of the sidekick as an extension of the hero. The sidekick cares more about his friend's interests and happiness than his own. When a crisis emerges, the sidekick supports him. When someone questions the hero—even when the hero makes mistakes and needs to be challenged—the sidekick defends him.

Literature and film are filled with memorable sidekicks. In The Bible, Moses found his ability to speak through Aaron. In mythology, Enkidu supports Gilgamesh and Patroclus supports Achilles. In Miguel de Cervantes's *Don Quixote*, Sancho acts as the practical counterpoint to Quixote's romanticism. In Daniel Defoe's *Robinson Crusoe*, Friday supports the leader of the isle of cannibals. In Arthur Conan Doyle's Sherlock Holmes stories, Watson helps the brilliant detective.

The sidekick offers an insider's view of the hero. He lives close enough to get an intimate view, but his perspective is limited. Not a hero himself, he does not understand many events until they're over—just like the readers of the story. Often, the sidekick offers the reader's perspective, affording closeup views of the hero but never knowing what will happen next.

• **Skeptic**: Standing outside the hero-sidekick alliance, the skeptic often gets jealous and even angry. He questions the hero and sidekick, whatever they say or do. Whatever the hero proposes and the sidekick disposes, the skeptic opposes. As Grouch Marx once says in *Horse Feathers*: "No matter what it is or who commenced it, I'm against it."

Skeptics doubt what they cannot see. In The Bible, the disciple Thomas resists believing that Jesus had been resurrected. "I have to put my finger where the nails were," Thomas says. "If I can put my hand in his side, then I'll believe you." When Jesus shows his wounds, Thomas believes him. But Jesus is disappointed in the doubting Thomas. "There will be many who do not see me and are still willing to believe," Jesus says. "These people are special to me."

Skeptics often dampen the spirits of other characters. When a hero begins a perilous journey, skeptics can be heard muttering that "it just won't work." Skeptics question and quarrel, ridicule and rant, sneer and scold.

But by asking tough questions, skeptics often play a constructive role. They help others to think through their actions: *Is this really the right job for you? Is he the right man for you? Do you think you should take this trip? Should you risk speaking out?*

Detectives offer compelling skeptics. They understand that no one tells the whole truth. Raymond Chandler's character Philip Marlowe and Dashiell Hammett's character Sam Spade see past the facade of deluded clients, corrupt cops, corner-cutting prosecutors, jealous spouses, and manipulative lawyers. "I don't know which side anybody's on," Marlowe cracks in *Murder, My Sweet*. "I don't even know who's playing today."

• **Mentor**: The hero needs wisdom for his journey. The mentor offers the knowledge and judgment that comes from a lifetime of experience.

Usually an older figure, the mentor has succeeded in his life but also fallen short. He has overcome his youthful flaws—impulsiveness, temper, irresponsibility, and grandiosity—and now offers his hard-won knowledge to his protege. In supporting the hero/protege, the mentor fulfills a deep need of his own. By passing along his knowledge and wisdom, he fulfills himself and, in a way, becomes immortal.

The mentor wants, above all else, for the hero to realize his full potential. And so he freely offers his time, listens to his dreams with empathy, and sets high expectations. The mentor challenges the protege to take on big challenges, prodding him to do the right thing, avoid shortcuts, and act by the highest standards. By doing things the right way, the mentor teaches, you give yourself the best chance to succeed—and, even more important, strengthen your moral core.

The mentor's name comes from Homer's *Odyssey*. Athena, the goddess of war, takes the form of an old man named Mentor to guide the young Telemachus while his father is away. "You should not be clinging to your childhood," Mentor tells Telemachus. Even without his father to guide him, Telemachus must become a man.

Often, a mentor's wisdom is captured in simple aphorisms. Consider the wisdom of Father Zosima in Fyodor Dostoevsky's *The Brothers Karamazov*:

> *"Love redeems and saves everything."*
> *"Many times, it is necessary to treat people as if they were children, or as if they were sick."*
> *"What is Hell? It is the suffering for being no longer able to love."*
> *"Everything passes, only truth remains."*

An elder in the monastery, Father Zosima heals the ill and guides younger priests. He wins the affection of the townspeople by living out his values.

To offer real guidance, the mentor also needs to follow his own wisdom. Shakespeare's Polonius offers sound advice. "To thine own self be true," he says in *Hamlet*. "Neither a borrower nor a lender be." But Polonius is pompous and vain; he speaks well but invites ridicule. While never perfect, a true mentor lives his ideals and does not bloviate like Polonius.

• **Tempter**: Opposing the mentor—and, usually, the hero's best interests—is a tempter. As the mentor guides the hero to make hard decisions and take difficult actions, the tempter offers easy answers. His message is as simple as it is dangerous: *Why work hard? Why consider other people's concerns? Take the easy way out!*

The greatest story of temptation comes from the story of Adam and Eve in the Garden of Eden. When a serpent urges Eve to eat from the Tree of Knowledge, to "be like God," she gives into temptation. Eve and Adam are then cast out of the state of innocence and purity, filled with shame. The New Testament shows the glory that comes from resisting temptation. Jesus resists the devil's temptation after he fasts for 40 days and nights. Each time the devil challenges him to show his special powers, Jesus resists.

The tempter sometimes plays a positive role, bringing lightness and laughter to the hero. In Shakespeare's *Henry IV, Part 1*, Falstaff lures Prince Hal into all kinds of merrymaking and pranks. Falstaff makes Hal a more complete man. But the partying cannot last forever. When Hal becomes king, his new responsibilities impel him to cast off Falstaff:

> *Presume not that I am the thing I was;*
> *For God doth know, so shall the world perceive,*
> *That I have turn'd away my former self …*

By following Falstaff, Hal enlivens his spirit. By later rejecting him, he becomes a man.

• **Mind**: The mind character takes a rational, intellectual approach to life. To this character, all problems can be reduced to cool calculation. When making a major life decision—whether to take a job, move to a new town, marry, have children—he focuses on the tradeoffs of time, money, and status.

Brainy characters understand that most problems require discipline and thought. Hermione, who plays the role of the intellect in the Harry Potter series, insists on the magic power of brains. "It's logic, a puzzle," she says. "A lot of the greatest wizards haven't got one ounce of logic. They'd be stuck in here forever."

The mind character often plays the key role in detective stories. In Edgar Allan Poe's "The Purloined Letter," Dupin uses logic to find a letter that a thief has used to blackmail a politician. Since he knows the thief is a poet, Dupin reasons that he would find a clever way to hide the letter—in a letterbox, in plain sight, where police would never look.

Lisbeth Salander, the computer hacker in Stieg Larsson's Millennium trilogy, uses her brains to defeat her abusers. She can hack any computer program, remember the details of everything she reads, and survive on the street. She also plots an ingenious strategy to defeat her sadistic guardian and overcome her evil father.

• **Heart**: Rather than reducing problems to rational calculations, the heart character understands the need to honor the deepest part of the soul.

With awareness of the heart, we all draw from our deepest wells of energy and intelligence. We can persevere when the odds are stacked against us. With empathy, we can understand what other people are experiencing—and how they fit into our lives. When we connect with other people, we grow and learn and act well ourselves.

People who know what they value, *emotionally*, act swiftly; they do not suffer a "paralysis of analysis." When they see someone doing something wrong, they respond instantly. Because they hold their values deeply, they do not hesitate when confronted with a moral challenge. They know what's right and what's wrong, and they act accordingly.

When you create a story—either real or fiction—keep these types in mind. Your story becomes complete only when you develop all these types and show how they interact with each other.

CASE STUDY: ROBERT MOSES AND JANE JACOBS

Who is the true visionary of the modern American city?

New York has long been the site of colossal battles over the shape of urbanism in America. Two forces have lined up to battle over the city's geography, development, economy, and social life. On one side, represented by Robert Moses, are the forces of giantism and regionalism. Moses created the vast landscape of modern New York: its highways, bridges, tunnels, public housing, parks, and beaches. On the other side, represented by Jane Jacobs, are the forces of intimacy and localism that make small-scale neighborhoods work. Jacobs inspired a grassroots movement to resist large-scale planning and to promote more organic development at the neighborhood level.

This ongoing battle is chronicled in two of the classic works on urbanism and politics. Robert Caro's *The Power Broker* details the remarkable life of Robert Moses. Jane Jacobs's book, *The Death and Life of Great American Cities*, offers an unsparing argument against large-scale planning. A more recent work, Anthony Flint's *Wrestling With Moses*, details how Jacobs fought Moses over his proposed Lower Manhattan Expressway.

The Moses-Jacobs dialectic—the constant tension between large-scale transformation and small-scale evolution, technocratic experts and grassroots activists, professional master planners and amateur protectors—still animates urban politics and planning in our day.

The Moses-Jacobs struggle resonates because the characters are so primal. Moses was the ultimate power broker, the visionary creator of a political empire that stretched across New York City to the region and the state. By controlling revenues of political authorities—and thus, contracts and jobs for countless people in city, state, and even federal politics for decades—Moses made himself untouchable.

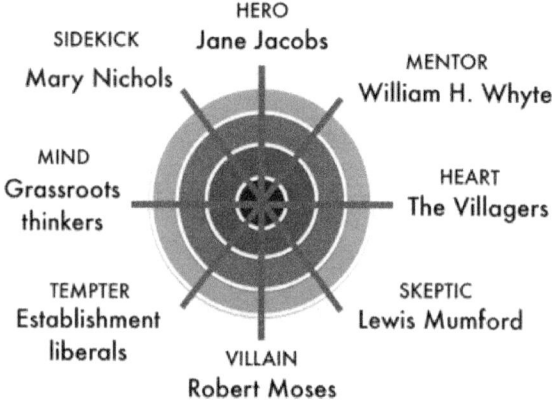

HERO
SIDEKICK Jane Jacobs
Mary Nichols   MENTOR
                    William H. Whyte

MIND
Grassroots   HEART
thinkers   The Villagers

TEMPTER   SKEPTIC
Establishment   Lewis Mumford
liberals   VILLAIN
                Robert Moses

Jacobs, meanwhile, was the quintessential grassroots activist, horrified by the abuses of Moses, his minions, and the servile politicians and bureaucrats who bowed to his power. With her keen observations of cities, from building stoops to public housing high rises, Jacobs developed a powerful critique of Moses.

With the help of likeminded neighbors in Greenwich Village, Jacobs rallied mothers, artists, shop owners, park advocates, and a growing band of activists to fight Moses's proposal to build a highway that would cut through the heart of the Village. This victory signaled the end of the Moses's total domination of New York planning and development.

The Moses-Jacobs battles involved all kinds of other character types as well. Casting Jane Jacobs as the hero and Robert Moses as the villain, let's look at some of those other characters.

- **Mentor**: William H. Whyte, a sociologist, explored the conformity of modern society and how cities were being demolished and rebuilt in the image of the "organization man."
- **Skeptic**: Lewis Mumford, the day's great urban historian, questioned whether Jacobs understood the massive forces shaping cities.
- **Sidekick**: Mary Perot Nichols, a reporter for *The Village Voice* who tracked the politics of Greenwich Village, explored the ins and outs of big-city politics with Jacobs.
- **Heart**: The residents of Greenwich Village, from the small shopkeepers to the mothers to the professionals.
- **Mind**: Jane Jacobs's intellectual influences included colleagues in journalism and architecture, friends and neighbors anxious to protect their community, and lawyers and zoning experts who taught her how politics works.

Missing from this list is a tempter. Perhaps Jacobs had none. Modest but determined, she could not be deterred from her vision of an old-fashioned people-oriented city, with its tightly knit communities and neighborly intimacies.

———

ELEMENT 8: SPIN THE WHEEL OF ARCHETYPES

One story's hero is another story's villain. Looked at in a different light, or facing a different set of challenges, a hero may begin to look less than heroic and a villain more than villainous. When we look at a character in a new way, in different circumstances, we can see a whole different set of qualities.

So develop your characters by casting them in unfamiliar roles. Show them contend with buried fears. Give them courage when they fret. Create a situation where the mentor tempts the hero. Depict the sidekick acting disloyally. Get the villain to behave well and the hero to behave badly. Whatever you think you know about a character, turn it upside down. Make your hero villainous and your villain heroic; give your sidekick fear and get your mentor to act impulsively; make your heart character think and your mind character feel.

If the eight basic character types can be seen as points on a wheel, see what happens when you spin the wheel and put the characters in unfamiliar roles.

To understand the power of switching roles, consider the concept of shadows. Carl Jung describes the shadow like this:

> The shadow is that hidden, repressed, for the most part inferior and guilt-laden personality whose ultimate ramifications reach back into the realm of our animal ancestors and so comprise the whole historical aspect of the unconscious.

A shadow also may hide the positive side of a personality. Sometimes characters are reluctant to admit their positive qualities because for fear of upending their self-image (as a tough badass, as a realist, or as a cynic) or upending others' expectations of them (this is common in gangs and other peer groups).

All of us deny our deepest desires, out of fear or shame. But those desires don't go away. They lurk beneath the surface. *That's the shadow.* Shadows give characters richness and complexity. No one can be heroic without wrestling with internal as well as external demons.

The shadow's greatest power comes from the character's refusal to embrace it. If we would all just acknowledge our deeper desires and fears, we could address them. But overcoming these desires and fears is scary.

Our shadow is, above all, insecure. Even if we are accomplished, decent, and good-looking, we think of ourselves as failed, flawed, and frumpy. When we look in the mirror, we see flaws. And we think that everyone else must see the same flaws and judge us harshly. Even egotists, when they see themselves as beautiful or smart or capable, fear that others might not acknowledge their positive qualities.

When you change characters' roles, you find deeper characters. And then, you have a chance to create a compelling story.

CASE STUDY: MOSES AND JACOBS, REDUX

Let us suppose, for the sake of argument, that Robert Moses was the hero of your story about the battle for the soul of New York City. As brutal as he could be, Moses played a major role in modernizing the city.

Think about it. Moses took a city of small urban villages, parochial and backward and set in their ways, and transformed them into a dynamic, integrated metropolitan engine. Like Baron von Haussmann in Paris and Vienna decades before, Moses understood that New York could operate on a grand scale only if it was willing to forge a massive, connected *system* out of a vast collection of small, insular communities.

Today's New York—a global capital of finance, technology, culture and the arts, education, medicine, and much more—is possible only because Moses was willing to use a "meat ax" to pursue big projects like bridges, highways, parks and beaches, and public housing.

With Moses as the hero, Jacobs takes the role of the villain. In this reading, she is a small-minded sentimentalist who understands intimate life of neighborhoods but does not appreciate the massive change that cities need to thrive in the modern world.

What about the other character types? Consider . . .

- **Mentor**: Governor Al Smith's top aide, Belle Moskowitz, mentored Moses early in his career. When his career as a civil service reformer faltered, she guided him to a more pragmatic approach to politics and policy. She helped him to see that good intentions are not enough. Power requires resources, connections, and strategy.
- **Sidekicks**: The "Moses Men"—the army of engineers, designers, financiers, lawyers, and managers who carried

out Moses's will—gave Moses their complete loyalty. They believed in him totally, devoting their lives to realizing his vision.

- **Mind**: As a college student, Moses studied British ideas about civil service and political authorities, which fired his imagination—first as a reformer and then as New York's ultimate power broker.
- **Heart**: Moses's emotional touchstone was Governor Al Smith, who guided him as a young man and gave him his first opportunity to build parks, roads, and bridges. Even at his most ruthless, Moses held a soft spot for the old Tammany Hall pol.
- **Skeptic**: Just as Lewis Mumford was skeptical of Jane Jacobs's rosy view of localism, he also doubted many of Moses's projects at a time when Moses was considered an untouchable hero by New Yorkers.
- **Tempters**: In 1934, Moses succumbed to the temptation of conventional political power and ran for governor. He lost badly. Had he won, Moses could not have created his massive machine. After this loss, Moses renounced the idea of elective office. But he never renounced his lust for power. By the end of his career, he pursued more destructive projects and disdained the democratic process.

Robert Moses's long career had a cast of thousands—a dizzying group of brilliant, driven, creative, and conflicted people. For most of his career, Moses exerted almost total control over the drama. Late in life, he faltered. Like all tragic heroes, hubris was his undoing.

———

AND ANOTHER THING . . .

An old literary debate asks: What matters more, character or plot? It's a tired debate. You cannot have characters without a plot, and you can't have a plot without characters. Characters and plot are two sides of the same coin. Still, pressed to say what matters most, I'd say character. Here's why: Nothing interests people more than the idea of people.

You can root for a hero and against a villain; you cannot root for plot twists.

We humans love looking at ourselves. In the story of Narcissus, a beautiful boy gets lost looking at his reflection in a pool. He confuses this image with reality. He spends his days gazing at his own image until he dies. Like Narcissus, we humans love to look at things with our own qualities, wherever we go.

This fascination with the human form carries over to inanimate objects. Consider the Old Man of the Mountain, an outcropping of rock on the White Mountains in New Hampshire. Viewed at an angle, the rock resembled the profile of an old man. For years, people fell in love with that jagged piece of rock. Government officials put the Old Man of the Mountain on the state's U.S. quarter.

Tourists traveled hundreds of miles to see it. When the outcropping fell off a few years ago, some New Hampshire residents began a movement to restore it.

Philosophers have a word for this kind of projection—*anthropomorphism*. We project human qualities onto all kinds of nonhuman things —animals, organizations, buildings, machines, and nature.

To win your reader's attention—and keep it—start by telling stories about *people*. Then help the reader to empathize with the characters. Arouse people by getting them to feel the actions of others. When you make the reader feel something, the reader *cares*.

CHAPTER 3
THE JOURNEY

Tell me a story of deep delight.

ROBERT PENN WARREN

RITA CHARON REMEMBERS the moment when she became the doctor she was meant to be.

Early in her career, Charon didn't always take time to understand her patients' lives and problems. Then along came a woman named Luz. When Luz complained about headaches, Dr. Charon prescribed acetaminophen. Later Luz asked Dr. Charen to fill out paperwork for disability benefits. Rushing to an appointment, Dr. Charon signed the forms. But she wondered about Luz's plans. She suspected that Luz might be abusing the system.

Feeling guilty about her brusque treatment of Luz, Dr. Charon asked her to come in for a visit. Luz then explained her real reasons for seeking disability benefits. The oldest of five girls who lived with her father and uncle in Yonkers, Luz had suffered sexual abuse since she was 12 years old. Now that she was 21, she wanted to rent an apartment in Manhattan and take her sisters with her. She wanted to protect them from the abuse she had experienced.

After learning Luz's real story, Dr. Charon enlisted social workers, emergency shelters, and support groups. She helped Luz find an apartment. She also continued to serve as her physician. She even cared for Luz's dying father.

That experience, Rita Charon says, made her realize that doctors need to understand their patients' stories in order to care for them. It's not enough, she decided, to isolate symptoms and disease for treatment. It's also not enough to analyze patterns of behavior, like diet, exercise, and relationships. Doctors need to understand how their patients' stories, how they got where they were. So Dr. Charon has become a leading figure in "narrative medicine," a movement to get doctors to write and tell stories about their experiences.

Stories can transform everything we do in life. Professionals in all fields often perform their assigned responsibilities well without understanding the people they work with. Administrators swim in seas of statistics and procedures, isolated from the larger dramas of life. Only when we use stories to engage people—doctors, patients, family members, friends, coworkers—can we serve others well and transform lives.

Stories offer all of us a way to create richer lives for ourselves. Stories make us human; they make us whole. Stories might not make all things possible. But they give all possible things a chance to come true.

––––––

ELEMENT 9: GIVE YOUR STORY A NARRATIVE ARC

Two and a half millennia ago, Aristotle outlined the basic imperatives of storytelling in his masterpiece *The Poetics*. This brief guide to the elements of drama remains the seminal work. In Aristotle's words:

- A whole is that which has a beginning, a middle, and an end.
- A beginning is that which does not itself follow anything by causal necessity, but after which something naturally is or comes to be.
- An end, on the contrary, is that which itself naturally follows some other thing, either by necessity, or as a rule, but has nothing following it.
- A middle is that which follows something as some other thing follows it.

Dividing all drama into a beginning, middle, and end might seem simplistic. And many authors violate the rule. The French filmmaker Jean-Luc Godard once quipped: "A story should have a beginning, a middle, and an end, but not necessarily in that order." But for most stories—and for other kinds of communication as well—readers need a journey that moves through these stages.

Aristotle's arc makes a story whole. Something important changes over the course of a story. That change produces a new understanding. The hero becomes a different person. Other characters do as well. As Aristotle explained, drama offers a complete, unified, and internally consistent story to explore the human condition.

Let's see how it works, step by step.

Act I: Into the World of the Story. Most stories begin with characters living ordinary lives in stable environments. This is the world of the status quo, the comfort zone, and *Ho hum, what's for supper?*

In Act I, we meet the main characters in this everyday, ordinary world. We see them interact with family and friends. We see them express, and pursue, their hopes and values. We learn their "back stories," the events that shaped their identity. We watch them playing their comfortable roles and embracing established values. They're "set," at least in their own minds.

Beneath the placid surface lie signs of trouble. A world that appears stable actually teems with contradictions and tensions. A priest hides a secret of abusing children. A ballplayer struggles with a deadly disease. A man has an affair. A student struggles with depression. A business partner embezzles company funds. A mobster struggles with his family. Something's gotta give.

Then a crisis rocks the hero's world. The hero—and other characters, too—are forced to deal with difficult challenges. Storytellers sometimes call this the "inciting incident." I call it the "trigger of trouble." Suddenly, the hero and other characters have to step out of their comfort zones. This moment must involve conflict—between the hero and other people, his community, and even himself. Conflict is essential. As the spy novelist John le Carré once noted, "The cat sat on a mat," is not the beginning of a story. "The cat sat on the dog's mat" is.

Sometimes a positive challenge rocks the hero's world. A new business opportunity (Steve Jobs starts Apple), a love interest (Prince Edward meets Wallis Simpson), a challenge on the ballfield (Jackie Robinson breaks the color line), a courtroom drama (Thurgood Marshall challenges school segregation in the Supreme Court), a petition to run for office (Ross Perot runs for president), a calling to serve God (Martin Luther King goes to seminary): All offer the hero a challenge that, when accepted, takes him in places he could not have imagined before.

With the arrival of trouble or a call to action, the story begins in earnest.

Act II: Crisis and Conflict. Most of us, even the most courageous among us, cannot face a crisis directly—not at first, anyway. It's like staring directly at the sun; we simply cannot handle the intensity. So in the beginning, we usually deny that the problem even exists. And even when we acknowledge the problem, we do not really confront it fully. We try to get rid of the problem without making any significant changes in our approach to life.

Just think of the examples from your life. Ask yourself: Have you ever known an alcoholic who went to AA as soon as his drinking problem caused problems in his life? Or a troubled couple who immediately sought counseling to address their marital tensions? Or a professional who sensed, right away, that his career was veering off track? How many people face their crises immediately, with an eagerness to learn and change? Maybe some, but not many.

Over time, after denying and then minimizing the crisis, the story's hero realizes that he cannot avoid the problem any longer. His wife leaves him or he gets fired or loses a good friend to addiction. So he confronts a *piece* of the problem. He refuses to acknowledge the whole problem; that would be too painful or difficult. So he tries to fix a piece of the problem, hoping that the rest of the problem will magically disappear. But the crisis doesn't go away; in fact, it gets worse.

Haltingly, the hero and other characters take on bigger and bigger pieces of the problem. Tension mounts. The greater the challenge, the greater the stakes. The greater the stakes, the greater the resistance. The greater the resistance, the more profound the experience. By making harder and harder choices—reluctantly, half-heartedly—the hero slowly transforms himself. He grows.

Toward the end of Act II, the hero recognizes a need to *transform* his life. Halfway measures, he now understands, cannot meet his challenge. To use Aristotle's terms, the hero reaches a moment of "recognition": He understands the full dimensions of the problem for the first time. Now, by embracing this whole problem rather than denying it, he gains the power to confront it. He reverses course.

In retrospect, the hero's problems seems so obvious. What takes so long for him to face his challenges? It's really quite simple. All of us struggle to face reality. We deny our problems not just to avoid them, but also because we need to break these problems into smaller pieces. The hero is no different. He *cannot* confront his crisis early in the story. He must face it, grudgingly, in stages. Eventually, after a long struggle, he transforms himself.

Act III: A new world is born: The story eventually reaches a resolution, which puts characters and issues in a new place.

Theater people call the final part of the story "the slow curtain." Characters settle their accounts—finish off foes, reconcile with friends and loved ones, embrace new roles and expectations. They say, in effect: *Ah, this is how life's going to be from now on.*

As you end the story, make sure you can capture the meaning of this resolution. You should be able to summarize it in a simple phrase. When Brian Piccolo dies at the end of *Brian's Song*, the resolution is not "Hero dies," but "Hero dies with courage, touching all who know him." When Willie Stark gets assassinated at the end of *All the King's Men*, the resolution is not "Politician gets killed," but "Corruption ruins politician and his whole world." When Dorothy returns to Kansas at the end of The Wizard of Oz, the resolution is not "Girl returns home," but "Girl returns home a mature, wiser young woman."

At every stage of the process, show the undercurrents of the story. For every scene, ask yourself: What are the emotional effects of this moment? A story is not just a sequence of events; it's the sequence of *meaningful* events. Make sure your narrative arc vibrates with emotional power.

With a strong conclusion, the story comes full circle. The point of the journey and its struggles becomes clear. To the story's hero–and to its reader–all the pieces come together to create something whole.

CASE STUDY: ANTHONY LEWIS'S *GIDEON'S TRUMPET*

American constitutional history is filled with tales of ordinary people who get caught in dangerous situations, often with no resources, who fought back against the system. Everyday heroes like Fred Kormatsu, Amy Rowley, Ernesto Miranda, Norma McCorvey, and Ellery Schempp fought all the way to the Supreme Court to seek their rights and changed history.

Another such figure was Clarence Earl Gideon, a 50-year-old drifter who was arrested in 1961 for breaking into a pool hall in Panama City, Florida, to steal money and wine. When brought to trial, Gideon asked for a lawyer but was denied. At the time, Florida guaranteed counsel only to defendants in capital cases and in cases with "extraordinary circumstances." When a jury found Gideon guilty, he went to jail. There, he petitioned the U.S. Supreme Court for a retrial. Eventually, Gideon won the case, which guaranteed the right of counsel to all defendants.

Let's step back and look at the narrative arc of this story.

• **World of the story**: On August 4, 1961, a police officer on patrol noticed something strange going on at the Bay Harbor Pool Room. When the cop investigated and contacted the bar's owner, the two of them discovered the vending machine broken and bottles of wine missing. A neighbor reported seeing a man emerge from the pool hall carrying a bottle of wine, his pockets jangling with coins, and getting into a cab. After the cab driver said he had picked up Gideon, the police found Gideon at a bar with $25 in change in his pockets and arrested him.

Gideon protested his innocence. When he could not meet bail, he was held for trial. In court, he asked the judge for a lawyer but the judge denied him, noting that this was not a capital case and it posed no "extraordinary" circumstances. The judge noted his request for the record.

• **Rising action**: At the trial, Gideon tried to defend himself, with some help from the case's amiable judge, but the jury found him guilty and the judge sentenced him to five years in jail. Behind bars, Gideon wrote to the U.S. Supreme Court, seeking a writ of *habeas corpus*. Because he was denied a lawyer in his trial, Gideon argued, he was being held unlawfully. In his writ, Gideon asserted (incorrectly, according to the law at the time) that the Constitution guaranteed him a lawyer under the Sixth Amendment. In fact, the amendment reads that "in all criminal prosecutions, the accused shall enjoy the right to have the assistance of counsel for his defense." The amendment offers no explicit guarantee of a lawyer if the defendant cannot afford one.

The Supreme Court agreed to take Gideon's case and appointed one of the nation's best lawyers, Abe Fortas, to represent him. Before the case began, 22 state attorneys general—led by future Senator and Vice President Walter Mondale—signed an *amicus curiae* brief urging the adoption of a uniform federal right to court-appointed counsel.

The case presented difficult issues of federalism: How much should the federal government require the state governments to do to assure a fair trial? Already, 45 of the 50 states guaranteed counsel to indigent defendants. Was it really necessary to mandate the others? And would a constitutional mandate create unnecessary burdens on state courts?

In the Court's hearing, Fortas rebutted that latter point. The existing requirement of counsel only in "special circumstances," he argued, actually imposed *more* of a burden to states than a blanket requirement would. Fortas's assistant, Abe Krash, noted: "What could be more of an irritant to state court judges than to have federal judges review and set aside their decisions on a case-by-case basis under so ambiguous a standard as 'special circumstances'?"

Bruce Jacob, who argued for the state of Florida, remembered the justices' obsession with the far-reaching consequences of the case. "They weren't concerned with precedents," he said. "They had all these hypothetical questions, trying to carry everything to its farthest point. I wanted to be honest. ... But the more honest I was, the more they kept putting me on the spot."

In a 9-to-0 decision, the Supreme Court ruled for Gideon and mandated that all defendants be given free counsel in criminal cases. In his opinion for the Court, Justice Hugo Black argued that *Betts* v.

Brady had never been the correct decision. "[A]ny person hauled into court, who is too poor to hire a lawyer, cannot be assured a fair trial unless counsel is provided for him," his decision stated.

• **Resolution**: Now entitled to a lawyer, Gideon got a retrial in the pool hall case. His new lawyer was able to puncture the prosecutor's claims. Gideon's conviction was reversed. Freed from jail, Gideon lived another ten years.

The Gideon case offers a perfect Aristotelian arc—from the moment in the beginning when the hero was denied his freedom … to the escalating battle over his claims until it reached its ultimate battleground and conclusion … until finally, in the end, the hero and other characters resumed their lives under new circumstances.

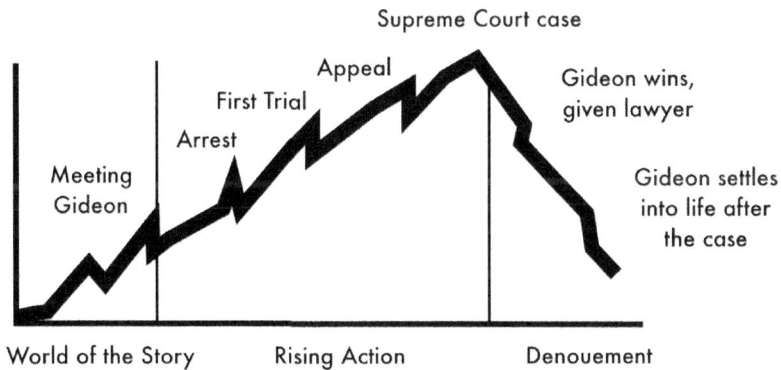

Supreme Court case

Appeal

First Trial

Arrest

Meeting
Gideon

Gideon wins,
given lawyer

Gideon settles
into life after
the case

World of the Story   Rising Action   Denouement

ELEMENT 10: STRUCTURE YOUR STORY, MOMENT BY MOMENT

In the last generation, Aristotle's classic narrative arc has gotten a makeover.

With the rise of Big Data and the quantitative analysis of stories, researchers have found ways to advance a story through three acts. These studies have identified specific moments that help define the characters and their quest.

To guide the storytelling process, I have examined a number of these studies. I have attempted to synthesize their points here.

The authors (and their books) who contributed to this analysis include

Joseph Campbell (*The Hero With a Thousand Faces*), Christopher Vogler (*The Writer's Journey*), Robert McKee (*Story*), Blake Snyder (*Save the Cat!*), Jessica Brody (*Save the Cat! Writes a Novel*), Jill Chamberlain (*The Nutshell Technique*), Jodie Archer and Matthew Jockers (*The Bestseller Code*), Michael Hauge (*Storytelling Made Easy*), and James Scott Bell (*Write Your Novel from the Middle*).

Act I: World of the Story

Act I introduces us to the hero, her likable qualities, and her flaws. By the end of this act, the hero plunges into a struggle that could transform her forever. The act takes up the first quarter of the story.

• **Establishing Shot** (0 to 1%): Something emotional has to happen right away. Show a single moment with the hero in a challenging place. In this moment, we start to care and root for the hero.

In this opening moment, the hero states her *belief* about her desires and how the world works. This "setup want" is superficial; it does not address the hero's true life challenge. Achieving this superficial goal will not solve the hero's problem; on the contrary, it will reveal the need to take on an even bigger, more existential problem.

This opening scene, then, hints at the hero's true need—as well as her flaw.

• **Statement of Value** (5%): In addition to knowing the character's superficial *want* or *desire*, we also need to understand her *deepest* desire —even if she doesn't fully realize it herself.

We can understand the hero's deepest desire in one of two ways. She might reveal it inadvertently, by saying something she does not really understand or acting in a way that expresses this desire.

Often, someone else—like the hero's mentor, sidekick, skeptic, for example—gives expression to the hero's deeper desire. Somehow, they know her passions better than she does. After all, she's in denial; they do not carry her same baggage, so they are free to see things clearly.

• **The Challenge/Catalyst** (10%): At some point, the hero faces a challenge. The mythology guru Robert Campbell calls this "the call to action." Others call it the "inciting incident."

That challenge can come from inside (e.g., the hero's own anxiety, insecurity, or restlessness) or outside (e.g., a broken relationship, job loss, terrible injury, and more). Whatever happens, the hero must—let me underscore *must*—do something to meet this challenge.

• **No Going Back** (20-25%): After an early period of doubt and debate, the hero moves out of her comfort zone, at least a little. She realizes she has to *act*. So she engages the battle—even though she has no idea where it might lead or how it will transform her life.

• **Hero, Meet Your Life Coach** (22%): As the character begins to struggle, she meets someone who can change everything: a friend, mentor, or lover who can push and prod the hero for the rest of the story. This character will force the hero to go deeper than she has ever had the courage to go before.

It's going to hurt. The hero's wounds are deep and she would rather anesthetize the pain, not confront its source. But this new life coach will not let her avoid the deeper reality forever.

Act II: Rising Action

Act II is a struggle over life and death—sometimes literally, sometimes metaphorically. This act, which takes up the middle 50 percent of the story, shows the hero taking on different aspects of her challenge—sometimes winning, sometimes losing.

• **Success! Or Failure!** (25%)—A quarter into the story, the hero gets what she wanted—or at least, what she *thought* she wanted. This inadequate victory shows that the early desire was superficial and avoidant.

Victory comes with a "catch." That catch points to the hero's authentic goal—and frontloads Act II with a batch of tougher, more meaningful challenges.

• **Halftime, or Throwing the Hat Over the Wall** (50%): As she struggles with her greatest challenge, the hero finally takes bold action. She asks herself: "OK, what's it going to be? More avoidance—or authentic growth?" She throws her hat over the fence; in other words, she moves forward in a way that she cannot go retreat. She's "in it to win it."

Halfway through the story, in the pursuit of her authentic goal, the hero will experience either a false victory or a false defeat.

• **Hitting Bottom** (75%): As the stakes and tension rise, nothing the hero does is enough. To become her best self, the hero needs to "hit bottom" and experience the full cost of holding on to her old ways. She needs to be knocked down, beaten up, and declared the loser. Not just once, but two or three times. Only then can she resolve to remake herself totally, from the inside out.

Now the hero faces a choice between Undesirable Option A and Even-More-Undesirable Option B. So the question is: Can she find a better Option C? Can she rise above the limitations and contradictions of the two unacceptable options? Either way, there is no going back, again. The struggle is unrelenting.

Act III: Resolution

In the end, the hero experiences success or failure. Either she learns and grows to become her best, most authentic self—or she squanders that opportunity. The hero's success or failure tells you everything you need to know about her character.

• **Depression and Brooding** (75% to 80%): At her nadir, the hero holds one last pity party. She mopes and complains and declares herself the loser. At the same time, she begins to realize that she needs to abandon her limiting beliefs and figure out how to solve her urgent life-or-death problem.

The time for rebuilding has arrived. Emotionally, the hero decides that she has to carry out a final process of transformation. She needs to fight for something that matters.

• **The Answer!** (80%): At last, the hero figures out (or fails to figure out) how to confront her deepest challenges. To begin a new life, she has to leave her old life behind. Every gain entails a loss. That's a hard lesson, but also the very essence of maturity and wisdom … and resurrection.

• **Plan and Execute** (80-90%): It's time to act. The hero has to assemble her posse, make plans, and mount a victorious (or losing) last stand.

• **The Final Battle** (95-98%): Finally, the climax: The hero's deeper desires and values finally prevail. She takes a less simplistic view of the world. She understands the world more profoundly and remakes herself accordingly (or fails to, in a tragedy).

• **The New Status Quo** (99-100%): In the end, we see the hero in her new world, with her new values and wisdom. Metaphorically, she has found the magic elixir (or, in a tragedy, finds herself defeated forever). In this final scene, we get an indication that a new approach might just work. No promises, of course. We might want a sequel, right?

CASE STUDY: ROBERT TOWNE'S *CHINATOWN*

A former Los Angeles cop named Jake Gittes, who removal from the force can be traced to nefarious deeds in Chinatown, thinks get gets just another case of marital infidelity when a woman calling herself Evelyn Mulwray asks to spy on her husband Hollis. When he takes the case, he discovers rape, murder, and the corrupt deals to wrest control of L.A. by greedy elites.

Hollis Mulwray, Gittes soon discovers, is the chief engineer for L.A.'s water system who is fighting plans to build a dam. The shale underneath the proposed dam will give way, he predicts, causing a catastrophic collapse of the structure. Because Mulwray opposes the dam, malevolent forces are out to get him; for a desert community like L.A., water is the most precious resource. The woman calling herself Mrs. Mulwray was in on the plot. Gittes has to find out why.

Chinatown, a noir detective film written by Robert Towne and directed by Roman Polanski, explores the dark side of politics: how greed and corruption can undermine the basic elements of a decent, fair, and just society.

Act I: The World of the Story

• **Establishing Shot** (0 to 1%): The story opens with Gittes showing a client photos of his wife having an affair, then comforting him. "She's no good," the client cries. "When you're right, you're right," Gittes says. Right away, we see that Gittes is cynical but also a little caring. Then a Mrs. Mulwray enters the picture, hiring Gittes to track Hollis to see if he is having an affair.

• **Statement of Value** (5%): Gittes attends a public hearing where Hollis Mulwray states his opposition to the dam. "The shale can't withstand the pressure," he says. "I won't build it." Farmers, desperate for water, create a spectacle by bringing sheep into the hearing.

• **The Challenge/Catalyst** (10%): One of his investigators shows Gittes photographs of Mulwray arguing with an old man named Noah Cross. We soon learn that Cross, Mulwray's former partner, abused his public position to enrich himself during the region's early boom years. Why did the two argue so intensely?

• **No Going Back** (20-25%): When Gittes goes to Mulwray's home, he meets the real Evelyn Mulwray. He wants to figure out who hired the fake Mrs. Mulwray to get dirt on Hollis. Evelyn asks Gittes to drop the matter but he refuses.

• **Hero, Meet Your Life Coach** (22%): Evelyn will lead Gittes to the truth, even though she will also withhold the critical pieces of the story. Her mystery—her beauty, passion, and determination—will drive Gittes forward.

Act II: Rising Action

• **Success! Or Failure! (25%)**: When Gittes goes to a dam to track down Mulwray, he is met by cops he once worked with. Gittes asks where Mulwray is. "I'd like to talk to him," he says. "You're welcome to try—there he is," a police lieutenant says as he points to Mulwray's dead body being dragged from the water. Now the case is more urgent —and dangerous—than ever.

• **Halftime, or Throwing the Hat Over the Wall** (50%): Gittes confronts Noah Cross: "When was the last time you saw Mulwray?" Cross pretends not to know. "Well, It was about five days ago," Gittes says. "You were outside the Pig 'n Whistle and you had one hell of an argument." Cross is surprised that Gittes is gathering information. Even though Cross is hiring Gittes to find the girl that Mulwray was with, the two are now enemies.

• **Hitting Bottom** (75%): After getting a late-night call from, his former police colleagues, Gittes goes to a house where the fake Mrs. Mulwray has been murdered. His former colleagues accuse him of a role in the killing. They demand answers. Gittes has been cornered. But who's behind it?

Act III: Resolution

• **Depression and Brooding** (75% to 80%): Gittes begins to analyze this complex situation. Nothing is as it appears. He needs answers. Noah Cross wants him to "find the girl," who has disappeared; Cross then tells Gittes that then girl is his daughter. Gittes struggles to sort the characters and their motivations.

• **The Answer!** (80%): Gittes finally learns that Hollis was killed because he discovered that sinister forces were diverting the flow of water in order to drive farmers out of business and buy their land cheaply—and then get the controversial dam built to raise the value of land in the area.

• **Plan and Execute** (80-90%): Gittes learns that Evelyn is leaving town with the girl. He tracks her down; convinced she was involved in her husband's murder, he calls the cops. Then he discovers the truth: Katherine, the girl, is Evelyn's sister *and* her daughter; Cross raped Evelyn when she was 15 years old. Now Evelyn is trying to save her from Noah's clutches. Gittes hurriedly makes plans to help Evelyn and Katherine escape before Noah can track her down.

• **The Final Battle** (95-98%): Cross catches up to Evelyn, in Chinatown, as she attempts to escape with her sister/daughter. As she drives away, cops fire at her car. They kill Evelyn. Noah takes Katherine into his arms. He gets what he wants.

• **The New Status Quo** (99-100%): Gittes is powerless. His old cop friends lead him away. "It's Chinatown, Jake," they say. The subtext is clear: In Chinatown, shady figures make shady deals and corrupt everyone in the process and no one is held responsible.

Chinatown is perhaps the best movie on politics and corruption—the power of elites, the behind-the-scenes scramble for power and money, the dirty characters behind it all, the complicity of officials, and the futility of trying to get good policy or justice. These key moments reveal the puzzles of this corrupt world.

———

ELEMENT 11: FOR COMPLEXITY, SHOW MORE THAN ONE ARC

A *good* story requires the hero to face a crisis and confront barriers, again and again, until he grows and becomes a better person.

A *great* story, however, requires at least two or three compelling characters to confront separate sets of barriers—and for them to cross paths along their journeys. These overlapping stories add richness and complexity to the drama. Sometimes the characters support each other; sometimes, they battle each other. These encounters create another dimension of conflict. The lives of different people come together and then separate, again and again, throughout the story. These overlapping arcs give the story complexity.

A love story, then, would not only follow the arc of the couple who meet and fall in love; it would also track the stories of their families, social circles, and careers (think: any Victorian novel). A political tale would not only follow the career of the president or union leader, but also his family's saga, his opponents' stories, and the communities or movements that he represents (think: *The Last Hurrah*). A family drama might revolve around the patriarch, with his children's struggles and conflicts (think: *Succession*).

Think of some common sets of arcs in stories:

- As one character succeeds in the world by cutting corners and making compromises, another struggles to do things the right way.
- As one character discovers and pursues his deepest desires, another rises by conforming to community ideals.
- As one character pursues a secret mission, her colleagues pursue their own goals without knowing about hidden drama.

Often one arc spins off another. The major arc gives rise to a character who goes her own way, only to cross paths with the main characters later on. To write storylines for arcs, create a set of "from … to…" statements for all the major characters. Consider, for example, these summaries of *Wizard of Oz*:

- Dorothy moves from innocence and helplessness to self-knowledge and strength.
- Dorothy's friends move from helpless, broken spirits to trustworthy and self-aware allies.
- The Wicked Witch moves from heartbreak and rage to a tragic fall.

The many arcs of a story—two or three or more—move forward independently. When the arcs intersect, they offer special tension and insight.

CASE STUDY: ROBERT CARO'S *PASSAGE OF POWER*

Three great tragedies of American politics can be found in the overlapping arcs of three great figures—John Kennedy, Lyndon Johnson, and Robert Kennedy. Robert Caro captures these arcs in *The Passage of Power*, his study of Lyndon Johnson's career between 1958 and 1964. Let's look at these three arcs:

JFK's arc: John Kennedy begins the story as a privileged playboy politician, a senator with a lackluster legislative record and no real promise of greatness. But Kennedy surprises people. He hustles and performs well in the 1960 primaries easily winning the nomination. As president, he inspires a new generation with his call to public service but stumbles in the Bay of Pigs fiasco and is humiliated by Soviet premier Nikita Khrushchev. In time, Kennedy finds his footing on the issues of space, civil rights, the economy, the Cuban Missile Crisis, and nuclear proliferation. Then, on November 22, 1963, he is assassinated. Kennedy dies a man of promise rather than a man of accomplishment, the essence of tragedy.

LBJ's arc: Lyndon Johnson begins the story as the most powerful congressional leader of modern times, ambitious to win the presidency. But Kennedy outmaneuvers him to win the Democratic nomination in 1960. When Kennedy offers him the vice presidency, Johnson accepts despite his long-smoldering resentment of the Kennedy family. "Power is where power goes," LBJ rationalizes. Once Kennedy wins the White House, Johnson is neutered. The Kennedys isolate him from the administration's important decision-making processes. LBJ fears his political career is over. But with Kennedy's assassination, Johnson becomes president and is transformed. He adopts the most ambitious agenda of any modern president, rejecting advice to avoid tough issues. "Well, what the hell's the presidency for?" he asks. Later, his presidency collapses; the Vietnam War and culture and race conflict rip the nation apart, leading to the election of Richard Nixon as president.

RFK's arc: Robert Kennedy begins the story as an arrogant aide to Joseph McCarthy and an ardent Cold Warrior. When his brother runs for president, he manages the campaign. As attorney general, he not only revives the moribund Justice Department but also serves as his brother's top deputy. RFK's resolve, more than any other factor, steers the world from nuclear war during the Cuban Missile Crisis. After his brother's assassination, RFK plunges into deep depression. But out of that depression he emerges one of the most transformative leaders of our time. He leads the race for the Democratic nomination in 1968—until, like his brother, he is felled by an assassin's bullet.

We might depict the overlapping arcs of these three figures like this:

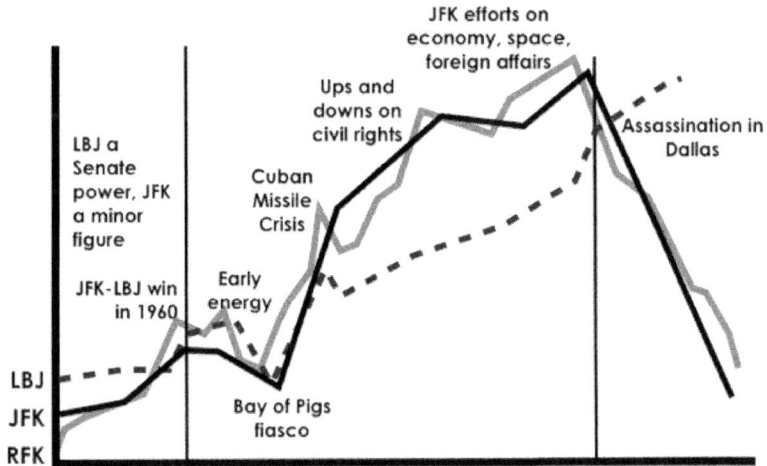

JFK efforts on economy, space, foreign affairs

Ups and downs on civil rights

LBJ a Senate power, JFK a minor figure

Cuban Missile Crisis

Assassination in Dallas

JFK-LBJ win in 1960

Early energy

LBJ

JFK

RFK

Bay of Pigs fiasco

Let's see the moments of overlap. The Kennedys pursued separate interests in the 1950s, when JFK was a senator and RFK served as a Senate staffer. But they came together when JFK vied for the vice presidential nomination in 1956. The Kennedys and LBJ followed separate tracks until 1960, when JFK outmaneuvered LBJ for the presidency but selected him as vice president. RFK froze out LBJ during the administration. After much delay, JFK embraced the civil rights movement—setting up a later triumph for LBJ. President Kennedy's assassination made LBJ president and led to RFK's isolation in the new administration—and his decision to challenge Johnson in 1968.

This Shakespearean tale reveals all the brightness and darkness of America in the 1960s. By tracking only one of the three narrative arcs, we would get a thin, superficial view of the era. But with all three, we get a vivid, complex view.

ELEMENT 12: SHOW CHARACTERS HITTING BRICK WALLS

In 2008, a computer scientist at Carnegie-Mellon University named Randy Pausch attracted national acclaim with his "last lecture." Dying of pancreatic cancer, Pausch spoke with joy about life and learning, family and friends. As his journey ended, he celebrated life.

Pausch talked about "brick walls," the barriers that we all face in our everyday lives. Those brick walls could be trivial (a traffic jam) or profound (a cancer diagnosis). Rather than lamenting them, Pausch called these them essential parts of our growth and development:

> Brick walls are there for a reason. The brick walls are not there to keep us out. The brick walls are there to show how badly we want something. Because the brick walls are there to stop the people who don't want something badly enough. They are there to keep out the other people.

What happens when characters hit brick walls? How do they deal with barriers? Do they get angry or accept the reality of the situation? Do they embrace responsibility or cast blame? Do they show a team spirit or angle for personal benefit? Do they adjust to changing circumstances or stubbornly cling to their old ways? Do they devise a strategy to climb over the wall or do they quit? Do they seek help from others?

By facing a series of crises, heroes and other characters stretch themselves to accomplish extraordinary feats.

All of literature's great characters—Oedipus and Odysseus, Hamlet and Macbeth, Don Juan and Tom Jones, Jane Eyre and Carrie Meeber, Santiago and Tomas, Holden Caulfield and Rabbit Angstrom, to name a handful—battle both external and internal foes to realize their potentials. Each faces daunting problems with limited powers.

"We only think," John Dewey reminds us, "when we are confronted with a problem." When we confront a brick wall, the story begins and deepens.

CASE STUDY: JOHN CANNAN, 'A LEGISLATIVE HISTORY OF THE AFFORDABLE CARE ACT'

Otto von Bismarck, the German statesman, once remarked: "If you like laws and sausages, you should never watch either one being made."

So many bits and pieces of junk enter both processes, Bismarck said, that people would be revolted if they witnessed what happened. So it was with the 2010 passage of the Affordable Care Act, popularly known as Obamacare.

For generations, health care advocates unsuccessfully lobbied for a program of universal access to medical care. More than 50 million people had no health care and faced ruinous bills or worsening illnesses. Hospitals, meanwhile, faced billions in extra expenses by providing free care in emergencies like car crashes, heart attacks, strokes, shootings, and overdoses.

Under President Barack Obama, a Democratic Congress finally passed health care reform in 2010. How it happened is a lesson in overcoming "brick walls" in the legislative process. Here are a few of barriers that Congress overcame:

- **Partisanship**: Democrats controlled both houses of Congress. But in the U.S. Senate, a hardy minority can use a filibuster to block action on legislation. A filibuster allows the minority to use a variety of delaying tactics to prevent a bill from combining up for a debate and vote. Filibusters can be broken when 60 or more senators vote for "cloture." The Democrats had those 60 votes until Edward Kennedy died and a Republican won the election to replace him. Now the G.O.P. could use a filibuster to kill the bill.
- **Committee system**: As a matter of course, all bills are assigned to a number of committees for their first consideration. The Senate sent the legislation to the committees for Finance and Health, Education, Labor, and Pensions; the House sent it to the committees for Education and Labor, Energy and Commerce, and Ways and Means. Each committee could hijack the process if they do not get what they want in the bill. Managing these fiefdoms posed a difficult challenge for Senate Majority Leader Harry Reid and House Speaker Nancy Pelosi.
- **Amendments**: Congress members introduced hundreds of amendments on issues ranging from abortion to taxes. Some of these amendments passed and some failed. Each one created a new barrier to the legislation. Often, the amendments steered the bill away from its core principles.

Consider the case of the "public option," which would allow consumers to choose from both private and public insurance plans. Health-care proponents were forced to abandon the public option in order to gain the support of insurance lobby. That was just one of dozens of sticking points for this complex legislation.

- **Reconciliation**: Under Senate rules, a minority can use a "filibuster" to prevent a bill from coming up for a vote. To force a vote, bill supporters need to get support from 60 out of 100 senators. Senate Democrats overcame this hurdle with "reconciliation," a process that allows budget bills to proceed without the 60-vote supermajority. Republicans cried foul, calling this maneuver a betrayal of the Senate's traditional mo0de of operations. This "nuclear" option ruined any chance for collaboration. The actual use of reconciliation also required a second vote on the legislation.
- **Industry and business opposition**: In 1965, Congress passed Medicare and Medicaid against the opposition of the American Medical Association and other industry lobbyists. President Obama and Democrats in Congress wanted their support, so they negotiated favorable provisions for interest groups in the health care industry.
- **Unifying approaches**: Traditionally, conference committees iron out differences in House and Senate bills. But Congress sidestepped this approach. Instead, a process called "ping-ponging" allowed members from one house to ask members in the other to resolve their differences before they passed their final versions. Later, Senate and House leaders worked with the whole House to settle differences outside the formal committee process.
- **Legal challenges**: As President Obama signed the new bill into law, the battle was just beginning. Opponents challenged the law in court. The Supreme Court upheld the law by a 5-to-4 vote, but certain provisions of the law were later declared unconstitutional.
- **The new regime**: When Donald Trump and Republicans swept to power in 2016, they set out to dismantle the law. Congress failed to repeal the law, but the Trump Administration used executive powers to undermine critical

provisions of the law. Most notably, the administration issued regulations against the "individual mandate" and public subsidies.

Obamacare was no small miracle, given the history of failed health-care bills going back to President Theodore Roosevelt and persistent attacks on health care by Republicans. But the law passed and remains the law of the land. For now.

———

ELEMENT 13: NEST JOURNEYS INSIDE JOURNEYS

Inside every great journey are a number of smaller journeys. Each of these smaller trips is a complete journey in itself; each one also moves the larger story forward.

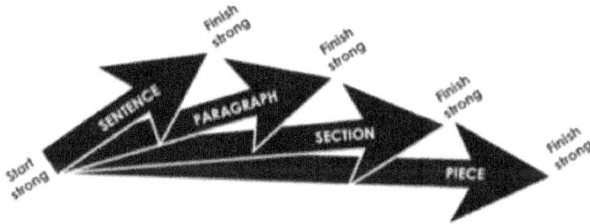

Think of a family vacation to the Grand Canyon from (let's just say) your home in Ohio. The first leg of the journey takes you to Indianapolis, where you go to the Indy 500 or visit the state capitol. Then you get to St. Louis, where you see the Cardinals or visit Forest Park. Then you go to Tulsa, Amarillo, and Albuquerque—at each stop, seeing historic and recreation spots—before arriving at the canyon in northern Arizona.

That's how writing works. Each section of the journey—every sentence, paragraphs section, and the whole piece—takes the reader on a complete journey. All of these pieces fit into larger journeys.

Part by part, journey by journey, the larger narrative takes form. Each part contains its own drama. The dramas of the parts contributes to the larger dramas.

The effect is powerful. The reader gets a whole experience. Each part offers its own value, with its own drama, but also contributes to a larger drama.

CASE STUDY: IAN FRAZIER'S 'THE BAG BILL'

In the next generation, the volume of plastic in the earth's waters will exceed the volume of fish life in these waters. Plastic pollution, on land as well as in the water, is not just an aesthetic concern. It is a matter of grave urgency to the ecosystem that sustains all life.

A bill to ban the use of plastic bags in New York City offered one response to this crisis.

In a profile for *The New Yorker*, the journalist Ian Frazier tracks the campaign to pass legislation to assess a 5-cent fee for the use of plastic bags in stores. That overall theme of Frazier's piece is simple: *In their effort to rid the city of an unnecessary scourge, environmentalists struggled against the public's lack of awareness and the well-funded campaign of the plastic lobby.*

Each of the article's eight sections support the overall theme of the article. Consider the controlling ideas of these eight parts:

- **The activist**: The story's protagonist, Jennie Romer, previously advised efforts to ban or charge for bags in California. Now she is lobbying New York's City Council to charge fees for bags.
- **The author**: Ian Frazier offers the backstory about his own efforts to combat the widespread litter of bags in public spaces.
- **The activist, then and now**: Romer's upbringing, which included regular family trips to recycling centers. Also: her rebuttals to bag bill critics and her frustration at the slow pace of progress.
- **Opposition**: Small shop owners claim that a bag tax would drive away customers.
- **Grassroots efforts**: Volunteers clean up bag litter in parks and other public places.
- **Pros and cons**: The arguments for—and against—recycling of plastics.
- **Going deep**: A visit to Staten Island, where Hurricane Sandy "inundated the park's woodland to a depth of perhaps 20

feet and left behind a vastness of shredded plastic in the
trees, like the pennants of a cast-of-thousands demon army."
- **Lobbying**: After a long campaign to persuade reluctant City
Council members, Mayor Bill de Blasio announces his
support.

Each of these eight pieces is a complete narrative that stands on its
own. But put together, they create a larger drama that affects not just
wastes in New York, but also the fate of waterways and landfills
beyond Gotham.

The uber-journey shows how an activist promotes her cause,
encounters opposition, and devises strategies to address every challenge she faces. Each section also creates its own journey, which nests
inside the whole piece Each paragraph also offers clear journeys,
which in turn contain sentences with their own clear journeys.

Let's go deeper, examining a couple of specific examples.

• **The level of the paragraph**: The first paragraph sets the tone for
the whole piece. The paragraph begins: "Jennie Romer moved from
California to New York about four years ago to save the city from
plastic bags." The paragraph ends: "She learned how better to advise
Los Angeles, which passed its own anti-bag ordinance, in 2012."

That paragraph offers a clear journey, which starts and ends
strongly. We begin with today's challenge; we end with the skills
Romer needs to meet that challenge, which she learned in L.A.

• **The level of the section**: The whole first section also offers a clear
journey that starts and finishes strongly. The section moves from
meeting the activist ("Jennie Romer moved from California to New
York ...") to an anti-reform group's distribution of misleading flyers:
"A representative of the [lobbying organization called the American
Progressive Bag Alliance], when told of this occurrence, said that it
would never do such an underhanded move." Welcome to the big city,
Jennie!

• **The level of the whole piece**: The overall piece also traces a clear
journey, starting and ending strongly.

Recall that the article opened by introducing Jennie Romer. Here's
how it ends: "If the bill passes, perhaps in may, as she now believes it
will, she plans to get a small plastic bag tattooed on her side, where it
generally will not be seen."

The article, then, takes us from the beginning to the end of Romer's

New York campaign—from getting to know her to seeing how she plans to celebrate victory when it happens.

Nesting narratives requires a strategic breakdown of a piece into smaller, whole sections. Each section should follow the Golden Rule and, at the same time, contribute to a larger work piece that also follows the Golden Rule.

———

AND ANOTHER THING . . .

The ultimate goal of storytelling is unity and wholeness.

A great story is not just, as the historian Arnold Toynbee once quipped, "one damned thing after another." You need more than characters, events, and backstories. You need to give it all *shape*.

The characters and events of a story, ultimately, force us to grapple with a great question. As a storyteller, your challenge is to force your character to face this question. So ask yourself: Where is your hero going? Is it toward home? Innocence? Redemption? Truth? Honor? How must he learn and transform to meet his challenges?

Emotions and values drive characters. Think of the great characters of literature. Would Beowulf matter as just another warrior recruited to kill a monster? Would Macbeth matter as just another rising figure in a royal administration? Would Huck Finn matter as just another young rebel looking for adventure? Would Don Corleone matter as just another mob boss who decides to stay out of the drug business? Without passion and complication, would we care about these characters?

WRITING TECHNIQUES
FOR PART TWO

CHAPTER 4
SENTENCES

IN *A MOVABLE FEAST*, Ernest Hemingway describes how he deals with the problem of writer's block:

> I would sit in front of the fire and squeeze the peel of the little oranges into the edge of the flame and watch the sputter of blue that they made. I would stand and look out over the roofs of Paris and think, "Do not worry. You have always written before and you will write now. All you have to do is write one true sentence. Write the truest sentence you know." So finally I would write one true sentence, and then go on from there. It was easy then because there was always one true sentence that I knew or had seen or had heard someone say.

If you can write "one true sentence," you can write anything. If you can't, you're doomed.

The sentence is, then, the most important unit of writing. If we did nothing else but study the sentence, we would all write better.

So what is a sentence, anyway? My online dictionary offers this definition:

> A set of words that is complete in itself, typically containing a subject and predicate, conveying a statement, question, exclamation, or command, and consisting of a main clause and sometimes one or more subordinate clauses.

This definition, alas, begs the question. A "set of words that is complete in itself" could include everything from a line of haiku to *War and Peace*. I like this definition offered by a legendary advertising copywriter named Eugene Schwartz:

> As much of your thought as you can effectively give the other person at one time.

This definition suggests a relationship between the writer and reader. It also suggests the importance of brevity. Too often, writers forget about the reader; they ramble on and on, using abstract and imprecise language that alienates the reader. Still, Schwartz's definition fails to break sentences into their essential parts. So try this definition:

> A complete idea that shows action or relationships, almost always using a subject and verb—and providing a building block for larger and larger ideas.

This definition, like Schwartz's, stresses the importance of keeping things simple, with the reader in mind. It also suggests that out is part of something greater.

Think of sentences as different kinds of paths. Imagine, first, a short path that moves quickly from one point to another. In this path, not much happens. You just take your subject (and reader) to a nearby place. Longer paths explore sights along the way; sometimes they veer off into different directions.

Like any journey, a sentence-path can be as simple or complex as you want or need it to be. The key words are *want or need*. You need to make conscious decisions to write a short or long, straight or curving, direct or meandering sentence. Our biggest challenge, as writers, is to take control of our work.

When in doubt, make sure your sentences are simple enough to be understood. Even in longer sentences, make sure the core idea is easy to understand. Whatever you do, avoid the pretension of academics and critics who want to show off with needless complexity.

"A lot of critics think I'm stupid because my sentences are so simple and my method is so direct," the novelist Kurt Vonnegut once said. "They think these are defects. No. The point is to write as much as you know as quickly as possible."

ELEMENT 14: FOLLOW THE GOLDEN RULE FOR SENTENCES

We hear a lot these days about the power of storytelling. Political pundits debate whether candidates offer a "strong narrative." Consultants earn small fortunes by schooling executives on the "hero's journey." Advertisers build compelling dramas into 30-second commercials. Narrative, narrative everywhere.

I would like to take the narrative imperative a step further. Every challenge of writing—creating great sentences and paragraphs, selecting the right words and images, getting the grammar right, editing with a sharp scalpel—should take a narrative form. Everything you write, in fact, should offer a complete drama.

Only when sentences move with all the elements of a great story—vivid characters, compelling goals, strong arcs, rising tensions, revealing twists and turns, and surprises—can they do their job.

To simplify the task, let me remind you of the Golden Rule of Writing:

1. Make everything a journey.
2. Start strong, finish strong.

Let's consider two key ideas.

First, the journey: Every sentence should take the reader from one state of understanding to another. Introduce every line with a compelling character, event, or issue. Set out a clear purpose or goal. In the march from the beginning to the end, show the reader one or more surprising ideas or images. And take only the steps you need to get to the destination.

Second, the start and finish: To write with power, start with a bang and end with a bang. Tell the reader, right away, who does what. Conclude the sentence with some kind of closure—completing the thought or action or offering a telling image or question.

Without clear starting and finish lines, we wander aimlessly. We can get lazy and write whatever comes to mind. Then the reader gets lost.

When my students first started to use the Golden Rule to write sentences, they thought it was too demanding: *Make every sentence a journey? Start strong, finish strong, in every sentence? Really?* But it's actually easy. The key is to focus on the structure of sentences, line by line.

CASE STUDY: COVERAGE OF NATIONAL CRISES

The best newspapers cover big stories with terse drama. Every line crackles with energy. Every detail paints a picture. Every aside puts the story into context.

So let's see how *The New York Times* reported three major news events: the Japanese attack on Pearl Harbor on December 7, 1941; the assassination of President John Kennedy, on November 22, 1963; and Al Qaeda's attacks on the U.S. on September 11, 2001.

- Sudden and unexpected attacks on Pearl Harbor, Honolulu, and other United States possessions in the Pacific early yesterday by the Japanese air force and navy plunged the United States and Japan into active war.
- America wept tonight, not alone for its dead young president but for itself.
- Today's devastating and astonishingly well-coordinated attacks on the World Trade Center towers in New York and the Pentagon outside of Washington plunged the nation into a warlike struggle against an enemy that will be hard to identify with certainty and hard to punish with precision.

Let's start with Part 1 of the Golden Rule: Make everything a journey. Let's map the *Times* report on Pearl Harbor.

The journey begins with a surprise attack on Pearl Harbor. Before we reach our conclusion—the start of active war—we need to understand the larger context. When we learn about the other attacks in the Pacific, we realize that Japan is pressing an all-out assault. When we then learn that Japan's air force and navy launched the attacks, we realize that the highest levels of government coordinated the attack. After years of tension, then, there is no alternative besides active war.

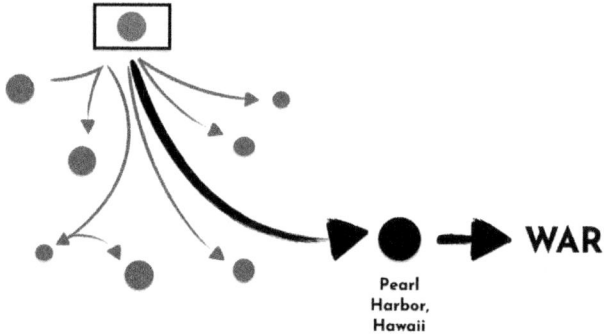

Pearl
Harbor,
Hawaii

Now let's consider Part 2 of the Golden Rule: Start strong, finish strong.

In all three examples, these opening sentences tell you what matters, right away. If fact, you get oriented in just four or five words. Then, the ends of the sentences offer a powerful thought, image, or question:

- Sudden and unexpected attacks …
- America wept tonight …
- Today's devastating and astonishingly well-coordinated attacks …

The endings complete the thoughts, as we see here:

- Sudden and unexpected attacks … plunged the United States and Japan into active war.
- America wept tonight … for itself.
- Today's devastating and astonishingly well-coordinated attacks … hard to punish with precision.

Even without the middles, each sentence makes sense, conveying the most urgent information. Each sentence puts the essential ideas where people are most likely to read them—at the beginnings and ends.

Does that mean we don't need the middle material? No. The middle offers the ideal place for bridges and brackets. Bridge provide paths from the beginning to the end. Brackets offer background information, such as context or attribution.

- … Pearl Harbor, Honolulu, and other United States possessions in the Pacific early yesterday by the Japanese air force and navy …
- … not alone for its dead young president …
- … on the World Trade Center towers in New York and the Pentagon outside of Washington plunged the nation into a warlike struggle against an enemy that will be hard to identify with certainty …

The middle of the Pearl Harbor sentences give us the context we need for the stories—where and how the attacks took place. The middle of the Kennedy sentence offers interpretation—gently casting doubt on what we think (that our sorrow is for Kennedy and his family) before concluding with another idea. The middle of the 9/11 sentence suggests the enormity of the crisis with information about its scope and its perpetrator.

In each sentence, *The Times* takes the reader to a new place. Each journey starts and finishes strongly.

———

ELEMENT 15: GIVE EVERY SENTENCE CLEAR BLASTS

All writing explores action and change. The verb offers the most important tool for that exploration.

The verb makes sentences move. The verb activates the sentence, generating the energy needed to drive the other parts of the sentence. The subject can't do anything without the verb. So give the verb special attention when constructing a sentence. Make sure the reader can visualize what happens. Most sentences state:

Who does what to whom?

Almost always, start with the subject: *Who or what.* Then say what happens: *Verb.* Finally, say what gets acted upon: *The object.*

Don't stop at one blast. Give your sentences, two, three, four or more verb forms. Once you get the reader's attention, don't let go. Create action, action, and more action.

Take a look at these sentences to see how a series of blasts—verb forms—can energize and inform the reader (author and title are indicated in parentheses, then the share of verbs to total words listed):

- "As Gregor Samsa *awoke* one morning from uneasy dreams he *found* himself *transformed* in his bed into a gigantic insect" (Franz Kafka, *The Metamorphosis*—3/20)
- "Jack *put* his arm out the window, *waving* his hat like a visiting dignitary, *backed* into the street, and *floated* away, *gentling* the gleaming dirigible through the shadows of arching elm trees, light *dropping* on it through their leaves like confetti as it *made* its ceremonious passage" (Marilynne Robinson, *Home*—7/47)
- "His fate *had taken* him off two trains this morning, *had raised* him to the surface at Whitehall Street, *had shown* him the *spinning* atoms, *unraveling*, the end of life, all of them people *tethered* by love, and habit, and work, and meaning, *tied* into a meaning suddenly *exploded*, because contrary to all he had *imagined*, being *tied*, being *known*, did not *keep* you safe" (Claire Messed, *The Woman Upstairs*—12/65)

To test whether your sentences contain enough blasts, take on the persona of Charles Kingsfield from *The Paper Chase*. Kingsfield is the professor at Harvard Law School who demands maximum effort and brooks no mental sloppiness. On the first day of class he challenges his students: "You teach *yourselves* the law. *I* train your *minds*. You come in *here* with a *skull* full of *mush*, and if you sur*vive*, leave *thinking* like a *lawyer*." Kingsfield emphasizes every three or four words, to force his audience to listen.

Use the Professor Kingsfield Test for verbs. When you *read* your writing aloud, *emphasize* the verbs in each of your sentences. When it *sounds* right—clear, energetic, informative—you *have succeeded*. When it *sounds* clunky or vague, you need *to rewrite* your passage around the bursts of action.

Make sure to put at least one blast in every sentence. Use active verbs to charge it full of energy. As a general rule, give the reader a blast right away—at the beginning of the sentence. If you don't put your blast at the beginning, make easy to find. Don't meander too long before delivering the blast. And then give another blast … and another … and another …

CASE STUDY: STEPHEN CRANE'S *THE RED BADGE OF COURAGE*

Take a look at this passage from Stephen Crane's *The Red Badge of Courage*, which shows a Civil War soldier's growing fear of battle:

> Previously he had never felt obliged to wrestle too seriously with this question. In his life he had taken certain things for granted, never challenging his belief in ultimate success, and bothering little about means and roads. But here he was confronted with a thing of moment. It had suddenly appeared to him that perhaps in a battle he might run. He was forced to admit that as far as war was concerned he knew nothing of himself.
>
> A sufficient time before he would have allowed the problem to kick its heels at the outer portals of his mind, but now he felt compelled to give serious attention to it.
>
> A little panic-fear grew in his mind. As his imagination went forward to a fight, he saw hideous possibilities. He contemplated the lurking menaces of the future, and failed in an effort to see himself standing stoutly in the midst of them. He recalled his visions of broken-bladed glory, but in the shadow of the impending tumult he suspected them to be impossible pictures.
>
> He sprang from the bunk and began to pace nervously to and fro. "Good Lord, what's th' matter with me?" he said aloud.
>
> He felt that in this crisis his laws of life were useless. Whatever he had learned of himself was here of no avail. He was an unknown quantity. He saw that he would again be obliged to experiment as he had in early youth. He must accumulate information of himself, and meanwhile he resolved to remain close upon his guard lest those qualities of which he knew nothing should everlastingly disgrace him. "Good Lord!" he repeated in dismay.

Start by counting the verbs in each sentence. This passage averages about four verbs per sentence. Even simple sentences—like "He sprang from the bunk and began to pace nervously to and fro"—thrust forward in bursts.

Now, as you read these sentences, state the verbs emphatically. What do you notice? When I emphasize the verbs in passages like this, I feel the energy driving forward. Each phrase gains its own power, and together the phrases build a complete thought.

Look at the variety of Crane's verbs: *had, felt, wrestle, taken, challenging, bothering, confronted, appeared, run, forced, admit, was* (three times), *knew* (twice), *allowed, kick, felt, compelled, give, grew, went, saw* (twice), *contemplated, failed, see, standing, recalled, suspected, to be, sprang, pace, is, said, felt, were, learned, would, obligated, experiment, accumulate, resolved, remain, disgrace,* and *repeated.* Crane gives us a lot of separate and distinct actions in a short passage.

This passage of 275 words contains eighteen sentences and forty-seven verbs. In this passage, then, sentences average about sixteen words and three verbs. So Stephen Crane uses one verb to move every four or five words.

———

ELEMENT 16: BUILD HINGE SENTENCES

So far we have sung the praises of the simple sentence—and for good reason. Simple sentences take the reader on a direct journey, without any confusing side trips. These sentences show who (or what) does what. And they show the object of that action, or when, where, why, or how it takes place.

But sometimes we need to pack more information into a sentence. We want a strong core in every sentence, but we also want to show relationships. For example:

> Leading scientists say global warming poses a threat requiring an international strategy, but the Trump Administration pressured the Environmental Protection Agency to halt action on climate change policies.

The core of this sentence is "Trump Administration pressured the Environmental Protection Agency." But the other ideas—that "global warming poses a real threat" and "requires an international strategy" and "to halt action on climate change policies"—provide important information. These ideas complete the thought.

If you look closely, you see a *hinge* in the sentence—a word that connects the first thought with the second thought. That hinge is "but." You can use seven conjunctions—what I call hinge words—to create hinge sentences. Those hinge words are *for, and, nor, but, or, yet,* and *so.*

You can remember these words with the mnemonic FAN BOYS. See how it works:

- I had to decide whether to go to a northern school like McGill *or* a southern school like Vanderbilt.
- To enjoy professional success, find work that excites you *and* dedicate yourself to mastering the core skills of that work.
- We have neither the urgency *nor* the imagination to confront our deepest flaws.
- Some say education is the source of economic success *but* others argue that access to a good education is a benefit of economic success.
- We can either continue on a path of fiscal discipline *or* force later generations to pay for our profligacy.
- Basketball favors the tallest athletes *yet* short players like Nate Archibald and Muggsy Bogues have found ways to thrive.
- Winning chess requires pursuing a variety of scenarios *so* many players study the classic games of the masters.

Other hinges include the semicolon (which bring together two complete thoughts) and the colon (which tells the reader to pay attention to what's coming next). So:

- I always loved reading detective novels; I was surprised to discover how much I also loved experimental fiction.
- To survive the coronavirus pandemic, people adopted whole new habits: masking, washing, and distancing.

Sometimes, the hinge hides in the beginning of the sentences. Words like *although, despite, without, before,* and *after,* to name a handful, set up a two-step thought:

- Although the Mets rarely win, they always provide entertainment.
- Despite losing the popular vote, Donald Trump won the 2016 Electoral College vote and became president.
- Without attention to the source of problems, we can only create partial solutions.

- Before running a marathon, train for at least six months.
- After eating heavy meals, gluttons turn to antacids for relief.

Hinge sentences bring two or more ideas together in the same thought. That helps you to explore complexity. When people write only simple sentences, research shows, they think in simple terms. Writing complicated sentences—not always, but when you need to express more complicated ideas or events—helps you understand the complexities of the world.

Teachers at New Dorp High School, in Staten Island, New York, found that getting students to write more complicated sentences dramatically improved their learning in *all subjects*. You can do the same with your writing. Remember to give each sentence a simple core: subject and verb. Then, when you want to show relationships or explore more complex ideas, build hinge sentences.

Need more convincing? Expressing complicated thoughts not only helps to develop your critical thinking but also helps to stave off Alzheimer's Disease and other cognitive disorders. To read about these benefits, read important articles in *The Atlantic* (bit.do/pegtyre) and *Time* (bit.do/nunstudy).

So far we have sung the praises of the simple sentence—and for good reason. Simple sentences take the reader on a direct journey, without any confusing side trips. These sentences show who (or what) does what. And they show the object of that action, or when, where, why or how it takes place.

But sometimes we need to pack more information into a sentence. We want a strong blast, but we also want context or background information. For example:

> Even though leading scientists say global warming poses a threat requiring an international strategy, the Trump Administration pressured the Environmental Protection Agency to halt action on climate change policies.

The blast of this sentence is "Trump Administration pressured the Environmental Protection Agency." But the other ideas—that "global warming poses a real threat" and it "requires an international strategy" and "to halt action on climate change policies"—provide important information. These ideas complete the thought.

These three formats offer room to provide just the right amount of context and nuance.

- **Simple sentence**: One complete thought (usually with a object, verb, and object). For example: *The architects examined the building.*
- **Compound sentence**: Two complete thoughts in the same sentence. For example: *The architects examined the building and their partners lined up financing.*
- **Complex sentence**: One incomplete thought connected to one complete thought. For example: *With a complete renovation in mind, the architects examined the building from top to bottom.*

Of course, you can go much further. Let's make the complex sentence even more complex:

With a modern design in mind, the architects examined the building—from the old, decaying roof to the rotting windows to the troubled foundation

As you add new material, make sure the ideas are clear. Read all your sentences aloud to make sure they roll off the tongue and—more important—to can easily understand the ideas. Don't allow extra information to take you off track. Keep the journey clear and the images vivid.

The best writers use all of these sentence structures. Sometimes you need to make simple, direct statements, both for pacing and meaning. Other times, you need to show relationships, twists and turns in thinking.

CASE STUDY: STANLEY FISH, *HOW TO WRITE A SENTENCE*

No one loves sentences more than Stanley Fish, the itinerant legal scholar and literary critic.

Fish loves short sentences just fine. But he also celebrates sentences that extend—forwards or backwards—into long streams of ideas and emotions. Fish expresses his love of the sentence with this 63-word beauty:

If you can write a sentence in which actors, actions, and objects are related to one another in time, space, mood, desires, fears, causes, and effects, and if your specification of those relationships is delineated with a precision that communicates itself to your intended reader, you can, by extrapolation and expansion, write anything: a paragraph, an argument, an essay, a treatise, a novel.

Could Fish have expressed the same idea with shorter, simpler, punchier sentences? Sure. But he wanted to express all of the challenges and rewards of writing great sentences under one idea: *If you can construct a great sentence, you can write well in all fields.*

Fish offers an example of the "additive" style ("…and then… and then… and then…") in this passage from Ernest Hemingway's *To Have and Have Not*:

A large white yacht was coming into the harbor and seven miles out on the horizon you could see a tanker, small and neat in profile against the blue sea, hugging the reef as she made to the westward to keep from wasting fuel against the stream.

Fish takes special delight in the left-branching style—so called because it consists of a bunch of contingent ideas at the beginning, then ends the sentence with the subject and verb. Here's what this sentence looks like graphically:

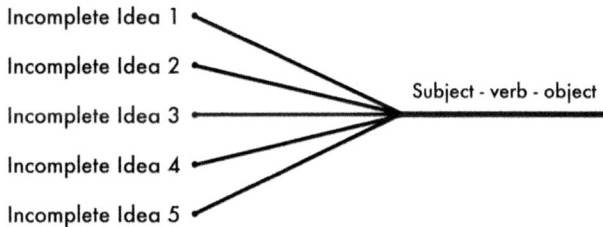

Incomplete Idea 1
Incomplete Idea 2
Incomplete Idea 3   Subject - verb - object
Incomplete Idea 4
Incomplete Idea 5

For rhetorical purposes, the author wants to make some points about the topic before saying who does what. Fish quotes from Martin Luther King's "Letter From a Birmingham Jail," the classic statement of civil disobedience. In a 315-word sentence, King offers 12 dependent clauses, each beginning with "when," to explain why blacks in 1963 should not accept the slow pace of progress on civil rights.

> But when you have seen vicious mobs lynch your mothers and fathers at will and drown your sisters and brothers at whim; when you have seen hate-filled policemen curse, kick, brutalize and even kill your black brothers and sisters with impunity; when you see the vast majority of your 20 million Negro brothers smothering in an airtight cage of poverty in the midst of an affluent society; when you suddenly find your tongue twisted and your speech stammering as you seek to explain to your 6-year-old daughter why she can't go to the public amusement park that has just been advertised on television, and see tears welling up in her eyes when she is told that Funtown is closed to colored children, and see the depressing clouds of inferiority begin to form in her little mental sky, and see her begin to distort her little personality by unconsciously developing a bitterness toward white people; when you have to concoct an answer for a 5-year-old son asking in agonizing pathos, "Daddy, why do white people treat colored people so mean?"; when you take a cross-country drive and find it necessary to sleep night after night in the uncomfortable corners of your automobile because no motel will accept you; when you are humiliated day in and day out by nagging signs reading "white" and "colored"; when your first name becomes "nigger," your middle name becomes "boy" (however old you are) and your last name becomes "John," and your wife and mother are never given the respected title "Mrs."; when you are harried by day and haunted by night by the fact that you are a Negro, living constantly at tiptoe stance, never quite knowing what to expect next, and plagued with inner fears and outer resentments; when you are forever fighting a degenerating sense of "nobodiness"; then you will understand why we find it difficult to wait.

Normally I'd preach against taking so long to get to the subject—in this case, "you," in the last line—but King makes his indictment the primary focus of the sentence. This long string of complaints creates a state of tension and anticipation. At the end, we know, as he says, "why we find it difficult to wait."

Like any good writer, Stanley Fish understands the power of short, well-stated sentences. But he also appreciates the power of the occasional longer journey.

————

ELEMENT 17: ALTERNATE SHORT AND LONG SENTENCES

Good writing requires a mix of short and long sentences. Too many short sentences, without a break, feel like water torture: *Drip, drip, drip.* Too many long sentences feel like a difficult hike through a dense forest.

Alternating clusters of short and long sentences gives writing a pleasant tempo. The reader stays alert, ready to take in everything that comes along. Sometimes it's easy; sometimes it takes work.

Physiologically, we need variety. Any time we do something—including reading—we trigger a complex chain of chemical reactions. When we hear the booming opening of a song on the radio, we are aroused. We cannot help but take notice. But if that booming style continues too long, we get exhausted. That's why, after that booming opening, the composer moves softly and sweetly. After developing those softer themes, he returns to harder themes.

That same process works in other forms of human expression and activity. Football games present a series of high-velocity, violent plays; between those plays, the players and fans get a respite as the quarterback huddles and the defense gets into position. Action movies also shift back and forth from action to respite (think about the car chases and gun fights in *48 Hours*, which alternate with quiet scenes of the partners sitting and talking in a car). Even still art forms, like painting and sculpture, alternate expressions of action and repose.

Varying sentence lengths also helps to convey different moods. Short sentences usually indicate rapid action; longer sentences indicate a more complex idea. Masters like Ernest Hemingway use both short and long sentences to capture the mood.

What counts as "short" and "long" has evolved over the years. In the last century, the average length of sentences has shrunk, as reading has become universal and the pace of life has quickened. The more people who read, the more writers must appeal to the attention spans of those readers. Take a look at the average length of sentences of notable authors over literary history:

- Philip Sidney, *Arcadia* (1590): 75
- Thomas Hobbes, *The Leviathan* (1651): 39.26
- John Bunyan, *The Pilgrim's Progress* (1678-1684): 31.61
- John Locke, *An Essay on Human Understanding* (1690): 49.8
- Jonathan Swift, *The Battle of the Books* (1698): 39.8
- David Hume, *History of England* (1754): 39.8
- Sir Walter Scott, *Ivanhoe* (1820): 32.1

Now look at the average sentence lengths of authors from the last century:

- Ernest Hemingway, *The Old Man and the Sea* (1952): 14.4
- Richard Feynman, *Six Easy Pieces* (1961-63): 21.2
- Martin Luther King, *Why We Can't Wait* (1964): 12.4
- Truman Capote, *In Cold Blood* (1966): 14.5
- Stephen Hawking, *A Brief History of Time* (1988): 15.2
- Ken Follett, *The Pillars of the Earth* (1989): 12.4
- Jon Krakauer, *Into the Wild* (1996): 18.9
- William F. Buckley, *Nearer My God* (1997): 20.5

Research shows that today's readers best comprehend sentences that average 17 or 18 words. So craft a bunch of short sentences, especially when you want to express action or break complex ideas into pieces. But write long sentences when you need to explain complex ideas or happenings. Move back and forth like a pendulum, from short to long sentences and back again. Overall, average 17 to 18 words per sentence. If you do that, you will never lose your readers.

CASE STUDY: ALEKSANDR SOLZHENITSYN, *THE GULAG ARCHIPELAGO*

How do you describe the horrors of totalitarianism, a system that insists that it has the answers to all questions? How do you capture the horror of a system that humiliates, crushes, and kills people who dare to express their own ideas?

Aleksandr Solzhenitsyn was one of the millions of Russians imprisoned in work camps for acts that Communist authorities deemed hostile to the Soviet Union. Solzhenitsyn had the temerity to criticize Josef Stalin, which was a violation of Article 58, paragraph 10, of the

Soviet criminal code. For this crime, Solzhenitsyn spent eight years at a labor camp.

Solzhenitsyn's *The Gulag Archipelago* describes, in awful detail, life in the camp. Each page presents, in unvarnished prose, the day-to-day reality of captivity. In this passage, Solzhenitsyn describes why various prisoners were arrested and convicted [the figures in brackets indicate how many words he used in that sentence]:

> The village club manager went with his watchmen to buy a bust of comrade Stalin. [15] They bought it. [3] The bust was big and heavy. [6] They ought to have carried it in a hand barrow, both of them together, but the manager's status did not allow him to. [23] "All right, you'll manage it if you take it slowly." [10] And he went off ahead. [5] The old watchmen couldn't work out how to do it for a long time. [14] If he tried to carry it out of sight, he couldn't get his arm around it. [16] If he tried to carry it in front of him, his back hurt and he was thrown off balance backward. [20] Finally he figured out how to do it. [8] He took off his belt, made a noose for Comrade Stalin, put it around his neck, and in this way carried it over his shoulder through the village. [28] Well, there was nothing here to argue about. [8] It was an open-and-shut case. [5] Article 58-8, terrorism, 10 years. [5]
>
> A shepherd in a fit of anger swore at a cow for not obeying: 'You collective farm whore!" [18] And he got Article 58, and a term. [8]
>
> A *deaf and dumb* carpenter got a term for counterrevolutionary agitation! [11] How? [1] He was laying floors in a club. [7] Everything had been removed from a big hall, and there was no nail or hook anywhere. [16] While he was working, he hung his jacket and his service cap on a bust of Lenin. [17] Someone came in and saw it. [6] Article 15, 10 years. [4]

Here's how the sentence lengths compare in these three paragraphs:

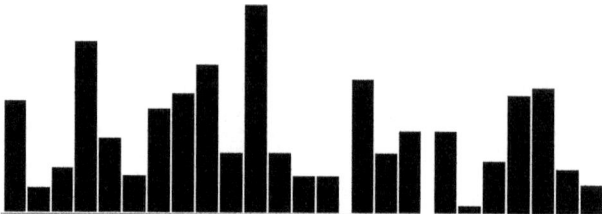

Read the passage again. How do alternating sentence lengths—from short to long and back again—affect the way you read and process the ideas? How do you feel after reading each sentence? How easy is it to follow those ideas? How much impact to the details make, not just in processing information but also in feeling the emotions of these awful cases?

AND ANOTHER THING . . .

Some writers rebel against the imperative of simple sentences. They say it robs them of the chance to develop their own style: *If William Faulkner can make long sentences work, why can't I?* Sure, Faulkner used meandering sentences to suggest the complexity of relationships and history and to evoke a Southern Gothic mood.

But wait. Before he broke away to create his meandering style, Faulkner mastered the fundamentals of simple sentence structure. Like Picasso, who mastered representational work before inventing cubism, Faulkner knew how to do all the basics before he broke away to create something new and different. Look at this passage from *Light in August*:

> They enter the kitchen together, though Mrs. Armstid is in front. She goes straight to the stove. Lena stands just within the door. Her head is uncovered now, her hair combed smooth. Even the blue garment looks freshened and rested. She looks on while Mrs. Armstid at the stove clashes the metal lids and handles the sticks of wood with the abrupt savageness of a man. "I would like to help," Lena says.
>
> Mrs. Armstid does not look around. She clashes the stove savagely. "You stay where you are. You keep off your feet now, and you'll keep off your back awhile longer maybe."
>
> The young woman does not answer at once. Mrs. Armstid does not rattle the stove now, though her back is still toward the younger woman. Then she turns. They look at one another, suddenly naked, watching one another: the young woman in the chair, with her neat hair and her inert hands upon her lap, and the older one beside the stove, turning, motionless too, with a savage screw of gray hair at the

base of her skull and a face that might have been carved in sandstone. Then the younger one speaks.

Faulkner's 16 sentences total 196 words, an average of 12 and a half words per sentence. The passage uses 145 single-syllable words, 44 two-syllable words, and seven three-syllable words. Simplicity itself.

Even when he wrote longer sentences, Faulkner delivered a series of clear blasts. You never get confused about who's doing or saying what to whom.

Faulkner was best known, stylistically, for his mastery of long and complex expression. But before he could develop his own style, he mastered simple expression.

CHAPTER 5
WORDS

The difference between the right word and the almost right word is the difference between lightning and the lightning bug.

MARK TWAIN

Words—so innocent and powerless as they are, as standing in a dictionary, how potent for good and evil they become in the hands of one who knows how to combine them.

NATHANIEL HAWTHORNE

OPEN a book or magazine to a random page and find a word you don't know much about. You might be amazed by the journey of discovery that follows.

I did that once and found *adumbrate*. Merriam-Webster's online dictionary says *adumbrate*, a verb, means "to foreshadow vaguely" or "to suggest, disclose, or outline partially." The word originated with the Latin *adumbrates*, a simple combination of *ad* ("to the") and *umbra* ("shadow"). The word was once in common use. A 1932 *New York Times* headline declares: "Events Adumbrate Happier Times."

As we consider adumbrate, look at its sister word *umbrage*. That word, meaning "vague suggestion" or "feeling of pique," also comes from the idea of a shadow. *Penumbra*, meaning the area of a shadow, offers another useful derivation. Americans learned this word when, in the 1974 *Roe* v. *Wade* decision, the Supreme Court ruled a woman's right to an abortion existed under the *penumbra* of the right to privacy.

Defining words is like going to a progressive dinner. You track down the meaning of one word, chew on it awhile, chat with other guests at the word feast, and then move on. You devour the next word, with all its flavors, and then move on again. At the end of the process, you understand a whole bunch of related words.

How many words do we actually need to communicate well? The average working vocabulary is 20,000 active words. For 95 percent of common texts—like newspapers, blogs, and memos—we use just 3,000 words.

Still, the greater your vocabulary, the more nuanced is your understanding of the world. Every word offers distinctive ideas and nuance. Even when words are close in meaning—like *spoon* and *scoop*—knowing both allows you to describe things with greater precision.

Just because you have a large vocabulary doesn't mean you need to flaunt it. I suggest thinking of words like utensils in a well-stocked kitchen. Your cabinets and drawers hold not just the basic pots and pans, spoons and knives, but also colanders, sifters, turners, whisks, tenderizers, and other tools. You would never use a sifter or a grater just because you owned it; you would use it only when it enabled you to do its assigned tasks. Likewise with vocabulary. Fill your cabinet, but only use words when they add value to your work.

Not many people spend time flipping through dictionaries and thesauruses. But it's not a bad idea to go on quests for just the right word, to look up the word you don't know—or don't know precisely—to build and refine your vocabulary. You might not see any need for a word like adumbrate right away, but knowing it stretches your mind and broadens your repertoire.

———

ELEMENT 18: USE SIMPLE WORDS, ALMOST ALWAYS

Given a choice of a simple or complex word, use the simple one. Given a choice of a short or long word, use the short one.

Simple words are democratic. Simple words invite more people to join the conversation. John Maeda, a designer at the MIT Media Lab, puts the matter, well, simply: "Complexity implies the feeling of being lost; simplicity implies the feeling of being found." When people feel "found," they can join the conversation.

When you use simple words well, you can also use more exotic, unfamiliar words without losing the audience. That was Shakespeare's approach. The Bard used twice as many words as other playwrights in Elizabethan England; he also invented whole new locutions, without bothering to define them. But he never confused his audience. He surrounded arcane references with common language and familiar situations. So even if a playgoer did not know the meaning of a particular word, he could still follow the action.

Linguists talk about "density" to describe the simplicity or complexity of language. Dense writing uses more "content" words, that is, specific, specialized terms. In their study *Writing Science*, M.A.K. Halliday and J.R. Martin detail the density of five sentences. Consider these sentences (with content words *in italics* and density scores in parentheses):

- But we never did anything very much in *science* in our *school*. (2)
- My *father* used to *tell* me about a *singer* in his *village*. (4)
- A *parallelogram* is a *four-sided figure* with its *opposite sides parallel*. (6)
- The *atomic nucleus absorbs* and *emits energy* in *quanta*, or *discrete units*. (8)
- *Griffith's energy balance approach* to *strength* and *fracture* also *suggested* the *importance* of *surface chemistry* in the *mechanical behavior* of *brittle materials*. (13)

We read the first few sentences easily. But the later sentences come hard. If we know only six of the eight content words in the fourth sentence, we might not understand the point. Even when we *do* know all eight terms, we might still struggle to understand the point. Too many content words overwhelm the reader.

When you need to use technical words, don't bunch them together. Take them one at a time, defining them with examples. If you define your terms well, they *become* simple for your reader. Take the term *atomic nucleus*. Until we reached high school chemistry or physics, that term was a complex, abstract term for most of us; afterwards, as it became familiar, it also became simple.

Given a choice between a simple word and a complex word, use the simple one. Say *use*, not *utilize*. Say *cause*, not *effectuate*. Say *worker*, not *personnel*. You get the idea. Simple words almost never trip up the reader; complex words often do.

Likewise, given a choice between a foreign and an English word, use the English one. Expressions like *rendezvous* (meeting), *bete noire* (something dreaded), *faux pas* (mistake), *gauche* (clumsy), *raison d'etre* (purpose for being), *wunderkind* (prodigy) do not, by themselves, damage a sentence. You can use them once in a while. But take care. They can annoy and distract the reader.

What about variety? Doesn't it make sense to use a whole menu of words, not just the ordinary dishes? The English poet William Cowper famously said that "variety's the very spice of life." Variety, of course, can add flavor to your writing. But variety for variety's sake just causes distraction. Use the simplest word possible for the occasion.

Consider one of the most useful verbs you'll ever see: *To say*. Novices often use different words to say *said*, especially when writing dialogue. So they say that a president *argues, declares*, and *cajoles*. A ballplayer *stutters, barks, muses*, and *mumbles*. A philosopher *cogitates, elucidates, complains*, and *demurs*. These synonyms disrupt the flow of ideas. Avoid that distraction; just say *said*. If someone says something interesting, you don't need to dress it up with synonyms.

CASE STUDY: JOHN MCPHEE, *THE CURVE OF BINDING ENERGY* AND *IN SUSPECT TERRAIN*

John McPhee, the master of long-form journalism, uses the simplest words possible to explain even the most technical subjects. Open any McPhee work and pick a random paragraph. I did just that with *The Curve of Binding Energy*, McPhee's book about nuclear proliferation:

> The material that destroyed Hiroshima was uranium-235. Some 60 kilograms of it were in the bomb. The uranium was in metallic form. Sixty kilograms, a hundred and 32 pounds, of uranium would be about the size of a football, for the metal is compact—almost twice as dense as lead. As a cube, 60 kilograms would be slightly less than six inches on a side. U-235 is radioactive, but not intensely so. You could hold some in

your lap for a month and not suffer any effects. Like any heavy metal, it is poisonous if you eat enough of it. Its critical mass—the point at which it will start a chain reaction until a great deal of energy has been released—varies widely, depending on what surrounds it.

On and on McPhee goes, describing the most complex scientific subjects with simple little words.

The trick is to relate the unknown to the known. To explain density, McPhee makes references to lead and footballs. To describe radioactivity, he reassures us that we can hold on our laps, without any danger, the same amount of U-235 that comprised the bomb dropped on Hiroshima.

Consider another example. In his book *In Suspect Terrain,* McPhee explains the geologic foundations underneath New York's skyscrapers:

The towers of midtown, as one might imagine, were emplaced in substantial rock, … that once had been heated near the point of melting, had recrystallized, had been heated again, had recrystallized, and, while not particularly competent, was more than adequate to hold up those buildings. Most important, it was right at the surface. You could see it, in all its micaceous glitter, shining like silver in the outcrops of Central Park. Four hundred and 50 million years in age, it was called Manhattan schist. All through midtown, it was at or near the surface, but in the region south of Thirtieth Street it began to fall away, and at Washington Square it descended abruptly. The whole saddle between midtown and Wall Street would be underwater, were it not filled with many tens of fathoms of glacial till.

McPhee sprinkles technical terms in this passage, but not so many that you need to scramble to find a dictionary. Anyone with a good high school or college education can understand this erudite, rich writing.

Here is how McPhee describes New York's deep, hard geologic foundation:

New York grew high on the advantage of its hard rock, and, New York being what it is, cities all over the world have attempted to resemble it. The skyline of nuclear Houston, for example, is a simulacrum of Manhattan's. Houston rests on 12,000 feet of montmorillonitic clay, a substance that, when moist, turns into mobile jelly. After taking so much money out of the ground, the oil companies of Houston have put hundreds of millions back in. Houston is the world's foremost city in fat basements. Its tall buildings are magnified duckpins, bobbing in their own mire.

Because his words are mostly simple, McPhee can offer unfamiliar terms (like *montmorillonitic*) when he wants to offer precision. Like all great writers, McPhee offers value to both specialists and lay readers. To understand new ideas, McPhee refers to common reference points.

Above all else, McPhee shows patience. He takes his time. If he needs to pause to explain an idea, relating it to something we already know, he will do so. In the long run, that's easier and faster than confusing us with abstract terms that we do not know.

———

ELEMENT 19: USE LONGER WORDS AS PRECISION INSTRUMENTS

"Everything is vague to a degree you do not realize," Bertrand Russell once said, "till you have tried to make it precise."

When you cannot express an idea precisely with short words, use longer ones. Don't worry about length or origin. Use the word that best states the concept you want to explore.

To describe a smooth, sweet flow of sounds, use *mellifluous*. To describe dominance of certain ideas in society, use the term *hegemony*. To refer to Gandhi's system of nonviolent direct action, use *Satyagraha*. To describe religious beliefs about the end of time, use *eschatological*.

These may not be common dime-store words. But they give us precision that other words lack. Most readers can handle esoteric words if you provide a simple definition or create the right context. Don't show off, but use big or exotic words when they do the work that small words cannot.

To explain a technical issue, you often need to deploy specialized vocabulary. An architect, for example, needs to use concepts like *articulation, massing,* and *fenestration* to explore design. A lawyer refers to *torts, prima facie evidence, liability, stare decisis, exculpatory,* and *interrogatories*. One more set from computer science and programming: *A.I., biometrics, algorithms, data mining, NoSQL, queries,* and *fuzzy logic*. None of the concepts is difficult when explained. Just be sure not to overwhelm your reader.

Beware of overwhelming your reader with too many many arcane, unfamiliar concepts, the reader gets overwhelmed. As long as you define your technical vocabulary—simply, at the moment of use—you won't overwhelm your readers.

Before using technical vocabulary, check each word's precise meaning. Start with the dictionary. You might be amazed what you discover. Because we usually learn vocabulary by hearing others use words, in print or in speech, we often miss the full meaning of those words. And so we use words imprecisely in our own writing.

Let me give an example. For years, I used the word *fulsome* to mean abundant or copious. And I was right. But fulsome also means, according to Merriam-Webster, "aesthetically, morally, or generally offensive." When I looked up the word, my understanding shifted. "Fulsome praise" refers not just to enthusiastic plaudits, but also to treacly or manipulative praise. I now remember both the positive and negative connotations.

While we're on the subject of *treacly*, which means sickly sweet or sentimental, let me relate another dictionary discovery. Treacly derives from treacle, which refers to a medicine used to treat poisonous bites. Treacle also refers to a blend of molasses, invert sugar, and corn syrup. Now that I know more than one dimension of treacly, I might deploy that word in new contexts.

A writer named Ammon Shea once spent a year reading the 20-volume *Oxford English Dictionary*. He discovered hundreds of words that work more precisely than common words. *Petrichor* refers to the loamy scent that comes after a spring rain, *prend* to a mended crack, a *vicambulist* to someone who wanders around cities, and a *kankedort* to an awkward situation. If such words can express a thought most precisely, sure, go ahead and use it. There is nothing wrong with sending the reader to a dictionary once in a while.

When you choose words, don't just consider the precise definition. Consider the sounds they make and the feelings and ideas they evoke. I like *kankedort* and *prend*, in part, because they sound like what they describe. *Kankedort* sounds clumsy, unsmooth: an awkward situation. *Prend* rhymes with *mend*.

To discover the most precise vocabulary, explore the language of experts. If you write about health, plunge into the details of cellular biology, nutrition, and energy. If you write about politics, go deep into all the areas of law, policy, rhetoric, and debate. If you write about sports, make a list of every move on the field, court, or rink. Every realm has a long list of precision words. Find them and use the ones most suitable to your audience.

CASE STUDY: THE AMERICAN SESQUIPEDALIAN

William F. Buckley spent a lifetime demonstrating the joy of lex. The question is: Did he go too far?

I have urged the use of simple words over fancy, English words over foreign, down-home words over Ivory Tower words. And yet, in a career spanning 50 years, Buckley demonstrated the value of stretching vocabularies and using words that hit their marks—even if those words befuddled the average reader. Why? Buckley explained with reference to music.

"Just as the discriminating ear greets gladly" an unusual note played with "just the right harmonic moment," Buckley said, "the fastidious eye encounters happily the word that says exactly what the writer wished not only said but conveyed [with] cadence, variety, marksmanship, accent, nuance, and drama."

Translation: Surprise and precision delight the reader.

Buckley played with words because he loved them. When he found words that performed magical feats, he put them on display. Educated readers—his audience—could understand what he was trying to say, even if they didn't know the meanings of all of his words.

Buckley especially loved his collection of verbs. He took delight in telling us who or what would *abjure, adumbrate, agglutinate, catechize, emplace, expiate, extirpate, hector, kedge, lucubrate, mollify, obtrude, polemicize, prescind, proffer, propitiate, pullulate, reinstitutionalize, remonstrate, subsume, taxonomize, traduce, and transubstantiate.* If Buckley caused his reader to pause, well, that was all part of the journey.

Did Buckley go too far? Remember how Shakespeare placed unfamiliar words among more common words so that he could keep the attention of mass audiences. Buckley did the same, usually.

Four questions determine whether Buckley and other sequipedalians should use long and obscure words:

1. Does the word say exactly what the author intends?

2. Does the context help the reader guess meanings even if he doesn't fully understand the words?
3. Can the reader keep up with the flow of ideas?
4. Does vocabulary add life to the writing?

If you answer yes to all four questions, go ahead and use Buckleyesque locutions. Otherwise, keep your words simple.

———

ELEMENT 20: USE ACTIVE VERBS, EVEN TO DESCRIBE PASSIVITY

Verbs power writing. Verbs show people doing things—cooking meals, throwing balls, shopping for clothes, singing songs, talking with neighbors ... everything that makes the world work.

Active verbs engage the parts of the brain involved in performing actions. When you use phrases like "She threw the ball" or "He warbled the melody," you activate the parts of the brain involved in kicking and singing. The mere use of the words arouses those physical sensations.

To make writing a physical experience, use active verbs. Stimulate the reader's brain by showing someone *dance, shuffle, skip*, and *amble; buy, sell, spend*, and *invest; sleep, dream*, and *wake; sit, lie*, and *lay; add, subtract, multiply*, and *divide; drink, sip, eat*, and *chew; love, hate, tolerate, ignore*, and *scrutinize; know, notice*, and *show; break, rip, fix, patch*, and *repair; sing, hum, twist* and *shout; teach, learn, listen, hear, accept*, and *ask; play* and *pray, run, gun* and *whisper; work, clean, put, organize, cut, hurt, heal, count*, and *draw; mess, straighten*, and *sort; travel, drive, park, speed, slow down, merge*, and *cut off*.

You get the idea. I listed all those verbs to suggest the wide range of actions in this world. Read those words again. Now note when those words produce a *physical reaction*. Interesting, isn't it, just how physically we respond when deciphering squiggles on a page?

Make a habit of searching for verbs in your reading. Read modern authors like Tom Wolfe, John Irving, Elizabeth Gilbert, Frank McCourt, Philip Roth, Dave Eggers, Jonathan Safran Foer, and Anne Lamott. See how they use verbs to create a motion picture in their work.

Pick up a dictionary and a thesaurus. Look for lists of verbs. I know, that sounds mechanical, contrived, and nerdy, but it isn't. It's just a way of acquiring more tools for your toolbox. A pulp novelist named Deanna Carlyle published *1,000 Verbs To Write By*, a collection organized by kinds of action—variations on the verbs *walk, run, jump, touch, took, pull, push, had, held, put, hit, was, react, sit, stand, smell, taste, think, say, hear, lie, enter, feel, seem, leave*, and *turn*. Scrolling such lists strengthens your word power.

Our world is one giant field of energy. Wherever we go, energy either bursts out or gets suppressed. The reader needs to see, feel, hear that energy. Give it to her.

CASE STUDY: PETE HAMILL, *DOWNTOWN*

For decades, Pete Hamill was the voice of New York, its neighborhood and bars, its politicians and working class, its loud conflicts and tender moments. Hamill's secret as a writer was twofold. First, he explored every corner of the city and talked to people at the street level. Second, he wrote with energy. In this passage, Pete Hamill remembers his early years as a reporter for the *New York Post*, exploring the streets of New York:

> On mornings when I had little money, or worked past the deadlines on other stories, I would leave the Post through the Washington Street exit and head for Broadway. The great street at that hour was usually thick with frantic people, bumping one another, dodging 'round one another, grumbling their apologies, then dashing across the paths of careening taxicabs. I loved plunging into the tumult, knowing that I was on my own while almost everyone else was going to work. My treks took me past Trinity and the Equitable Building, where I had lounged away so many lunch hours, then into the rushing infantry rising from the subways at Fulton Street. In a coffee shop with a street counter, I'd buy a cardboard cup of coffee and a cheese Danish. I had the morning papers with me, but usually I also had a book. On days of decent weather, I'd head for City Hall Park. There I'd bow my head in reverence to the Woolworth Building (often humming some lines from the tune "Million Dollar Baby"), find a bench, sip the coffee, and gaze at the vanished majesties of Park Row.

Look at the verbs in this paragraph: *had, worked, leave, head, was, bumping, dodging, grumbling, dashing, loved, knowing, plunging, was, going, took, lounged, rising, buy, had, had, head, bow, humming, find, sip,* and *gaze.*

Out of 26 verbs, only five are forms of *to be* or *to have.* All the rest are action verbs, which show Hamill living life to the fullest.

―――――

ELEMENT 21: USE THE VERBS *TO BE* AND *TO HAVE,* SPARINGLY

Overusing the verbs *to be* and *to have* ruins more writing than any other habit. *To be* and *to have* do not show people actively doing things; they just indicate some state of existence. I call them couch-potato words. They just lie around, passively, while the rest of the world acts with purpose.

Most writers cannot resist using these verbs. In fact, seven forms of the verbs *to be* and *to have* rank among the 35 most-used words in the English language, according to the *American Heritage Word Frequency Book.* That's *one in five* words. No other verbs appear on that list.

Let's look at some passages from business memos and college papers. Start with this passage from an insurance analyst:

The last year showed the major risks we *have* to cope with. There *were* a number of severe earthquakes. The hurricane season *was* also eventful —it *was* just fortunate that the tracks of most of the storms remained over the open sea. … The severe earthquakes and the hurricane season with so many storms demonstrate once again that there must *be* no slackening of our efforts to analyze these risks in detail and provide the necessary insurance covers at adequate prices.

This clunky passage contains only five instance of *to be* and *to have.* But those passive verbs pull the passage away from simple, clear thinking. So the passage wanders on, for 81 words. These 22 words convey the ideas much more clearly:

The earthquakes and hurricanes of 2010 reveal the costly risks of severe weather—and the need to analyze risks to insure property.

Simple and clear. Two verbs—show and analyze—enliven the

shorter passage. The verbs act like magnets, giving shape to the filings of the other words.

Consider the following pairs of sentences. The first set shows sentences using *to be* and *to have*; the second set shows sentences with strong action verbs. Which sentences work better?

Sentences Using Passive Voice
- The Episcopal Church was caught between rival factions of the gay marriage controversy.
- Immigration officials have a hard time patrolling the Mexican border.
- Joe Biden's choice of a running mate is expected before the convention.

Sentences Using Active Voice
- Conservative and liberal factions of the Episcopal Church disagreed about the ordination of gay priests.
- Coyotes and drug smugglers overwhelm immigration officials at the Mexican border
- Joe Biden will pick his running mate before the convention.

The sentences in the second set, with active verbs, convey more precise information. They also force us to look for more details, which help to bring the scene to life. You know who's doing what to whom.

In my years as a college teacher, I struggled to get my students to use action verbs. Despite my preaching the power of action verbs, my students continued to use *to be* and *to have* without much thought. Habits die hard, right? Without a concerted effort to stop, most of us maintain bad habits. We do what's easiest. We take the course of least resistance. One day, at wit's end, I banned the verbs *to be* and *to have* from the next paper assignment. I knew it was a radical step. It's unnatural to remove the two most common verbs from your vocabulary. But I wanted to force my students to look for active verbs that conveyed exactly what they wanted to say.

When I first issued the ban, students grumbled and complained. "All kinds of great writers use *to be* and *to have*!" they cried. "This makes writing even a simple sentence hard!"

True, true. But sometimes you need an artificial constraint to develop a skill. Musicians, athletes, surgeons, actors, standup comics—

everyone who wants to do something well—achieve mastery by practicing skills, deliberately, one at a time. They focus, intently, on changing their behavior, converting lazy actions into purposeful actions. Coaches call it "deep practice." Such work helps to transform bad habits into good habits.

The ban worked. The students wrote the strongest sentences I had ever seen in college papers. The previous week's batch of papers contained dozens of unclear sentences. This new batch contained not one. And so we continued the ban all semester. Under the ban, no student gave me a single paper with an unclear sentence.

The ban, I must admit, produced some silly passages. Instead of saying "She *had* an impressive library," you'd get "She *possessed* an impressive library." Does "possessed" really work better than "had"? In this case, no. I'd like to see something like this: "She owns hundreds of books in a number of disciplines—psychology, philosophy, history, and fiction." Or: "She accumulated an impressive library."

So what happened to the ban? After a few weeks, amended it. I allowed students to use *to be* and *to have*—but only when they explained, in a footnote, why it worked better than other possibilities.

Once you kick the *to be/to have* habit, you can go back to using these verbs when they work best. But stay on guard. Do not let passivity creep back into your work. Every time you write a draft, search your document for all forms of these verbs—*am, is, are, was, are, were, been, has, have, had*. If possible, replace them with verbs that convey action.

CASE STUDY: GILBERT GAUL, *THE GEOGRAPHY OF RISK*

Global warming, arguably, poses the the greatest challenge of our time. Within a generation, major cities on waterfronts could be under water. Heartland cities and towns could be parched for water or suffering regular 100-year twisters and hurricanes.

This issue demands clear, energetic prose. To understand the full dimensions of this crisis—viscerally—we need to feel the dangers. Consider this account of a visit to Clearwater, Florida:

> We began on the barrier islands in Clearwater Beach and Honeymoon Island and worked our way south toward Indian Rocks and Treasure Island. Towering hotels and condos crowded the shoreline. Hine

pointed out one condo that draped over an inlet. The owners had pumped in sand and built a seawall to save their investment. But the water kept rising. It was unclear how long it would last. In the meantime, the nearby beaches were being starved of sand because of the seawall.

Look at the verbs: *began, worked, crowded, pointed, draped, pumped, built, save, kept rising, would last, being starved.* Each one paints a picture. We see action, not just states of being.

Sometimes the verb *to be* works fine:

"Humans beings are lousy planners," Hine said. "They're not bad people. But they are sloppy."

Instead of using the verb *to be* in these sentences, Gaul could say that people *plan poorly* and *develop sloppy habits.* But in this case, the verb *to be* works best. To make sense of how people respond to crisis, we need to know what they *are,* deep down. But to see the issue's drama, we need to use action verbs. Consider this next passage:

Houses and bungalows filled the interior of the barrier islands. … Many sat at ground level and would no doubt be sacrificed to rising water in the future. It could take until the middle of this century or possibly longer. So much depends on the warming climate and the ice sheets in the north. Thousands of years ago, during the last ice age, the shoreline here extended seventy to one hundred miles from where it is today, Hine pointed out. Then the ice sheets and glaciers retreated, and the seas rose.

And here:

Hine described one barrier island we drove along as "a three-thousand-year-old bulge of sand wrapped around a limestone ridge." Cranes and bulldozers dotted the eroding beach. The Corps of Engineers was busy pumping sand. Hine wasn't opposed to replenishing beaches, he said, even though it is "a stopgap measure." There were other things that could be done, he said, but first the politicians and developers had to stop thinking in "political time" and start thinking in geologic time—and stop attacking the scientists for delivering bad news.

Think of writing as presenting a series of pictures—or, better yet, *videos*. Moment by moment, show your reader how things *move and change*. Use vivid nouns and action verbs. Show the reader, moment by moment, what's happening.

———

ELEMENT 22: AVOID BUREAUCRATESE AND EMPTY-CALORIE WORDS

A glut of gross and pretentious words is the curse of our bureaucratic age.

Bureaucrats avoid simple speech for three reasons—to provide shorthand for insiders, to obscure and avoid difficult questions, and to avoid the hard work of simple expression.

• **Shorthand**: To write for broad audiences, professionals use quick references (e.g., "people," "low-income," "test scores") and acronyms (e.g., SES, ROI, FAR, at-risk). This kind of shorthand is useful. But when use too much jargon, we lose focus on the subject. We make even the most concrete matters abstract.

Professionals also put *-ize* at the end of nouns to make them into verbs. "Let's prioritize our goals," a government planner says. "Parents need to regularize their routines," a child psychologist says. "Managers need to systematize their organizational structures," consultants say. What's wrong with that? Simple: It prevents us from thinking through what we want to say. Avoid *-ize* by saying that "Let's decide what's most important" or "Parents need to set routines" or "Managers need systems to make their projects and people."

The *-ism* ending, common among academics, is almost as bad. It oversimplifies everything. Look at this collection of *-ism*s: liberalism, conservatism, fascism, communism, socialism, capitalism, Marxism, Maoism, feminism, pacifism, Bushisms, and a hundred more. As catch-all terms, *-ism*s indicate a general idea. Too often, though, these broad terms avoid the details that matter. If I had a dollar for everyone who talked about Marxism without understanding anything about Marx, I would be living in luxury.

• **Avoidance**: To avoid controversy, bureaucrats and professionals steer clear of language that might, in some way or other, offend one group or another.

We dance around words about race, sex, religion, handicap, age, class, and even beauty. We don't want to insult anyone with bluntness or crudeness, but as a result we avoid speaking the truth.

Consider how we address people we once called crippled. Because the word started to sound awkward or mean, we replaced it with *handicapped*, then *disabled*, then *physically challenged*, and finally *differently able*. But a writer named Nancy Mairs, who happens to be handicapped, insists on calling herself crippled. "I refuse to pretend that the only differences between you and me are the various ordinary ones that distinguish any one person from another," she writes. The euphemisms, she says, amount to avoidance at best and a patronizing and superior attitude at worst.

In his classic *1984*, George Orwell coined the term "Newspeak" to indicate language that deliberately mislead. Politicians and bureaucrats use Newspeak to deny unpleasant truths. So *taxes* become *revenue enhancements*, terrorists become *freedom fighters*, deaths of civilians become *collateral damage*, and an invasion becomes an *incursion*.

• **Laziness**: Bureaucrats and specialists also use gross and pretentious language because they get lazy. Consider the following pairs of words.

Help—Facilitate
Set priorities—Prioritize
Near—In proximity to
About—Approximately
Give—Distribute
Use—Utilize
If—In the event that
Size—Magnitude
About—Approximately

The first words in these pairs are simple, clear, and sprightly. The second words are long, clumsy, and overblown. Too often we use the second of these expressions. The question is why.

Bureaucratese is common most big organizations, where orientation is now called "onboarding," pay is called "compensation," firing is called "letting go," mass firing is called "downsizing" or (worse) "rightsizing," unstable market conditions are called "headwinds," and cutting whole departments is called "outsourcing." These euphemisms result from avoidance of the truth, but also the egos of people in charge. When you work with such people, it's easier to use the ugly words than simple, sprightly words. We get lazy and our language suffers.

How we speak, as George Orwell argues, determines whether we think clearly enough to maintain our freedom. "If you simplify your English, you are freed from the worst follies of orthodoxy," he said. "[W]hen you make a stupid remark its stupidity will be obvious, even to yourself."

To understand anything well, we need to strip it down to its essentials. To do that, avoid bureaucratese and words that lie.

CASE STUDY: GEORGE ORWELL, 'POLITICS AND THE ENGLISH LANGUAGE'

What makes bad writing bad? George Orwell finds an answer by comparing two passages. The first is a verse from Ecclesiastes; the second is a translation of that verse into modern bureaucratese.

> I returned and saw under the sun, that the race is not to the swift, nor the battle to the strong, neither yet bread to the wise, nor yet riches to men of understanding, nor yet favour to men of skill; but time and chance happeneth to them all.

> Objective considerations of contemporary phenomena compel the conclusion that success or failure in competitive activities exhibits no tendency to be commensurate with innate capacity, but that a considerable element of the unpredictable must invariably be taken into account.

Why does the first delight and the second confuse and discourage the reader? The first passage, Orwell notes, is simple and visual. All but seven of 49 words contain just one syllable. The passage contains six vivid images, which bring the reader into the middle of a scene. The second passage, by contrast, contains 22 polysyllabic words but, as Orwell notes, "not a single fresh, arresting phrase." It actually presents less information.

To combat abstract, lifeless prose, Orwell proposes that we think in pictures before we express ideas in words. Rather than trying to find the right word, right away, he suggests conjuring up images in our mind's eye. Try not only to see, but also to feel and hear what's going on in the scene. *Then* look for the right words.

In other words, think like a filmmaker. Create a series of scenes, which show people acting and responding. Provide vivid descriptions of places and actions. Bring the reader into the world of the story, moment by moment. Whatever you do, *get specific*.

————

ELEMENT 23: AVOID AGGRESSIVE ADJECTIVES AND ADVERBS

Do you want to write smart, clever, witty, creative, insightful, brainy, surprising, fresh, analytic, engaging, scintillating, and even thrilling prose?

Then avoid using adjectives like those in the previous paragraph. Use adjectives only to express something specific, to set up a description, or to surprise the reader. The French philosopher Voltaire once called adjectives the "enemies of nouns." Rather than coming up with just the right nouns, we fall back on blah nouns and dress them up with adjectives. Mark Twain once had good advice for editing: "Substitute 'damn' every time you're inclined to write 'very'; your editor will delete it and the writing will be just as it should be." Try the same trick for adjectives.

Adjectives fail us for two reasons: They are vague and exhausting.

1. Vague: Too often, adjectives just wave at meaning. Consider the following adjectives: *big, strong, smart, unique, tall, tired, quick, fat*. Those words raise the question: Compared to what?

Take a look at these sentences that rely on adjectives:

- They live in a huge house.
- The company agreed to a complicated settlement.
- Vanderbilt has a rigorous liberal arts curriculum.
- Molly is an accomplished girl.

Now look at sentences that use specific information.

- The 6,000-square-foot house sits in five acres of woods.
- The company agreed to a 329-page settlement, which details 16 separate provisions and defines 46 terms.

- Vanderbilt students must take at least two courses in seven out of eight "core" subject areas.
- In addition to winning a National Merit Scholarship, Molly plays soccer, edits the student newspaper, and performs in a local theater.

Which provides the best view of the subject? It depends on your goal. To make a cursory point and move on, use the sentences in the first group. But to offer a clear picture, use those in the second group.

2. Exhausting. Adjectives do the most damage in clusters. When we use bunches of adjectives, we risk dizzying the reader. Consider Thomas Wolfe's *Look Homeward, Angel*:

> The nostalgic thrill of dew-wet mornings in Spring, the cherry scent, the cool clarion earth, the wet loaminess of the garden, the pungent breakfast smells and the floating snow of blossoms ... inchoate sharp excitement of hot dandelions in young earth ... good male smell of his father's sitting-room ... smooth worn leather sofa, with the gaping horse-hair rent ... blistered varnished wood upon the hearth ... the brown tired autumn earth ... fat limp underdone bacon ... large deep-hued string beans smoking-hot ...

Exhausted? Me too.

Of course, we need adjectives. Consider the passages "He wore a red hat" and "Young jockeys prefer experienced horses." These adjectives perform useful work. Why? "Red" refers to something *specific*; "young" and "experienced" make clear *comparisons*. As summary statements, these adjectives work fine.

Adjectives work when they provide:

- **A setup**. Adjectives often perform a useful service introducing a complex idea. Consider the following passage: "Vanderbilt has a rigorous liberal arts program. Students must take at least two classes in seven core subject areas. The adjective "rigorous" gives you a general idea; "two classes in seven areas" explains that idea.
- **Precision**. Adjectives work best when they refer to a one-and-only thing. The adjectives *unique, first, blue, stationary,* and *transitory* say something precise. *Unique* means one of a

kind. *Blue* is a specific color (*royal blue* or *baby blue* or *periwinkle* might work better). *First* refers to a singular position. *Stationary* contrasts with something in movement. *Transitory* means something that does not last.

- **Sensation**. Sometimes adjectives evoke useful sensations. Wolfe's phrase "wet loaminess of the garden" works. But for this phrase to resonate, the reader needs a moment to soak up the sensation. When the adjectives come fast, one after another, readers cannot process all the sensations. So don't use too many at once.
- **Surprise**. Adjectives work best when they surprise the reader. I smiled when I read Thomas Lynch's description of a vacation on the beach at Santa Barbara, California: "The Pacific was pacific." The Book of Jeremiah talks about a "basket of naughty figs." Maybe, once in a while, it makes sense to use adjectives in unfamiliar contexts. So we might talk about an "impatient smile" or an "ambitious fear." In these examples, the adjective serves as a metaphor.

Now, about those adverbs . . .

Years ago, Gabriel Garcia Marquez started going to AA—Adverbs Anonymous. Admitting that adverbs held a power over his writing that he could not control, he stopped using adverbs altogether.

Adverbs—modifiers of verbs, usually ending in *-ly*—damage writing even more than adjectives. If you use an adverb, it means you're probably not using an action verb. Consider the following passages:

> She walked briskly down the street.
> He eyed her knowingly across the bar.
> He hungrily ate the Chinese food.
> She eagerly plunged into the consulting project.

Words like "briskly," "knowingly," "hungrily," and "eagerly" do not tell us anything specific. When we say that someone ate hungrily, for example, we have an idea that he attacked the plate with zeal. But what does that mean? Did he eat a whole meal in ten minutes? Did he eat food he normally refuses? Did he eat so quickly that he got indigestion? Did he eat faster than everyone else? Did he eat off others' plates?

Even when adverbs *seem* to describe something, they often just repeat ideas; presumably, a person would not eat food unless he was hungry. If he eats for other reasons—boredom, frustration, nervousness—make sure to show or tell the reader.

When you find an adverb in your drafts, cut it and see if the sentence loses meaning. The verb probably does enough work on its own. If not, consider using a different verb, which conveys action. "He ran to get to the meeting" beats "He moved quickly to get to the meeting." One more example: "The crowd greeted the speaker with boos and catcalls" beats "The crowd treated the speaker rudely."

Search your drafts for these common adverbs: *again, also, always, constantly, down, even, ever, frequently, generally, hardly, here, how, however, in general, increasingly, just, more, most, mostly, never, no longer, normally, now, occasionally, off, often, on, once, only, out, over, rarely, really, regularly, so, sometimes, still, then, there, too, twice, up, usually, very,* and *well.*

Occasionally adverbs offer brevity, a virtue. "The bicyclist deftly avoided the runner," then, might work better than "The bicyclist moved off the sidewalk to avoid the runner." Whatever you do, do so *consciously.*

CASE STUDY: THE RHETORIC OF DONALD TRUMP

What happens when a real estate mogul, brand-name pitchman, and TV celebrity—a man who lacks the patience to read even one- or-two-page briefings—decides to run for president? What happens when people ask him about the nuclear triad, tariff rates, and foreign intelligence?

For Donald Trump, the answer is to speak in generalities—with lots of adjectives and superlatives. With a surfeit of adjectives, Trump could speak loudly and confidently without any detailed knowledge of any subjects.

In speeches and more informal remarks, Trump regularly praises people and places things that are *amazing, beautiful, best, big league, brilliant, elegant, fabulous, fantastic, fine, good, great, happy, honest, incredible, nice, outstanding, phenomenal, powerful, sophisticated, special, strong, successful, top, tremendous,* and *unbelievable.*

When perturbed about people or events, he calls them *boring, crooked, disgusting, dishonest, dopey, dumb, goofy, horrible, no good, obsolete, out of control, overrated, pathetic, ridiculous, rude, sad, sorry, stupid, terrible, unfair, weak,* and *the worst.*

Trump loves adjectives so much that he uses them as nouns as well. "We have to get very, very tough on the cyber," he says. Cyber what? Talking about various global threats, Trump muses about possible responses. "It could mean nuclear," he said. Nuclear what? Another time he said "we want to battle drug addiction and combat opioid." Opioid what? By using only adjectives in these passages, Trump uses power words without specifying what exactly he's talking about.

The constant use of adjectives, with no real scale or precision, gives Trump the appearance of certainty. His brash talk pleases supporters and flummoxes everyone else. Because Trump speaks so constantly—in rallies and fundraises, photo-ops and spray events, Twitter and TV —no one can keep up with him. We are left in a cloud of *amazing* and *very* and *beautiful* and *totally* and *bigly.*

As a writer, you do not have permission to overwhelm readers with such meaningless hyperbole. You need to describe things with precision. You need to paint pictures, define complex terms, describe processes, explain cause and effect. So, please, don't be like Donald Trump.

———

AND ANOTHER THING . . .

Picture a child curled up on a window bench reading a book. Or a commuter as she grabs a bar on a subway while reading a newspaper. Or a college student peering into a computer screen to read a blog or document.

Reading looks passive, but really it's physical. Our job, as writers, is to provide enough energy—and enough emotion—to keep the reader physically engaged.

Specific, precise words help us to get the reader physically and emotionally involved. Abstract words create a distance between the subject and the reader. If I read about the "collateral damage" of war, I will approach the subject with detachment (which, by the way, is the point); if I read about guerrillas or drones blasting innocent people, I get a sense of the violence and feel empathy for the victims. If I hear abstract arguments about global warming, I feel detached; if I see the human tragedies of the hurricanes Katrina or Sandy, I respond emotionally.

But emotions don't just prompt us to care. They also prompt us to *think*.

Consider debates about diet. When we think of "meat" or "poultry" abstractly, as just another commodity in the grocer's refrigerator, we think shallowly. But when we understand how chicken farms operate—when we see the animals confined in small spaces without light, pumped with hormones, made so fat they cannot even stand, then boiled alive—we develop a deeper understanding of the issue. The only way to think precisely is to gather and express precise ideas and then use them to engage emotions as well as ideas.

Use words that connect the reader with the subject, vividly and intimately. Then you'll be able to combine the best of both heart and mind.

PART THREE
DEPICTING A PLACE

Show me a place—the streets and neighborhoods, the parks and office parks, the downtowns and strips and malls, the highways undergrounds—and I'll show you that the character of the people who live and work there.

Places not only *contain* everything we do. They also *shape* everything we do. They help to forge our identity. Wherever we are, places help us to create meaning. They help (or hinder) our ability to forge relationships with other people, explore how the world works, and how it might work better. Place helps us to discover who we are and what we might become.

In *The Timeless Way of Building*, the architect Christopher Alexander called the sum total of these attributes the "Quality Without a Name," or QWAN.

QWAN speaks not just to a place's physical makeup but also its values and aspirations. It reflects the *soul* of a place.

Great places do not just provide the opportunity for people to *do things*. Homes don't just provide containers for us to rest, eat, sleep, and get ready for life outside. Parks don't just provide containers for play. Schools don't just offer containers for learning.

Great places also create *meaning*. They help people to nurture relationships with others. They help us to explore how the world works—

and how it might work better. In great places, we discover who we are and what we might become.

Descriptions of a place begin with an account of its physical layout and the way people use it. Start with its physical contours. What is the shape of the place? How big is it? Where is it located? What's nearby? What are the boundaries, the focal points, the pathways, the furniture, the nooks, the lookouts? What places attract what people? Why?

Most of us only notice the obvious aspects of places. We see what we essential for us to know or what is unusual in some way. When we focus on one aspect of a place (like a path overlooking a pond or a garden in a city park) we don't focus on other aspects (the hidden nooks, service buildings, unused passageways). To succeed as a writer, you need to train yourself to see like a movie camera, spanning the space, zooming in and out, looking high and low.

Whether you're describing an intimate place (like a bedroom or a chapel), a public place (like a street scene or a building), or a remote place (like a desert landscape), don't be satisfied with what you see right away. Push yourself to *see more*. Then push again … and again.

That's the challenge of this unit of our writing program: Learn how to look with fresh eyes so that you can see for your reader. Don't be satisfied with what you see right away. Push yourself to *see more*.

THE PLAN OF ATTACK

As before, we'll start with two content skills, with a focus on understanding the places where people live:

- Chapter 6: The World of the Story
- Chapter 7: The Senses

Then we move on to two more skills of writing mechanics:

- Chapter 8: Paragraphs
- Chapter 9: Wordplay

Earlier, I said that the sentence is the most important unit of writing. But mastering the paragraph might improve your writing more than any other skill. Why? Because people are confused about what a paragraph is and what it does. We've got the answer here.

CHAPTER 6
THE WORLD OF THE STORY

> The center of reality is wherever one happens to be, and its circumference is whatever one's imagination can make sense of.

> MARGARET ATWOOD

PICTURE A GRAY STONE mansion on a hill. A rusted iron gate, chained and padlocked, surrounds the property. Inside, a long driveway leads to the massive structure. The house stands lifeless; no smoke comes from the chimney and the windows look shabby and neglected. Grass and moss have overtaken the driveway. Woods crowd the mansion's edges.

With every detail, you sense tragedy and loss. That mansion was once full of love and life. Windows glowed with light and curtains danced in the soft breeze. Inside people ate great meals and sang into the night. A beloved matron ran the house while her husband tended to the affairs of business. As the seasons came and went, people played tennis and swam, picnicked and tended gardens, received visitors and embarked on trips.

The whole history of the people—their spirit, their identity—is captured by this place. So is the tragedy that befell the household with the death of the matron and the vengeful anger of the housekeeper.

You might recognize this scene from Daphne du Maurier's 1938 Gothic novel *Rebecca* (or the 1940 movie version, starring Laurence

Olivier and Joan Fontaine). From the book's very first line—"Last night I dreamt I went to Manderlay again"—we experience the mysterious power of this place.

Great stories focus on people, their passions and struggles. But to know people, you need to know the places of their lives. Places not only contain the characters and action, but also set the boundaries and basic rules for action. In a sense, the setting is the "extra" character of your story, creating possibilities and barriers, just like the flesh-and-blood characters.

Alfred Hitchcock, who directed the film *Rebecca*, sometimes plotted his films by first deciding the places where scenes would take place. Once he identified the locales, he developed characters and storylines to fit those places. Hitch explains:

> Of course, this is quite the wrong thing to do. But here's an idea: select the background first, then the action. It might be a race or might be anything at all. Sometimes I select a dozen different events and shape them into a plot. Finally—and this is just the opposite of what is usually done—select your character to motivate the whole of the above.

Hitchcock built *The Man Who Knew Too Much* this way. He later recalled this thinking:

> I would like to do a film that starts in the winter sporting season. I would like to come to the East End of London. I would like to go to a chapel and to a symphony concert at the Albert Hall in London.

Once he had a setting, Hitchcock figured out which characters belonged and what they would do in that setting.

Whether or not you use Hitchcock's approach, survey all the possible locations as you develop your story. If you write about sports, consider the stadium, practice fields, locker rooms, bars, and after-hours nightclubs. If you write about the civil rights movement, start with the streets, lunch counters, churches, schools, and jails. If you write the life of a high school, think about classrooms, corridors and stairwells, pizza joints and Saturday night party spots.

Place matters. So create the settings that reveal the values of the people and periods of the story.

ELEMENT 24: CREATE SMALL, KNOWABLE PLACES

Recall a time you went to a big city, like New York, Chicago, or Los Angeles, for the first time. How did you cope? Probably by finding a place apart from the hubbub—a coffee shop, a library, a friend's apartment—to collect yourself and figure out what to do next. Small settings provide predictable containers for action. We can only pay attention to a few things at a time. In order to think or act, we need to focus.

Likewise, your story needs small, knowable places. The less distracting the settings, the more readers can pay attention to characters and action.

TV dramas and sitcoms shows succeed, in part, because they depict the action in small, predictable spaces. Characters gather in living rooms, bars, offices, and other limited spaces. Because these places are so familiar, the audience can focus on the characters and storylines. Predictable places never disorient the viewer.

These small, knowable places reflect the characters' values and status. The working-class Bunkers of *All in the Family* live in a drab row house in Queens, their living room focused on a TV. The upper-crust Huxtables of *The Cosby Show* live in an elegant brownstone in Brooklyn Heights, their living room a showcase for antiques and art. In *Friends*, the characters meet in hip singles' apartments and a coffee bar. In *The Office*, the characters work together in the drab regional branch office of Dunder-Mifflin.

Even when a story's action extends far and wide, small spaces still contain the action. In Homer's *Odyssey*, as the hero sails all over the Mediterranean, he and his crew regularly repair to their ship. In Jack Kerouac's *On the Road*, Sal rides his motorcycle to New York, San Francisco, Los Angeles, Denver, Chicago, and Mexico City. In *Blue Highways*, William Least Heat Moon drives an RV across America. The vehicles not only contain the stories, but also offer symbols of the characters' values.

As you describe your settings, pay attention to things that shape or symbolize people's behavior there. When possible show how people use props. Every prop reveals something about the characters, their community and culture. Objects provide something for the characters to use; they give us an excuse for action. Look at this passage from "Fun With a Stranger," a short story by Richard Yates:

> Miss Snell kept a big, shapeless old eraser on her desk, and she seemed very proud of it. "This is my eraser," she would say, shaking it at the class. "I've had this eraser for five years. Five years." (And this was not hard to believe, for the eraser looked as old and gray and worn-down as the hand that brandished it.) "I've never played with it because it's not a toy. I've never chewed it because it's not good to eat. And I've never lost it because I'm not foolish and I'm not careless. I need this eraser for my work and I've taken good care of it.

A simple prop—an ordinary object in a classroom, a small knowable place—offers instant insight into a stern, dreaded primary school teacher.

I realized the full power of props when listening to a radio interview with the economist Barry Bluestone. Talking with Tom Ashbrook of NPR's "On Point," Bluestone described working at a Ford plant in during his college summers in the 1960s. Bluestone brought an object for show-and-tell. "This is a two-barrel carburetor from 1964," Bluestone announced, as if the audience could see. "It went into a Mustang and there's a good chance that I built that thing." Bluestone then recounted watching a worker at a McDonald's restaurant a few days before. "I'm looking at a guy operating a fryolator and he's going through the exactly same motions that I went through, but he's making one-fourth what I made."

When I heard this, I was amazed. Simply bringing an object into the conversation, acting as if listeners could see it, Bluestone activated the visual parts of our brains and our memories. He put us on that assembly line in Roseville, Michigan, and in that fast-food restaurant in Boston, Massachusetts. The power of props to enliven a scene—*even when you can't see them*—is profound.

Wherever you set your story—at home or work, out in the larger world or on the road—create a meaningful and limited container for the characters and action. Show the characters develop themselves there. Put objects around them; better yet, put objects in their hands.

Once your characters have established themselves in small, knowable places, they can venture into the big, unruly world outside.

CASE STUDY: FACEBOOK'S WAR ROOM

In the White House it's called the Situation Room. In hospitals, emergency shelters, and police departments, it's called the Crisis Center. At Facebook it's called the War Room.

In a world of constant crises and threats, major institutions use these well-equipped places to manage chaos. They bring specialists together in one place, enabling face-to-face discussions and rapid responses to the crises.

When Mark Zuckerberg started Facebook at his college dorm at Harvard, he could not have imagined that his website would attract hundreds of millions of users—or that the site could be weaponized to spread lies and propaganda. But that's just what has happened. In response, Facebook established a war room to track future threats and shut down trolls and bots.

Facebook monitors cyber threats in a 25- by 30-foot conference room, off the hallway connecting Building 20 and Building 21, in the middle of the company's Menlo Park headquarters. Desks for 24 people fill the middle of the room. On the edges, 17 vertical screens emit the steady hum of cable TV news and data streams from Facebook. Whiteboards fill in the spaces along the edges. Cables and wires hang from the open ceiling, just above an American flag.

Facebooks's War Room represents 20 different units in the company, with experts from threat intelligence, data science, engineering, research, operations, legal policy, and communications.

All day long, staffers inspect data for spikes in hate speech, spam, or other fake information. The screens monitor how people share Facebook messages across other platforms like Twitter, Reddit, and Instagram. Data are depicted in bar graphs and scattergrams and maps. When staffers see something suspicious—like fake reports of long lines at voting stations, which are intended to discourage voters from going to the polls—they alert appropriate public officials.

Facebook's first line of defense is its programmers' ability to detect malicious bots and actors and to drive them out of the system electronically. But the threat is so big—and the enemies are so clever—that Facebook also needs a live human response as well.

In a world where someone in Hong Kong can speak to someone in Washington in real time, why does Facebook need to gather experts in one room? Because direct, personal communication still works best.

"When every moment counts, the decision making needs to be fast," says Samidh Chakarabarti, the head of civic engagement at Facebook. "There's no substitute for face-to-face, in-room interaction, so we felt this physical war room to be able to coordinate teams."

The threats are endless. The Internet has proliferated the opportunities for mischief-making in all realms of life—not just politics, but also commerce, intimate relationships, even warfare. Malicious actors, from Vladimir Putin in the Kremlin to punks in basements, have developed sophisticated strategies to find holes in computer systems.

"We know that the bad actors out there who are looking to interfere in elections, they are definitely well funded," Chakarabarti said. "They're committed and they are getting increasingly sophisticated. So as one example, I think they've been getting better at being able to mask the location that they're coming from."

Facebook and other online media—not to mention the IRS, political party organizations, banks, and other corporate and political agencies —need to monitor their systems constantly. Even one hole in the system can compromise the data of hundreds of millions of people.

Public and private entities need to develop a systemic process to defend themselves against hackers. If Facebook does not block the scammers, bots and fakers will dominate the everyday discourse of Americans. Hence, the War Room.

————

ELEMENT 25. MAP THE CHARACTER'S 'CIRCLES OF LIFE'

Nothing reveals the characters, their ideals, and the possibilities of their lives more than the places where they spend time. The Zen aphorism "You are what you pay attention to" applies to place. The places in your life cause you to focus on some things and not others. To plot a story, then, get an overview of the many places where the characters spend their time.

We live in four basic kinds of places. Think of these places as a circles:

Home: Home is not only where you eat, sleep, and build a life. It's also where you experience your intimate relationships and forge the values that guide the rest of your life. "Home is the place to go that, when you have to go there, they have to take you in," Robert Frost famously said. Home is the place where everyone knows your flaws and still loves you.

So what does the home look like? What does the home reveal about your values, your dreams and aspirations? How do you decorate your home? How clean or dirty is it? Are you a neat freak or a hoarder, or something in between? Is the home filled with books or video games or pizza boxes? Is the kitchen a place of love and creation? Are there places for hobbies, like woodworking or sewing or sports?

And where is the home located? On a gritty city street or in a leafy suburb? Is it a diverse community, teeming with people of all ages of many racial and ethnic and religious backgrounds? Or is it monochromatic and blandly conformist? Is this community full of activity and adventure? Or do people move from home to work to school to church without any stopping in between?

Work: We spend most waking hours at work. Whether or not we like our jobs or coworkers, we accommodate ourselves to them. Does workplace reflect the company's organizational structure—its strict hierarchy or its loose collection of work groups? Do people work alone in offices, buzz in cubicle hives, or gather for group sessions in open spaces? Or do they work in one vast connected system, like a factory or warehouse? Or maybe a showroom or boutique?

Do people have accidental encounters in hallways and lunchrooms and meeting rooms? Are the open spaces full of energy and conversation or do they hum with the quiet productivity of people coming and going? Is the environment energetic or enervating? What makes the work spaces distinctive from other workplaces?

The Third Place: Sociologists use this label for the places that attract people in their "off" hours—bars and bookstores, churches and fraternal organizations, gyms and cinemas, coffee houses and retreats, to name just a handful. When you think of a "third place," think of the bar in the TV show *Cheers*, where "everybody knows your name" and where relationships range from the superficial to the intimate.

So what happens in the third places of your stories? Why do people gather there? To get away from work or to fraternize with work friends? Are these places full of family? How many people gathering there are regulars? How many are locals and how many are outsiders?

Out There: When not in these three core places, we circulate among strangers in cars, trains and planes, parks and hiking trails, sidewalks, and public buildings. Sometimes we interact with strangers but more often we avoid them. So what's "out there" like? Is it open and free or tight and constrained? Safe or dangerous? A place of play or commerce? Diverse or homogenous? Does it feel welcoming or repressive?

Generations ago, children spent most of their free time outside, playing and exploring the world with friends and siblings. Now we plan "play dates" and sign kids up for camps and enrichment programs. Or we leave 'em alone to sit in front of a TV or computer screen. So "out there" is a different place now.

Asked how to construct a story, the journalist and author Gay Talese responded: "Scene, scene, scene." Use circles of different sizes to show how much time your characters spend in what places.

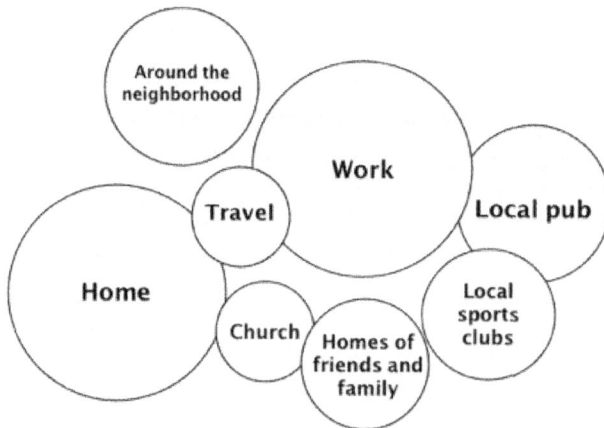

As an example, map out the circles of a hypothetical factory work-er's life. The character in this story, I would say, leads a balanced life. What do you think?

Where we spend time evolves over the course of our lives. Our circles revolve around school and home in our growing years, college and adventures in our young adulthood, work and third places in our twenties, and back to home and work as adults. Some of us spend a lot of time in the community, while others avoid the public sphere.

The circles of our lives shape the way we act. Each circle has its own values and norms; many have strict rules. We behave differently in a bar with old college friends than we do in a church with family or a professional office or the gym where we work out. Some places encourage loving and supportive behavior, while others encourage bullying or abuse—and most places encourage something in-between.

Our lives need a balance of different kinds of circles. Often, we spend too much time in some circles and not enough in others—by choice or by necessity. We avoid some circles because we feel uncomfortable there. We gravitate to others because they offer "comfort zones," where we do not have to prove ourselves.

To develop ourselves fully, we need to choose our circles well. We need many and varied activities—and we need to surround ourselves with people who make us better. We need to avoid circles where people manipulate and undermine us and spend time in circles where people support and challenge each other.

CASE STUDY: ROBIN NAGLE, *PICKING UP*

Robin Nagle, an anthropologist, has always been fascinated with garbage.

No city, after all, could survive without reliable garbage pickup. Cities are the densest centers of production and consumption and someone has to remove the trash. Every day, workers with the New York Sanitation Department travel 6,000 miles of streets, removing 11,000 tons of household trash and 2,000 tons of household recycling. Known as "sans," the sanitation workers also sweep those streets and, in the winter, they help to plow streets and remove snow.

After years of effort—phoning, emailing, visiting, networking—Nagel got permission to accompany sanitation workers on their daily rounds. Then she decided to become a san herself. Her exploration of the sanitation workers takes us to a number of distinct circles of life.

To start, Nagle spends lots of times on the highways and streets that connect the city's neighborhoods:

I am heading south during the evening rush hour on the Major Deegan Expressway in New York City, carrying a load of densely packed garbage to the dump (more properly called a transfer station). As I thread the truck's 35-ton bulk through thick traffic, well aware that no one is glad to see me, the engine's steady keening aligns with my own sense of caution. Though I own the road—few motorists will play chicken with a garbage truck—50 miles an hour is plenty fast enough for me.

From the city's highways and streets, she drives into the transfer station to dump her load for the day:

Piercing backup beeps and roaring hydraulics are accompanied by shrieks of metal against metal, and the acoustic onslaught reverberates off the walls like a physical force, so intense that it takes on a kind of aural purity. Workers who spend their shifts inside the facility wear fat red headphones, but those of us only passing through must suffer the cacophony. The best way to communicate is with hand signals.

To become a san herself, Nagle was required to take courses and pass a series of tests:

"Good morning," yelled a loose-limbed man in a sanitation worker's uniform. Mo Ragusa could be a tall Mickey Rooney. He was standing before us in a long cinder-block classroom, its yellow walls made yellower by the usual wash of fluorescence. When we muttered an anemic reply, he looked at us with contempt. It was just past 6 on a hot Monday in early summer. Our class of 77 men and two women sat alphabetically in rows of nine tables, simultaneously sleepy and tense.

Every day, she explores the city's neighborhoods:

Bart's collection truck moved steadily up the street, its many backlights and reflectors bright against the dark evening. I was directly behind him in my own truck, the doors folded open for the warm breeze. We were on the Grand Concourse, one of the city's celebrated thorough-fares and a defining landmark of the Bronx. ... Pedestrians crowded the sidewalks, their arms heavy with shopping bags or schoolbooks. Thick traffic slowed our pace. Bart signaled a left turn and I did the same; a short block later, he signaled another left, heading us back the way we'd just come. Again.

In her work, Nagle has discovered that sans are really a community, with their own informal fraternal organizations:

They gather on the last Thursday of the month at a social hall in Maspeth, Queens, greeting one another with hearty embraces. The loudest welcomes are given to the most recently retired, not yet so far from the daily life of the job; their smiles are wide and their cheeks flush as they endure huzzahs and backslaps. Almost all are men. Their sartorial choices run from T-shirts and jeans to sport coats and dress pants, though a few wear tailored suits.

Wherever she goes, Nagle discovers that she is invisible. Sans are, in the words of one sociologist, an "unmarked" element of city life.

You are picking up garbage in a residential neighborhood when a man walks up to you and tells you he thinks sanitation workers have no right to be in unions because if they did their jobs right they wouldn't need to organize in order to be treated fairly. He then adds a bag to his pile of trash and goes back into his house. You are a union supporter. What should you do?

In her work, Robin Nagel answers her own question every day. As a student of cities, she has shared the world of this most vital and invisible band of public servants. And we are the richer for it.

———

ELEMENT 26: USE PLACE TO EXPLAIN CHARACTER AND IDEAS

"First we make the place," Winston Churchill once remarked. "Then the place makes us."

To portray people and their journeys, we need to show both sides of that equation. The places where we live not only contain the stories of our lives; they also shape them. Characters understand the world from these places—and then turn around and shape these spaces.

As you write your stories, consider those settings as extra characters. Make your places "act" on the characters—enabling them to do this, preventing them from doing that, and shaping their hopes and fears. Consider how the place influences characters in their everyday lives—and in their fateful decisions. Does the place foster energy? Connections? Imagination? Hope? Morality? Or does it foster dread? Lassitude? Fear? Confusion? Conflict?

Consider a few possibilities. New York offers infinite variety and frenzied activity; smaller communities like Missoula, Montana, offer 360-degree access to the splendors of nature. Yale offers the grandeur of an Ivy League school; community colleges offer bunker-like settings but also a leg up for immigrants and left-behinds. A McMansion offers all the trappings and isolation of modern affluence; a saltbox house in a New England town offers a warm home and access to town squares.

Can you imagine Mario Puzo's *The Godfather* without Don Corleone's compound or the streets of New York? Can you picture David Schearl, the lead character in Henry Roth's *Call It Sleep*, outside the rough ghettos of Brooklyn and lower east side of Manhattan? Or Holden Caulfield, the hero of J.D. Salinger's *The Catcher in the Rye*, outside Pency Prep or New York? These places shape their stories and offer important information about the characters and their struggles.

When you know a place, you can get to understand the people who live and work there. So give your story a vivid, meaningful place.

CASE STUDY: ROBERT CARO, *THE PATH TO POWER*

When the Pulitzer Prize-winning biographer Robert Caro first saw the hill country in central Texas, he knew he had found the key to the character of Lyndon Johnson.

On an unforgiving swath of empty space, Caro saw a "huddle of houses," where the 36th president was born and raised. It was a lonely, desolate spot. Back when LBJ was a kid, people would sit by the side of the road for hours, waiting for a single car to drive by. It was as isolated as any place in America. The question arises: Why did Johnson's forebears move to such a vast, isolated place?

See how Caro answers the riddle:

> The Hill Country was a trap—a trap baited with grass.
>
> To men who lived in the damp, windless forests of Alabama or east Texas and then had trudged across 250 miles of featureless Texas plains —walking for hours alongside their wagons across the flat land toward a low rise, and then, when they reached the top of the rise, seeing before them just more flatness, until at the top of one rise they saw, in the distance, something different: a low line that, as they toiled toward it, gradually became hills, hills stretching across an entire horizon—to these men the hills were beautiful. …
>
> The air of the highland was drier and clearer than the air on the plains below; it felt clean and cool on the skin. The sky, in the clear air, was a blue so brilliant that one of the early settlers called it a "sapphire sky." Beneath that sky the leaves of Spanish oaks, ancient and huge, and of elms and cedars sparkled in the sun; the leaves of the trees in the hills looked different from the leaves of the scattered trees on the plains below, where the settlers' wagons still stood—a darker, lush green, a green with depths and cool shadows.

The grass promised settlers a lush and fertile land for farming and a hospitable place for living—but it was a false promise. The grass had grown long and thick, but the topsoil offered just a thin blanket over a foundation of limestone. So when people settled and trod on that turf, the lush grass gave way to a dusty, bare expanse. In just a short time, this lush landscape would turn into a dustbowl.

The desolate hill country, in turn, yielded poverty, hopelessness, and isolation. It also gave rise to Lyndon Johnson's ambition and impatience, his drive to escape Texas to gain power in Washington, D.C.—and his burning desire to transform the area, bring it technology and education and money.

———

ELEMENT 27: USE PLACE TO EXPLORE IDENTITY

The places where people live, work, and play leave hints about their characters—how they present themselves to the world, what they do to motivate themselves, and what gets lost in the shuffle.

Consider three questions that a place answers:

Who am I? We decorate our homes, offices, and even our cars to advertise our values and aspirations. When we hang art, arrange books, drape curtains, display knickknacks, tack snapshots, or post affirmations, we tell people, "This makes me *me*."

Some places allow little opportunity to advertise our identity. College dorms, army barracks, high-rise apartments, and tract housing limit how you can express yourself. Many housing developments restrict how homeowners may decorate their own homes. Offices constrain expression even more. Still, most people try to give their places a distinctive flavor. When they settle into their homes, people paint this and remodel that, landscape here and plant there. People advertise their identity, wherever they go.

When I was in college, a guy named Dave lived down the hall in my dorm. Rather than accepting the dorm's bland furnishings, Dave brought his own desk, chairs, shelves, and curtains. He installed a big fish tank. He put down a plush rug. When you entered his room, the sounds of Miles Davis and Charlie Parker caressed you. With this setup, Dave told everyone, in a sense: "This makes me *me*."

Whatever you describe in your pieces, look for the things that characters use to express themselves.

What do I aspire to? Sometimes we arrange our space to put ourselves in the mood to work, relax, play, or interact with others. We surround ourselves with furniture, art, music, and mementos that help us to focus on what matters in our daily lives.

People arrange their homes and offices to evoke just the right aspirations. Photos and vacation souvenirs provide reminders of carefree days. A "conversation corner" with comfy chairs guides us to read or chat. A recreation area with a TV or stereo calls us to chill and get social. A work nook inspires us to focus.

Aspirations mark our public spaces too. Civic art, parks, architecture, even bus shelters and signage, tell the world about the community's aspirations. Can you imagine Paris without the Eiffel Tower, St. Louis without the arch, Seattle without the space needle?

Even fakery advertises our aspirations. Back in the 1980s, New York City Mayor Edward Koch wrapped the exteriors of abandoned buildings with massive pictures of lively brownstones. Critics said Koch glossed over the area's socioeconomic problems with this architectural wrapping paper. Exactly! By changing people's images of this bombed-out area, Koch encouraged people to imagine something better.

What do I neglect? With the first two questions, people consciously shape the worlds where they live, work, and play. But people also behave less consciously, leaving behind hints about their character.

The things we leave behind without thinking—books, clothing, unopened mail, shopping bags, dishes, and more—offer clues about what we take for granted, how organized we are, and what we do in our day-to-day lives.

Sloppy people cannot be bothered to manage their space. They put a priority on work or play instead of placemaking. (Or they're just lazy.) Neat freaks' spaces also reflect the order of their minds. They pay attention to one thing at a time. They can be more efficient, but may also be also less creative. Their places help to tell the story.

Hoarders make up a whole different class. Often lost in the past, they refuse to part with old objects—even worthless old newspapers and bags, broken or outdated equipment, tattered clothing, souvenirs and tchotchkes, outdated records and papers, and more. Many have piles of unopened booty from long-ago shopping trips. When asked to toss or give away objects, hoarders experience anxiety and fear.

Things have stories to tell. So let every piece of furniture, every belonging, every arrangement tell something about your characters.

CASE STUDY: SYBILLE BEDFORD, *THE FACES OF JUSTICE*

No place is set up for dramatic impact—*controlled* dramatic impact— quite like a courtroom. From the bench where the judge sits down to the witness stand, counsel tables, and spectators' seats, the courtroom displays the power and majesty of the law.

Consider this description of Old Bailey in London:

Above the dais, the ornate chair, the robe, the still head of the judge rises above the court as if suspended.

"Thirty-two cheeses, my Lord, valued at 300 pounds, four shillings, and nine pence."

The first moments inside a court of law are like the first moments at a play—the eye notes the scene, sound begins to reach the ear, then words. Sense converges later.

The judge's head does not stir...

"With respect—" Another gowned figure has leapt to his feet. "My learned friend is perfectly aware that the cheeses were never found." ...

The jury shifts a little. Twice six persons, three of them women, fitted to two benches, one above the other, in an open box that seems just to hold them. They also seem much alike, grey, absent-faced, thin-suited people: civilians firmly stuck to their place at this scene of adorned, articulate and accomplished men. ...

The pit, the few square feet of center floor free of pews and boxes, is filled with two large tables, stained biscuit-brown like all the other boarding, aflutter with a snowstorm of documents ...

An usher moves slowly, careful not to trip. A handful of extraneous and upset-looking people sit neatly in three more short rows of beach squeezed by the entrance door. ...

At the far end of the court, in the largest box of all, on an axis with the Judge's chair, sits the prisoner in the dock ... In the dock with him, like an idle umpire in the ring, sits a warder in uniform, bulky, relaxed, unconcerned. ...

In her account of a simple case of theft, Sybille Bedford describes the courtroom with details that others might miss. She shows how the room reinforces power relations with its pyramidal organization, from the judge on top to the spectators below. To show how the setting controls people's behavior, she describes the movements of the judge, jury, lawyers, defendant, and spectators.

The room symbolizes the status of everyone in the judicial system: All are equal under the law, but some are "more equal" than others. If status details reveal people's character, then the architecture and orna-mentation of this room reveals the hierarchy of the modern system of justice in the Western world.

———

ELEMENT 28: PLACE STORIES IN A LARGER WORLD

Suppose you're a city planner. You're designing a park in a residential neighborhood. What do you put in the park? Benches? Gardens? Fountains? Statuary? Play equipment? Athletic fields? A stage for plays? Picnic tables and grills? Kiosks? Bathrooms?

It depends, doesn't it? You cannot design a park—or anything else —unless you understand the broader context. You need to know about the people who live nearby, the daily flows of traffic, business and social life, schools and other parks. To design the park, you need to understand the larger territory.

The same goes for describing settings in stories. To understand any place, you need to understand how people move in and out of the story, from intimate spaces to social spaces, from confined urban spaces to the open expanses of nature. However important the main setting, we also need to see the story's larger landscape. That landscape supplies the complete cast of characters that moves in and out of the story.

So if you write a story about a school, show the neighborhood surrounding the school, the students' homes, the places they work and volunteer, the sports fields and theaters, the malls and pizza parlors where they hang out, and more. If you write about a business, show the workplace but also outside meeting places, factories, sales stops, tax offices, homes, and more. If you write about sports, show the players and their fans on the field but also in the locker room, homes, player hangouts, fan events, and more.

You get the idea. Moving back and forth, from the inside to the outside of the place, helps us to glimpse the characters' psychology. The home shows the characters' intimate life. Workplaces and "third places"—bars, clubs, and other places where people meet friends— show characters playing their social roles.

People usually behave more intimately inside—but not always. Children from abusive or deprived families, for example, often hide in fear at home and find their real opportunity for expression in schools, playing fields, and churches and youth hangouts. "Third places"—the places between home and work, like bars, union halls, churches, theaters, and sports clubs—sometimes offer more warmth and security than home. Friends confide in each other more than intimates.

Wherever you take your characters, use those places to reveal the states of their hearts and minds. Let those places reveal their psychology and understanding.

————

CASE STUDY: JOAN DIDION, *THE WHITE ALBUM*

To understand the planning process of the California Department of Transportation, Joan Didion toggled back and forth from the small office of planners from Caltrans to the sprawling highway system they were trying to manage.

Zooming in: In a windowless room at the Caltrans operations center at 120 South Spring Street in downtown Los Angeles, planners sat staring at computer consoles, observing streams of information about the traffic on the city's infamous freeways.

Zooming out: On the 42-mile "Loop," the concrete triangle formed by the Santa Monica, San Diego, and Harbor freeways, drivers get clogged even on good days. This is why transportation planners are desperate for any tweaks that could save time and cost for the millions of motorists who travel to work, school, shopping, and sports and entertainment.

Zooming in: Back in the Caltrans offices, analysts tracked traffic in real time by analyzing data from sensors installed along the highway. In this small, featureless room, planners looked for patterns that might help them to understand the way people drive. Every twenty seconds, these sensors record activities ranging from swerves to jackknifed trucks.

"There's a heart attack," someone says.

"We're getting the gawk effect," someone else says.

At the time of Didion's visit, the Caltrans officials were assessing the impact of a new policy intended to reduce traffic on the freeways. To encourage ride-sharing, the state set aside Diamond Lanes for cars carrying three or more people. The hope was to "pry John Q. Public out of his car," as one Caltrans official said.

Zooming out: Alas, the result of this policy was more congestion, not less. Angelinos resisted the Caltrans experiment. To see how, Didion shifts our attention again to the outside world:

> Citizen guerrillas splashed paint and scattered nails in the Diamond Lanes. Diamond Lane maintenance crews expressed fear of hurled objects. … To understand what was going on it is perhaps necessary to have participated in the freeway experience, which is the only secular communion Los Angeles has. Mere driving on the freeway is in no way the same as partici-pating in it. Anyone can "drive" on the freeway, and many people with no vocation in it do, hesitating here and resisting there, losing the rhythm of the lane change, thinking about where they came from and where they're going. Actual *participation* requires a total surrender, a concentration so intense as to seem a form of narcosis, a rapture-of-the-freeway. The mind goes clean. The rhythm takes over. A distortion of time occurs, the same distortion that characterizes the instant before an accident. … The moment is dangerous. The exhilaration is in doing it. "As you acquire the special skills involved, … the freeways become a special way of being alive."

In this piece, Didion tells a tale of two worlds: the world of techno-cratic planners and the world of the drivers who must navigate the region's notorious freeways.

Everyone, Didion notes, is stubborn. Even when highway improve-ments could improve their driving experience, drivers resist change. Even when their experiment yields disastrous results—the number of accidents in a six-week period typically range of 49 to 72; in this exper-iment, the number of accidents was 204—the planners refuse to yield..

As the drivers cling to the romance of the open highway, Didion muses, planners "have their own rapture at 120 South Spring, and it could be called Perpetuating the Department."

———

AND ANOTHER THING …

Place matters. But how much?

In the 1950s, the psychologists Abraham Maslow and Norbett Mintz designed an experiment to find out. The researchers set up three rooms—one beautiful (with large windows, comfortable furniture, and soulful art), one ugly (set up like a janitor's closet, with drab walls and clutter), and one "average" (clean and functional but not especially attractive). Maslow and Mintz then asked experiment subjects questions about the energy and well-being of the people in pictures.

Participants in the beautiful room judged the people in the pictures to be vibrant and full of life; participants in the ugly room judged the same people to be tired and unhappy. The researchers assisting Maslow and Mintz had similar experiences. The researchers who worked in the ugly room experienced "monotony, fatigue, headache, sleepiness, discontent, irritability, hostility, and avoidance." They also made poor decisions in the ugly rooms.

The world of the story—the places where people spend their lives —shapes how they feel and behave and how others perceive them. Well-designed places make it easier for people to do what they want to do. They boost people's energy and focus. Poorly designed places disorient people, sap their energy, and alienate them from others.

Put your characters in different places. Note how they change as they go from home to school to work, from the mall to the ball field to the theater, from the pizzeria to the pub. Place determines possibilities. Create settings that make the characters who they are.

CHAPTER 7
THE SENSES

Good writing is supposed to evoke sensation in the reader. Not the fact that it is raining, but the feeling of being rained upon.

E.L. DOCTOROW

IMAGINE WALKING HOME one day and pausing at a gourmet candy shop to buy a piece of dark chocolate.

You spy the chocolate behind the curved glass shield running along the counter. You see deep brown chunks, darker than the darkest dirt, lying next to light chunks of milk chocolate. The saleswoman wraps the chocolate in white tissue paper, puts it in a cream-colored bag, and hands it to you. Later, you sit in your quiet dining room and open the bag. You hear a dog barking in the distance, but all else is silent. You take the chocolate out, feeling its hardness and rough shape beneath the tissue. You see three smooth edges and one jagged edge. You see a pale dust on the candy's surface.

Then you bring the chocolate to your mouth. You bite a corner. You feel the chocolate's density and resistance. The break sounds like pieces of a plastic toy snapping apart. Before the chocolate breaks, you taste its bitterness with the tip of your tongue. As you move that piece around your mouth, the taste moves with your tongue. The chocolate begins to melt. As the ooze spreads, you savor the chocolate's bitterness, saltiness, sweetness, and oiliness.

In that one small act of tasting chocolate, you experience all of the senses. You see its shapes and colors. You feel its texture and size. You assay its density. You hear it snapping and then melting and moving around your mouth.

To describe any scene, describe all the senses. Show what something looks, sounds, and feels like.

Pay attention to how people express themselves. Visual people use expressions like, "Oh, yes, I see what you mean" and "Watch what he does," and use visual cues like maps and charts. Auditory people say, "Oh, yes, I hear what you're saying" and "Listen, that's just not right." Kinesthetic people say, "I know how you feel" and "Let's crunch the numbers," and ask for a demonstration or a chance to try something out.

Tap into all the senses to connect with readers. Think of yourself as a method actor. Close your eyes and remember how you felt at similar moments. *What did it feel like? What did you see? What were the colors and the lighting like? What did you hear? How warm or cold was the air?* When you feel those emotions, then you can write about them.

The senses affect us so powerfully that we often use one sense to describe another. We use physical words—for heaviness and lightness, hardness and softness—to describe colors. We use visual words—for brightness and darkness, focus and blurriness—to talk about sounds. So we use metaphors to describe metaphors.

Bring all of the senses into your writing. Help the reader see, hear, and feel the action.

———

ELEMENT 29: HELP THE READER TO SEE

When you give the reader something visual, you arouse the most active parts of the reader's mind. Just as a fireworks display offers many different kinds of stimulation—and potential for clashing values—so does vision.

No visual details reveal as much as the face, with its telling signs of our minds and emotions—whether we're truthful or deceitful, relaxed or nervous, alert or dazed, creative or one-dimensional.

So practice observing faces. Look at people you know or love. Or just find a photograph or painting. Search for clues. Do facial muscles hang on the skull tightly or loosely? What can we tell from the shape of the face, the chin and lips, the forehead and eyebrows? How do the eyes reveal about character? What can we tell from an involuntary twitch or a look away?

Scholars have identified hundreds of "microexpressions," facial movements that appear for just fractions of seconds. Cops, teachers, counselors, supervisors, and investigators all study body language. In an emergency situation—a standoff during a robbery, a hostage taking, or a gang member's threat—interpreting microexpressions can be a matter of life and death.

Go beyond facial expressions to read body language. How we carry ourselves—not only our faces, but also our arms, hands, legs, and trunks—reveals our moods. When we lower our center of gravity and clench our fists, we subconsciously prepare for attack. When we draw in our chin, close arms and legs, we prepare to defend ourselves. When we open ourselves, we invite others into our world. Consider these basic indicators from body language:

- **Eyes looking up**: Pondering something. Often the sign of a visual thinker.
- **Arms crossed**: Defensiveness, creating as barrier with other people.
- **Looking directly**: Confidence, with nothing to hide.
- **Looking indirectly**: Submission or lack of confidence.
- **Looking sideways**: Distraction or auditory style.
- **Glancing and grazing**: Sizing up the other person, perhaps as a partner.
- **Squinting**: Focusing, intently, on how well ideas and feelings fit together.
- **Body shift**: Disagreeing with the speaker. Often indicates a desire to get out of the "space" that the speaker creates with his remarks.

Color sends signals about mood. Take the color red, which indicates not only anger but also physical readiness: well-oxygenated and ready to fight. No wonder red signals emergency and alarm. Let's see how all of the major colors symbolize emotions:

- **Red**: Power, aggression, and sexuality.
- **Yellow**: Cowardice, but also joy.
- **Blue**: Tranquility and patience, but also coldness and depression.
- **Orange**: Courage and confidence.
- **Purple**: Extreme anger, sadness, and mourning.
- **Green**: Money and nature, but also sickness, fear, and jealousy.

Rather than appealing only to the mind, the best writers also appeal to the heart. Color gives you one powerful way to do so.

If you use enough visual detail to excite the reader's imagination, you will enlist that reader in completing the picture.

CASE STUDY: TIMOTHY CROUSE, *THE BOYS ON THE BUS*

During the 1972 presidential campaign, Timothy Crouse spent hundreds of hours on buses and airplanes, at rallies and hotels press rooms, to explore how the mass media packaged the everyday events of political campaigns.

One of Crouse's most memorable characters was a reporter for the Associated Press named Walter Mears. Few reporters were easier to miss—or at the same time more influential—than Mears. Others, like Johnny Apple of *The New York Times* and David Broder of *The Washington Post*, were famous. But by giving every day's story a clear angle, Mears had more influence. He drove the coverage of the campaign.

Crouse offers this image of Mears at work:

Mears' way with a lead makes him a leader of the pack. Covering the second California debate between McGovern and Humphrey, Mears worked with about 30 other reporters in a large, warehouse-like press room that NBC had furnished with tables, typewriters, paper and phones. The debate was broadcast live from an adjacent studio, where most of the press watched. For the guys who didn't have to file immediately, it was something of a social event. But Mears sat tensely in the front of the Press Room, puffing at a Tiparillo and staring up at a gigantic monitor like a man waiting for a horserace to begin. As soon as the program started, he began typing like a madman, "taking transcript" in shorthand form and inserting descriptive phrases every four or five lines: "Humphrey started in low key," or "McGovern looks a bit strained."

After watching Mears up close, Crouse moves back to examine the whole scene:

The entire room was erupting with clattering typewriters but Mears stood out as the resident dervish. After the first three minutes, he turned to the phone at his elbow to call the AP Bureau in L.A. "He's phoning in a lead based on the first statements, so they can send out a bulletin," explained Carl Leubsdorf, the No. 2 AP man, who was sitting behind Mears and taking backup notes. After a minute on the phone Mears went back to typing and didn't stop for a solid hour. At the end of the debate he jumped up, picked up the phone, looked hard at Leubsdorf, and mumbled, "How can they stop? They didn't come to a lead yet."

Finally, Crouse zooms in again to show how reporters from other news organizations took their signals from Mears. Because Mears wrote fast—and because he wrote for a wire service trusted by newspapers across the country—others copied his news angles.

Two other reporters, one from New York, another from Chicago, headed toward Mears shouting, "Lead? Lead?" Marty Nolan came at him from another direction. "Walter, Walter, what's our lead?" he said.

Mears was wildly scanning his transcript. "I did a Wallace lead the first time," he said. … "I'll have to do it again." There were solid, technical reasons for Mears' computer-speed decision to go with the Wallace lead: it meant he could get both Humphrey and McGovern into the first paragraph, both stating a position that they hadn't flatly declared before then.

"Yeah," said Nolan, turning back to his Royal. "Wallace. I guess that's it."

Moment by moment, Crouse show the boys on the bus in '72 took their cues from the nondescript man puffing on a cigarillo. From such moments, presidents are selected.

———

ELEMENT 30: HELP THE READER TO HEAR

No one knows exactly how language evolved, but one theory holds that people started naming objects with the sounds those objects evoked. Sharp or rough objects, therefore, got names that sounded sharp or rough—*clash, clang bang, rough, jagged, zip*. Soft or curved objects got names that sounded soft or rounded—*bulbous, smooth, spray, sprinkle, whisper*.

Even when we read silently, we hear the textures and tones of the author's voice. If we cannot hear something—or if the word's meaning does not fit its sound—we struggle to make sense of it.

Some linguists say that the meanings of words come from their smallest sounds. The long-e sound of *here, near,* and *teeny*, for example, suggests something diminutive. Low-pitched vowels (like a and o) sound wide and describe bigger things, like *large, far,* and *storm*.

When the words sound like what they describe, the reader absorbs them quickly. Look at Edward Daily's account of the tense atmosphere of prisoner of war camps during the Korean War:

> Just prior to my falling asleep, a low flying single-engine airplane flew overhead. Could it be an American fighter plane lost and seeking a place to land? Not too far in the distance I heard several explosions and shortly the airplane flew overhead again. Then the sound of the airplane disappeared into the night darkness. … I dozed off to sleep. I was awakened in the early morning of August 29 by large sounds of shouting coming from the South Korea cell. The door was rapidly opened as the enemy soldiers equipped with burp guns moved inside the cell to single out certain South Koreans.

Listen to all the sounds in this passage—the quiet of dozing off … the drone of the low-flying plane … the explosions … the plane's drone again … shouting … the door opening … the movement of soldiers into cells … the calls that identified POWs for execution.

Now listen to this description of an atonal Soviet-era composer's work: "An affair of shrieking cluster chords, sputtering streams of pizzicato, siren-like glissandos, and other Xenakis-like sounds." If ever writing should sound discordant, it's in a passage describing discordant music.

Speech often provides the most important sounds in a story. Speech offers a kind of voiceover. Whatever your characters say, they offer a unique interpretation of events.

Speech reveals something about people's character. Their levels of confidence, clarity, their smoothness, certainty, and self-awareness, how quickly they speak, and their accents all offer insight into their minds and hearts.

A little prompting helps readers to hear your characters' accents and rhythm. Tell me that the speaker uses an Irishman's brogue, an Arkansan's twang, a New Yorker's Brooklynese, or a French woman's singsong, and I can imagine the rest.

So how do you capture someone's accent and dialect? Should you record it or imitate it? No; better to offer some quick hints of its shape. In *Nobody Turn Me Around*, my book about the 1963 March on Washington, I wanted to capture Martin Luther King's accent. But I knew that excessive use of dialect would create a distraction. So I offered short phrases from King's speech:

> King's Southern accent, softened by time spent in his family's bourgeois circles and tempered by years in the North, put a special emphasis on his words: "in the *his-tor-eh* of *ow-a* nation" … "a *gret* American" … "symbolic *shadda*" … "a *gret beckon* light."

With just a handful of words, we get a taste of the speaker's accent. That's enough. Anything more could be a distraction.

Go someplace and let the sounds wash over you. Go to a ballgame and hear the murmur of the crowd, the *crack* of the bat and the *thwap* of the ball hitting the glove. Go to a library and listen for the *creaking* of furniture or the heating register *rattling* or the windows *vibrating*. Go someplace noisy, like a cafe or school, and listen for the layers of sounds near and far. Walk down the street, ride a bike path, or venture into the woods. Just listen. You might be amazed what you hear.

But beware: In lesser writers, too much sizzling of sibilant sounds can be overwhelming. Consider this passage from a *New York Times* essayist named Verlyn Klinkenborg:

It is late afternoon as I write. There is blundering beyond the tree line. Soon the tuberous blunder heads trundle over the horizon; then begin to "wampum, wampum, wampum" until at least they're vrooming nearby, just down the valley. Or perhaps they're harrumphing and oomphing, from the very emphasis of the storm.

Clever, for sure. But sometimes, too much of a good thing is a bad thing.

CASE STUDY: LAURA KUNREUTHER, 'SOUNDS OF DEMOCRACY'

How people speak—not just what they say—plays a critical role in politics and everyday life. A guttural bellow sends a different message than a smooth tenor or a low whisper. Nearby sounds also affect communication. Ambient noise—distracting murmurs, chairs squeaking, doors opening and closing, even the moments of silence as audience members look at their phones—can distract speakers and listeners.

Laura Kunreuther, an anthropologist living in Kathmandu, tracked the sounds of the Occupy movement as it spread from New York City across the world. Often, the most forceful sounds come not from speech or chant but from restless and angry sounds in the crowd. Here, she describes an Occupy event in India:

> Activists sought to disrupt the status quo by transforming all kinds of noise into signs of protest. Each day the activists turned the side of the road in front of the prime minister's residence into a stage where, in addition to the usual repertoire of political slogans and banners, numerous performances took place. These ranged from poetry slams to performance art and silent protests; from banging plates and chimes, blowing whistles, and asking people to honk in support to staging a so-called Superman rally that mocked contemporary politicians by walking in procession in front of the police academy while wailing.

With these disruptive sounds, the protesters insisted that people should be seen and heard everywhere. By occupying that space—loudly—these protesters demonstrated that they were a force to be reckoned with.

Just about every sound can send a message. Most drivers honk their horns to send signals as they weave through traffic. But in the midst of a protest, honking can mean much more. "The honks and whistles of protest are ... much longer in duration and volume, signifying a difference from driving as usual," Kunreuther notes.

To understand any political event—whether it's a spectacle like a protest or a more intimate moment like a fundraising event or bargaining session—pay close attention not just to the main speakers and their messages but how those messages are delivered and heard. Note the tone and tenor of the speakers. Note also the surrounding sounds and whether they support or disrupt whatever else is happening at the time.

———

ELEMENT 31: HELP THE READER TO FEEL

The next time you see people—at work or school, in streets and parks, at the theater or ballpark—pay attention to how they experience interact with objects.

When people want to see something, they focus their attention on the object. They concentrate, lean forward, turn their head, and *think*. When people want to hear something, they also focus on the source of the sound, turn their heads, and work to separate the sound they want to hear from those that want to screen out.

Feeling is different, as the philosopher Walter Benjamin noticed. "Tactile reception," he says, "comes about not so much by way of attention as by way of habit." Feeling is an everyday experience that we often take for granted. We often miss the implications of feeling things. So we as writers, we need to work hard to bring tactile sensations into our writing.

To connect with your reader, then, pay attention to the physical dimensions of your subject. How? Start by remembering moments of physical pleasure or excitement, pain or anger, loneliness or togetherness. Then describe those moments, physical detail by physical detail.

Think of a breeze drifting across your face. Recall burning a finger on a hot skillet or plunging a hand into a bucket of ice. Remember smashing a softball, falling from a bicycle onto gravel, or swinging an ax against a hard tree. Remember the feeling of embracing a loved one, mixing fingers with dirt as you pull weeds, or sitting on a park bench on a hot summer day. Then connect those feelings with emotions.

Now, when telling stories, tap into these kinds of memories. Describe, moment by moment, the feelings you imagine.

Before the Battle of Bull Run, during the Civil War, a Union soldier named Sullivan Ballou sent a love letter to his wife Sarah. A century and a half after the war, the letter still moves us. Why? See how Ballou evokes emotions by tapping into physical sensations

> But, O Sarah! If the dead can come back to this earth and flit unseen around those they loved, I shall always be near you; in the garish day and in the darkest night—amidst your happiest scenes and gloomiest hours—always, always; and if there be a soft breeze upon your cheek, it shall be my breath; or the cool air fans your throbbing temple, it shall be my spirit passing by.

Ballou uses specific moments to describe feeling: *If the dead flit ... if there be a soft breeze upon your cheek ... if the cool air fans your throbbing temple. With these physical moments,* the reader can put herself in Sarah's position. We can imagine being with Sarah, years later, when a breeze cools catches her on a warm day—and when that breeze causes her to remember her late husband.

Use sounds that describe texture. Hard consonants sound rough and sharp, while soft consonants sound smooth. The word *crackling* sounds rough, while *luminescent* and *slither* sound smooth.

Read this passage from Charles Dickens's *A Tale of Two Cities*, which describes the storming of the Bastille:

> Flashing weapons, blazing torches, smoking wagon—loads of wet straw, hard work at neighboring barricades in all directions, shrieks, volleys, execrations, bravery without stint, boom, smash and rattle, and the furious sounding of the living sea; but, still the deep ditch, and the single drawbridge, and the massive stone walls, and the eight great towers . . .

This passage helps you experience the tactile sensations of the battle scene. It's not just the sights or sounds. It's also the heaviness of the weapons and the heat of the firing and the penetration of the volleys.

Don't just describe a person, place, or event with sights and sounds. Use the words that give the reader a physical experience.

CASE STUDY: CHRIS HEDGES, *WAGES OF REBELLION*

The half century beginning in the 1960s was the age of protest. From civil rights to women's rights, from environmentalism to arms control, activists have forced the formal political system to address issues it would rather ignore. Protest has become so ubiquitous, in fact, that we sometimes don't notice; we're like the fish in water who has no understanding of what water is.

Often, protesters get frustrated that their efforts to raise issues get ignored by the public, media, and public officials. Some of them, desperate to dramatize their concerns, take extreme actions. Such is the case with a brand of activism sometimes called "eco-terrorism."

Here's how the author Chris Hedges describes Wiebo Ludwig, a radical environmentalist who desperately tries to confront the fracking industry:

> Ludwig's first acts of sabotage were minor. He laid down nails poking up out of boards on roads to puncture the tires of the industry's trucks. He smashed solar panels. He blocked roads by downing trees. He disabled vehicles and drilling equipment. But after two leaks of hydrogen sulfide gas from the nearby wells and after the destruction of two of his water wells, he declared open war on the oil and gas industry. He began to blow up oil and gas facilities. He said he had to fight back to "protect the children."

Hedges evolves physical feelings in this passage: nails *poking* up to *puncture* the tires, *smashed* solar panels, the *blocked* roads, *downing* trees, *leaks* of gas, *blow up* oil and gas facilities.

Later, Hedges describes the effects of isolation in prisons:

> The techniques of sensory deprivation and prolonged isolation were pioneered by the Central Intelligence Agency ... One example of causing self-inflicted pain is to force a prisoner to stand without moving or to hold some other stressful bodily position for a long period. ... Sensory disorientation combines extreme sensory overload with extreme sensory deprivation. Prolonged isolation is followed by

intense interrogation. Extreme heat is followed by extreme cold. Glaring light is followed by total darkness. Loud and sustained noise is followed by silence.

Practically every phrase evolves physical sensations: deprivation, isolation, self-inflicted pain, disorientation, overload, extreme heat and cold, grating light, total darkness, loud noice, and silence. The passage hurts to read. Hedges succeeds in at least making the reader aware of the physical pain sadistically inflicted on prisoners.

In both of theses examples, Hedges tells the reader just enough to imagine being in the position of the prisoner: unnatural stillness, sensory overload, sensory deprivation, isolation, heat, cols, light, darkness, noise, and silence.

———

AND ANOTHER THING . . .

To experience the world, we need to use all our senses. Our lives are as rich as our sensory experiences.

Research confirms something that should be obvious: Sensory experience is essential to life. Children in a rich sensual environment—and the opportunity to explore that environment—learn better than children in a barren environment. Infants and toddlers need to crawl, bump and feel, smell and taste, listen and laugh. Children in sensually impoverished environments do not develop the neural connections in their brains to learn well and act creatively.

By tapping our physical experiences, sensory language helps us understand even the most complex ideas.

Concrete words (such as "spoon" or "water") take less time to process than abstract words (like "justice" or "moral"). Concrete words activate more parts of our brain, tapping into the rich networks of experiences that we all have.

Using physical words is like watching a movie in hi-definition, full-color, 3-D, surroundsound. Using abstract words is like watching a black-and-white movie with poor lighting and a cone camera.

Consider an experiment devised by a psychologist named Elizabeth Loftus. She showed two groups a videotape of a car accident. She asked one group how fast the cars traveled when they *smashed*; she asked another how fast the cars went when they *contacted* each other. The *smashed* group said 41 miles per hour; the *contacted* group said 32 miles per hour. Then Loftus asked whether the video showed broken glass. Three times as many people from the *smashed* group remember broken glass, though the video showed no broken glass.

A single choice of words can transform the way readers experience your writing.

WRITING TECHNIQUES
FOR PART THREE

CHAPTER 8
PARAGRAPHS

The paragraph [is] a mini-essay; it is also a maxi-sentence.

DONALD HALL

If you rewrite a paragraph fifty times and forty-nine of them are terrible, that's fine; you only need to get it right once.

TANA FRENCH

HERE IS the first thing you need to know about the paragraph: It evolved as a tool of convenience.

Until the invention of the printing press, writers did not use paragraphs, at least as we know them now. Ordinary people got their stories orally. The storyteller paused at critical moments, giving the reader a chance to absorb and anticipate ideas. Readers, who were rare, concentrated intently as they read page after page of dense text.

A break in text was first indicated by the use of a horizontal line called a *paragraphos*, then by placement of an enlarged first letter in the left margin, and then by a mark called a *capitulum* or *pilcrow* (¶). By the seventeenth century, indentation became the standard way to signal to readers, "OK, here comes a new idea."

By the late nineteenth century, with the rise of public education, "paragraphing" was central to writing instruction. The purpose of a paragraph was simple—to develop ideas in depth, one at a time. Many writers numbered their paragraphs, marking an explicit progression from the first to the last idea.

These days, the paragraph has become something of an orphan. Harvard's rock-star linguist Stephen Pinker dismisses the very idea of the paragraph. "Many writing guides provide detailed instructions on how to build a paragraph," Pinker says in his book *The Sense of Style*. "But the instructions are misguided, because there is no such thing as a paragraph."

No such thing as a paragraph? Seriously? True, people disagree over when to end one block of text and start another. But it seems odd to dismiss such an important element of writing altogether. The best Pinker can do is note the paragraph offers "a visual bookmark that allows the reader to pause." But that's a copout. We can do better.

Language mavens before Pinker not only defined the paragraph succinctly, but also detailed a whole range of types of paragraphs. The best definition comes from Fred Newton Scott and Joseph Villiers Denny, in a 1902 book on composition:

> A paragraph is a unit of discourse developing a single idea. It consists of a group or series of sentences closely related to one another and to the thought expressed by the whole group or series. Devoted, like the sentence, to the development of one topic, a good paragraph is also, like a good essay, a complete treatment in itself.

Scholars identified a wide range of paragraph types: propositional (statement and proof of an assertion), amplifying (further developing an idea), preliminary (laying out the plan of analysis), logical (laying out an inductive or deductive explanation), periodic (saving the theme for the last sentence), and so on.

We can avoid these complications with this pithy definition:

> A paragraph is the statement and development of a single idea.

Pin that to your computer screen. If you follow that basic idea, your writing will never meander or get lost.

Before we proceed, I need to make reference to one irregular form of the paragraph, which I call the "paracluster." A paracluster is a collection of lines of dialogue that, together, express one idea. Consider the following passage from F. Scott Fitzgerald's *The Great Gatsby*:

> "You're a rotten driver," I protested. "Either you ought to be more careful, or you oughtn't to drive at all."
>
> "I am careful."
>
> "No, you're not."
>
> "Well, other people are," she said lightly.
>
> "What's that got to do with it?"
>
> "They'll keep out of my way," she insisted. "It takes two to make an accident."
>
> "Suppose you met someone just as careless as yourself."
>
> "I hope I never will," she answered. "I hate careless people. That's why I like you."

In this scene, Nick describes his squabble with Jordan, a selfish woman who cheats and lies when it suits her. The collection of lines in this dialogue, arranged as eight paragraphs, should be considered a single paragraph. This paracluster expresses one idea: *Dishonest people exploit honest people*.

Enough preliminaries. For now, let's resolve to revive the idea of the well-constructed paragraph.

ELEMENT 32: MAKE EVERY PARAGRAPH AN 'IDEA BUCKET'

When we write, our minds often wander. We start with one thought, which sparks a new thought—so we write it down. That new thought sparks another new idea—so we write that down. Then we think of something else again—so we write *that* down.

Before we finish any thought, we veer off course. And sometimes we never get back to the point we started to develop in the beginning.

So I would like to issue a simple command: *State and develop just one idea in every paragraph*. Think of a paragraph as a bucket. Develop one idea in each bucket, along with whatever information you need to explain that idea. Never put two or more different ideas into the same bucket.

Figure out what point you want to make in every bucket. Usually, the opening sentence states that idea. So ask yourself: Do the subsequent sentences all support or develop that idea? Does each sentence take the idea one step further? Or do you veer off in different directions?

If the paragraph contains more than one idea, cut the extra ideas. If you state three ideas in a paragraph, break the paragraph into three parts. Keep the parts that add to your overall point and delete the extraneous parts. To repeat: Develop one idea per paragraph, with as much detail you need to develop that idea.

Labeling ideas in paragraphs: Writing one-idea paragraphs requires discipline and effort. So here's a simple trick: In your drafts, label each paragraph. Put the label at the beginning of each paragraph, in bold face, the way I do in this paragraph. Summarize the main idea in a short, zippy phrase. If anything in the paragraph veers away from the label, cut it.

Write labels that read like tabloid newspaper headlines. To make those headlines sprightly, use punchy puns, exaggerated language, and plays on words. By writing tabloid headlines, you'll think harder about the point of each paragraph.

Let me give you an example. Here are the tabloid headline labels I might use for the paragraphs so far in this section:

- Wanderers
- Lost
- The Idea Bucket
- What's the Point?
- Ruthless Cutting
- Labeling ideas in paragraphs
- Tab It Up
- Tab Examples

Crafting tabloid headlines only takes a few moments but yields three major benefits:

- Assuring that every paragraph contains and develops just one idea.
- Testing whether each paragraph takes you, clearly, from the beginning to the end.

- Seeing all of the major ideas in a piece, instantly, in just a few moments.

Yes, I know, making tabloid-style headlines for your paragraphs takes a few extra minutes to your writing process. But these labels can save you hours over the long run. They will save you from veering off the point—and that will save lots of time having to figure out and fix the paragraphs later. So do you want to spend a few minutes tabbing your paragraphs along the way? Or do you want to write a confusing piece—and then, later, have to figure out what you wanted to say and then fix your passages?

Some writers kid themselves by thinking they can produce a stream-of-consciousness draft and "sort it out later." But if you lose control of one paragraph, the next one could get on the wrong track too. The ideas of one paragraph inevitably carry over to the next. If you state three separate ideas in paragraph one—losing the train of thought—you will probably stay off track in paragraph two. And the idea you develop in the second paragraph might be the one that doesn't belong anywhere in the piece.

So work hard, paragraph by paragraph, to state and develop just one idea at a time.

CASE STUDY: JOURNALISM FRAGMENTS

Consider these two paragraphs. Which one best expresses and develops a single idea? Which one overwhelms the reader with several separate ideas?

Even though he lacked experience in national politics, Barack Obama won the 2008 election because of his impressive powers as a communicator. Obama served for eight years in the Illinois legislature and lost one race for Congress before he won election to the U.S. Senate in 2006. His dazzling appearance at the 2004 Democratic National Convention —not to mention his best-selling memoir, *Dreams from My Father*—won him adoring fans all over. Obama assembled an unprecedented fundraising machine, which enabled him to outlast Hillary Clinton in the 2008 primaries and trounce John McCain in the general election.

Even though he lacked experience in national politics, Barack Obama won the 2008 election because of his impressive powers as a communicator. After flailing in early debates, Obama showed mastery of public policy in the debates with his Democratic rivals. When the controversy over Jeremiah Wright threatened his campaign, he gave a powerful address at Independence Hall to reclaim the moral high ground. In interviews with reporters, Obama showed an ability to synthesize complex issues into terms that played well with ordinary voters. Though especially articulate in big speeches, he also communicated well in small groups. Obama also looked more confident—and seemed to have a greater command of issues—than John McCain in the fall debates.

The first paragraph seems fine, at first glance anyway. We open with a sweeping statement about Obama's strengths and weaknesses. But the paragraph wanders, talking about Obama's wins and losses, his fundraising ability, past elections. The paragraph focus on Obama but lacks real focus. We want to ask: *What about Obama?*

In the second paragraph, each sentence supports the argument about *Obama's eloquence*. We see lots of examples of his eloquence at work. We don't wander into discussions of past elections or fundraising. We stay on message—eloquence, eloquence, eloquence. We might the paragraph like this:

Eloquence trumps experience.

If you can state the paragraph's main idea that simply—and then support it throughout the paragraph, avoiding all temptation to wander off on tangents—you will write brilliant paragraphs. And, of course, if you write brilliant paragraphs, you will write brilliant stories, essays, and analyses.

––––––

ELEMENT 33: FOLLOW THE GOLDEN RULE IN EVERY PARAGRAPH

The paragraph does not just express and develop a single idea. The paragraph also offers a *journey*, which starts and ends strongly. Whatever you write—fiction or nonfiction, business reports or technical papers, for general or specialized audiences—take the reader from one specific place (the beginning) to another, different place (the end).

The journey could depict physical movement, changes in emotions or other states of being, or a new understanding of a topic. But somehow, something has to change from the beginning to the end.

When you map the journey, pay attention to the moments when you could go off track. Digressions pose the biggest challenge for most writing. Too often, we start on one path and get distracted. It's OK to take side trips, when they offer important information. But always —*always*—get back to the main road.

To chart your journey, remember the second part of the Golden Rule: *Start strong, finish strong*. A quick reminder of what that means:

- **Start strong**: In the first line, tell the reader something important, right away. Focus on the subject of the paragraph. Whether you want to explore a person, place, event, or idea, get right to the point. Be specific. Describe what's happening with that subject. Sometimes, open with a brief setup to establish the context.
- **Finish strong**: In your last line, clinch your point. Say what happens with the person, place, event, or idea. Make sure that something changes over the course of the paragraph-journey. Sometimes, conclude with a memorable question or image, some worthwhile idea or phrase.
- **Brackets and bridges in the middle**: Use the middle sentences to progress toward the final line of the paragraph. You might use a long series of sentences or just a few. Make sure every sentence leads to the next one. Make sure every sentence adds an important piece of information.

In the discussion of the Landscape View ("The Core Idea"), I suggested writing just one sentence per line. The main virtue of that approach, as we discussed, is focusing attention on each sentence, one by one. The line-by-line approach helps you to track the *progression* of sentences, from the beginning to the end of every paragraph. You can tell—step by step, in every paragraph—whether you're making progress toward the defining idea of the paragraph.

Paragraphing is an art. Most writers have their own style for paragraphs, just as they have their own style for whole pieces. To develop that style, follow the Golden Rule. Take the reader, line by line, from one distinct place to another, different place.

CASE STUDY: TE-NEHISI COATES, 'THE CASE FOR REPARATIONS'

In an essay for *The Atlantic*, Te-Nehisi Coates calls for the payment of reparations to African Americans to repair the damage of slavery and racism in America. To make the case that slavery is not some long-ago anomaly of America history, Coates uses detailed stories to show its ongoing power in modern life.

In Coates's hands, every paragraph offers a complete drama, with relevance far beyond the immediate characters and setting. Consider three paragraphs that begin his essay. First, he introduces the Ross family:

> Clyde Ross was born in 1923, the seventh of 13 children, near Clarksdale, Mississippi, the home of the blues. Ross's parents owned and farmed a 40-acre tract of land, flush with cows, hogs, and mules. Ross's mother would drive to Clarksdale to do her shopping in a horse and buggy, in which she invested all the pride one might place in a Cadillac. The family owned another horse, with a red coat, which they gave to Clyde. The Ross family wanted for little, save that which all black families in the Deep South then desperately desired—the protection of the law.

Line by line, Coates shows a man of decency, whose family worked hard and achieved a measure of prosperity. We visualize the land and the farm animals, we feel pride for their achievement, and we celebrate their goals for the future. At the end, we face the ominous truth that the family's commitment and hard work are vulnerable.

What kind of system would make such good people so vulnerable? Coates continues:

> In the 1920s, Jim Crow Mississippi was, in all facets of society, a kleptocracy. The majority of the people in the state were perpetually robbed of the vote—a hijacking engineered through the trickery of the poll tax and the muscle of the lynch mob. Between 1882 and 1968, more black people were lynched in Mississippi than in any other state. "You and I know what's the best way to keep the nigger from voting," blustered

Theodore Bilbo, a Mississippi senator and a proud Klansman. "You do it the night before the election."

Here, we confront a harsh truth: Mississippi was a state constructed for the privileged few to steal from the vulnerable many. Step by step, the story gets harsher—from taking away the vote to threats of lynching to the ugly boast of a bigot. That boast, closing this paragraph-length narrative, provides a fearful image and more foreboding. Then, in the next paragraph:

> The state's regime partnered robbery of the franchise with robbery of the purse. Many of Mississippi's black farmers lived in debt peonage, under the sway of cotton kings who were at once their landlords, their employers, and their primary merchants. Tools and necessities were advanced against the return on the crop, which was determined by the employer. When farmers were deemed to be in debt—and they often were—the negative balance was then carried over to the next season. A man or woman who protested this arrangement did so at the risk of grave injury or death. Refusing to work meant arrest under vagrancy laws and forced labor under the state's penal system.

See how Coates develops the narrative with that last paragraph: from the statement of the problem ("robbery of the purse") to a step-by-step explanation of its meaning (perpetual slavery) to the ultimate use of force and law (imprisonment for anyone seeking to break free).

Each of these paragraphs uses the 1-2-3 format that Aristotle outlines in *The Poetics*. In each of these passages, we see a complete drama. The drama opens with a description of the world of the story, then explores how people struggle in their everyday lives, and concludes with a glimpse of the inevitable tragedy.

Each paragraph starts strong and finishes strongly. We open with an intriguing setup and end with the drama's inevitable outcome. In between, we see the steps to move the story from one place to another.

Ta-Nehisi Coates has become one of America's leading literary figures because of his fierce vision and truth-telling. But that vision and honesty would falter if Coates could not craft such strong paragraphs. The paragraphs give the reader a series of important journeys.

––––––

ELEMENT 34: 'CLIMB THE ARC' IN MOST PARAGRAPHS

The paragraph offers an opportunity to create drama in your writing. Whatever you write—a story, summary, or analysis—the paragraph can take your reader on a compelling journey.

So follow Aristotle's "narrative arc" in every paragraph. Open in the "world of the story," by introducing the reader to an important person, place, action, or idea. Then, line by line, move to increasingly dramatic or important moments or ideas. Finally, conclude by resolving the paragraph's issues.

If you give every paragraph a sense of drama, the whole piece will gain power. Most readers will not notice how you create such drama. But they will *feel* it—and be impelled to stay with you for the whole piece.

Sounds demanding, right? I can almost hear you responding: *Are you actually telling me to build an Aristotelian arc into every paragraph? Every paragraph?* But it's not so hard. Just take every paragraph, sentence by sentence. Structure your paragraphs to fit the three-part narrative arc.

- **World of the Story**: In the first line or two, show the reader what you want to talk about. Preview the issues you want to explore. You can even hint or even tell the reader where the journey will end. In other words, show the beginning of the journey—setting the stage, raising the issues, "hooking" the reader.
- **Rising Action**: Next, show the paragraph's journey, step by step. With each line—each sentence—reveal something new. Raise the stakes of the story. Start simply, then move to more important and dramatic ideas. Whenever you need to define terms or name the issues or players, do so. Then return to the focus of your paragraph. Line by line, develop your ideas, showing complications and complexities. Move toward a resolution of the issue.
- **Resolution**: Finally, complete the journey. Take your reader to the end. Finish saying what you want to say. If possible, conclude with something vivid that launches the reader to the next paragraph.

You might not create a perfect Aristotelian arc for every paragraph. Some paragraphs, after all, just supply information. Other paragraphs take a reader along for only part of a journey.

But in every paragraph, you can create meaningful movement, from the beginning to the end.

CASE STUDY: MARTIN LUTHER KING'S 'MOUNTAINTOP' SPEECH

In February 1968, two Memphis sanitation workers were crushed to death by a malfunctioning truck. That tragedy prompted workers to renew a long battle for better wages and working conditions. They held marches and appealed to the public to support their cause. After police and thugs attacked the marchers, Martin Luther King came to Memphis in April to rally the workers.

At a public meeting, King delivered the final speech of his life. Look at the last lines of the speech, line by line:

> *We've got some difficult days ahead.*
> *But it really doesn't matter with me now.*
> *Because I've been to the mountaintop.*
> *And I don't mind.*
> *Like anybody, I would like to live a long life.*
> *Longevity has its place.*
> *But I'm not concerned about that now.*
> *I just want to do God's will.*
> *And He's allowed me to go up to the mountain.*
> *And I've looked over.*
> *And I've seen the Promised Land.*
> *I may not get there with you.*
> *But I want you to know tonight, that we, as a people, will get*
>   *to the Promised Land!*
> *And so I'm happy, tonight.*
> *I'm not worried about anything.*
> *I'm not fearing any man!*
> *Mine eyes have seen the glory of the coming of the Lord!*

This paragraph taps people's emotions as well as their minds by providing a clear narrative. Reread the passage and figure out where King opens his mini-story. How does he place the audience in the "world of the story"? Then see how he advances his ideas, one by one, till he reaches a peak. Finally, see how he concludes the narrative.

- **World of the Story**: King begins by setting the scene. He summarizes his thoughts by noting the "difficult times ahead" and the prospect of getting to "the mountaintop."
- **Rising action**: Then King describes a set of values worth pursuing—living a long life, doing God's will, reaching the Mountaintop, and finally, "as a people," getting to the Promised Land. Each value is greater than the previous ones. As King moves through his account, he moves closer to his goal of redemption.
- **Resolution**: King concludes by expressing his lack of fear or worry—and his gratitude for what God has allowed him to do: "Mine eyes have seen the glory of the coming of the Lord!"

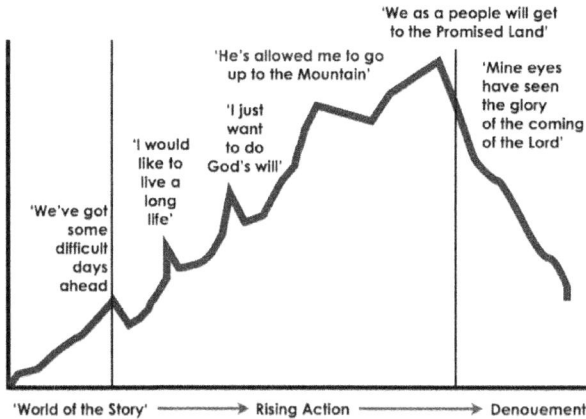

In this paragraph of simple words and ideas, King creates a complete drama—a complete story. He gives the reader, on a small scale, Aristotle's narrative arc. With each line, he takes us to higher and higher levels—until, at the end, he resolves all of the tensions.

(Side note: To understand King's power, not not just his narrative. Note also that King uses short, declarative sentences, which average just 7.75 words. Then, note that he uses simple words. Finally, note that he makes literary allusions to the Bible and "The Battle Hymn of the Republic.")

———

AND ANOTHER THING . . .

Like other crafts, writing changes with technology. The paragraph has always played a leading role in the evolution of writing.

The creation of the printing press transformed writing by breaking ideas into pieces that we could absorb, one by one. Now, the computer, Internet, and ebook revolutions are producing new formatting techniques. The trend is clear: The more you can break up text, the better.

The process started with bullets. People had used bullets for years in memos, reports, and other professional documents. But the rise of the personal computer made bullets ubiquitous. Why? Three reasons:

- People produce longer documents in professional settings. Bullets enable readers to skim the documents to find pertinent points.
- Software programs—from Word to standard email systems —make bullets easy to produce.
- PowerPoint has become the primary tool for making presentations in business and government.

Bullets, alas, make us lazy. Bullets encourage us to make endless lists, rather than thinking through the logic of our ideas.

On the Internet, most paragraphs are separated by spaces (like this one). This format looks odd in traditional publications like books and magazines, which indent new paragraphs. But separating paragraphs with spaces makes sense for web sites and professional documents.

The Internet also allows for hypertext, which allows readers to jump to a whole new document with a simple click. This enables authors to provide more detailed background information, references, and explanations. With hyperlinks, the author can give the reader choice about how much information to absorb.

Whatever the format, writers need to compose paragraphs that explore a simple topic fully and take readers on a complete (if short) journey.

CHAPTER 9
WORDPLAY

Genius is play, and man's capacity for achieving genius is infinite, and many may achieve genius only through play.

WILLIAM SAROYAN

CONJURE UP AN IMAGE of animals chasing each other in a park, athletes clashing on a field, teenagers teasing and flirting at a mall, or improv actors discovering their lines as they speak them.

Each is a form of play. Each is a joyful activity that occurs not for a "rational" purpose but to take delight in living. Play is a pervasive—and essential—part of the experience of all animals. When we play, as when we dream, we release thoughts and emotions that otherwise get suppressed. We also explore. We engage in a game of trial and error to discover how the world works.

Ironically, play requires rules. Think of kids playing ad-hoc street games like Capture the Flag or Kick the Can. Before the games, they earnestly set ground rules. With the rules set, they can play with abandon. Or think of kids playing make-believe. When one plays out of character, others get upset: "You're not supposed to do it that way." To enter the special "space" of play, we need special rules and procedures.

Now think of the playful things writers do with words. Think of the jazzlike improv of Will Shakespeare or Walt Whitman or Herman Melville or James Joyce. Think of the quips of Gertrude Stein or Mae

West or the clever puns of a Marx Brothers movie. Here's Groucho
Marx in *Animal Crackers*:

> One morning I shot an elephant in my pajamas. How he got in my
> pajamas, I don't know. Then we tried to remove the tusks. The tusks.
> That's not so easy to say. Tusks. You try it some time. As I say, we tried
> to remove the tusks. But they were embedded so firmly we couldn't
> budge them. Of course, in Alabama the Tuscaloosa, but that is entirely
> ir-elephant to what I was talking about.

No one was punnier than Shakespeare. Hamlet calls his uncle
Claudius, who murdered his father and married his mother, "a little
more than kin, and less than kind." Claudius, irritated at Hamlet's
mourning, asks: "How is it that the clouds still hang over you?"
Hamlet responds: "Not so, my lord, I am too much in the sun." Later,
someone asks about Polonius, who has been murdered. Hamlet
responds that he is at supper—"not where he eats, but where he is
eaten."

In *Romeo and Juliet*, after a jokester named Mercutio is accidentally
stabbed, he cannot resist one last quip before he dies: "Ask for me
tomorrow and you shall find me a grave man." Shakespeare's work is
filled with sexual puns, including the last word in the title *Much Ado
About Nothing*, which refers to the female genitalia.

Wordplay requires the reader to do more work. Readers need to
think through the puns and the twists, the odd couplings and the irregular sounds.

When you master wordplay, magic happens. With the right rhythm
and cadence, words send readers' imaginations into unpredictable
spins of delight. Writing does more than simply communicate. It
changes thinking and feeling.

Wordplay begins with rhythm. Life moves in rhythm, from the
turning of seasons to the tides of the ocean, from the rhymes of a
poem to the movements of a dance. Ancient literature, like Homer's
Odyssey and *Iliad*, took the form of verse. In an oral tradition,
without written records, storytellers used a distinctive meter,
melody, wordplay, and imagery to remember the lines of the epic
tales.

Too much wordplay, though, taxes readers' patience. So mix your
wordplay with simple language. Put on a display of linguistic

pyrotechnics, then back off and give your reader a chance to absorb the fireworks.

———

ELEMENT 35: TAP INTO LIFE'S EVERYDAY RHYTHMS

Our lives rhyme. Without trying, we create cadences in our language. We use rhythm to emphasize points—but also because it just sounds pleasing. We delight people with the cadences of our speech. Even the simplest conversations hop along rhythmically, like this exchange I heard before the 2015 Super Bowl:

> *"You like the* Patriots!
> *I* hate *the Patriots!*
> *Tom Brady is such a* fake! *And Bill* Belichick?
> *Give me a* break!"

> *"Hey, the Patriots are the* best team!
> *You're for the* Jets?
> *All you can do is* dream!"

In fact, we find speech without rhythm annoying. People who speak in monotones sound robotic. Their flat and unrhythmic speech lacks life. It's sometimes hard to know what they think—even when they *say* what they think—because they don't emphasize any words or ideas. Some do the opposite, punching every word and thereby emphasizing none. *I … remember … how … former … Vice … President … Dan … Quayle …. used … to … emphasize … every … single … word.*

Rhythmic creates a "we" feeling, engaging audiences word by word, phrase by phrase, sentence by sentence, and paragraph by paragraph. When we speak in rhythm, other people follow. If I talk in sprightly phrases, you will get into my rhythm. When speech moves ins predictable bursts, people wait till a moment of quiet to respond.

Rhymes reinforce ideas. In an experiment at the University of Texas, researchers asked volunteers to read a collection of aphorisms. Some of the aphorisms rhymed and others did not. The volunteers remembered the rhyming aphorisms ("Early to bed, early to rise, makes a man healthy, wealthy, and wise") more than the non rhyming aphorisms ("You can kill a man but you can't kill an idea"). Why? The rhymes could be absorbed whole. The rhythm, pace, and sounds give them "handles" that make them easy to grasp and hold.

Consider one notorious example. In the O.J. Simpson murder trial, his attorney, Johnny Cochran, told jurors: "If the gloves don't fit, you must acquit." Cochran was wrong, of course. But it didn't matter. Jurors remembered the phrase in their deliberations. Despite over-whelming evidence against Simpson, the jury acquitted him.

Why do rhymes affect people's hearts and minds? Every rhyme brings a sense of wholeness. Compare two simple rhymes. First: "Roses are red, violets are blue, it's Valentine's Day, and I love you." Then: "Rose are red, violets are blue, some poems rhyme, but this one doesn't." Because the first ends in a rhyme, it sounds complete. Because the second one doesn't, it feels like a violation.

To understand rhythm, observe language, line by line. Find a passage from a great writer. Read sentences aloud, with rhythm. See how the pacing draws you in and holds your attention? Now, compose your own passage. Write one sentence per line, using the Landscape View. Then read whatever you just wrote. When you stumble—or get bored or confused—revise and rewrite.

With a regular rhythm, you can carry the reader smoothly through any story or essay. Get into the rhythm, delivering images and ideas with the steady pace of a heartbeat. Then you will engage the reader on the deepest possible levels. Then, the occasional deviation will surprise and delight the reader.

CASE STUDY: LINCOLN'S GETTYSBURG ADDRESS

In the July of 1863, after the Civil War had raged for more than two years, the Confederate General Robert E. Lee planned a great attack on the North, in Gettysburg, Pennsylvania. Lee had just won a major conflict in Chancellorsville, Virginia, when he decided to move north-ward through the Shenandoah Valley. He was met in Gettysburg by the Union forces of Major General George Meade.

What followed was the bloodiest battle of the war and a turning point for the Union. The Blue and the Gray clashed for three days. The Confederates successfully attacked Union positions on hills. Then the Confederates massed 12,500 soldiers for a great attack at Cemetery

Hill. After one of the bloodiest fights in the war, the Union repelled Lee's forces, which then retreated back to Virginia.

The carnage at Gettysburg was unprecedented. Upwards of 51,000 troops from the two sides were killed. The battlefield was strewn with bodies blasted with artillery or slashed with bayonets. The stench of the corpses was unbearable. The surviving soldiers were traumatized for the rest of their lives. The defeat was devastating for the Confederacy, but even victory was not sweet for the Union.

To commemorate the awful moment, President Abraham Lincoln spoke at a dedication of a cemetery. The result was the greatest speech in American history, which not only honored the dead but rededicated the warring nation to its founding ideals. Read these lines from Abraham Lincoln's Gettysburg Address, set out in verse form:

> Four *score and seven* years *ago*
> *our* fathers *brought forth on this continent*
> *a* new nation, conceived *in Liberty,*
> *and* dedicated *to the* proposition
> *that* all *men are created* equal.
> Now *we are engaged in a* great *civil war,*
> *testing whether* that nation,
> *or* any nation *so* conceived *and so* dedicated,
> *can* long *endure.*
> *We are met on a* great *battle-field of that war.*
> *We have come to dedicate a* portion *of that field,*
> *as a* final *resting place*
> *for those who here gave their* lives
> *that that nation might* live.
> *It is altogether* fitting *and* proper
> *that we should* do *this.*

Lincoln uses rhythm to pace his prose: variations of ta DUM ta da DUM da DUM. He speaks in brief bursts, each of which evokes a clear vision or sound. He uses alliteration—like *four score, fathers,* and *forth*— to join key ideas. He repeats key terms—like *nation, so, conceived, dedicated/dedicate, lives/live, battlefield/field*—to create a flow and connect ideas.

Lincoln grew up reading works that moved in poetic rhythm—like The Bible, Bunyan's *Pilgrim's Progress, Aesop's Fables,* poetry of Robert

Burns, and Edward Gibbon's *Decline and Fall of the Roman Empire*. By bringing the rhythm of these works into his own language, Lincoln began the long process of binding the warring nation's wounds.

———

ELEMENT 36: USE METAPHORS AND SIMILES TO ORIENT AND DISORIENT

We make sense of the world by saying one thing *is* something else—or is *like* something else—even when it isn't. When two things share similar shapes, textures, or sounds, we use metaphors and similes to make the comparisons.

The metaphor says X *equals* Y; the simile says X *resembles* Y. So what's the difference? "Metaphors are forceful," Poet Laureate Ted Kooser notes. "Similes are, like, casual." A metaphor insists that a leader is a lion; a simile suggests, more tentatively, that the man acts *like* a lion. A metaphor says X=Y. A simile says X≈Y.

Both metaphors and similes work by orienting and disorienting the reader at the same time. They make the familiar unfamiliar and the unfamiliar familiar. Unfamiliarity makes us curious; familiarity helps us to understand. Put the two together and you get insight.

Suppose I tell you that the X-1 rocket—something that most people reading this have never seen—has a needle for a nose. Or suppose I compared a megachurch to a floating crap game. You'd get the idea, right? A familiar image helps us understand something unfamiliar.

Take a look at Michael Oakeschott's metaphor for the possibilities and limits of politics:

> In political activity, then, men sail a boundless and bottomless sea; there is neither harbor for shelter nor floor for anchorage, neither start-ing-place nor appointed destination. The enterprise is to keep afloat on an even keel; the sea is both friend and enemy; and the seamanship consists in using the resources of a traditional manner of behavior in order to make a friend of every hostile occasion.

Now look at the simile that C.S. Lewis uses in his memoir of grieving his late wife:

> Grief is like a long valley, a winding valley where any bend may reveal a totally new landscape. ... Sometimes the surprise is the opposite one; you are presented with exactly the same sort of country you thought you had left behind miles ago. This is when you wonder whether the valley isn't a circular trench.

As these passages show, metaphors and smiles come to life with movement. Both take the reader on journeys—Oakeshott to some unknowable place, Lewis's back home to familiar terrain. Both images work because they take us, the readers, to new places and new insights.

Metaphors often distort our judgment. Consider two experiments. Researchers at Yale and Colorado, pretending to struggle with piles of folders, asked subjects to hold their cup of coffee. When asked to describe a person later, subjects holding warmer cups gave warmer descriptions; subjects holding cooler cups gave cooler descriptions. In another experiment, a Yale researcher asked subjects to describe a person based on a resume held in a clipboard. Subjects holding heavier clipboards described the person in more serious terms than those holding lighter clipboards. The qualities of objects like coffee (hot or cold) and clipboards (heavy or light) become metaphors for something completely separate (people's personalities).

The power of metaphor extends far and wide (that's a spatial metaphor, if you didn't notice). That, ultimately, is the work of all language—to engage us completely to express ideas and feelings.

CASE STUDY: RACHEL MADDOW, *BLOWOUT*

For more than a century, fossil fuels have dominated the global economics and politics. The oil and gas industry is, in the words of Rachel Maddow, "the most consequential, the most lucrative, the most powerful, and the least-well-governed major industry in the history of mankind."

Oil and gas created the world we live in, with a sprawling land-scape of highways, suburbs, airports, and refineries. Oil has also dominated the American political system, dictated the key tenets of foreign policy, and contributed to the global warming crisis that threatens civilization. Oil's impact is everywhere, from Russian to Saudi Arabia to Venezuela and everywhere in-between. Companies from Standard Oil to Gazprom have remade the world to suit their needs for extraction, refinement, and sale of the slick fuels. Oil is, Maddow says, the "key ingredient in the global chaos and democratic downturn we're now living through."

What's the best way to understand this pervasive and overwhelming force? Maddow, best known for her news program on politics on MSNBC, explains the whole complicated mess by telling stories. She travels all over the world to meet the people working inside the industry and struggling with its impacts in the community. To make sense of these stories, Maddow uses metaphors and similes. A few examples:

> I believe there is one *narrative thread that can compass the greater part of that tragedy*—a thread that wraps its way around the globe: from Oklahoma and Texas and Washington, D.C., to London, Kyiv, Siberia, Moscow, Equatorial Guinea, and the Alaskan Arctic …
>
> There were countless stories in the local papers about [American Energy Partners CEO] Aubrey McClendon spreading his wealth. "Asking me what to do with extra cash is *like asking a fraternity boy what to do with the beer*" …
>
> The Wall Street-induced Great Recession had thrown the American economy into *free fall*, but the fracking-driven energy boom was *like an unexpected net appearing underneath a doomed trapeze artist, mid-tragedy.* …
>
> "Insiders say that Igor Sechin [Vladimir Putin's top deputy] is *like a cyborg.* He can go without sleep for days on end and works standing up; it's even said he cured himself of cancer." …
>
> [McClendon's] profligacy and his *addiction to huge helpings of debt*—which sounded nicer when you called it "leverage"—had finally caught up to him. …
>
> His [McClendon's] misdeeds at Chesapeake (real and alleged) still trailed him *like unsightly toilet paper stuck to the heel of his tasseled loafer.* …
>
> "I've been doing it for forty years, and I'll tell you what farming in Oklahoma is. It's a gamble. Farming in Oklahoma is *like going to Vegas every year.*" …

Each of these metaphors evokes something vivid and physical. They help us to understand the ideas and connections Maddow needs to tell her rollicking, important story about the power of oil in the modern age.

———

ELEMENT 37: PLAY IMPROV WITH WORDS

You've probably seen improvisational actors at comedy clubs or on TV shows like "Whose Line Is It Anyway?" Given a prompt, two or more actors make up a scene. The improv actors are not allowed to reject anything someone says; they have to say, "Yes, and…" So each statement or action feeds on the others.

Writing can be like that. You need enough confidence in your abilities to go with the flow. Improv—on stage or at the keyboard—requires some vision, a willingness to take chances, and lots of play, all supported by mastery of all the basic skills of the trade. In the end, you discover things you could not have imagined.

Improv works because it pulls down into your subconscious for ideas. When you let go and let the words flow, you never know what you're going to write. You will discover ideas and images that lurked just below your cognitive surface. Rather than editing yourself as you write—disciplining yourself like a schoolmarm—you will have a chance to play and discover.

Let's check out three essential parts of improv for writers, one by one:

(1) Create a sensual experience. Start off by looking for vivid details. Describe those details with precision. As you construct a scene, think of all the ways that we see things—their colors, brightness, and shadows; their shapes, size, and scale; and their arrangements and alignments. Then pick the ones that most casual observers would miss.

See how Robert Penn Warren, in *All the King's Men*, introduces us to the heat and monotony of highways in Louisiana, the kingdom of the corrupt governor Willie Stark:

> You look up the highway and it is straight for miles, coming at you, with the black line down the center coming at you, black and slick and tarry-shining against the white of the slab, and the heat dazzles up from the white slab so that only the black line is clear, coming at you with the whine of the tires, and if you don't quit staring at that line and

don't take a few deep breaths and slap yourself hard on the back of the next you'll hypnotize yourself and you'll come to at just the moment when the right wheel hooks over into the black dirt shoulder off the slab, and you'll try to jerk her back on but you can't because the slab is high like a curb, and maybe you'll try to turn off the ignition just as she starts the dive.

This stream-of-consciousness passage—146 words in one sentence —puts the reader in the car on one of those endless, mind-numbing trips that define the politician's life. We feel the heat, hear the sounds, experience the monotonous blur of stripes on the highways, and feel the car drifting as the driver dozes off in boredom.

To evoke sounds, play with onomatopoeia, words that sound like what they're describing. *The bus hissed away from the curb. The ball smashed the window. He told her to shush. The snake slithered through the grass.*

Alliteration, the repetition of consonant sounds, also engages the reader and produces memorable phrases. Consider the work of masters like Shakespeare ("I grant I never saw a goddess go") or Robert Frost ("I have stood still and stopped the sound of feet") or Alfred Lord Tennyson ("Fly o'er waste fens and windy fields") or George Manley Hopkins ("swift, slow; sweet, sour; adazzle, dim"). Politics and mass media—professions dedicated to selling ideas and products—use alliteration too. Remember Spiro Agnew's attack on liberals as "nattering nabobs of negativism"? Or commercials for Reese's ("rich rushing butter cups") or Fila ("Functional, Fashionable, Formidable")?

Don't just get the sounds right; play with the unusual ways they come together. In his portrait of the elder George Bush, Richard Ben Cramer imitates Bush's whiny, fractured, faux-folksy (*fauxsy*?) voice to reveal Bush's evasions over the Iran-Contra scandal.

> Jeezus! What did they want? They wanted an answer on Iran-contra: *What did Bush know ... and when did he know it?*
>
>   For more than a year, ever since late '86, Bush had been holding the line: *I did what I did ... I told the President what I told the President. ... And honor forbids me to say more.* Bush had said that so many times, he was frustrated. He thought he had answered *every conceivable nuance.* Of course, he never actually said anything.

But once he'd made his point ... well, anyone who insisted on bringing it up was just *rehashing* ... try'na make him *look bad*.

They were, you know, acting like bullies. And the old school code treats a bully with ... contempt. That's why he couldn't believe—wouldn't hear it!—when his white men warned that Dan Rather was going to jump him ... . "No," said the Veep. "Dan's a friend." (He'd known Rather since Texas—Dan was just a local newsman, Bush was in the oil bidness ... Jeez, it'd been more than 20 years!)

Cramer merges his own voice with Bush's to capture the vice president's impatient, calculating, *fauxsy* voice: *Jeezus, try'na, bidness, Jeez*. But notice that Cramer doesn't overdo it. He uses ordinary expressions to pad the jazzy, funky phrasing that demands more of the reader's attention.

(2) Speculate, with real information. When in doubt about details, speculate about them. Even when you cannot answer a question definitively, you can still offer possibilities. We don't know what Washington experienced as he crossed the Delaware River, what Civil War soldiers felt as they saw a brother die, or how athletes felt when they won an Olympic medal. But we can explore plausible scenarios. When we do, we excite the reader's imagination.

Look at *The Big Bam*, Leigh Montville's biography of Babe Ruth. As much as we know of America's most famous athlete, we know few basic facts about his early years. So Montville combines what he *knows* with what he *doesn't know* to create intimate images of young George Herman Ruth:

Behind that moon face with those small eyes, that fat nose, those big lips that will be captured in any instantly recognizable portrait in a blue New York Yankees cap, the boy will forever hide. He is only a shape, glimpsed here, glimpsed there, lost again. No one has found that boy at the beginning of it all, touched him, gotten to know him. No one ever will. If the right questions ever were asked, the answers never were given. Time has finished the job. There is no one to talk to now. No one is around.

By playing with unknown facts—saying "Yes, and..."—Montville helps us see, better than ever, this unknowable boy. Montville allows us to join in the speculation. Montville turns a deficit of information to his advantage. When he suggests possibilities, he invites the reader to project their own images and ideas into the scene.

(3) Put everything into action. Show people doing things. Action speaks louder than description. If we pay close attention to everyday actions, and describe them in detail, we see just how complex and surprising life can be.

Tom Wolfe, the master of modern nonfiction improv, uses action to explore abstract ideas. In *From Bauhaus to Our House*, Wolfe describes the absurdities of modernist architecture. In 155 words, he shows how elites embrace modernism—and then, alarmed at its sterility, spare no expense to cover it up. See how Wolfe uses movement to make his point:

> Every great law firm in New York moves without a sputter of protest into a glass-box office building with concrete slab floors and seven-foot-ten-inch-high concrete slab ceilings and plasterboard walls and pygmy corridors—and then hires a decorator and gives him a budget of hundreds of thousands of dollars to turn these mean cubes and grids into a horizontal fantasy of a Restoration townhouse. I have seen the carpenters and cabinetmakers and search-and-acquire girls hauling in more cornices, covings, pilasters, carved moldings, and recessed domes, more linenfold paneling, more (fireless) fireplaces with festoons of fruit carved in mahogany on the mantels, more chandeliers, sconces, girandoles, chestnut leather sofas, and chiming clocks than Wren, Inigo Jones, the brothers Adam, Lord Burlington, and the Dilettanti, working in concert, could have dreamed of.

Wolfe puts details into motion. Rather than *explaining* the buyer's remorse of Modernism, he shows people scrambling to replace Modernist foofaraw with classic materials. Read that passage again and mark the action verbs and precise verbs. If brevity is the soul of wit, as Shakespeare once remarked, then specificity is the soul of improv.

One last point. Once you've tried some improv lines—once you've departed from straightforward description and decided to dazzle your audience—make sure the passage reads well. Improv pulls the reader out of familiar paths and rhythms. That can be jarring, in a good way. Just make sure your wordplay does not become a distraction. Read everything aloud. If it sounds right, you might—*might*—have something worth keeping.

Improv requires discipline. That's the most important lesson of all: Play all you want, but then work hard to make sure the play engages, rather than distracts, the reader.

CASE STUDIES: GARRISON KEILLOR AND P.J. O'ROURKE

For decades, Garrison Keillor delighted Americans with his evocation of the special community of Lake Wobegone. In his radio program "A Prairie Home Companion," Keillor spun yarns about the residents of this imaginary hamlet in Minnesota, where "all the women are strong, all the men are good-looking, and all the children are above average."

But like the characters in Lake Wobegone, Keillor also had an edgier side. In his essays about American politics, he was a biting critic. In "We're Not in Lake Wobegone Anymore," Keillor eviscerates the modern Republican Party:

> The party of Lincoln and Liberty has been transmogrified into the party of hairy-backed swamp developers and corporate shills, faith-based economists, fundamentalist bullies with Bibles, Christians of convenience, freelance racists, misanthropic frat boys, shrieking midgets of AM radio, tax cheats, nihilists in golf pants, brownshirts in pinstripes, sweatshop tycoons, hacks, fakirs, aggressive dorks, Lamborghini libertarians, people who believe Neil Armstrong's moonwalk was filmed in Roswell, New Mexico, little honkers out to diminish the rest of us, Newt's evil spawn and their Etch-A-Sketch president, a dull and rigid man suspicious of the free flow of information and of secular institutions, whose philosophy is a jumble of badly sutured body parts trying to walk.

Like all great improv artists, Keillor strings together details and images to reveal new sides of his subject. With a string of provocative details, Keillor draws a devastating portrait of the G.O.P. that he says threatens basic the American ideals of freedom, individuality, and respect for law and democracy.

And now, for equal time…

P.J. O'Rourke brings the same biting humor—and eye for details—

to his description of the oddball crowd at the 1988 Democratic National Convention:

> Democrats are also the party of government activism, the party that says government can make you richer, smarter, taller, and get the chickweed out of your lawn. Republicans are the party that says government doesn't work, and then they get elected and prove it. ...
>
> The Democratic Party is, to be polite about, broad-based. It's the Cat-Canary Love Association, Dogs and Mailmen United. Some people say the only reason Lloyd Bentsen is a Democrat is to keep Republicans from being embarrassed by their ties to big business. And Jesse Jackson —if you listen to what he says rather than how he says it—sounds like Fidel Castro's Jimmy Cricket. ...
>
> Then there was Michael Dukakis. Dukakis wasn't a right-winger or a left-winger. He was ... Well, he sort of ... I mean ... um ... mmmm ...
>
> Excuse me, I dozed off for a moment and went face down into the typewriter keys.

Pay attention to the similarities and differences of Keillor and O'Rourke's writing techniques. See how they gather details and then twist them for effect.

By going off the grid, stylistically, Keillor and O'Rourke lampoon the maddening absurdity of politics. Their riffing creates a dreamlike and almost hallucinatory state, where we are free to let go and laugh a little when we might otherwise cry.

———

ELEMENT 38: REMEMBER THAT GOOD IS GREAT

Every complex thing is really a collection of simple things. "Nature is pleased with simplicity," Isaac Newton said. "And nature is no dummy." Everything—every great structure, work of art, scientific proof, business plan—contains concatenation of simple things.

Remember the Periodic Table of Elements, which organizes 118 basic chemical elements according to their atomic number, electron configurations, and recurring properties. Everything in nature is comprised of some combination of these elements. From a limited number of inputs, nature creates unfathomable complexity.

Complex writing works like that. Every great sentence and paragraph, every great passage, is really a combination of simple pieces:

- Specific (and, if possible, unusual) subjects and verbs.
- Precise, sensual details that evoke images, sounds, and feelings.
- Rhyme, alliteration, onomatopoeia, consonance, anaphora, parallels, and other poetic devices.
- Terms that refer to shared knowledge and ideas.

Gather these pieces, one by one. Pay close attention to the character, place, and scene—and to ideas, contradictions, and puzzles. Then record and arrange those details in ways that pull the reader into the story, moment by moment.

All *great* writing, in fact, is just a collection of *good* elements. So when you want to create great language, remember this: *Good is great.*

To capture anything with fresh insight—whether it's a look, a movement, a feeling, a sound, a smell, or an idea—gather small observations. List them. Mull them. Think metaphorically. Look for *unexpected* sights and sounds and ideas.

And then put the pieces together, one by one. String those phrases together in unusual ways, like Charlie Parker or Miles Davis. Combine shapes together like Picasso and use colors like Monet. Do the little things well and you'll surprise yourself.

CASE STUDY: TOM WOLFE, *FROM BAUHAUS TO OUR HOUSE*

Look once again at Tom Wolfe's screed against modernist architecture (contained in the previous section on improv). Now look at the passage, broken this passage into pieces:

> *Every great law firm in New York*
> *moves without a sputter of protest*
> *into a glass-box office building*
> *with concrete slab floors*
> *and seven-foot-ten-inch-high concrete slab ceilings*
> *and plasterboard walls*
> *and pygmy corridors*
> *—and then hires a decorator,*

gives him a budget of hundreds of thousands of dollars
to turn these mean cubes and grids
into a horizontal fantasy
of a Restoration townhouse.

And so on. Look at the passage, line by line. What do you see? Simple phrases, each with a precise image or action. Separately, each of these lines is simple. Added together, they are anything but simple.

Wolfe creates this vivid scene because he collects countless details that other observers might miss. Wolfe achieves something great, with simple goodness, line by line.

———

AND ANOTHER THING . . .

Playing with words takes you places you could never imagine before the journey.

Rather than following a straight and simple path, ideas and images bloom and fly in strange, even surreal, ways. The reader makes associations that challenge the normal ways of thinking.

When jazz musicians improvise, they move into a dreamlike trance; they turn off their inhibitions and self-censorship. At the same time, they rev up the parts of the brain that allow for free expression. Improv —in acting or music or writing—is a wild process of discovery. It's a literary Mardi Gras—exuberant, creative, wild, sometimes out of control.

Still, even the wildest improv requires some basic order. The improv offers a crazy counterpoint to the main line. Listen to Willis Conover, the host of a jazz program on Voice of America for 41 years. "Jazz is a cross between total discipline and anarchy," Conover told an interviewer. "The musicians agree on tempo, key, and chord structure but beyond this everyone is free to express himself. This is jazz. And this is America. That's what gives this music validity." Improv is freedom but it requires discipline.

Get the words and rhythm, the sounds and the cadences, right. For one moment, forget about rules and restrictions. Let loose with the improv at the keyboard.

PART FOUR
DESCRIBING ACTION

Life, ultimately, is action. So is writing.

People and places are not static. They change constantly. They act on the world and the world acts on them. So to describe the world, we need to put people and places into action.

So how do you describe action? Let me offer a simple formula:

First, … Then, … Then, … Then, … Finally, …

To show action, break movements down into parts. Every action is really a collection of smaller actions. If I take a walk in the park, I am really performing a series of discrete activities—walking in, surveying the area, looking for clues on who's doing what and where, listening intently, making a decision on Path A versus Path B, deciding whether to sit on a bench or on a patch of the lawn, and so on.

Consider, for example, William Whyte's classic *City: Rediscovering the Center*. Whyte and his research team used time-lapse photography to capture how people use a variety of public spaces. They recorded people's actions, moment by moment, in and around parks, plazas, sidewalks, street corners, building lobbies, fountains, benches, chairs, and more. By watching the actions, moment by moment, they discovered how people use different spaces. It was data-based analysis at its best.

Whyte's job was to help readers to see the dynamics of urban space, moment by moment. By using time-lapse photography, he could find the right speed to explore space. To describe lightning-fast actions, he could isolate specific moments for detailed observation. To describe long processes, which take hours or days or longer to unfold, he could speed things up and compress long, drawn-out actions into short descriptions.

Action, please note, does not mean just *movement*. It means *movement with meaning*. Something as subtle as a nod is action if it has meaning for the story. Something dramatic as a car crash is not action if it lacks meaning for the story.

THE PLAN OF ATTACK

As a student of politics, you need to understand all of the elements of action. To do that, we have broken down action into two parts:

- Chapter 10: Action and scenes
- Chapter 11: Details

Now that we understand how actions work, we need to deepen out understanding of writing techniques. And so we explore two new topics:

- Chapter 12: Grammar
- Chapter 13: Editing

Writing instructors usually make grammar and editing too abstract and complex. I have a different approach. I see grammar as a set of "rules for the road." When you walk or drive, for example, signs tell you when to stop, pause, yield, look forward, and more. In a way, grammar performs the same tasks for writers and readers.

Just as action is really a set of smaller actions—and a scene is really a set of actions—editing requires that we break things down into appropriate pieces.

CHAPTER 10
ACTION AND SCENES

Human beings must have action; and they will make it if they cannot find it.

ALBERT EINSTEIN

ON FEBRUARY 26, 1972, a flood of water and waste overwhelmed the West Virginia community of Buffalo Creek. For decades, the Buffalo Mining Company had piled sludge from coal mines on the edges of town, creating mountains 40 to 60 feet high and more than 450 feet long. One local likened the spongy mass to a "mound of mashed potato." The walls created a dam, but that dam was so soft and spongy that it could not contain the flood.

Suddenly, after days of late-winter rain, Buffalo Creek flooded and the wall collapsed. See how it happened, moment by moment:

- The entire lake of black water, all 132 million gallons of it, roared through the breach in a matter of seconds.
- It was already more than water, full of coal dust and other solids, and as it broke through the dam and landed on the banks of refuse below, it scraped up thousands of tons of other materials, the whole being fused into a liquid substance that one engineer called a "mud wave" and one witness described as "rolling lava."

- The wave set off a series of explosions as it drove a channel through the smoldering trough of slag, raising mushroom-shaped clouds high into the air and throwing great spatters of mud three hundred feet up to the haul road where a few men were returning from the mines.
- The rock and debris dislodged by those explosions were absorbed into the mass too. By now, there was something like a million tons of solid waste caught up in the flow.

This passage from Kai Erikson's *Everything In Its Path* offers a model for action writing. I broke one paragraph into pieces so you could see how Erickson describes, moment by moment, this catastrophe. We see the flood overwhelming this community, hear the explosive sounds, and feel the power of the water and debris. We see the flood from the perspectives of workers, engineers, housewives, children, and retirees. The image of the mushroom cloud evokes disaster.

Erikson describes the scene, moment by moment. Rather than rushing into generalizations—a common habit for writers—he breaks the action down into discrete pieces. He creates suspense by ratcheting the tension, moment by moment.

The flood destroys not just the physical environment, but also the community's social fabric. Before the flood, Buffalo Creek was considered a tightly knit, caring place. Friends and neighbors left doors unlocked, loaned possessions to each other, stopped by for unscheduled visits, and gathered for supper and church. After the flood, they became suspicious and untrusting. Many bickered with old friends and neighbors. Some sank into alcoholism and depression. Others left the area. Some even committed suicide.

Erikson's vivid scene raises a powerful question. Did the flood destroy the community? Or did the community's weak foundation undermine the people's ability to deal with the disaster?

Reread Erikson's passage and pick out the action verbs. Then pick out the specific nouns. Look for the words that describe sights and sounds and smells. By focusing on details, Erikson makes the scene come alive.

———

ELEMENT 39: DEPICT SPECIFIC, DELIBERATE ACTIONS

Action offers the potential of changing the world in unpredictable ways. As the philosopher Hannah Arendt notes, action "has an inherent tendency to force open all limitations and cut across all boundaries." Whenever someone acts, they unsettle the world. Action makes stable things unstable. That's why stories need action. Stories are about discovery and change.

Let us define action like this:

> The fact or process of doing something, which influences something else, usually as a result of a deliberate choice.

A Dutch linguist named Tuen Van Dijk offers a number of sentences to explore action. Let's start with these five sentences:

- Leaves are green.
- Peter is ill.
- The train from Paris arrives at 5 o'clock.
- John recovered quickly from his heart attack.
- Mary could not pay her income tax.

Something happens in these sentences, but we do not actually *see* anyone acting. I would call these "summary statements." These kinds of statements offer important context for action. But they are informational, not action-oriented.

Now take a look at these three sentences:

- Harry found a briefcase with ten thousand dollars.
- George hesitated whether he would stay or not.
- Laura stared out of the window.

In these passages, we get closer to action. We can conjure an image of Harry encountering a briefcase someplace—maybe in a coffee house or a cloakroom—but we have no real information about his action. We can visualize George in the moment before he *might* act, but we still do not see him acting. Laura staring out the window looks more like action. We can picture her, standing, looking intently. But she remains still.

Now take a look at four more sentences:

- Ann cleaned the windows.
- Hans repaired my watch.
- Barbara accused him of murder.
- Larry refused to let him go.

We are getting closer. In each one, we can visualize someone putting his or her body into motion in order to change something. We might imagine Ann reaching up to get spots off the glass, Hans using tools as he leans over a table, Barbara pointing her finger, and Larry holding or blocking someone from leaving. But, again, we get no specific images or actions.

Now look at these sentences:

- Ann leaned into the window, pressing her damp rag to remove the soot from the pane.
- Hans peered through the magnifying glass and gently adjusted the spring of my watch.
- Barbara stood, shaking, as she raised her voice and made her accusation: "*You* killed him!"
- Larry stepped into the doorway, stopping his movement.

Finally, we get real action—vivid images of people using specific, discrete movements in order to change their part of the world.

As a storyteller, your job is to show the reader as much action as possible. Here's a simple test for every scene you write: *Could you use the sentences to draw a detailed picture?*

Don't summarize what people do or think, how they're positioned, or what's happening around them. Answer the following questions: *Who do you see—specifically? What do you see him doing—specifically? What is he acting on—specifically? What visible actions inform us about his goals—specifically?*

Show the sequence of movements needed to act. To describe a woman's commute, then, don't say: "She drove to work." Put details into a sequence, like this: "Leila balanced her leather briefcase and coffee while opening the door of her crimson Honda Civic. She tossed the briefcase onto the passenger seat and slid in behind the wheel.

Then the car crept out of the driveway and into the street..." See the difference?

To create action, get specific about who does what, *moment by moment*. Give your reader *moving pictures*.

CASE STUDY: ROBERT PENN WARREN, *ALL THE KING'S MEN*

Robert Penn Warren's *All the King's Men* offers a gripping tale of power and corruption in Louisiana in the 1930s. Governor Willie Stark takes command of the state and transforms it by building roads and hospitals and offering jobs and benefits to the state's poor and forgotten people. He uses demagoguery and brute force to get his way. In the process, he creates smoldering resentments.

In this scene, a prominent doctor named Adam Stanton, disgusted by Stark's corruption, murders Stark. The scene is narrated by Jack Burden, the governor's aide:

> He took a step toward us, but still did not look at me.
>
> Then the Boss veered toward Adam, and thrust out his hand in preparation for a handshake.
>
> "Howdy-do, Doctor," he began, holding out his hand.
>
> For an instant Adam stood there immobile, as though about to refuse to shake the hand of the man approaching him. Then he put out his hand, and as he did so I felt a surge of relief and thought: "He's shaking hands with him, he's all right now, he's all right." Then I saw what was in his hand, and even as I recognized the object, but before the significance of the recognition had time to form itself in my mind and nerves, I saw the two little spurts of pale-orange flame from the muzzle of the weapon.
>
> I did not hear the report, for it was lost and merged with the other more positive staccato series of reports, on my left. With his right arm still extended Adam reeled back a step, swung his reproachful and haggard gaze upon me and fixed it, even as a second burst of firing came and he spun to the floor.

Every moment matters in this scene. We open with the bonhomie of a back-slapping pol. The governor expects nothing more than glad-handing from a prominent citizen. That citizen ignores Jack—a minor surprise, but apparently insignificant—then moves toward Stark. All is going well, apparently. Then Jack sees something in Stanton's hand—and it's such a surprise that he can't react till it's too late. When the gun fires, everything changes.

Now look at this slow passage, earlier in the book, which describes the protagonist Jack's grad-school apartment:

> He even took a relish in the squalor, in the privilege of letting a last crust of buttered toast fall to the floor to be undisturbed until the random heel should grind it into the mud-colored carpet, in the spectacle of the fat roach moving across the cracked linoleum of the bathroom floor while he steamed in the tub. Once he had brought his mother to the apartment for tea, and she had sat on the edge of the overstuffed chair, holding a cracked cup and talking with a brittle and calculated charm out of a face which was obviously being held in shape by a profound exercise of will. She saw a roach venture out from the kitchen door. She saw one of Jack Burden's friends crush an ant on the inner lip of the sugar bowl and flick the carcass from his finger. The nail of the finger itself was not very clean. But she kept right on delivering the charm, out of the rigid face. He had to say that for her.

Not much happens. A piece of toast falls, a roach moves, a tub steams, a mother visits, and a friend crushes an ant, the mother recoils. So what's the drama? It's not as dramatic as the gun scene. But in this series of minor movements, enough happens for us to visualize the scene and to understand why it matters.

————

ELEMENT 40: USE SPEECH ACTS TO PROPEL THE STORY

We usually think of speech as a way to exchange ideas. As we adjust and combine ideas, we develop better explanations for understanding the world. U.S. Supreme Court Justice Oliver Wendall Holmes called for a "free trade in ideas" because, he said, "the best test of truth is the power of the thought to get itself accepted in the competition of the market."

But not not all speech is intended to engage others in a discussion. Sometimes people speak not to persuade others, but to get others to *do* something or *not do* something. Speech often works as *action* more than *expression.* Consider the following kinds of speech and how they foster action as much as communication:

- **Order**: "Get that report done by Monday" could be an invitation to discuss when the report can be finished. But more likely, it is an act of power or control.
- **Request or demand**: A request or demand, likewise, is a power move. "I'd like that report done by Monday" could be the beginning of a conversation but it could also be a form of coercion.
- **Apology**: By righting a wrong, an apology often resets a relationship. When grievances hang over a relationship, both sides are stuck. Offered sincerely, an apology offers a way out of the conflict.
- **Promise**: In some contexts, promises are as legally binding as a formal contract. A promise requires that one or more people perform a specific action.
- **Answer**: By answering a question, the speaker often exerts power or changes an arrangement. "Yes, I am leaving you," for example, may initiates a divorce. It does not just contribute to a dialogue.
- **Complaint**: When people exchange thoughts about a relationship—for example, in therapy or mediation—a complaint could be part of a constructive dialogue. More often, it is an action intended to gain moral power or leverage over another.
- **Warning or threat**: Usually delivered just before some form of enforcement, a warning or threat sets the stage for a power move. Warnings and threats pack a punch only when backed by the real possibility of action.
- **Refusal**: Saying "no" often begins, escalates, or ends something. Consider the meaning of "no" to the following requests: "Get back to work," "Remove your troops from the country," and "Will you marry me?" "No" in each case is an action more than a part of dialogue.

Speech-acts, you see, often work as forms of power and control. When they provoke a response, it's usually a power response--though skilled thinkers can at least try to shift the dialogue from power moves to dialogue.

CASE STUDY: JENNIFER MERCIECA, *DEMAGOGUE FOR PRESIDENT*

Few politicians have used language with as much blunt force as Donald Trump. America's 45th president uses words as weapons, as bludgeons to move people physically and emotionally more than intellectually.

Of course, almost all politicians use rhetoric to move their audiences. Few politicians resist demagoguery altogether. But most use language in a process of thinking things through, presenting sequences of ideas and facts to show how the world works. However self-serving, they explain strings of cause and effects, with two or more variables. When engaged, they consider alternative analyses, bring more relevant facts to bear, and explore possible exceptions. They bargain over policies and ideas.

Trump is different. He uses words not to explore ideas but to move people to feel, act, and react. Trump does not read, so he absorbs little information about the complex issues that he faced as president. And he has no interest in the mutual exploration of ideas. For Trump, language is a means of acting on other people. It is an instrument of blunt force.

In her work on Trump's 2016 campaign, Jennifer Mercieca identifies six rhetorical maneuvers that we might consider speech acts. Three of these maneuvers are designed to ingratiate Trump with this supporters.

- *Ad populum*: Using assertions of popularity as "proof" of the superiority of an idea or approach. When Trump claimed that he could "stand in the middle of Fifth Avenue and shoot somebody and I wouldn't lose any voters," he used his supporters' enthusiasm to dismiss any arguments people could make against his policies. He was saying, in effect: *The details don't matter, only my popularity matters.*
- *Paralipsis*: Putting forth an idea without accepting responsibility for that idea's veracity: "I'm not saying, I'm just saying." Trump often makes outrageous comments, eliding responsibility for those comments with lines like

"people are saying" and "a lot of people tell me." He also retweets offensive and racist content and then refuses responsibility for the remarks.
- **American exceptionalism**: By declaring America "the best," and "great," with success "like never before," Trump makes broad claims for success without any evidence. Patriotic fervor substitutes for facts or analysis.

Three other strategies are designed to alienate Trump and his tribe from other people:

- *Ad hominum*: Attacking a person's character in order to invalidate their ideas. Trump's nicknames for opponents (e.g., "Lyin' Ted," "Liddle Marco," "Low Energy Jeb," "Crooked Hillary," "Crazy Nancy," "Low IQ Maxine," "Sleepy Joe") instantly brand and dismiss anyone who might disagree, shutting down discussion.
- *Ad baculum*: Using words as threats or calls to violence. After falsely claiming that Hillary Clinton would seize guns, Trump seemed to call for violence if she won the election. "If she gets to pick her judges, nothing you can do, folks. Although the second amendment people, maybe there is, I don't know." In 2020, he tweeted "LIBERATE MICHIGAN" and "LIBERATE VIRGINIA" when those states' Democratic governors adopted policies to contain the coronavirus pandemic. Trump's followers responded. Soon after these tweets, the FBI discovered plots to kidnap governors from those states.
- **Reification**: Speaking in ways that take away someone's humanity, depicting them as objects. Trump regularly shuts down discussions by attacking people's character. He has attacked opponents—especially woman and minorities—as ugly, stupid, and pigs. He regularly uses words like "scum," "animals," "monsters" to describe people who criticize him.

Human communication requires both sides to respect each other, consider each other's ideas, break ideas down into pieces, and seek common ground. But Trump's speech acts tend to make such communication impossible. He uses speech as a bludgeon.

Not all speech acts undermine communication. Patriotic appeals can rally the nation not just to act but also to explore strategies for achieving common goals. Franklin Roosevelt's statement that "the only thing we have to fear is fear itself" was not just a statement of an idea, but a challenge. George W. Bush's admonition to first responders at Ground Zero after 9/11—"I can hear you! The rest of the world hears you! And the people who knocked these buildings down will hear all of us soon!"—was designed to rally followers more than to exchange ideas with them.

When you describe what people say, make sure you take note of the speaker's *intent*. Is it to inform people or engage others an a mutual exploration of ideas? Or is to stifle thought and prompt them to act or shut down?

———

ELEMENT 41: BUILD ACTIONS INTO SCENES

If an action is the basic unit of a scene, a scene is the basic unit of a story. A scene unfurls a complete set of actions. Moment by moment, a scene shows action and conflict, usually in a single place in a limited period of time.

Scenes take place in homes and workplaces, shops and restaurants, streets and cars, and churches and schools. They also take place on highways and shops, ballparks and legislative chambers, and about anywhere that people gather.

The range of possible actions is limitless—talking, arguing, canoodling, fighting, ignoring, playing, working, singing, fighting, loving, and more. What matters is what *changes* the story ... or what changes our *interpretation* of the story.

Every scene poses some dilemma that plays out in three stages, which we can plot on Aristotle's narrative arc. First, we survey the scene through a distinctive point of view. Second, the character debates whether to act. Third, the character takes action.

A clear point of view

The reader needs to know: Through what vantage point do we experience this scene? Do we experience the scene through the perspective of the main character, an opponent, a sidekick, or a mentor? Or do we see the happenings through the viewpoint of an invisible character, ignored by everyone else in the room?

Let us first consider the omniscient narrator, who hovers over every scene, knowing everything about everyone. This narrator shows reveals details that the characters themselves might miss. He reveals the characters in both public and private settings, revealing thoughts and emotions that most other characters cannot see. He even gets inside their heads, revealing their internal thought processes.

Now consider the first-person point of view, which offers a more intimate view of the story and characters. Through the eyes of one character—often the hero or his sidekick—we get a partial view of the goings-on. We see the hero sympathetically because we are so close to her, guessing her moves and responding to them with a sense of excitement or wonder.

Consider two classic examples of this intimate approach. In Mark Twain's *The Adventures of Huckleberry Finn*, Huck narrates. We see this boy's character—his ignorance and his decency—through his unselfconscious comments about his abusive father, his overweening aunt, and his friend Jim. In the Sherlock Holmes series, Arthur Conan Doyle uses the first-person POV of Watson, the detective's sidekick. This view offers an intimate perspective but prevents the audience from getting ahead of the story.

You can also tell a story from more than one point of view. If you switch perspectives, be sure to make the shifts in perspective clear at the beginning of every scene, right away. Signal that you are shifting POV by referring to a different situation. Use one of four basic techniques to indicate your point of view:

- **Place**: "The situation was different in Los Angeles…"
- **Time**: "Years later, the police found new evidence that…"
- **Person**: "After he graduated from college, Alex set his sights on Washington…"
- **Perspective**: "The Irish families from South Boston saw the situation from a different angle…"

Truman Capote's *In Cold Blood* uses a number of different perspectives: those of Herbert Clutter and his family, the murderers Dick and Perry, the detective Al Dewey, the townspeople at a diner and post office, even secondary figures like hitchhikers and the murderers' families.

Whatever POV you use, make sure the reader understands it right away—unless, that is, you want to surprise the reader.

Moments of debate and hesitation

Before people act, they need to *decide* to act. By considering the pros and cons of different options, they reveal their character. Choosing one option alters the course of the story.

Show the moment before the character makes his fateful decision—when he could stop or reverse course but decides to move forward.

In the "calm before the storm," we see the character's vulnerability. In these moments, the character is often more honest than at other times. The moment of pause allows us to see how the character weighs his knowledge and values and deals with the outside pressures.

The moment of decision could happen long before the story's action. In his account of the Buffalo Creek disaster, Kai Erikson explains how mining companies piled wastes from the mines into vast mountains of coal sludge, then covered up evidence of the danger. Company leaders knew that their actions risked a disaster, but they failed to do anything to prevent the inevitable destruction.

Show your reader that distinct moment of pause, which clarifies what's at stake.

Irrevocable action

After debate comes action. Once the characters weigh the pros and cons, they need to act—and they cannot go back. Deciding to go forward means abandoning the possibility of returning to old ways.

In taking a fateful action, characters can behave in one of two ways. They can either act with all their attention and energy, focusing on their goal without distractions and doubts. When you act with such commitment, solving problems becomes easier. Or they could act distractedly and half-heartedly. This, alas, is how we normally act. We take actions with only partial attention, every day, without fully considering the consequences.

The key issue with action, then, is how conscious people are when they do something. That is the heart of all stories (and other kinds of writing as well): Did the character mean to do something, or did they act in a lazy and unthoughtful way?

CASE STUDY: WILLIAM SHAKESPEARE, *MACBETH*

The hero of Shakespeare's great tragedy *Macbeth* is a man of valor and triumph. Macbeth's success on the battlefield opens up new possibilities for his career in the Kingdom of Scotland. But spurred by the prophesy of witches and his wife's unyielding ambition, Macbeth decides to kill the king to hasten his rise to the throne.

Let's see how Shakespeare tells the story:

• **Clear POV**: Shakespeare hovers above the story, offering an omniscient point of view. He shifts from one group of characters to another—the witches, Duncan and his aides, Macbeth and Banquo, Macbeth and Lady Macbeth, Duncan and others, the guards, Fleance and Banquo, Macduff and others, Malcolm and Donalbain, and so on.

Shakespeare could have presented *Macbeth* in a different way: through the eyes of Macbeth, Lady Macbeth, Banquo, or even the guards. But with those limited perspectives, he would lose important moments. If we saw the story through the eyes of other characters, we might not understand the witches, the rising opposition to Macbeth, or Macbeth's own desperation.

• **Deliberation and debate**: As he ponders the plot to kill King Duncan, Macbeth expresses his desire to finish the ugly deed ("t'were well that it were done quickly"), worries about cosmic justice ("even-handed justice commends the ingredients of our poison'd chalice to our own lips"), and frets about the monstrousness of killing one of his own kind ("I am his kinsman and his subject").

When Lady Macbeth arrives, he tells her: "We will proceed no further in this business." She dismisses his doubts. Fight for what you want, she says, or be "a coward in thine own esteem." He begs for mercy. She rejects his plea, questioning his manhood. He wonders about the possibility of failure. Again, he got no sympathy from the wife: "But screw your courage to the sticking place and we'll not fail."

Macbeth could go either way. His conscience and fear are at war with his ambition and his wife's determination.

• **Irrevocable action**: After Lady Macbeth badgers him—stoking his ambition while questioning his manhood—Macbeth finally decides to carry out the assassination. The plan is to stab Duncan, pretend to discover the king after he has been killed, and then frame the guards for the murder.

After killing Duncan, Macbeth returns to Lady Macbeth. "I have done the deed," he cries. The couple then discuss the consequences of the murder. "This is a sorry sight," Macbeth says, looking at his bloody hands. "A foolish thought, to say a sorry sight," Lady Macbeth retorts. This tension—between fear and boldness—continues as the kingdom plunges into civil war.

Macbeth's mental state is precarious before and after the murder. Before the deed, Macbeth hallucinates, seeing the murder weapon floating before him:

> *Is this a dagger which I see before me,*
> *The handle toward my hand? Come, let me clutch thee.*
> *I have thee not, and yet I see thee still.*
> *Art thou not, fatal vision, sensible*
> *To feeling as to sight? or art thou but*
> *A dagger of the mind, a false creation,*
> *Proceeding from the heat-oppressed brain?*

Later, after committing the murder, Macbeth is distraught. He asks Lady Macbeth if she heard screams. "I heard the owl scream and the crickets cry," she says, distancing herself from her husband's action and his misery.

––––––––

ELEMENT 42: CREATE MYSTERY TO SURPRISE THE READER

History, Kurt Vonnegut once said, "is merely a list of surprises."

Surprise is the secret sauce of storytelling. People make predictions, all day long, based on what happened before. We predict what family, friends, coworkers, neighbors, and even strangers will do, based on what they have done before. When predictions come true, over and over, we become blasé. So when surprise comes, we react emotionally. Surprise is the root of all learning and memory, all emotion and creativity.

So how do we give readers surprises? A simple formula, it turns out, shows how to create surprise of any kind—comedy or tragedy, farce or insight, subtle or raucous humor. The formula looks like this—

$$E/N$$

—where E stands for the expected, or normal, event, and V stands for a direct violation of that expectation.

Think of the great surprises in literature and art. Think of Oedipus's discovery that he killed his father and had sex with his mother. Think of Darth Vader's declaration to Luke Skywalker: "I am your father." Or think of *The Crying Game*, when Dil reveals to his lover Fergus that she was really a he.

Ponder some of the surprises of history. Visualize the Wright brothers alighting off the hills of Kitty Hawk with their aircraft. Think of the discovery, so improbable that it was denied for years, that mold produces antibiotic properties. Recall Eisenhower's deception of the Nazis to stage a successful invasion of Normandy. Remember the sneak attacks on Pearl Harbor and the Twin Towers.

Each of these events occurred when, at a specific moment, events violated reasonable expectations: E/N.

Now let's see if we can provide a reliable technique to create expectation and then violate it. It's simple, really. Just hide crucial information from whomever you want to surprise. Create a false or incomplete understanding of the scene. Then, moment by moment and piece by piece, reveal the truth.

Before you write a scene, list all the events or information that a person would need to understand the situation. Then shield one or more characters—or the reader—from that information. The longer the sequence, the more opportunities to hide information and then reveal that information.

You can embed surprise not just in sequences of action, but also in details of things. In the opening scene of Orson Welles's *Citizen Kane*, the New York publishing baron Charles Foster Kane utters the word "Rosebud" as he drops a snow globe. What does that mean? Only late in the story do we learn that Rosebud is the name of a sled that Kane owned in his troubled childhood, a symbol of the insecurities that drove him to lust for power.

The more information you hide in a story, the more opportunity for surprises. Even a slow non-story, like *Oblomov* or *Waiting for Godot*, the authors create surprises when they reveal long-ignored details.

You can also create surprise by focusing attention on the wrong things. Detective stories often use such red herrings. In *The Mysterious Affair at Styles*, Agatha Christie offers two characters who so despise each other they would never collaborate on anything—except, as we learn at the end, they collaborate on a murder. In Christie's *The ABC Murders*, the obvious suspect for the murder of a shopkeeper is her drunken, threatening husband. But he's not the one, as a string of other murders reveals.

Surprise comes after seeing some details of the story but not others. As a writer, you have the power to conceal and to reveal, whatever and whenever you want. Make a list of all the people, places, things, and moments that reveal something about the subject. Hide them at the beginning of the story, and then reveal pieces of them, one by one.

CASE STUDY: THE SENATE VOTE TO REPEAL OBAMACARE

If politics is a story of drama and consequence, the seven-year effort to kill the Affordable Care Act, also known as Obamacare, was one of the most consequential dramas in modern congressional history.

Congress passed Obamacare in 2010, when big Democratic majorities in the House and Senate overwhelmed the Republican opposition. After taking control of Congress in 2011, Republicans voted at least 70 times to repeal the law. Those anti-Obamacare votes were easy because they produced no consequences. President Obama vowed to veto any repeal that reached his desk.

When Donald Trump became president in 2017, with Republican majorities in both House and Senate, the drama changed. If the G.O.P. could discipline its members, it could repeal the law. But at that moment of truth, many Republicans hesitated. Did they really want to be responsible for denying medical coverage to 30 million people? What would happen to those people? And how would they explain the repeal to voters in the 2018 election?

When the House passed a bill to repeal major provisions of Obamacare in the summer of 2017, the Senate took up the bill. After weeks of lobbying, two Republican senators—Lisa Murkowski of Alaska and Susan Collins of Maine—decided to vote against the repeal. Since the Republicans held a 52-to-48 Senate majority and

Democrats were united to save the law, the repeal could not survive another GOP defection.

But no one knew how John McCain of Arizona would vote.

McCain, a self-style "maverick," had long opposed Obamacare. But he was disturbed by the legislative process that led to this vote. Neither house had given the issue its due diligence in hearings. And the repeal had no provisions for dealing with the millions of people who would lose their insurance. Philosophically, McCain favored repeal; practically, he was concerned that this bill was a reckless, punitive measure.

As the votes were tallied on the floor of the Senate, the mystery and drama increased. McCain had just flown in to Washington from Arizona, where he was receiving treatment for brain cancer. When he got to Capitol Hill, both sides lobbied him. He listened, respectfully.

The floor was crowded on the night of the Senate vote. Vice President Mike Pence went to the Senate chamber to manage the process for the Trump Administration. One by one, Pence buttonholed Republicans, seeking to keep them united. Then he went to look for McCain.

Susan Collins was talking with Lisa Murkowski when McCain approached them. He pointed at the two "no"-voting Republican colleagues and said, "You two are right." But no one besides these two antis knew McCain's intentions.

Pence talked with McCain for 30 minutes. He told him the president wanted to speak with him too. McCain took the president's call in the cloakroom. Republican leader Mitch McConnell was ready for McCain to vote against the repeal. "He's pretty much a contrarian in a lot of ways," McConnell mumbled.

The chamber buzzed with suspense. Would McCain, in his dying days, buckle under the pressure of his own party leaders? Senator Joe Donnelly of Indiana, who could not resist that pressure, knew McCain was made of tougher stuff: "He was a prisoner of war for five and a half years!" Vietnamese torturers could not pressure McCain to betray his country. How much difference could Trump *et al.* make?

Finally, McCain reentered the chamber. "He comes around that corner," Senator Elizabeth Warren remembered. "No fuss, no muss, waiting for his name again."

When he appeared, the chamber turned silent. Then there were gasps.

When he heard his name, McCain moved forward with gusto and declared "No!" as he gave a thumb's down signal.

Gasps were again audible.

Afterward, McCain explained his vote. "I've stated time and time again that one of the major failures of Obamacare was that it was rammed through Congress by Democrats on a strict party-line basis without a single Republican vote," he said. McCain did not want to see such a party-line vote to repeal the law, especially for a program that helped millions of Americans.

McCain called for a return "to the correct way of legislating." With any major piece of legislation, Congress needs to "hold hearings, receive input from both sides of the aisle, heed the recommendations of the nation's governors, and produce a bill that finally delivers affordable health care for the American people." In passing Obamacare, three House committees and two Senate committees held hundreds of hours of hearings and considered detailed data on the potential impact of the new law. In in their effort to repeal the law, Republicans short-circuited the process. Mark Peterson of UCLA, an expert on the policymaking process, said that he "can't recall any major piece of legislation that was completely devoid of public forums of any kind." That was McCain's concern as well.

The mystery and drama were over. We now knew how it would turn out—and why.

———

AND ANOTHER THING . . .

Want a surefire way to test whether the pieces of your scene fit together? Work backwards.

When we work from the end to the beginning, we see the sequence of actions in a fresh way. Too often, when we tell a story from beginning to end, we fail to see the inner logic of the story. Starting from the beginning, you only see the evidence available. So work with the end in mind—with all the pieces of information necessary to create a whole story.

Figure out your conclusion first—how the story is resolved. Then work backwards, to the previous sections when the hero makes a decision to change his life. Then develop the previous scenes, when the hero comes to understand the issue. Continue to work backwards, until you introduce the hero and the world of the story.

Read this passage from Martin Amis's novel *Time's Arrow* to see just how jarring—and revealing—backwards movement can be:

> First I stack the clean plates in the dishwasher. ... So far so good: then you select a soiled dish, collect some scraps from the garbage, and settle down for a short wait. Various items get gulped up into my mouth, and after skillful massage with tongue and teeth I transfer them to the plate for additional sculpture with knife and fork and spoon. That bit's therapeutic, at least, unless you're having soup or something, which can be a real sentence. Next you face the laborious business of cooking, of reassembly, of storage, before the return of these foodstuffs to the Superette, where, admittedly, I am promptly and generously reimbursed for my pains. Then you tool down the aisles, with trolley or basket, returning each can and packet to its rightful place.

Amis narrates this 165-page novel backwards. The story begins at the end and ends at the beginning. Because Amis shows his characters acting in reverse, we notice things we ordinarily would miss.

You don't need to tell a backwards story. But by looking at your story's events in reverse order, you can find fresh ways to narrate events, with revealing details about the people and places, choices and actions, and the logic of the story.

CHAPTER 11
DETAILS

When you walk into a room and you get a certain feeling or emotion, remember back until you see exactly what it was that gave you the emotion. Remember what the noises and smells were and what was said. Then write it down, making it clear so the reader will see it too and have the same feeling you had.

ERNEST HEMINGWAY

WHAT HAPPENS when you see an object or a scene? How do your eyes work? Can we train our eyes to see better? Can we train ourselves to observe better?

Look at this chart. Read the letters, one at a time. Move from the top to bottom letters in each column, one by one. Then move from the second to third letters in each column, one by one.

T E L M N
S F R T N
O W I I G
H E E E T

Spend only as much time as necessary to notice what letter you have landed on.

This is a variation of a game called Super Saccades. Eye specialists devised the game to help people exercise their eye movements so they can see better—or, to be more accurate, to *construct images* from the tiny fragments that they actually see.

When we view a scene, our eyes jump around three to five times a second, viewing tiny fragments of the scene at a time. These movements, which see about 15 degrees of the scene, are called saccades. In saccades, our eyes jump to the most interesting pieces of the scene. What's interesting? Usually something with an unusual shape, color, or texture. As we quickly view these tiny pieces, our brain searches its memory for similar pieces and scenes. The brain creates a complete picture by combining the fragments it sees with the fragments of memory of past experiences.

"We can't perceive an entire visual scene simultaneously," University of Virginia psychologist Daniel Willingham notes. "We can pick out one object if it has some distinctive feature (e.g., a red car amidst a lot of white ones). But to appreciate a bunch of complex objects, you've got to serially process them."

Observation requires deliberate, patient work. We humans are not cameras, capable of recording all of a scene's details at once. What we see depends on what we look for—or what stands out—as our eyes dart from point to point. We have to scan, stop, look; then scan, stop, and look again; over and over, we scan, stop, and look.

ELEMENT 43: FIND DETAILS BY LOOKING INSIDE-OUT

Finding details requires learning how to observe in new ways. Start with a photograph of a fiddler from long-ago Asheville, North Carolina:

Right side up, you instantly recognize an older man, wearing a coat, about to play a fiddle. You still recognize him upside-down, but it takes a moment of work. Without the picture's wholeness and familiarity, you process the image differently. Observed from an unfamiliar angle, you pay attention to shapes and shades. You consciously *determine* what's in the picture. Rather than instantly thinking "fiddler," you look at the elements of the image, one at a time. In this way, you find the telling details. This is active observation.

Betty Edwards, the author of *Drawing on the Right Side of the Brain*, teaches her students to draw by turning pictures upside-down. Since they don't get distracted by the whole image, they can pay close attention to the lines and shapes, solids and voids, colors and shadings.

You can also focus on details by envisioning a picture on a grid. Rather than paying attention to the whole picture, note the simple shapes inside the boxes.

To you describe a person, scene, or action, break down your picture into segments. Observe the picture, square by square. Notice the colors, texture, shapes, and definition. Don't try to make sense of the whole picture. Look at the whole only after you have discovered the details in the squares. Consider the image of the fiddler again, this time with a grid overlay.

Why do these strategies work? The brain, as Daniel Siegel notes, "has a bias for making the world appear solid and stable." The brain wants to make sense of the whole and therefore misses the parts. You job, then, is to slow down the brain's instinct to construct something whole. Rather than automatically deciding that the picture shows a fiddler, zoom in on the details first. As you accumulate these micro-details, you will understand the whole better.

A writer's job is to make find the details that show something new or important to the reader. The writer makes the familiar unfamiliar and the unfamiliar familiar. When you find something that's familiar, don't write about what the reader would know already. Instead, find some details that would surprise the reader.

CASE STUDY: ISABEL CHENOWETH'S 'THE WOMEN'S MARCH'

On January 21, 2017, more than 5 million people across the world joined in one of the greatest political demonstrations in history. The Women's March was organized by activists who wanted to protest the rise of Donald Trump, who was inaugurated as president the day before.

One of the biggest gatherings was in New York, where the photographer Isabel Chenoweth captured this scene:

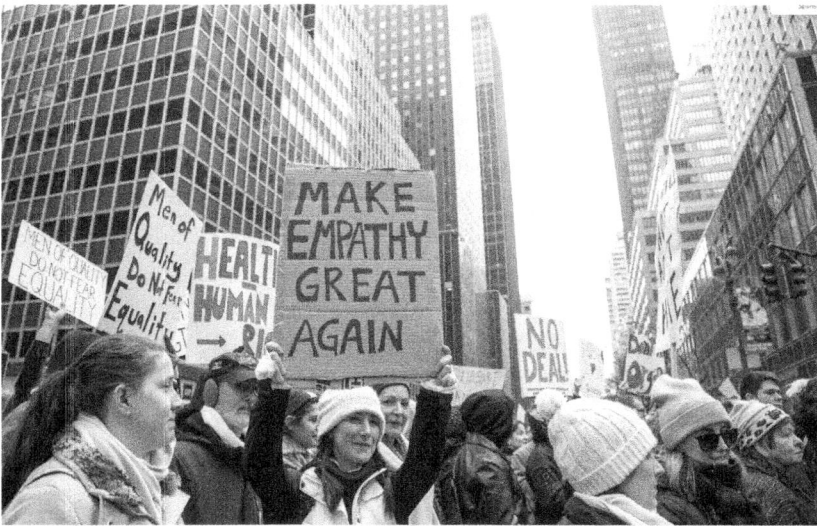

Look at the image carefully. Start by focusing on the subject. Then look around the subject. Then search for more details. Keep looking. Even when you think you have identified all the important details, keep looking.

The focal point is the woman with the cardboard sign about empathy. She looks relaxed, as do others in the picture. After months of shock and dismay, the protesters came together to share their commitments and to support each other. This was a moment of catharsis. The simple act of saying "No" to the new administration offered an emotional release and allowed, for the first time in months, a sense of hope for the anti-Trump resistance.

Now, look along the edges of the image. See how Chenoweth frames the picture. New York's great skyscrapers form a canyon that contains the multitudes. Massive crowds flowed into the city's narrow passageways like a river. People moved with a steady, rhythmic pace, full of energy and life.

Pay attention to the shapes and colors. Note that the signs were handmade. In the greatest demonstration of the civil rights movement, the 1963 March on Washington, organizers mass-printed the signs so that protesters would make statements that would embarrass the civil rights movement. Signs were means of control as well as expression. But here, no one attempted to censor any voices. Marchers were free to express their ideas on a range of issues: women's rights, health care, education, racism, corruption, and more.

Now imagine the sounds being made when Chenoweth clicked her camera. Imagine the chants ("This is what democracy looks like!") and the murmur of pleasantries below ("Oh, what a beautiful sign!" "Thanks for coming!" "What a day!"). Imagine the movement of the crowd forward, how people accommodated each other, in a great mass dance, on the streets and sidewalks.

What else do you see? To look at the image in greater detail, go online (bit.do/womensmarch2017). Now let me ask you: What's the story?

Is it the buoyant spirit of the day?

Or the sense of dread the marchers felt?

Or the determination to resist the new administration?

Or the power of organizing?

Or something else?

If you were reporting on this event, you would look all around, not just to get the "big picture" but also to find the small, telling details. Then you would talk with the marchers about why they came, what they hoped for and what they feared, and how they planned to act. By exploring this picture—and everything in this scene—you could tell a whole story about this historic moment.

———

ELEMENT 44: ISOLATE DETAILS TO MAKE BIG POINTS

Consider this great paradox. The more specific your observations and thoughts—about characters, scenes, places, actions, moments—the more readers relate to it. "In the particular," Anton Chekhov said, "is contained the universal."

Specific details tap into your reader's memories and emotions. When you provide vivid details, you trigger a chain of associations. The reader recalls moments that somehow relate to those details: childhood moments, traumatic events, moments of ecstasy, images and sounds, feelings and emotions.

When you offer surprising details—the small nods and sighs, the light in the room and the color of the paint on the wall, the sound of the brook or the smell of the soil—your reader trusts you. Why? Rather than telling your reader what to think, you offer information that she can use to make her own judgments.

Details lend authority to stories and arguments. Even if a character's paisley blouse, layered hair, and magenta lip gloss don't matter much, they show that the writer was attentive. And so the writer gains credibility.

To describe a person, place, or action, look for *unusual* details, especially those that others might not notice. If you walk into a party, don't just look at the friends and family who shout "Surprise!" Look at the people on the edge of the room. Look for someone who seems out of place. Look for someone with a surprising reaction. Look for the different ways that people interact after the moment of surprise. Likewise, when you describe a familiar person—like Washington or Lincoln or FDR—don't repeat the details we know already. Show us something we don't know.

Look at the photograph of Richard Nixon. In most ways, Nixon was an ordinary looking man. He resembled most other middle-aged men of his time.

Nixon differed from most other men only in minor ways: the ski-jump nose, the beady eyes, the patchy hair, the bushy brows, and the jowls. Cartoonists exaggerated Nixon's distinctive features because they knew that, to recognize something, we need to look for *what's different.*

Think about it. Has anyone every described someone like this: "Oh, you can't miss him—he's the one with two eyes, a nose, and a mouth"? To describe people, place, action, or idea, focus on what's *different.*

Attention, as the neuroscientist Cathy Davidson has noted, "is about *difference.*" We pay attention to things that lie outside our normal everyday experiences. We notice things, Davidson says, when they are "*not* part of out automatic repertoire of responses, reflexes, concepts, preconceptions, behaviors, knowledge, and categories and other patterns both mental and physical."

So find the details that surprise the reader. Use colors, sounds, textures, shapes, and utterances that startle, amuse, or disturb the reader. Move from the predictable to the unpredictable.

CASE STUDY: *THE NEW YORK TIMES* 'PORTRAITS IN GRIEF'

In the aftermath of the terrorist attacks of September 11, 2001, *The New York Times* published brief portraits of people killed at the World Trade Center, the Pentagon, and the crash in Somerset County, Pennsylvania. Over time, *The Times* memorialized more than 2,500 people. Standard eulogies, which make generalizations about a person's "good nature" or "interest in the arts" or "devotion to family," often sound hollow. To avoid such blandness—and to convey something memorable about the ives lost on 9/11—*The Times* instead offered a few intimate details:

Dianne Bullis Snyder: Before leaving on trips, she used to post life lessons on her children's doors. "Don't wait for tragedy, say it today," one of them read. "I love you and I'm glad you're alive." She made quilts, taught herself French, and timed the cookies to come out of the oven as the children arrived home from school.

Maurita Tam: Fun-loving? She was frisky and gregarious. Her mother, Julie Tam, chided her halfheartedly about her unladylike giggle. "She would giggle at every little thing and kick both legs up in the air," Maurita's mother recalled. Her room at college was a hangout for friends who giggled with her, teased her about a pinup poster of an Asian performer, and picked her brain for ideas about assignments and projects.

John P. Lozowsky: Using a big nail, he tethered a self-propelling mower to a cinder block, "so he could lie back and sunbathe so the mower could do its job." During the weekdays, he biked to work. On long weekends he drove four hours to upstate New York in a $450 car that he painted with his son, niece, and nephew.

Giann Gamboa: The last time anyone saw Giann, he was on the 78th floor, getting ready to squeeze into a crowded elevator as the building was being evacuated. He offered his spot to a young woman who was crying and anxious to flee. "I'll just take the next one," he told a friend, as the elevator doors shut.

Jan Maciejewski: An avid soccer and tennis player, Jan was always running. He would run from his main job as a waiter at Windows on the World to catch the subway to his other job as a computer consultant. He would run back to the subway to get home to his wife in Astoria, Queens. The pockets of his pants always had Band-Aids he wore on his calloused feet.

Sadie Ette: When her cousin Ben packed up Sadie's Manhattan apartment after 9/11, he saw a Bible on her pillow, which she had apparently read before going to work on 9/11. It was open to the 91st Psalm: "With His wings He will cover you and beneath His wings you will find refuge; His truth is a shield, a full shield. You will not fear the terror of night, nor the arrow that flies by day."

Portraits of Grief provided an emotional balm to New Yorkers and others struggling to make sense of the attacks of September 11. They showed not just the terrible tragedy of that day but also the great gifts that these people's lives offered the world. *The Times* portraits succeeded by noticing the little things.

––––––

ELEMENT 45. USE STATUS DETAILS TO REVEAL EGO AND DESIRE

As social creatures, we care about our place in the status system. We want to fit in, but we also want to stand out. So we send signals—in our dress, cars, homes, work, schools, hobbies, and speech—about how we want others to see us.

How important is status? So important that we sense pain and threat when it's challenged. To explore this point, Naomi Wiesenberger, a brain researcher at UCLA, asked study subjects to play a video game of dodge ball. Halfway through the game, two of the on-screen players rejected a third by turning away to play a private game of catch. So how did the real-life player at the computer respond? With intense pain, that's how. The part of the brain that processes physical pain—the dorsal region of the anterior cingulate cortex—was activated. "Those who felt the most rejected," Wiesenberger reported, "had the highest levels of activity in this [pain] region." Even in a computer simulation!

Status comes both from conformity and difference. Conformity connects us to others. As social creatures, we depend on others for affirmation of our value. We need others to tell us that we're OK. We need to say, in effect, *I'm just like you.* On the other hand, we need to separate ourselves from the pack. Lost in the sameness of the group, we lose our sense of self. So, while *fitting in*, we also want to *stand out*.

Some years ago, I worked with teachers at an independent school in Connecticut. While I waited for a meeting, I stood in a hallway and watched the teenaged students arrive. It was homecoming week, when students dress in different period costumes every day. One day they wore togas, another they wore colonial garb. On this day, they wore western clothing. As the students climbed the stairway, they strutted in anticipation of their friends' *oohs* and *aahs*. One by one, they showed off their jeans and prairie dresses, plaid shirts and cowboy hats, head-dresses and leather skirts and vests. What was different seemed to matter most. But look again. All these kids conformed to contemporary norms. They sauntered the way teenagers do. The boys wore baggy pants and styled their hair like Tom Brady. The girls wore tighter clothes and styled their hair like *Seventeen* models.

We want a sense of adventure, but we also want the stability of social norms. We care about appearances, status and style, how we look, what people think about us. We want to look like the other members of our tribes. We want to signal to the world—with what we wear and drive, how we walk and talk—how we fit into the social order.

Tom Wolfe coined the term "status details" to describe the telling markers of social position. Status details, Wolfe says, involve

> the recording of everyday gestures, habits, manners, customs, styles of furniture, clothing, decoration, styles of traveling, eating, keeping house, modes of behavior toward children, servants, superiors, inferiors, peers, plus the various looks, glances, poses, styles of walking and other symbolic details that might exist within a scene. Symbolic of what? Symbolic, generally, of people's status life, using that term in the broad sense of the entire pattern and behavior and possessions through which people express their position in the world or what they think it is or what they hope it to be. The recording of such details is not mere embroidery in prose. It lies as close to the center of the power of realism as any other device in literature.

Status details offer a glimpse into the character's ego. Status details display the whole community's swirl of egos, with the tensions between individual expression and group conformity. These details also tell us something about that moment in time: its technologies, trends, and fads.

The swirl of status symbols also tells us about the greatest struggle of all: To be genuine. Ralph Waldo Emerson once wrote: "To be yourself in a world that is constantly trying to make you something else is the greatest accomplishment." Use status details to make that struggle —both the internal and the external struggle—a key part of your story.

CASE STUDY: STEVEN ARONSON, 'NEW YORK APOGEE'

The leitmotif of Donald Trump's life, by all accounts, is the striving for success, adulation, privilege, and luxury.

Growing up, Trump was pulled in two directions. First, he aimed to please his father Fred, a housing developer in the Queens borough of New York City. A harsh and aggressive man, Fred Trump was known for his hard-edged business tactics, his brusque style with family, and his ties to shady business partners. Second, Donald Trump sought to escape his father's world by moving to the glamour of Manhattan. There he could build glittering skyscrapers that outshined his father's pedestrian, low-slung housing complexes.

Trump's greatest achievement, by all accounts, was Trump Tower, the 58-story, 664-foot building on Fifth Avenue, between 56th and 57th Streets. In his other business endeavors—in real estate, sports, casinos, "Trump University," airlines, food and spirits, even beauty pageants—Trump's attention wandered. But Trump stayed focused and clear about his vision for Trump Tower. He was especially engaged on the design of the top three stories that became his home.

Trump Tower, the mogul told *Architectural Digest*, is "the finest apartment in the top building in the best location in the hottest city in the world." He elaborated: "In the real estate business we have a generic term for the best location, wherever it is: the Tiffany location. And Trump Tower is literally that—it looks down on Tiffany's, which I purchased the air rights to a number of years ago."

Trump's apartment itself was a seven-bedroom triplex penthouse with a two-story living room. *Architectural Digest* provided a seven-page tour of the apartment, filled with glossy images of the rooms and Trump posing with his first wife, Ivana. Steven Aronson writes:

> Everything in the Trumps' two-story living room savors of the luxurious: from the understated chairs and sofas to a banquette covered with a fabric painted in 24K gold; to the antique Venetia-style mirror and the brown marble fireplace; up, up, up to the gold-leaf ceiling. "It's close to 20 feet," Donald Trump notes, "about as high as any ceiling in any new building in years." …
>
> The city literally ripples in the glass, flowing by day and flashing by night, its rivers and bridges caught in the crossweave of time and space. …

[T]he bedroom … overlooks the living room and through that the city. "Ivana wanted a very feminine feeling up here," [the designer] Angelo Donghia said. "And she got it—peach-pink mirrors, peach suede walls. It's soft, comfortable, and modern." …

The top floor offers guest rooms—not used very often since Trump owns the Grand Hyatt, the St. Moritz and the Barbizon Plaza hotels. The top floor also houses space for the three kids, with a nanny's quarters and kitchen and dining room. …

"We're turning the entire roof of the building into a private park for our children," Donald Trump says. "It's going to have statues, waterfalls, gazebos, and everything else we can think of. We also own the duplex next to our triplex and we're converting it into a gym and play area for the kids. The space will also yield a huge library and a dining room for big buffets."

Every aspect of the penthouse expressed Trump's outsized aspirations and ego, his ideas about the good life, and his beliefs about success. To paraphrase Dorothy in *The Wizard of Oz*: "Toto, we're not in Queens anymore."

––––––

ELEMENT 47: PUT DETAILS INTO ACTION

When you seek details, look for movement.

To observe movement, isolate the different parts of a scene. Watch animals play in a field or marsh. Watch a crowd sway at a ballgame or concert. Watch the wind bend the trees. Watch the rhythms of people moving around a town square. Watch how friends cluster together at parties.

Movement activates the senses. By seeing movement, the reader can see, hear, feel, and even smell the action. Seeing details in motion reveals *relationships*. You get a sense of what causes what. You can also explain something complex, moment by moment.

Think back to the saccade chart. No matter what we view, our eyes dart from point to point to construct the whole picture.

To describe movement, create a "track" in your mind. Don't just assemble a mental picture of the scene; look for the elements that change over time.

- **Approach and frame**: Focus on the subject—a person or animal, a car or other vehicle, a ball or other object of action. Isolate her from everything else in the scene. Show her, either still or in motion, so that we can get a sense of her character.
- **Zoom**: Move in to explore the details that offer important details. Don't settle for the general description. Find telling and surprising details. Isolate the character's expressions, appearance, clothing, and behavioral tics.
- **Track**: Follow a character as she moves, whether she's doing something active (like running a race) or passive (like sorting through memorabilia). As you track the movement, notice how the action affects things nearby. Think of your subject like a motorboat moving through water. How and where does the character move? What changes over the course of the movement? What kind of a wake does the movement produce? How does that wake affect other elements of the picture?

Even still pictures can be dynamic. A verbal snapshot of a moment in time can show all kinds of relationships. A sequence of those shots can tell a whole story.

CASE STUDY: JOURNALISM FRAGMENTS

To see the power of details in action, let's look at four brief strategies, with passages from exemplary works of journalism.

• **Approach**: In her story on ocean dumping, the journalist Susan Casey follows a seaman named Charles Moore. As he sails in the Pacific Ocean, Moore discovers massive piles of nonbiodegradable garbage. This passage shows Moore approaching a mountain of junk; as he gets closer, his shock becomes palpable:

> This was an odd stretch of ocean, a place most boats purposely avoided. For one thing, it was becalmed. "The doldrums," sailors called it, and they steered clear. So did the ocean's top predators: the tuna, sharks, and other large fish that required livelier waters, flush with prey. The gyre was more like a desert—a slow, deep, clockwise-

swirling vortex of air and water caused by a mountain of high-pressure air that lingered above it.

Moore had never seen a sight as chilling as what lay ahead of him in the gyre:

> It began with a line of plastic bags ghosting the surface, followed by an ugly tangle of junk: nets and ropes and bottles, motor-oil jugs and cracked bath toys, a mangled tarp. Tires. A traffic cone. Moore could not believe his eyes. Out here in this desolate place, the water was a stew of plastic crap. It was as though someone had taken the pristine seascape of his youth and swapped it for a landfill. How did all the plastic end up here? How did this trash tsunami begin? What did it mean?

The details unfold, moment by moment—moving into the doldrums, spotting the ghosts of plastic bags, then seeing the whole ugly landfill out in the ocean.

Moore's discovery offers a perfect setup for Susan Casey's report on ocean dumping, which brings plastics into the food chain. Casey's moving account helps us to visualize and make sense of a complex topic.

• **Zoom**: In *The Right Stuff*, Tom Wolfe zooms in on the rocket Chuck Yeager piloted at the speed of sound:

> The X-1 looked like a fat orange swallow with white markings. But it was really just a length of pipe with four rocket chambers in it. It had a tiny cockpit and a needle nose, two straight blades (only three-and-a-half inches thick at the thickest part) for wings, and a tail assembly set up high to avoid the "sonic wash" from the wings.

Wolfe starts with a distant, simple image, complete with color. Then he adds a detail that shifts our attention to the basic structure of the thing. Finally, he moves in to observe small details, including the effects of flying at the speed of sound.

• **Track**: In *The Suicide Index*, a memoir of her father's suicide, Joan Wickersham searches her father's belongings for a suicide note:

I went though the bureau drawers and found a broken gold pocket watch in an old jeweler's box from Wiesbaden, and packets of pins and needles from when he'd been president of the family business, and foreign coins, and breath mints, and, beneath a pile of boxer shorts, a couple of issues of *Penthouse*.

Asa we see this scene, we see not just the materials in the drawer; we also imagine Wickersham's response. She gets us rummaging through the drawers with her. We join her as a voyeur in search of answers about the puzzle of suicide. It's a slow scene, but our attention shifts with every new movement and detail.

The bottom line is the same for all of these maneuvers: Show the details that matter. Use details that add fresh insight, a new way of looking at the world.

AND ANOTHER THING . . .

When I was a young reporter for United Press International in the 1980s, I wrote a feature story about a Vanderbilt University medical researcher named Pierre Soupart. A pioneer of *in vitro* fertilization, Soupart spent as much time battling politics—the Reagan Administration's determination to block his research—as he spent working in the lab. Soupart's story offered a fascinating glimpse into the politics of science.

When I submitted my article, my editor asked one question: "What's he look like?"

I didn't understand why that mattered. Wasn't the article supposed to explore the controversies surrounding Soupart's research? Shouldn't I focus on the battles involving the Reagan Administration, the Christian Right, the medical community, and federal bureaucrats? Why did Soupart's *appearance* matter?

Here's why: The reader needs to *picture* Soupart to *care* about him. The details I added—he was a short, slight man with salt-and-pepper hair and a mustache, a chain smoker who always wore white lab coats —enable the reader picture Dr. Soupart moving around the lab, clipboard in hand, conferring with his young researchers. These details give him life.

Small details give us a sense we are in the subject's company. And remember, as social creatures, readers like to be in someone's company.

Observing carefully, in order to find telling details, requires slowing down the brain. You need to clear away distractions and avoid making assumptions. Then you will be able to pay attention to the elements of a picture you otherwise might miss.

Psychologists call this quieting process "mindfulness." To see the world in a mindful way requires carefully observing thoughts, feelings, perceptions, and sensations. A mindful person works to avoid automatic responses. A mindful writer sees and describes each person, thing, or incident carefully, avoiding judgmental attitudes. By leaving behind judgment, you allow yourself to see things with a fresh eye.

WRITING TECHNIQUES
FOR PART FOUR

CHAPTER 12
GRAMMAR

If you can remember all the accessories that go with your best outfit, the contents of your purse, the starting lineup of the New York Yankees or the Houston Oilers, or what label "Hang On Sloopy" by The McCoys was on, you are capable of remembering the differences between a gerund (verb form used as a noun) and a participle (verb form used as an adjective).

STEPHEN KING

NOAM CHOMSKY WON fame a half century ago with his theory that language follows a universal grammar. How we use language—how we put words into sequences—is as basic to humans as how we eat, socialize, or reproduce. Here are some of Chomsky's basic observations about the elements of grammar:

- All languages use vocabularies with many thousands of words.
- All languages use subjects and predicates.
- All languages use nouns and verbs.
- All languages use sets of sounds—but each language uses just a small share of the total sounds that humans can hear.
- All languages categorize distinctions in meaning in similar ways.

On top of those basic building blocks, the structure of language varies according to the needs and histories of communities. Early punctuation, like the comma, colon, and period, was originally indicated orally, with pauses and emphases, to indicate rhythm in speech. Later these tools were brought to the page and took the form that we know now. Necessity, then, was the mother of punctuation.

Like other activities, communications requires a common set of rules. Just as drivers need to follow the "rules of the road"—when to stop, change lanes, yield, turn, and so on—writers need rules to guide their own journeys. At the same time, they need some freedom to express themselves with clarity, energy, and creativity.

ELEMENT 47: MAKE SURE THE PARTS OF SPEECH GET ALONG

Like the members of a family taking a road trip, the different parts of speech need to stick together and get along. The nouns need to cooperate with the verbs and the pronouns. The modifiers have to stay close to the things they modify. Verbs and helping verbs also need to stick together.

A handful of simple rules will keep all your words working together. Think of these rules in three parts. Start by saying *who's who and what's what*. Then *show the action*. Finally, *make everything whole*.

Rule 1: Say who's who and what's what.

Nothing matters more than the subject. So follow these simple rules to make the subject—*who and what*—clear.

• **Make nouns agree with verbs**. The principle is simple: Singular nouns get singular verbs, and plural nouns get plural verbs. But applying the rule can get tricky.

Before we get to the tricky stuff, let's review the simple application of the rule. It's usually easy to match noun and verb:

- The dog *jumps* up and down; the dogs *jump* up and down.
- The most important criterion for the job *is* experience; the criteria for the job *are* difficult to meet.

Sometimes, whether a noun is singular our plural depends on the context:

- Data *is* the key to better policing; data *are* to be found in response times, shift reports, and parole records.

Now, on to the tricky stuff.

Modifiers that mislead: The greatest cause of noun/verb confusion is the modifier—specifically, the prepositional phrase. Prepositions are words that indicate relations, like *over, under, with, beside, next to, before,* and *after*. A prepositional phrase modifies a noun, like this:

- The team of veteran athletes plays its first game on Tuesday.
- The bridge over the river and park has a spectacular view.
- The house with a new kitchen and sunroom is for sale.

When we use prepositional phrase, we sometimes confuse the modifier for the subject. Here's a trick: Every time you see a prepositional phrase, put a bracket around it to determine the actual subject, like this:

- The team [of veteran athletes] plays its first game on Tuesday.
- The bridge [over the river and park] has a spectacular view.
- The house [with a new kitchen and sunroom] is for sale.

Focus on the subject—not the items within the prepositional phrase—and you'll always get it right.

Plural noun problems: Plural nouns also make noun-verb agreement tricky. Most words linked by *and* create a plural noun—and therefore require a plural verb. Thus:

- The president and Congress *were* at loggerheads over the coronavirus legislation.

But hyphenated words are considered a singular noun. Thus:

- Give-and-take *is* required for passage of legislation.

Some words ending in *s*, like politics, sports, and headquarters, seem plural but are actually singular.

Oddball rules: Use singular verbs for *each, either, everyone, everybody, neither, nobody, no one*, and *someone*. *None* is singular when it refers to a singular noun and plural when it refers to a plural noun: "None of the apartment was painted" says that no one part of the *apartment*—not the living room, not the dining room, not the bedroom—was painted. "None of the apartments were painted" says that none of the many *units* in a building—were painted.

• **Make nouns agree with pronouns**. We face a similar problem matching nouns and pronouns. We need to match singular verbs with singular pronouns and plural verbs with verbs pronouns.

People often treat a collective entity—like a school, team, or family —as a plural noun. So we see sentences like this: "In 2008, Ohio State won their first five games." But in fact Ohio State is a single entity, so it should be "Ohio State won *its* first five games." When you use the team's nickname, it's plural: "The Buckeyes won *their* first five games."

• **Use possessives correctly**. The big challenge here is to avoid confusing possessive words with contractions.

Possessives: To indicate a singular noun's possession of something, use an apostrophe and the letter *s*. For example:

- Prince Charles's marital problems
- James MacGregor Burns's study of leadership
- The witch's demise

To indicate the possessive of a plural noun, usually just add an apostrophe. Thus:

- The Democrats' electoral chances

With letters and digits, plurals look like singular possessives. So:

- The A's have a good chance to win the pennant.

Possessives get confusing when you talk about two or more people or entitles. Consider the characters in the slapstick movie *Bill and Ted's Excellent Adventure*. Written this way, the title refers to a single adventure that both characters enjoyed. Bill and Ted comprise a single entity.

If this pair enjoyed several adventures together, say "Bill and Ted's Excellent Adventures." If each character enjoyed separate adventures, give both of them possessives: "Bill's and Ted's Excellent Adventures." If they separately enjoyed the same adventure—if, for example, each time-traveled to the French Revolution in separate time machines—say "Bill's and Ted's Excellent Adventure."

Contraction confusion: Now that we know how to use possessives, let's discuss the dangers of confusing possessives and contractions.

A contraction combines subject and verb. We use contractions to sound informal. Instead of saying, for example, "Bill Clinton is a native of Arkansas," we say "Bill Clinton's a native of Arkansas." Formal writing usually avoids such shortcuts; more casual writing doesn't hesitate a moment to use a contraction.

Rule 2: Show the action.

The ultimate goal of all writing is to show action. Even when exploring ideas that are abstract and unseeable—like *freedom* or *fission* —we need to show something happening.

• **Get the tenses right**: Compared to other languages, English tenses are simple.

Start with inflections, the endings to verbs that change tense and meaning. English verbs use only four inflections for regular verbs. So we say, for example, that we *play*, he *plays*, he or we *played*, he is or we *are playing*. Simple enough: add *-s, -ed, -ing*, or nothing, and you can describe almost all action. By comparison, Latin verbs use 120 inflections.

Still, English poses its share of complications. Irregular verbs, for example, do not follow standard rules. Consider these examples:

Base form — Past tense — Past participle
Beat — Beat — Beat/beaten
Begin — Began — Begun
Blow — Blew — Blown
Fall — Fell — Fallen
Dive — Dived — Dived
Get — Got — Gotten
Keep — Kept — Kept
Know — Knew — Known

Lay — Lain — Laid
Lie — Lay — Lain
Ring — Rang — Rung
See — Saw — Seen
Sink — Sank — Sunk

These verb forms are oddballs, with no obvious logic. Unfortunately, you need to memorize these—or at least be aware that you need to look them up.

• **Choose the tense that makes your writing clear**. Use tenses clearly and consistently. Specific historic events and past practices usually require the past tense: *Martin Luther King rallied garbage workers in Memphis* and *Thomas Edison failed 10,000 times to develop a storage battery.*

Past perfect: To indicate an event that happened before a past event, use the *past perfect* tense: *X had happened before Y happened.* So you could say: *Martin Luther King* had gone *to Memphis when he was assassinated.* The past perfect tense talks about two different moments in the past. But be careful. If you litter your prose with past perfect usages, it gets hard to write simply. So use the past perfect tense sparingly. Usually use it to make a transition in time, then revert to simple past tense, like this:

Martin Luther King *had gone* to Memphis when he was assassinated. In Memphis, he *conferred* with leaders of the sanitation workers. He also *reached out* to city leaders to find middle ground. Just before his assassination, he *gave* the speech known as the Mountaintop speech.

Subjunctive: References to imagined past circumstances require a verb form known as the *subjunctive*: *If Abraham Lincoln had lived, the nation would have avoided the bitter conflicts of Reconstruction.* Other imagined situations also require the subjunctive. I might say, for example, *If I were Superman, I would fly to work.* I will never be Superman, so the situation is purely imagined.

Also use the subjunctive to express extreme improbabilities: *If I were a Rockefeller, I would give away millions for cancer research.* Someone could become a Rockefeller by marriage, of course, but it's not a real possibility for most people.

• **Avoid double negatives, usually**. Double negatives require the reader to spend too much time figuring out the meaning of a statement. Double negatives also say what isn't, rather than what is. The reader usually wants to know what is, not what isn't. Double negatives leave too many possibilities open.

Take this statement: *Senator Patty Murray was not displeased with the education bill.* So what does the senator think? The phrase tells us about the *absence* of something (displeasure) but not the *presence* of its opposite (pleasure). Was the senator pleased? Thrilled? Indifferent? Intrigued? Uncertain? The reader cannot know.

Besides creating uncertainty, double negatives produce gloom. Psychologists report that using negative words actually depress people. Unlike math, where two negatives multiplied produce a positive, writing with double negatives usually produces confusion. Sio avoid it.

• **Avoid splitting infinitives, usually**. To understand a split infinitive, consider the distraction that occurs when a phone call interrupts a conversation. Suddenly, the conversation is broken. And it's often difficult to restart the conversation.

A split infinitive occurs when a word (usually an adverb) gets between a verb and helping verb.

Consider this: *Kate Smith liked to really sing loudly.* We know the meaning of this simple sentence. Kate liked to sing loudly. How much damage can *really*'s interruption of *to sing* cause? Not much, usually. In fact, a growing number of language mavens scoff at the old-fashioned ban of split infinitives. In her book *Grammar Snobs Are Great Big Meanies*, June Casagrande declares "only windbags fuss over split infinitives."

Split infinitives may, as Casagrande argues, add panache to a sentence. She uses the example of the *Star Trek* TV series, which opens like this: "To boldly go where no man has gone before." Getting to "boldly" sooner rather than later gives the passage panache. So we should not get too upset, right? Still, I wonder. Would "To go boldly where no one has gone before" lack pizzazz? What about "Boldly going where no one has gone before"? Both phrases work for me. Maybe we should heed the split-infinitive ban after all.

• **Use contractions, selectively**. Avoid contractions, unless you want to create a casual mood or quote someone else using contractions.

Formal documents like academic papers and legal documents usually avoid contractions because they sound unprofessional. Using contractions in a formal document is like wearing Bermuda shorts to a wedding or funeral. It is better to fit the style to the context.

In more conversational pieces, contractions help you sound real. You would not want to say "Let us suppose," would you? Don't irritate your reader with stuffiness. As a rule of thumb, use contractions when doing otherwise sounds stiff. Of course, that is a judgment call. Or should I say "that's a judgment call"?

Rule 3: Make everything whole.

The best writing gives the reader a satisfying sense of completeness. The story is not just a collection of events, but something that adds up to something whole and unified. An incomplete story produces frustration. Likewise with grammar. When someone raises a point, but fails to complete it, we feel frustrated.

So consider a few grammatical tips to make sure you complete your thoughts:

• **Almost never use sentence fragments and run-on sentences**. A sentence fragment is an incomplete thought. Like this. A run-on sentence goes on and on, often changing subjects, which gets confusing, because the writer should break it up into parts, and the reader will understand the thoughts better, and the writer won't confuse the reader, like this.

These days, even academic writers use fragments to make writing conversational. Look how the Yale historian Edmund Morgan describes Benjamin Franklin trying to unmoor his ship:

> Franklin strips to his shirt and wades out into the water and mud up to his waist but finds the boat chained and locked to a staple in the stake. He tries to wrench out the staple. No go. He tries to pull up the stake. No go. Back to shore, and the three start looking for a farmer's haystack to sleep in.

Morgan uses these brief phrases—"No go" (twice) and "Back to shore"—to pace and redirect the passage. Morgan makes his youthful subject sprightly. But be careful. Too many short, telegraphic passages annoy the reader. If you're in doubt, tell yourself: *No go.*

Avoid run-on sentences, except, on rare occasions, when you want to describe long and meandering trains of thought that connect the present with the past or move from the here-and-now to some imagined or real place or even describe an event or process that meanders and weaves its way, like a path that winds up a steep mountain and ...

As your "default" style, write simple sentences. Only when you master simple structures can you command complex structures.

• **Don't dangle your participles**. Participles are verb phrases that provide setup information.

Consider this example: *Having served as supreme allied commander during World War II, Dwight Eisenhower understood the complexities of bureaucracy.* The participial phrase "Having served as supreme allied commander during World War II" offers useful information about Eisenhower.

But participial phrases often breed confusion. Sloppy writers often forget what phrase they mean to modify. Consider this sentence:

> Winning the states of the old Confederacy, the electoral system tilted toward the Republican Party after Richard Nixon's 1968 campaign.

That participial phrase should modify the Republican Party, not the electoral system. So try this instead:

> Winning the states of the old Confederacy, the Republican Party gained electoral dominance starting with Richard Nixon's 1968 campaign.

Do you know the political adage "Keep your friends close and your enemies closer"? Try this grammatical parallel: Nouns should keep their verbs close and their modifiers closer.

Writers err when they lose track of *what belongs with what.* They forget what subject goes with what verb, what modifier goes with what subject or verb, what noun goes with what pronoun, what noun or verb with what adjective or adverb.

At the end of every passage, just ask yourself what belongs with what. Bracket the modifiers to make sure you know what's the subject and what's the verb. Move the pieces around until you find the right matches.

CASE STUDY: APPROACHES TO HIS/HER

Gender presents a tricky problem. Often, we want to refer to someone without indicating whether that person is male or female. Consider this common sentiment:

> Every person deserves the opportunity to discover *his/her/their* passions and follow them wherever they take *him/her/them*.

What to do? Oldtimers choose the male pronoun (in this case, *his* and *him*), insisting that they are "gender neutral." Enlightened moderns look for an inclusive approach, to make sure we don't ignore or stereotype girls and women.

Let's explore a few samples to analyze this problem. The first sample comes from James Allen's classic self-help book, *As a Man Thinketh*:

> A man only begins to be a man when he ceases to whine and revile, and commences to search for the hidden justice which regulates his life. And he adapts his mind to that regulating factor, he ceases to accuse others as the cause of his condition, and builds himself up in strong and noble thoughts ...

Why Allen seem to exclude women from this passage? He seems to imply a special quality to male character traits. Could Allen make a similar point with gender neutrality? I think so. Try this wording for the first sentence: "We reach maturity when we cease to whine and revile..."

For a second sample, let's turn to the *Annals of Behavioral Medicine*, where researchers at Stanford use two separate approaches to avoid gendered language.

> Whether one is engaging in a health promoting activity such as exercise or is living with a chronic disease such as asthma, he or she is responsible for day-to-day management. Gregory Bateson once said, "one cannot not communicate."

At first, the Stanford researchers use the universal "one." This approach, alas, sounds stiff and formal. So they try "he or she" and "his or her." This approach sounds OK for one or two phrases; but used again and again, it gets clunky and confusing. And so, to be consistent and balanced, some writers collapse "he or she" into "he/she" or "s/he" and "his or her" into "his/her." That might work for legal documents but fails to engage the reader warmly.

For a third sample, turn to the political theorist Richard Flathman, who overturns the male bias in language by using female pronouns for all general references. Look at a few passages from Flathman's book *The Philosophy and Politics of Freedom*:

- The Stoic defines *herself* by reference to society. *Her* studied indifference to the merits of *her* society's arrangements testifies to the hold society has upon *her*.
- Nothing in this stance denies that what A is and does now is in part a result of *her* past interactions.
- Even a person in a tight-fitting straitjacket or mummy case can may be able to wiggle *her* toes, blink *her* eyelids, flex certain of *her* other muscles, and so forth.

Some of Flathman's colleagues go further, giving higher values to the feminine. In his book *Contingency, Irony, and Solidarity*, for example, Richard Rorty uses the feminine for arguments he endorses and masculine for arguments he rejects.

Word mavens have long sought a gender-neutral pronoun for these circumstances. For a while, writers used the word *non* as a catch-all phrase for "his or her." I would love to see *non* catch on; so far, however, it's a non-starter.

To skirt the his-or-her question, I use plurals whenever possible. Rather than saying that "the student has until November to complete his college application," for example, I say, "Students have until November to complete their applications."

When I need to use a singular pronoun, I try to mix up *he* and *she* and *his* and *her*. So: "A lawyer must keep track of her billable hours" or "A chef needs ready access to his spices."

Which brings us to "they." To avoid the sexism of male pronouns and the awkwardness of "he or she," many writers use "they" for their second references. So you might say, "The professor told their students to turn in their papers." That sounds wrong to me, but so do other alternatives. Let's face it. Language evolves to fit changing needs and tastes. If something solves a problem, why fight it?

_____

ELEMENT 48: USE PUNCTUATION TO DIRECT TRAFFIC

If all sentences are journeys, which take the reader from one place to another place, punctuation offers traffic signals to manage the traffic.

Punctuation tells the reader whether to stop (period), slow down (comma), look both ways (question mark), look forward (colon), yield (semicolon), or proceed slowly (ellipses).

Let's explore these signs in some detail.

Use periods to stop the action.

The period is the writer's best friend. By marking the end of the sentence, the period prompts is to stop one thought and proceed to the next.

The British call the period the "full stop." The term is more than a label; it's also a command, with a theatrical air. The message is simple. If you can learn to make a simple statement, and then stop, you will become a good writer.

A liberal dose of periods would solve many writing problems. Bad writing often results when the writer wanders away from the subject. The easiest answer is to write short sentences—at least until you get the knack of longer sentences. When in doubt, end your sentences.

Take it from Mark Kramer, the former director of the nonfiction writing program at Harvard University's Nieman Fellowship. Kramer used to hold out his cupped hands to his students. "Here's an unlimited supply of periods," he would say. "Use 'em all you want. No limits!" You could almost see those dots filling his hands, as dense and rich as black caviar.

Use commas to pause the action.

If good writing depends on flow, the comma is the writer's second best friend. Commas create pauses, giving the reader a brief moment to sort ideas and images.

The comma's first function is to separate items in lists, so we don't get lost in a long train of nouns. To make lists in a sentence, just insert a comma after every item. So: *Willie Mays could hit, hit with power, catch, run, and throw.*

Some editors say you can delete the last comma, known as a serial comma or an Oxford comma. I disagree. Without that last comma, "run and throw" sound like a single skill. Most people, of course, understand running and throwing to be separate skills. But why risk even a brief moment of confusion? Consider the line from Robert Frost's poem "Stopping By Woods on a Snowy Evening":

The woods are lovely, dark[,] and deep.

The line's meaning varies depending on the use of the last comma. With the serial comma, the phrase "lovely, dark, and deep" refers to three separate attributes of the woods. Without the serial comma, "dark and deep" modifies "lovely."

The comma's second function is to offer space to make an aside or a parenthetical comment. Therefore: *Willie Mays, a first-ballot Hall of Fame member, is baseball's greatest living player.* Mays's status as a Hall of Famer comes as a parenthetical idea.

In both cases—separating items in a list and making a parenthetical point—commas offer the pause the refreshes. But be careful not use commas to pause too often. With too many pauses, you lose tempo. Consider the following 70-word sentence from *The New Yorker*:

> The first time that Sam Popkin, a political scientist at the University of California at San Diego, who, along with his wife, the China scholar Susan Shirk, has known Hu [Shuli] for many years, watched Hu report a story, it reminded him of the portrait of the *Times* reporter R. W. Apple in *The Boys on the Bus*, when "Apple used to make something like a hundred calls a day," Popkin said.

Nine commas shatter a simple idea (Hu is manic!) into a dozen pieces. Look how we might express the same idea with fewer commas:

> With her frenetic pace, Hu Shuli resembles the legendary *Times* reporter Johnny Apple. As Hu's friend Sam Popkin notes, "Apple used to make something like a hundred calls a day."

In 29 words—two sentences, 12 and 17 words long, using two commas—the new passage says what matters. Surplus commas fragment the idea under discussion. The new version avoids those tangents.

Use colons to look ahead.

When you look through the viewfinder of a camera, you narrow your perspective to whatever lies in front of you. The colon acts in much the same way. The colon offers a prompt to pause a moment to look ahead. So:

> Before he ran for president, Barack Obama had the same political experience as Abraham Lincoln: eight years in the state legislature and two years in Congress.

A colon also sets up a list:

> Winter is coming, so get out your cold-weather gear: coats, hats, gloves, boots, and earmuffs.

When a sentence contains two passages that could stand alone as sentences, do not use a colon. Instead, use a period or a semicolon.

Use semicolons to make a complex list; also use them to combine complete thoughts.

The semicolon's only mandatory function is to make lists within lists. In this sense, the semicolon acts as a super comma. Therefore:

> To win the presidency, Democrats need to win Northeastern states, like New York, New Jersey, and Connecticut; Rust Belt states, like Ohio, Michigan, Wisconsin, and Illinois; and liberal bastions, like California, Oregon, and Massachusetts.

The semicolon's second function is optional. The semicolon creates a break—and a connection—between two complete thoughts in the same sentence. So:

William Buckley was a polymath; he was a writer, editor, speaker, activist, harpsichordist, and sailor.

Think of those independent thoughts as separate roads coming together. The semicolon provides the Yield sign that allows traffic to merge.

We could express those thoughts in two sentences or restructure the sentence with a comma (*William Buckley, a polymath, was a writer, editor, speaker, activist, harpsichordist, and sailor*) or a colon (*William Buckley was a polymath: a writer, editor, speaker, activist, harpsichordist, and sailor*). The semicolon offers a middle ground, with a pause longer than a comma but shorter than a period.

Some people hate this odd-looking little symbol. Novelist Cormac McCarthy calls the semicolon "idiotic." A copy editor at *The Washington Post* once called it "an ugly bastard." The novelist Kurt Vonnegut called semicolons "transvestite hermaphrodites representing absolutely nothing."

Mercy. Why such emotional revulsion to this little wink of ink? Why not put an extra tool into your toolbox? Sometimes you want to express two related thoughts without the period's abrupt, severe break. If so, the semicolon works wonders; it does the job. See?

Hyphenate words to combine ideas.

Hyphens offer a way to combine two or ideas into one. Consider the following sentence: "East-coast liberals like AOC differ from west-coast liberals like Jay Inslee." We could say, "liberals from the west coast," but that's not as pithy.

Of course, connecting too many things with hyphenation can get silly. Thus: "The first-term African-American junior-senator from south-side Chicago made his first-ever run for the White House in 2008."

These hyphenated expressions often lead to whole new words. After combining separate words with a hyphen, people used to using the words as a single idea. The word for the America's national pastime, for example, began as *base ball*, evolved to *base-ball*, and finally took the modern form of *baseball*. More recently, *electronic mail* transmogrified into *e-mail* and then into *email*.

Use em-dashes—like this—to make asides.

If you want to set off whole phrases or lists, use an elongated hyphen known as the em-dash. Look at this sentence:

> The Chicago Cubs' inability to win a World Series for 108 years—a period that saw 19 different presidents—caused angst among fans.

The em-dash helps the author make an parenthetical remark. The em-dash tells the reader to pause, as if to say, "Hey, check this out."

Critics say the em-dash cheapens writing by encouraging a loose, informal style. To be sure, overusing any tool can be annoying. When we use the em-dash too much—like here—it distracts—and annoys—the reader. But in moderation—again, not like this—the em-dash offers a useful—and even fun—way to emphasize a point.

Use ellipses to show thoughts trailing off ... or indicating gaps in speech ...

Every time I see an ellipsis, a set of three dots, I hear the sound of harp music. Ellipses (plural of ellipsis) suggest thought trailing off, pondering, open-ended ideas. Ellipses allow us to drift for a moment ...

A case in point: "Dorothy considered her challenge: 'If only I could see the Wizard of Oz ...'" We see the girl with braided hair, looking off into space, in her own world, lost in thought.

Ellipses also perform a more technical task: marking gaps in quoted passages. People rarely speak in compact packages, so writers some-times need to stitch together comments made at different moments. To indicate gaps in a passage, use an ellipsis. So we might quote John F. Kennedy's inaugural address this way:

> Ask not what your country can do for you—ask what you can do for your country. ... Let us go forth to lead the land we love, asking His blessing and His help, but knowing that here on earth God's work must truly be our own.

Ellipses allow us to use just the words that convey the thought.

(Psst: Use parentheses to make asides.)

Sometimes, you want to offer a tidbit of related information. That information might strengthen the argument (providing details or context) or simply offer an aside (as part of a conversation).

When you want to provide examples of a several things, use parentheses rather than saying "for example" over and over. When Barack Obama assembled his administration in 2008, he drew his team from America's elite universities. Here is how *New York Times* columnist David Brooks described Obama's advisors:

> January 20, 2009, will be a historic day. Barack Obama (Columbia, Harvard Law) will take the oath of office as his wife, Michelle (Princeton, Harvard Law), looks on proudly. Nearby, his foreign policy advisers will stand beaming, including perhaps Hillary Clinton (Wellesley, Yale Law), Jim Steinberg (Harvard, Yale Law) and Susan Rice (Stanford, Oxford).

Here an elite, there an elite, everywhere an elite. Brooks uses parentheses to make this point nicely.

Profligate use of parentheses makes writing choppy. On the other hand, sometimes you want to show just how choppy the world can be. "So are my parentheses part of my style?" Ben Yagoda asks (rhetorically). "Actually, yes. I am drawn to them in part because they express my belief that the world and language are multifarious, knotty, and illuminated by digression."

(Any questions?)

Use quotation marks to say exactly what someone said.

To indicate the use of someone's exact words, use quotation marks. So:

> "Ask not what you country can do for you," President Kennedy said. "Ask what you can do for your country."

Always use the speaker's exact words. If you want to use bits and pieces of someone's speech, put quotation marks around the precise phrasing and use your own words to connect the phrases. So:

After challenging the nation to "ask what you can do for your country," President Kennedy challenged other nations to "ask not what America will do for you, but what together we can do for the freedom of man."

Punctuation and quotation: In American English, punctuation marks usually belong inside quotation marks. Therefore: *"Ask not what your country can do for you," Kennedy said.*

Sometimes you need to quote someone quoting someone else. To do that, use single quotation marks inside double quotation marks, like this:

> "I went back to the doctor and he says, 'Henry, I told you, you can't make it, you're going to die in that mine.' I said, 'Well, Dr. Craft, let me try it one more time,' because I had some debts I wanted to pay."

What about a quote inside a quote inside a quote? Switch back and forth, from double quotation marks (") to single quotation marks (') and back to double marks ("), like this:

> "I met Joyce at the civil rights march, and she called out to me, 'Let's sing something. How about "Ain't Gonna Let Nobody Turn Me Around"? Let's do that one.'"

The power of quotation comes from our innate desire for inside information or intimacy. Whether we want to eavesdrop or hang on the words of an expert or wordsmith, quotations give writing extra depth and style.

Use exclamation marks—rarely!—to show excitement or emphasize your points.

I once worked with someone who used exclamation marks, lots of them, all the time!!!! Even when discussing something mundane, she ended every sentence with a throng of these happy marks!!!! I guess it's not much different from someone who agrees with you all the time, or says "have a nice day" no matter what's happening!!!! But I think it's too much!!!! So annoying and distracting!!!!

Sober wordsmiths avoid exclamation marks, except to show someone shouting. The novelist Elmore Leonard suggests using no more than two or three exclamation marks every 100,000 words (the length of a book). And I agree. Mostly! To evoke real emotion, tell a great story rather than use perky punctuation.

Every rule, of course, has an exception. I so admire Tom Wolfe that I tolerate his use of exclamation marks. By one count, Wolfe's novel *The Bonfire of the Vanities* contains 2,343 exclamation marks in 659 pages. "I'm trying to restore punctuation to its rightful place," Wolfe once explained. "Dots, dashes, exclamation points were dropped out of prose because they 'reeked of sentiment.' But an ! shows someone getting carried away. Why not? The writer carefully not using this punctuation doesn't bother to convey what's exciting to the reader."

CASE STUDIES: DAVE EGGERS'S *THE PARADE* AND ROBERT CARO'S *THE PASSAGE OF POWER*

Some authors use little punctuation besides the period and comma. Others create a parade of punctuation, phrase by phrase.

Start with a novel by Dave Eggers. In his account of a fictional nation that just concluded a civil war, Eggers describes a project to build a highway that runs from the nation's south to its north. Look at the simple, spare prose that Eggers uses to describe the city at the end of the highway:

> After an hour he saw a bright silver roof of corrugated steel. It was far larger than any structure he'd seen since he'd arrived. A roof like this was rare in this country; he assumed the building was both new and built by people with means. Indeed, as he drew closer, he saw that it was an NGO, one he had not heard of. As the RS-80 passed slowly, he saw staff moving in and out of the building. One man, in a khaki suit, left the building and got into a gleaming white Range Rover and, without acknowledging Four [one of the lead characters in this story], drove up the embankment and onto the just-paved highway, speeding south on it as if it had been finished for years, not minutes.

Until the end of the passage, Eggers uses simple, declarative prose. In the first five sentence he uses five periods and four commas; in the sixth sentence, he uses five commas to pace and parse his long thought.

Now look at a monster sentence, full of twists and turns and lookouts and rotaries, in Robert Caro's *The Passage of Power*. In this passage, Caro explores the controversy over John Kennedy's selection of Lyndon Johnson as vice president in 1960:

> In attempting to understand why, [Kennedy] declared to his journalist friend Charles Bartlett that his offer to Johnson has been merely a gesture ("I just held it out like this, and he grabbed at it")—a statement at direct variance not only with Johnson's account of the conversation but with what Kennedy himself told O'Donnell, O'Brien, Governor Lawrence and others immediately after it took place—one possible explanation is that since he had allowed unequivocal "promises ... assurances" to be given in his name to liberals and labor leaders that Johnson would not be offered the vice presidency, the easiest way to explain why the offer had been made was to say that he hadn't really offered it, had only "held it out like this" and that Johnson had, "to his shock," "grabbed at it," and he, Kennedy, then had no choice but to let the offer stand.

This 148-word sentence uses every punctuation mark but the exclamation mark! Caro pulls the reader through a long stream of consciousness. He wants the rush of words, interrupted and diverted in surprising ways, to bring the story's details into one place.

As a writer, you enjoy some discretion in your use of punctuation. Your sweet spot probably lies closer to Eggers than to Caro.

——————

ELEMENT 49: SELECT THE RIGHT WORD

Details matter. Any time you create the possibility of confusion—especially by choosing the wrong word—you risk losing your reader.

Beware of words sound alike but mean different things. For a comprehensive list of these "false twins," check a style guide like *The Chicago Manual of Style*. Meanwhile, learn the distinctions among the following sets of words:

Affect and effect: Used as a verb, *affect* describes how one thing influences another. So: *Hillary Clinton's popular-vote victory did not affect Donald Trump's conviction that he won a mandate.*

Used as a noun, *affect* describes a person's emotional capacity. So: *The killer showed a shocking lack of affect when confronted with his crime.*

Effect, a noun, refers to consequences. So: *The effects of the Civil War included a stronger federal government and the end of slavery.*

Alternate and alternative: As a verb, *alternate* means taking turns. So: *Writers should alternate writing clusters of short and long sentences.* As a noun, it means a substitute for another. So. *His alternate taught the class.*

Alternative means a choice between two or more things. So: *Getting old beats the alternative.*

Comprise and Compose: Approach with caution; these two words confuse even the most careful writers.

To comprise is "to be made up of, to consist of, to include." The whole comprises the parts. So: *The United States comprises 50 states.*

To compose is "to make up, to form the substance of something." So: *The parts compose the whole.* To remember this, think of the musician who pulls together different musical ideas to *compose* a piece of music.

Farther and further: Use *farther* to describe physical space. Think of "far" to remember it as a distance word. So: *I ran farther today than yesterday.*

Use *further* to refer to a figurative distance. So: *Walker advanced further in his violin lessons than Leila.* Or: *Let's examine this further.*

Its and it's: *Its* is possessive; it shows that something belongs to something else. So: *Its customer base includes senior citizens and boomers.*

It's is a contraction of *it is*. So: *It's a truism that Republicans have a "lock" on the states of the old Confederacy.*

Its and their: *Its*, again, refers to the possession of a singular entity. So: *The University of Connecticut women's basketball team had its best years under Coach Geno Auriemma.*

Their refers to the possession of a plural entity. So: *The Connecticut Huskies had their best seasons under Coach Geno Auriemma.*

Lay and lie: *Lay*, a transitive verb, refers to the act of putting something down. When you lay something else down—a hammer, book, platter—you act on that object. *Lay* always takes an object. So: *I lay the book on the desk.*

Lie, an intransitive verb, does not take an object. *To lie* means to recline, or place your own body in a certain way. (The past tense is *lay*. Sorry. These rules do seem contradictory sometimes.) So: *Oblomov decided to lie in bed indefinitely.*

Less and fewer: *Less* refers to a smaller amount of something, without discrete units of measurement. So: *After the 2020 election, Donald Trump had less power than Joseph Biden.*

Fewer refers to smaller numbers of things that can be counted. So: *Donald Trump won fewer votes than his Democratic opponents in 2016 and 2020.*

Lose and loose: To *lose* is to go down to defeat; *loose* means slackness. So: *The Mets got so loose at the end of the 2007 baseball season that they started to lose a lot of games.*

That and which: Quick, explain the different meanings of these two sentences:

- Bill Clinton favored welfare reforms that provided incentives to work.
- Bill Clinton favored welfare reforms, which provided incentives to work.

The first sentence, using *that*, is restrictive. It means that Clinton favored only those welfare reforms that went hand-in-hand with work incentives. *That* connects the noun and its descriptor. According to this passage, Clinton can support only reform with work incentives.

The second sentence, using *which*, makes a looser connection to the noun. In this example, *which* simply modifies "welfare reforms." We do not know whether Clinton would insist on the work provisions, only that work provisions are connected to welfare reform.

The comma offers the marker we need to make the distinction. A comma never precedes *that*; a comma always precedes *which*. Think of the comma as a pause for parenthetical information.

There, their, and they're: *There* refers to location, *their* to ownership, and *they're* to a group in the state of being. So: *As long as you are there, tell me if they're finished planting their gardens.*

Who and whom: Ask not for whom this question matters; it matters for thee.

Who serves as a subject; *whom* serves as an object. Just remember this simple question: *Who does what to whom?* If you remember that, you'll always remember the distinction.

Laissez-faire grammarians do not care about the who/whom distinction anymore because, they say, we can tell what the speaker means in either case. Use of whom, furthermore, sounds stiff, especially to the casual ears of 21st-century Americans. *Whom would you like to ask to the school dance?* That sounds a little prim, right?

Still, I think it makes sense to stick with this simple rule. When you see *who*, you know it's a subject. When you see *whom*, you know it's an object. I don't care who you are or for whom you write. Use these words precisely.

These grammatical distinctions sometimes seem picky. But they still matter. More precision beats less precision, every time.

CASE STUDY: WILLIAM SAFIRE, 'ON LANGUAGE'

For three decades, William Safire reigned as America's popular arbiter of usage. With a grammarian's precision and a dash of humor, Safire pronounced on everything from the parts of speech to sentence structures, from Newspeak to neologisms, from pithy quotations to complex rules of grammar.

In his "On Language" column for *The New York Times*, Safire offered a list of 16 "fumblerules"—mistakes that illustrate rules of proper English—including:

- No sentence fragments.
- It behooves us to avoid archaisms.
- Also, avoid awkward or affected alliteration.
- Avoid commas, that are not necessary.
- Verbs has to agree with their subjects.
- Writing carefully, dangling participles should not be used.
- Never use a long word when a diminutive one will do.
- Last but not least, avoid clichés like the plague.

All of which raises a question: Just how fixed are the rules of grammar? Like the U.S. Constitution, the English language is a living thing. It evolves with new ideas and habits.

Consider one example that rankles American word mavens: the use of *their* for singular entities. Proper American English requires that we say Harvard won *its* game against Yale; in Britain, they say Oxford won *their* match against Cambridge. But in everyday speech, most Americans follow the Brits; they say *their* when referring to a collective such as a country, university, team, or business. Americans also now say *their* to refer to people of indefinite gender: "The next mayor's going to have their hands full." I don't like it, but I can't prevent it. Besides, we have bigger problems to solve.

Some people resist language's evolution. The purists correct you when you talk about your son's school or its principal with a *they*. If they don't correct you, they grimace.

The casual speaker will shrug and get on with their life. They know they're on the winning side.

———

AND ANOTHER THING . . .

To succeed in any field—sports, music, speaking, cooking, or writing, to name a handful—you need to perform a number of actions automatically. When you do, you free your mind for creative work.

Grammar should come automatically, almost all the time. When you construct a sentence, you need to use proper grammar and punctuation without thinking too much. If you must stop to think about the basics, you lose your focus on what you want to say.

Grammar offers a simple system to structure writing. When you know how use periods, commas, colons, and other punctuation, you don't have to think too much. You can concentrate on the action or ideas you want to describe.

To be sure, rules of grammar sometimes seem arcane and pointless. Rules sometimes contradict each other—and sometimes they make simple communication difficult. George Eliot called grammar "the slang of prigs." Winston Churchill agreed. He famously mocked the rule against ending sentences with prepositions: "This is the kind of tedious nonsense up with which I will not put."

Grammar irritates and vexes almost everyone. But it also makes communication possible. It provides the rules of the road. If you follow the core rules, you can focus on reaching your destination.

CHAPTER 13
EDITING

Whenever you feel an impulse to perpetrate a piece of exceptionally fine writing, obey it—wholeheartedly—and delete it before sending your manuscript to press. Murder your darlings.

SIR ARTHUR QUILLER-COUCH

A MAN ARRIVES at his new apartment, eager to settle in. He looks around, imagining life in his new home. The movers arrive. They bring chairs, tables, wardrobes, a bed, boxes of books, and art. Quickly, the apartment fills up. But the boxes and furniture keep coming. Before long, the man can no longer move around.

> Gentleman: *What is it that's left?*
> First Furniture Mover: *Wardrobes.*
> Gentleman: *The green and purple ones?*
> Second Furniture Mover: *Yes.*
> First Furniture Mover: *And that's not all. There's more to come.*
> Second Furniture Mover: *The staircase is jammed from top to bottom. Nobody can get up or down.*
> Gentleman: *The yard is cram-full too. So is the street.*
> First Furniture Mover: *The traffic's come to a standstill in the town. Full of furniture.*

In his absurdist play *The New Tenant,* Eugene Ionesco captures this dilemma of modern society. We have too much stuff; we are, as one critic has noted, "stifled in a sea of inert matter." We do not know how to control our environments or lives. We let things and events control us.

The same problem happens in writing. In the age of the computer, we produce endless screens of words—emails and memos, texts and tweets, social media comments and more. *It just keeps coming.* Like the man in the apartment, we struggle to move through that clutter.

The writer's primary job is to help the reader see the world clearly. Only when you clear away junk can the reader understand your point.

Writers usually say too much in first drafts. The best writers revise their work, over and over, cutting and rewriting words, phrases, sentences, and paragraphs. William Faulkner once teased Thomas Wolfe for his wordy prose: "You're a putter-inner and I'm a taker-outer." Go ahead, put in all you want. But be a relentless taker-outer too. All of which leads us to the most important single fact about writing. No writer just writes. A good writer needs to be a good editor too. As Fran Lebowitz has said, "all writing is editing."

Critique every word, sentence, and paragraph—over and over. You will be in good company. Ernest Hemingway rewrote the ending to *A Farewell to Arms* 39 times. James Thurber rewrote "The Train on Track Six," 15 times. "There must have been close to 240,000 words in all the manuscripts put together, and I must have spent 2,000 hours working on it," he said. "Yet the finished version can't be more than 20,000 words." Do the math. That's one hour for every ten words.

The goal of editing? To make every word do work. William Strunk and E.B. White, in their classic *The Elements of Style,* explain:

> Vigorous writing is concise. A sentence should contain no unnecessary words, a paragraph no unnecessary sentences, for the same reason a drawing should contain no unnecessary lines and a machine no unnecessary parts. This requires not that the writer make all his sentences short, or that he avoid all detail and treat his subjects only in outline, but that *every word tell.*

Use only the words you need and leave the rest behind.

Editing often feels tedious. But it offers an adventure, if you have the right attitude. Like a detective searching for clues, a good editor seeks out clumsy phrases, passive voices, unnecessary words and phrases. After finding them, he rewrites or cuts clunky or superfluous passages. He clears away the dross, making it possible to see what matters.

Take time off after you write a draft. Clear your head before editing. When you work on a piece for a long time, you suffer familiarity blindness. You do not what's in front of you because you've been looking at it for too long.

————

ELEMENT 50: SEARCH AND DESTROY, FROM BIG TO SMALL

Suppose you wanted to remodel your kitchen. Which approach would you take?

- **Option 1**. Remove whatever walls, cabinets, and flooring you want to replace; rewire and replumb the room; replace the walls, cabinets, and flooring; install appliances; paint the walls; put in light and electrical fixtures.
- **Option 2**. Paint walls, remove the walls, remove and replace cabinets, install fixtures, replace the plumbing, remove and replace flooring, retool electrical systems, and so on.

Option 1 works best. Why? First, by starting with the big tasks, you avoid repeating work. If you paint before removing and replacing walls and cabinets, you will need to paint again. Second, by moving from one discrete task to another, you avoid overwhelming your brain. We work best when we give a task our total attention. When we try to do more than one thing at a time, we struggle.

Most editors review drafts paragraph by paragraph, chapter by chapter. As they edit their pieces, they check for structure, word choice, noun-pronoun-verb agreement, accuracy, verb tenses, hanging participles, punctuation, spelling, style, and so on.

That's fine with short pieces or near-perfect drafts. But when we try to do too many tasks at once with rougher drafts, we get overwhelmed and lose focus. We simply cannot deal with the full range of issues—from the basic structure down to the minute details—all at once.

The brain loves simple, clear tasks. When you only search for one problem at a time, you stay sharp. You spot problems better and don't run out of energy. Therefore, follow this simple approach to editing: Start big, working your way to smaller issues, one challenge at a time. Let's see how to do it.

Start by blocking sections. Most writing—even pieces as short as a two-page memo or a newspaper op-ed article—consists of a number of chunks. Each chunk presents a distinct idea.

Put a label on each major section. It's easier to manage a handful of well-marked sections, each with well-marked parts, than a piece with 75 unmarked parts.

For each section, express a clear "umbrella" concept. Everything in that section should fall under the umbrella. If you veer off topic, cut it or move the stray pieces.

Make sure your whole piece starts and end strongly. Make sure all its sections do as well. Consider writing the first and last paragraphs before anything else. If you know the beginnings and endings of your journeys, the pieces in the middle sort themselves out easily.

Label ideas in paragraphs. Every paragraph should take the reader on a simple journey, starting and finishing strongly. Make every paragraph a mini-journey, following Aristotle's narrative arc. Make sure you can explain each mini-journey with a simple tabloid headline. Make sure just glancing at your paragraph labels reminds you, instantly, about what journey it takes the reader. (More on this point in a moment.)

Check sentences for the Golden Rule. Make sure every sentence takes a journey, starting and finishing strongly.

Find the modifiers that make sentences run on and on. Sometimes it seems that crafting a simple sentence is the toughest chore of writing. As our minds whir with ideas, we get tempted to veer off track. Then we fail to make our simple points.

Often, we get off track with prepositional phrases. Prepositional phrases offer details about the subject; they modify the topic under discussion. Prepositions, remember, express relationships between things. The most common prepositions—*of, to, in, for, on, with, out, from, by*, and *out*—are among the 37 most commonly used words in the English language. Notice how the prepositions work:

- Franklin Roosevelt was the son *of* a wealthy family *from* Hyde Park.

- Jimmy Carter came *from* a town *in* southern Georgia.
- I once lived *in* a house *by* the side *of* the Mississippi River.

These prepositional phrases provide useful information. But when you put too many of these ideas into a sentence, you lose sight of the main action—*who's doing what to whom*. The reader struggles to keep up with the twists and turns.

Let's look at an example from an academic history journal:

> After the Second World War, the general drift of American public opinion toward a more liberal racial attitude that had begun during the New Deal became accentuated as a result of the revolution against Western Imperialism in Asia and Africa that engendered a new respect for the nonwhite peoples of the world, and as a result of the subsequent competition for the support of the uncommitted nations connected with the Cold War.

In this 72-word sentence, the author uses 16 prepositions—*after, of, toward, during, as, of, against, in, that, for, of, as, of, for, of,* and *with.* Each one adds a new thought, but pulls the passage off course. It's overwhelming, like asking a driver to turn 16 times to travel a short distance. To rewrite that passage, I broke it up. Look at this new version:

> After World War II, Americans adopted more liberal attitudes about race. The New Deal began this process. Revolutions against imperial powers in Asia and Africa created new respect for the nonwhite populations. The Cold War also prompted the U.S. to consider how racial strife damaged America's image.

The revision breaks one monster sentence into three ordinary sentences. The new passage uses 47 words, 25 fewer than the original passage. And it uses only five prepositions—*about, against, in, for,* and *in*—instead of 16. That's fewer than two prepositions per sentence—a more manageable number of twists and turns for the reader.

Root out repetition and needless words. Most drafts contain meandering, repetitious, and clumsy phrasing.

Too often, writers repeat ideas by using just slightly different words for the same thing. Politicians say they will care for "each and every" voter. Business executives tell us that "first and foremost," we have to cut costs. Advertisements offer a "free gift" for opening a bank account. We also hear people talk about *future plans, end results, armed gunmen, unconfirmed rumors, living survivors, past history, actual experience, advanced planning*, and *natural instincts*. Each of those expressions repeats a simple idea. So cut 'em!

Eliminate hedges and emphatics. Too often, when we want to emphasize a point, we use vague language.

An emphatic shows strength of conviction but lacks adequate evidence or certainty. Emphatics assert something without showing it. *As everyone knows* is a classic emphatic. So are *of course, naturally, understandably, usually, almost always, interestingly*, and *surprisingly*. Consider this passage from a portrait of Andrew Carnegie:

> The Carnegies were poor—very poor—but not quite destitute. Their home was a hovel, but not quite a hellhole. Allegheny, Pittsburgh, and the environs were ugly and just plain awful. But there were worse places in the world then, and there are now.

The passage tells us little. The author wants to emphasize points with locutions like "very poor" and "just plain awful"; he backs off his points when he refers to "a hovel, but not quite a hellhole." The author would do better note the food the Carnegies ate, the clothes they wore, the size and furnishings of their home, and whether they had heat and water. Details, not emphatics and hedges, offer a clear picture.

A hedge makes a grand statement and then backs off that statement. By expressing conditions or exceptions, the hedge tells the reader, in effect, "I'm not *completely* sure what I'm going to tell you." Hedges include words like *almost, virtually, perhaps, maybe*, and *somewhat*. Such words pretend to modify a point, but give the reader little real information. Writers use them to avoid taking a clear, distinct stand.

Address details, one by one. Now address all the other problems: spelling and punctuation, noun-verb and non-pronoun agreements, adjectives and adverbs, dangling modifiers, passive verbs and imprecise nouns.

As you move from big to small problems, you'll see something amazing. By fixing the big problems, many smaller problems disappear. Why? When we structure a piece poorly—with the wrong chapters or sections, arranged poorly—we lose clarity about the smaller points. Because we're fuzzy on the big stuff, we're fuzzy on the little stuff. So when we get the big pieces right, the smaller pieces take care of themselves.

CASE STUDY: ROY BHASKAR, *PLATO, ETC.*

For four years, the journal *Philosophy and Literature* conducted a contest to identify the worst academic prose published the previous year. Roy Bhaskar "won" the prize in 1996 with this passage:

> Indeed dialectical critical realism may be seen under the aspect of Foucauldian strategic reversal—of the unholy trinity of Parmenidean/Platonic/Aristotelean provenance; of the Cartesian-Lockean-Humean-Kantian paradigm, of foundationalisms (in practice, fideistic foundationalisms) and irrationalisms (in practice, capricious exercises of the will-to-power or some other ideologically and/or psycho-somatically buried source) new and old alike; of the primordial failing of western philosophy, ontological monovalence, and its close ally, the epistemic fallacy with its ontic dual; of the analytic problematic laid down by Plato, which Hegel served only to replicate in his actu-alist monovalent analytic reinstatement in transfigurative reconciling dialectical connection, while in his hubristic claims for absolute idealism he inaugurated the Comtean, Kierkegaardian and Nietzschean eclipses of reason, replicating the fundaments of positivism through its transmutation route to the superidealism of a Baudrillard.

OMG, I'm speechless. How do you make sense of this monstrosity? Let's get to work.

First of all, note that this 130-word sentence contains 23 preposi-tional phrases (beginning with prepositions like *under, of, in, for,* and *to*). Each prepositional phrase modifies something.

The sentence has two main parts. In the first part (from "Indeed" to the em-dash), Bhaskar introduces the idea of the Foucauldian reversal. In the second part (from "of the unholy" to the end), he says what gets reversed. You can state his whole argument with the simple sentence:

> Foucault's approach [subject] reversed [verb] previous philosophical traditions [object].

Ah, simplicity! But hold on. Stated that way, the whole passage looks pointless. So let's dig deeper. To start, should Bhaskar lump together all of these figures: Parmenides, Plato, Aristotle, Descartes, Locke, Hume, Kant, Comte, Kierkegaard, Nietzsche, Hegel, and Baudrillard? I mean, seriously. Why not throw in the Marx Brothers too?

Bhaskar wanted to say that Foucault challenged a wide range of thinkers and ideas. Great. I agree. Bhaskar also wants to say that competing traditions shared some underlying assumptions. Again, great.

Bhaskar gets lost because he wants to talk about too many ideas at the same time. To fix this passage, he needs to say what he means, point by point. In this case, start by looking at all the philosophical traditions that Bkaskar says Foucault *et al.* reversed:

- The Parmenidean/Platonic/Aristotelean "unholy trinity."
- The Cartesian-Lockean-Humean-Kantian paradigm.
- Foundationalisms.
- Irrationalisms.
- "The primordial failing of western philosophy, ontological monovalence, and its close ally, the epistemic fallacy with its ontic dual."
- Plato's "problematic," which "Hegel served only to replicate," blah blah blah.
- Other stuff.

Whew. Did I get that right? I'm not sure, but at least we have a clear statement of the different targets of Foucault's work. The next step is to "chunk" related ideas. Here, we organize the ideas into two groups (indicated below with italics):

Foucault's approach undercut the *ancient debates* about idealism and materialism. Foucault also challenged the *extensions of those debates*— including Kant's demand for rationality, Descartes' separation of mind and body, and Nietzsche's appeal to primal urges.

The most important lesson: Take your time. Keep it simple. If you have to explore a lot of ideas, take them one by one. There's no rush. So describe your ideas, as simply as possible, one at a time.

ELEMENT 51: FIX PROBLEM PARAGRAPHS WITH TABLOID HEADLINES

"Writing, like life," Henry Miller once said, "is a voyage of discovery." In that voyage, we often get tempted to wander off the path.

You begin writing a paragraph with one idea in mind. That reminds you of another idea, which reminds you of another idea, and so on. Before you know it, you have veered far from the first idea—without offering adequate evidence for it. You might not even remember where you intended to go. And if you don't remember your destination, how can the reader?

How should we deal with unruly paragraphs? The solution is simple. Just *label every idea in every paragraph*. Come up with a short label—three to five words—that describes the idea. When a paragraph contains more than one idea, break it up into as many paragraphs as ideas.

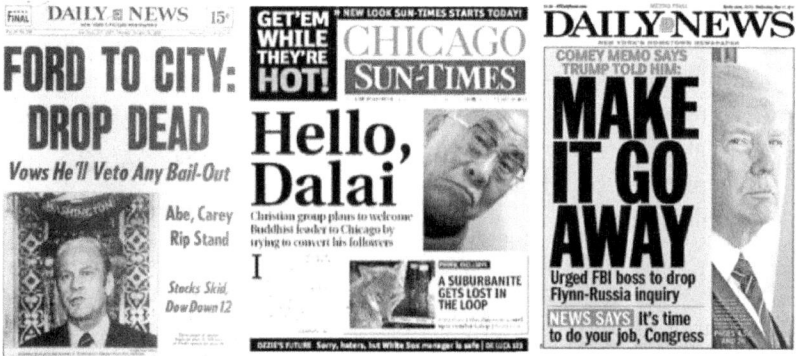

Write your labels like tabloid headlines. At their best, tabloid headlines capture the essence of the story. They also give stories sizzle and intrigue. Take a look at these three tabloid headlines. The first reports President Gerald Ford's rejection of federal loans to New York City during the 1975 fiscal crisis. The second reports the Dalai Llama's trip to the U.S. The third reports President Donald Trump's frustration with the FBI investigation of his campaign's collusion with Russia.

Labeling paragraphs *always* works. When you put pithy tags on paragraphs, you can quickly grasp all the ideas in a piece. When you repeat myself or veer off course, you can see it—and then fix it.

CASE STUDY: JOHN STUART MILL, *ON LIBERTY*

A century and a half ago, John Stuart Mill published *On Liberty*, the classic manifesto of freedom of conscience and expression. Mill argues for a philosophy called utilitarianism—which endorses policies that promote "the greatest happiness for the greatest number"—rather than natural rights.

See how Mill makes his case. See if you can identify a single idea that unites the paragraph—or whether Mill actually expresses several ideas:

> It is proper to state that I forego any advantage which could be derived to my argument from the idea of abstract right as a thing independent of utility. I regard utility as the ultimate appeal on all ethical questions; but it must be utility in the largest sense, grounded on the permanent interests of man as a progressive being. Those interests, I contend, authorize the subjection of individual spontaneity to external control, only in respect to those actions of each, which concern the interest of other people. If any one does an act hurtful to others, there is a *prima facie* case for punishing him, by law, or, where legal penalties are not safely applicable, by general disapprobation. There are also many positive acts for the benefit of others, which he may rightfully be compelled to perform; such as, to give evidence in a court of justice; to bear his fair share in the common defence, or in any other joint work necessary to the interest of the society of which he enjoys the protection; and to perform certain acts of individual beneficence, such as saving a fellow-creature's life, or interposing to protect the defenceless against ill-usage, things which whenever it is obviously a man's duty to do, he may rightfully be made responsible to society for not doing. A person may cause evil to others not only by his actions but by his inaction, and in either case he is justly accountable to them for the injury. The latter case, it is true, requires a much more cautious exercise of compulsion than the former. To make any one answerable for doing evil to others, is the rule; to make him answerable for not preventing evil, is, comparatively speaking, the exception. Yet there are many cases clear enough and grave enough to justify that exception. In all things which regard

the external relations of the individual, he is *de jure* amenable to those whose interests are concerned, and if need be, to society as their protector. There are often good reasons for not holding him to the responsibility; but these reasons must arise from the special expediencies of the case: either because it is a kind of case in which he is on the whole likely to act better, when left to his own discretion, than when controlled in any way in which society have it in their power to control him; or because the attempt to exercise control would produce other evils, greater than those which it would prevent. When such reasons as these preclude the enforcement of responsibility, the conscience of the agent himself should step into the vacant judgment-seat, and protect those interests of others which have no external protection; judging himself all the more rigidly, because the case does not admit of his being made accountable to the judgment of his fellow-creatures.

How did you do? Did you struggle to tease out Mill's main argument? Did you get confused when he changed the subject?

By my count, Mill makes six distinct arguments in this 477-word paragraph. He explores one point, then moves into another, then another, and so on. In Mill's day, this style worked well. Readers— almost always educated elites—took time to concentrate on their reading. They did not contend with the information overload of the 21st century. But we modern readers struggle to read long, dense paragraphs like this.

When I have taught Mill's work in my college classes, I encouraged my students to note each distinctive idea in the margins. That way, they could track Mill's argument, point by point. Most readers are unwilling to take such an active role reading and marking a piece of writing. It's the writer's job to sort ideas for the reader.

Here's how a modern-day Mill might have broken up this passage. Each of the new paragraphs, as you can see from my tabloid-style labels, explores a distinct point.

Forget rights! Utility's the way to go: It is proper to state that I forego any advantage which could be derived to my argument from the idea of abstract right as a thing independent of utility. I regard utility as the ultimate appeal on all ethical questions; but it must be utility in the largest sense, grounded on the permanent interests of man as a progressive being.

Do no harm: Those interests, I contend, authorize the subjection of individual spontaneity to external control, only in respect to those actions of each, which concern the interest of other people. If any one does an act hurtful to others, there is a *prima facie* case for punishing him, by law, or, where legal penalties are not safely applicable, by general disapprobation.

When force is OK: There are also many positive acts for the benefit of others, which he may rightfully be compelled to perform; such as, to give evidence in a court of justice; to bear his fair share in the common defence, or in any other joint work necessary to the interest of the society of which he enjoys the protection; and to perform certain acts of individual beneficence, such as saving a fellow-creature's life, or interposing to protect the defenceless against ill-usage, things which whenever it is obviously a man's duty to do, he may rightfully be made responsible to society for not doing.

Sometimes it's what you *don't do* that matters: A person may cause evil to others not only by his actions but by his inaction, and in either case he is justly accountable to them for the injury. The latter case, it is true, requires a much more cautious exercise of compulsion than the former. To make any one answerable for doing evil to others, is the rule; to make him answerable for not preventing evil, is, comparatively speaking, the exception. Yet there are many cases clear enough and grave enough to justify that exception. In all things which regard the external relations of the individual, he is *de jure* amenable to those whose interests are concerned, and if need be, to society as their protector.

When to let 'em off the hook: There are often good reasons for not holding him to the responsibility; but these reasons must arise from the special expediencies of the case: either because it is a kind of case in which he is on the whole likely to act better, when left to his own discretion, than when controlled in any way in which society have it in their power to control him; or because the attempt to exercise control would produce other evils, greater than those which it would prevent.

Do the right thing: When such reasons as these preclude the enforcement of responsibility, the conscience of the agent himself should step into the vacant judgment-seat, and protect those interests of others which have no external protection; judging himself all the more rigidly, because the case does not admit of his being made accountable to the judgment of his fellow-creatures.

Organized in these compact paragraphs, Mill's argument hops nicely from point to point. His writing is too flowery and wordy for modern readers, but he makes each point well.

―――

ELEMENT 52: EDIT BY READING ALOUD AND BACKWARD

For most of history, storytellers told their tales aloud. They recounted, from memory, great myths, histories, comedies, and tragedies. Audiences served as focus groups. When audiences responded well to a phrase or a passage, it stayed; when readers got bored or confused, the storyteller revised the piece.

These days, alas, writers usually labor in isolation. We write our drafts, in isolation from others. Sometimes we share drafts with friends and colleagues. But rarely do we read our pieces aloud.

As we review drafts, we glide over passages. Because of "familiarity blindness," the tendency not to notice details we have seen over and over, we don't pay careful attention to the the details. The more we know something, the less we pay attention to it. We skim. So we miss details. Did you notice, for example, that I used the word *the* twice in a row in this paragraph? Most people don't.

Consider two options for active editing. Read your drafts aloud, fast or slowly, to yourself or to others. Or work backwards.

Read aloud: Reading aloud helps you find clumsy or ungrammatical passages. Any time you stumble while reading a passage, something's wrong.

When you read aloud, ask yourself: *Does one idea lead to the next? Can you follow the story or argument? Does the piece stay on track?* Also pay attention to the technical issues, like typos and clumsy, wordy, or vague passages. As you read a piece, mark the clunky phrases and errors. Then you can go back and make corrections.

Pick up a great book—a classic—right now. Read something by Truman Capote or John McPhee or Toni Morrison. Find the poetry of Wordsworth or Shakespeare or T.S. Eliot or Isabel Wilkerson. Or find a well-edited magazine, like *The Atlantic*. Read a passage aloud. Notice how the words glide.

Speed editing: Try reading fast. In fact, readitsofastrunningallthewordstogetherthatyoustumble. Speed-talking reveals the clunky passages better than reading at a normal pace. You can read good writing fast, but flawed writing causes you to stumble. When you read fast, you are forced to activate your whole brain. You have to concentrate. Your whole body gets into it.

Read backwards. To combat familiarity, read backwards. Read the last paragraph first, then the paragraph before that, then the one before that, and so on. You will be surprised at how easily you can spot—and kill—bad and repetitive writing.

By reading backwards, you also see the piece's outline . Does paragraph 17 logically follow paragraph 16? Does paragraph 7 develop the ideas of paragraph 6?

To master their skills, athletes often work backwards. They imagine the result they want—say, a tennis ball landing just beyond the reach of the opponent—and then think backwards. After imagining the ball landing, the player imagines the ball flying across the net ... hitting the ball ... bringing the racket back ... and getting into position.

The ancient Greeks knew the importance of building from the end. Herodotus said: "One should always look to the end of everything, how it will finally come out." Think of writing that way. Think of how you want to complete a passage, and then what came before, and then what came before that, and so on.

CASE STUDY: SARAH KENDZIOR, *THE VIEW FROM FLYOVER COUNTRY*

Read this passage, sentence by sentence:

> Do not rejoice at the fall of the mall. The setting may have been artificial, but the people in it were real.
> [D]owntowns [were] replaced by malls [which were] replaced by nothing. ...
> Our connections and commerce are [now] dependent on our screens. Pay attention, pay attention, to the men behind the screens.
> Malls were once castigated for turning consumers into zombies. Now, the zombie is the ideal online retail employee, unthinking and robotic. Advice by algorithm, delivery by drone: This is what a dehumanized landscape looks like. ...
> The fall of the mall is a problem for the consumer: With local

> *businesses decimated and chain stores departed, those*
> *without Internet access and credit cards can struggle to*
> *procure goods. But the fall of the mall is a bigger problem*
> *for low-skill workers. …*
> *Between 2000-2011, suburban poverty surged 67 percent,*
> *as gentrification forced city residents from their homes.*
> *Mid-tier malls that depended on middle-class shoppers*
> *faltered, as the middle class shrank. …*
> *The rise in online shopping has been blamed for the demise of*
> *the mall. But some economic analysts see a more basic*
> *problem [of rising inequality].*

You might find the experience odd, but you get Sarah Kendzior's point. She is arguing that the decline of the shopping mall was a sign of economic loss for poor and working class people. Malls disappear because people nearby no longer have the money to spend in them. When people stop spending, stores close; when mall stores close, they lay off hundreds of people at a time.

Now read the passage backward. Actually, I must confess: When you read it backward, you will actually be reading it in the order that Kendzior composed it.

When you read something backwards, it usually makes sense. But its slight oddness, its unfamiliarity, slows you down. That causes you to pay greater attention to sentence structure, grammar, and spelling. That's what you want to do as an editor: Slow down, so you can see what you might otherwise miss.

————

ELEMENT 53: MURDER YOUR DARLINGS

Something extraordinary happens when we write. We develop a relationship with our words. We fall in love, with all the blindness that love brings.

When we write well—or just *think* we write well—we treat our paragraphs, sentences, and even phrases with affection. When we turn a phrase well, or offer a telling detail about a person or place or action, we look on our passages with reverence.

But sometimes we need to delete a well-turned phrase—or even a whole section, consisting of many well-turned phrases.

Why? As noted before, we often veer off track. The process of discovery takes us into unexpected territory. We start a project thinking that X is the most important idea, only to discover that Y or Z are interesting too. And so we veer off track to talk about Y and Z.

Act other times, eager to persuade the reader, we accumulate too much detail and evidence. We don't select the most telling or persuasive information; we use it all. Lawyers often do this in legal arguments. Knowing that judges and juries will not necessarily respond to the essential point, they throw everything into their briefs and arguments. But don't follow the lawyer's approach. Make a point, offer evidence, and move on.

If you think you have written something beautiful, be careful. Your emotional attachment to that passage might signal danger. You might love a phrase or an idea so much that you don't realize that it actually *stinks*.

The ultimate test of any passage—any sentence, paragraph, or section—is whether it states a clear idea and then provides supporting evidence. Track down the unnecessary passages and words and ruthlessly excise them. When you cut a passage, even one you adore, you give room for other passages to shine.

You're still reluctant o cut too much, right? If you worked on a passage and really like it, even if it does not contribute to your point, you don't want to kill it forever. The answer is simple. Create a files for the stuff you cut. I call these files my "darling" files—after the comment by Sir Arthur Quiller Couch at the beginning of this chapter.

CASE STUDY: NYCEDC, 'NEW YORK WORKS'

In the spring of 2017, I wrote a draft report for the New York City Economic Development Corporation, outlining a strategy to create 100,000 middle-class jobs in the next decade.

Writing government reports is a tricky proposition. The report's major goal is to speak to the people of the city—to create a dialogue about our common challenges and how we can work together. But every passage of a government report is fraught with political danger. Innocent-sounding words and phrases can alienate key constituencies. So if you write for government or corporate entities, be ready to murder your darlings. In my draft, this passage got cut:

The area around Grand Central Station is one of the most important legal and financial centers in the U.S., with a growing tech sector as well. With 70 million square feet of office space, 200,000 workers, and the city's greatest transportation center, Midtown East is home of some of urban America's greatest landmarks, from the Lever House and Roosevelt Hotel to the Chrysler Building. But the area's office buildings have become outdated, with low ceilings and outdated technology. To compete with other Class A office centers around the world, the district needs to build new structures and update its existing stock.

Rather than rezoning the whole area, the city and community have agreed to rezone a Grand Central subdistrict. The process comes at an auspicious time. Two transit projects—the Second Avenue subway line and the East Side Access—improve connections to the rest of the city and region. The Second Avenue line began operation in 2017 along six stops; it will expand in coming years. The East Side Access, scheduled to open in 2019, will bring the Long Island Rail Road lines from Penn Station to Grand Central.

The strategy strikes a balance between historic preservation and the need for state-of-the-art Class A office buildings. To leverage this change, the plan uses air rights and FAR bonuses to provide incentives for new development and rehabilitation.

Now, here's how we rewrote that section in the final report:

The Greater East Midtown business district is one of the largest job centers in the region and provides many of the world's highest-profile business addresses. It contains more than 60 million square feet of office space, more than a quarter million jobs, and numerous Fortune 500 companies. However, the area faces a number of long-term challenges: aging building stock, limited recent office development (and few available office development sites), an existing zoning framework that hinders new office development, and public spaces and transit infrastructure that are stretched to capacity.

Gone is the background information about landmark buildings and zoning processes. When I drafted this report, I thought these details offered important context. But the powers-that-be in New York's city government decided otherwise. Too much history, they said, detracted from the urgent message. To quote Joe Friday on *Dragnet*, the old TV series, they wanted "just the facts, ma'am." So we cut this passage. We murdered my darling.

————

AND ANOTHER THING . . .

Editing is hard for two reasons. First, we don't like to admit our mistakes. Even when we want to catch errors, we get defensive when we realize that our writing is clumsy or confusing.

Second, when we read a text from beginning to end, we have a hard time spotting many problems. Why? Take a look at this passage and count the number of times you see the letter F.

FINISHED FILES ARE THE RESULT OF YEARS OF SCIENTIFIC STUDY COMBINED WITH THE EXPERIENCE OF YEARS.

Most people find only three F's because they glide over the three instances of the word "of." Hence the great challenge of editing: the difficulty in noticing familiar words, phrases, and punctuation.

If you have a hard time finding F's, you will experience even more difficulty spotting other problems. When you edit, after all, you need to check for a wide variety of issues—verb use, noun-verb agreement, punctuation, excess verbiage, precision of word choice, and a number of stylistic issues. It's just too much.

The answer? Break down the problem, from big to small pieces. Then, piece by piece, check one issue at a time. Don't try to check and fix all of the potential problems at the same time. You will only burn yourself out—and all kinds of errors and problems.

William Faulkner deserves the final word on editing. An interviewer for *The Paris Review* once asked him to provide a formula for becoming a good novelist "Ninety-nine percent talent," he said. "Ninety-nine percent discipline. Ninety-nine percent work. He must never be satisfied with what he does. It never is as good as it can be done."

So it takes 297 percent effort to be a great writer. Daunting, yes, but doable.

PART FIVE
EXPLAINING A PROCESS

Once we can describe simple actions, we can describe the more complex processes that shape our world.

A *process* is a complex *sequence of related actions*. Processes might include weather systems, streams of traffic converging into a city, strategies for teaching a foreign language, planning for a banquet, and the spread of a virus in a population.

Suppose we wanted to explore the life of a city park—the park's uses, designs, support, activities, meaning, and related matters. Think of the parks as a collection of a number of different actions and processes—or *vectors*. Understanding the complex processes of parks might look like this:

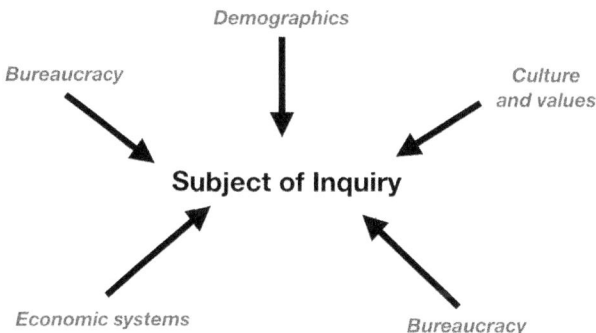

Demographics

Bureaucracy

Culture and values

Subject of Inquiry

Economic systems

Bureaucracy

For each vector, we might describe a set of actions. For demographics, for example, we might describe how different groups (male and female, young and old, professional and working class, students and visitors, and so on) use the parks. To explore culture and values, we might observe how people with different backgrounds, interests, group identifications, and so on, interact in the park.

The trick is to identify the relevant sequences and relationships, gather information about how they work, and then organize them in a logical way. The trick is to organize your thoughts into separate pieces, so the reader can absorb information without feeling overwhelmed. Describe one sequence at a time, with the most important sequences first.

Avoid too much generalization. Describe what you can observe, action by action.

THE PLAN OF ATTACK

As always, we will start with two skills of gathering and understanding content. Specifically, we want to learn how to focus on a topic and how to follow its movements.

- Chapter 14: Framing
- Chapter 15: Rhythm and Beats

Then we will take on two new skills of writing mechanics:

- Chapter 16: Composition
- Chapter 17: Numbers

A complex process is really a collection of simple actions. The trick is to identify those actions and put them in the right sequence. Make sure to organize those sequences in a logical way, so the reader can absorb the information without feeling overwhelmed. Describe one sequence at a time, with the most important sequences first.

CHAPTER 14
FRAMING

When you can measure what you are speaking about, and express it in numbers, you know something about it; but when you cannot measure it, when you cannot express it in numbers, your knowledge is of a meager and unsatisfactory kind; it may be the beginning of knowledge, but you have scarcely in your thoughts advanced to the state of Science, whatever the matter may be.

LORD KELVIN

THE WORLD IS A COMPLEX PLACE. To understand that complexity, ironically, we need to pretend it's simple.

That's why we use maps. A map condenses reality into a small, manageable piece. A wall map of San Francisco, for example, reduces 47 square miles to about six square feet. By focusing on a few features —roads, parks, landmark buildings—we can understand what we need to know. At the same time, we purposely ignore a lot more.

Could we do more? Could we add some lush details, like the size and shapes of homes or the pathways in parks? Sure. Different maps emphasize different things: roads, buildings, parks, utilities, population. But if we pack too much information onto the map, it loses its power to display patterns clearly.

Lewis Carroll expresses this dilemma in an absurdist story called

"Sylvie and Bruno." A character named Mein Herr explains his idea for a full-scale map:

> "And then came the grandest idea of all! We actually made a map of the country, on the scale of a mile to the mile!"
>
> "Have you used it much?" I enquired.
>
> "It has never been spread out, yet," said Mein Herr. "The farmers objected: they said it would cover the whole country, and shut out the sunlight! So we now use the country itself, as its own map, and I assure you it does nearly as well."

Analysts simplify the world in three ways. First, they listen to experts reduce complex things into pithy summaries. Second, they conduct mind experiments. Third, they build and use models to express complex ideas simply.

The key is finding the right "frame." A frame determines what we look at and what we don't. Just as a picture frame draws our attention inward, mental frames tell us where to focus. Whatever lies outside the frame is considered unworthy of attention, at least at the moment.

Suppose we go to a dinner party. When we arrive, we see the host greeting guests, with an exaggerated bonhomie. Meanwhile, her partner earnestly talks with other guests while he finishes preparing dinner in the kitchen. The couple's child, oblivious to both parents, sits in the TV room immersed in a video game.

What do we see? With one frame, we might see a happy family taking delight in having company. With another frame, we might guess that the man and woman are in the midst of a fight—separate from each other, pretending they're happy but doing everything possible to avoid each other. With another frame, we might see the child alienated from his parents . . . or as an autistic unable to engage other humans . . . or just as a happy kid doing his thing.

The frame we select determines the view we see.

Finding the right frame—the right lens or model or map—can be devilishly difficult. When you simplify the world, you leave out considerations that may matter. A roadmap may work fine for drivers but not for runners, who need to know about sidewalks and hills. A figure ground map, which shows "solids" and "voids," does not distinguish the different kinds of buildings and open spaces. You can distinguish neither the solids (homes, businessses, parking garages, and so on) not the voids (parks, parking lots, streets, and so on).

When you analyze something, try different frames. Try to be conscious of the frame you use—and the ones you do not. Look for your frame's flaws.

————

ELEMENT 54: USE TESTIMONY OF EXPERTS AND OTHERS

Sometimes, the best way to begin a journey is to ask people who know the territory. Testimony from experts often lends more insight than a long and detailed explanation. Think of their insights and advice as shortcuts for your journey. You get the experience and wisdom of a trusted authority, in a pithy form.

When you quote experts, you tap years of their study and analysis. When Nobel laureate Paul Volcker discusses interest rates or deregulation, you listen. When Stephen Hawking describes the black holes, you listen. When Twyla Tharp talks about modern dance, you listen. Experts, of course, disagree on many issues. But expertise deserves respect. When hordes of experts endorse a point of view—when, for example, scientists affirm the dangers of global warming—their testimony deserves even more notice. Still, remain skeptical.

But don't just use quotations for expertise. Also use quotations to lend your writing a fresh voice. Albert Einstein offers a chilling warning about the nuclear age: "I know not with what weapons World War III will be fought, but World War IV will be fought with sticks and stones." Ronald Reagan warns about the fragility of political liberty: "Freedom is never more than one generation away from extinction. We didn't pass it to our children in the bloodstream."

The worst quotations state the obvious. Tautologies—saying that one thing equals or causes that same thing—waste people's time. Athletes often say that "we just need to score more than the other side" to win. I have heard economists tell us that people with more liquid assets have more cash available to spend. And I have heard psychologists explain that couples' arguing indicates danger for their marriages. Do we really need expert testimony on these matters?

(Well ... *sometimes*. Consider that last point about marital arguments. Psychologist John Gottman has found that arguing can *improve* relationships. Couples who argue, and then address their differences constructively, do better than couples who do not argue at all. Gottman can predict a marriage's prospects by watching *how* couples argue, whether they attack each other personally or work to deal with their mutual problems.)

To decide whether to use a quotation, ask yourself: Does the speaker lend special credibility to the issue? Does the quotation's language offer something provocative? Does the quotation reflect something unique about the speaker or issue? If the answers to any of these questions are yes, the quotation might add value to your piece.

CASE STUDY: THE DEBATE OVER GLOBAL WARMING

No issue sparks more controversy—and more invective—than global warming. To Al Gore and other environmentalists, climate change poses the greatest threat civilization has ever known. To skeptics, global warming is a hoax perpetrated by junk scientists, ideologues, and supporters of global government.

Here's what James Hansen, the director of NASA's Goddard Institute for Space Studies, says:

> Our global climate is nearing tipping points. Changes are beginning to appear, and there is a potential for explosive changes with effects that would be irreversible — if we do not rapidly slow fossil fuel emissions over the next few decades. Tipping points are fed by amplifying feedbacks. As Arctic sea ice melts, the darker ocean absorbs more sunlight and speeds melting. As tundra melts, methane, a strong greenhouse gas, is released, causing more warming. As species are pressured and exterminated by shifting climate zones, ecosystems can collapse, destroying more species.

Richard Lendzen, a geophysicist at MIT, disputes Hansen's argument:

> The notion of a static, unchanging climate is foreign to the history of the earth or any other planet with a fluid envelope. The fact that the developed world went into hysterics over changes in global mean temperature anomaly of a few tenths of a degree will astound future generations. Such hysteria simply represents the scientific illiteracy of

much of the public, the susceptibility of the public to the substitution of repetition for truth, and the exploitation of these weaknesses by politicians, environmental promoters, and, after 20 years of media drum beating, many others as well. Climate is always changing.

What are nonexperts to think of his dispute? What pieces of evidence can we trust? Do these passages clear up any issues? Can these scientists agree on *anything*?

We quote experts and lay people not just to get their opinions, but also to see how they frame issues. To frame the issue of global warming, Hansen uses images of chain reactions and tipping points. Lendzen, meanwhile, scoffs that anything more than an "anomaly" is talking place. He frames global climate as a vast phenomenon, which has always experienced shifts over time—not necessarily because of human influences.

These approaches to problem solving guide us to explore the issue further. We can, for example, read more about the chain of events that Hansen says are responsible for our current dilemma. When did that chain of events begin? At what point did it read a critical mass? Was there a tipping point? Is there a point of no return? How might we know?

Who to believe? Not for me to say. But when you gather the data and frame the issues well, you can move toward at least a provisional answer.

––––––

ELEMENT 55. CONSIDER HYPOTHETICALS AND SCENARIOS

Hypothetical situations—imaginary or "what if" stories—often clarify complex problems. A hypothetical says something like this: *What if X happened?* Sometimes these questions are fanciful. But by imagining things that have not happened, you can open your mind.

Much of western philosophy is based on hypotheticals. Philosophers from Thomas Hobbes to John Rawls ask: What would happen if people were to create a government from scratch? What kind of government would people choose? But hypotheticals go beyond philosophical what-ifs. Psychologists test their hypotheticals to discover how people think about choices in their lives. Consider these scenarios from the research of psychologist Daniel Pink:

- How do people respond when offered a choice between deluxe Lindt truffles for 15 cents and Hershey's Kisses for free?
- Why do people switch to a expensive coffee like Starbucks after paying less for a middling brand like Dunkin' Donuts?
- How does a consumer's past behavior affect future choices?

In these hypotheticals, Pink and others try to understand the major causes of people's behavior. Pink does not really care whether you choose Lindt truffles or Hershey's Kisses. He cares about a bigger issue: When do irrational habits trump rational calculation?

Scenarios offer a more robust process for analyzing complex issues. In a scenario, you gather troves of data and attempt to imagine a wide range of possible futures. In a typical scenario exercise, people are asked to consider three possibilities.

- What would happen if everything went gloriously right?
- What would happen if everything went horribly wrong?
- What would happen if things stayed pretty much the same?

The point is to prepare participants—businesses, policy makers, communities, teams—for even the most extreme possibilities. If we can respond well to both extremes, we can probably respond well to the middle scenarios as well.

Peter Schwartz, a leading theorist of scenario-building, explains the scenario process in *The Art of the Long View*:

> Scenarios are not predictions. An old Arab proverb says that "he who predicts the future lies even if he tells the truth." Rather, scenarios are vehicles for helping people learn. Unlike traditional business forecasting or marketing research, they present *alternative images of the future*; they do not merely extrapolate trends of the present.

Policy analysts use scenarios to explore a whole range of important issues. What if terrorists target subway systems for chemical attacks? What if scientists discover a prohibitively expensive cure for cancer?

What if global warming increases average temperatures around the world by 1 degree in the next 20 years? What if China's protectionist policies lead to U.S. retaliation? What if Americans do not get off their "SAD" diet of grease, sugar, and salt?

The scenario-building process moves through three stages:

- **Research**: Collect rafts of information about what we know: company records (investment, labor costs, sales, growth rates, use of technology, market shares) and customer information (demographics, geography, buying habits, brand loyalty).
- **Consider all possibilities**: Consider *all* possible events. Imagine the best and worst scenarios. What would happen in the worst-case scenarios? What about the best-case scenario? And what about the vast middle ground?
- **Plan for all contingencies**: When you see all the possibilities, devise a menu of responses for the worst- and best-case scenarios and everything in-between.

Consider the debate over energy policy. In the summer of 2008, U.S. gas prices passed $4 a gallon. Senator John McCain proposed expanding offshore drilling. Looser environmental regulations, he said, would produce enough extra crude oil to drive down prices. But would that happen? How much extra drilling would looser regulations allow? How much extra supply would drive down costs to, say, $3 a gallon? How about $2.50 or $2 a gallon? How quickly could that happen? Would this greater supply necessarily benefit American motorists, or might oil companies sell extra supply to Japan and other foreign markets? The answers, of course, depend on a number of complex questions about war and peace, world oil supplies, American conservation policy, breakthroughs in technology, and environmental issues.

By sketching several possibilities—great, awful, and the vast middle—scenarios create room for the creative, open thinking. Scenarios help us to imagine a wide range of responses to future events.

CASE STUDIES: SOCIAL CONTRACT PHILOSOPHERS

Philosophers often use hypothetical situations to theorize about government and politics. Suppose people could create a system of government from scratch. What would they do? What principles would they use to design that government? How much power would they give to the government? On what issues would they allow the government to rule? How might they restrict government powers?

Consider three classic "social contract" models and a contemporary answer to this fundamental set of questions:

- **Thomas Hobbes**, believing humans to be selfish and aggressive, argues that chaos would result without a strong central authority. Without a strong ruler, we would live in a constant state of insecurity. We would worry that a neighbor would steal our goods or marauding hordes would attack us on the roads. Our lives would be "solitary, poor, nasty, brutish, and short." By creating basic order, a strong ruler offers the best chance for individual freedom to flourish.
- **John Locke**, believing people to be industrious and constructive, argues for limited government. In Locke's view, government serves two basic roles. First, it protects people's right to property. People should be free to use natural resources, create things of value, and sell them on the marketplace. Second, government acts as an umpire, an authority to settle disputes. When the government performs these two roles well, it allows people the freedom to make their own decisions about how to live their lives.
- **Jean-Jacques Rousseau**, imagining people to be good but vulnerable to corruption, argues for a communal style of government. Left alone, Rousseau's speculated, people would behave selfishly. So Rousseau advocates small, tight-knit communities where everyone contributes and benefits from joint efforts. The individual would identify with his or her community—and avoid the dangers and selfishness of Hobbes's and Locke's individualist worlds.
- **John Rawls**, a contemporary philosopher, focuses on "distributive justice." He asks: What is the best way to distribute goods in a world where people have different

abilities and backgrounds? He offers a clever scheme called the "difference principle." Under this principle, inequality is acceptable as long as it contributes to the wellbeing of the "less-well-off" groups in society. When giving more to the 1 percent increases the welfare of the 99 percent, it is just.

These models ask us to imagine a world free of entrenched rules and prejudices. They take us out of our comfort zones, out of our tendency to take things for granted.

———

ELEMENT 56: FIND A SUPER MODEL TO GUIDE ANALYSIS

"We are pattern seekers, believers in a coherent world," says the Nobel laureate Daniel Kahneman. Simple models offer a powerful tool to begin to decipher a complex world. Before we can understand something complex, we need to simplify it; then we can look at its pieces and appreciate the complexity.

Consider the model airplane. It's a small version of the real thing. Done to scale, the plane actually looks like it could take flight. Of course, it can't. It lacks an engine and the distribution of its weight could not allow the wings to gain the right lift. The body and wings also lack the strength to handle the stresses of a flight.

But we love model airplanes because they help us to envision the real thing. We hang them on a ceiling or hold them in our hands and imagine the real silver birds zooming at speeds of 600 miles an hour. Those models often help non-hobbyists. During World War II, the War Department recruited teenagers to build models of Italian, Japanese, German, and Russian airplanes for use by American fighter pilots. By studying the shapes of planes, fighting men could identify enemy aircraft.

We might think of intellectual models the same way. We use models to simplify reality. A model is a simplification of reality, which helps us to identify patterns in recurring events. Because they strip out many details, they can offer insights into complex situations. And we can use those insights to solve real-world problems.

A model makes a generalization: *If X tends to happen, Y tends to result.* Models help us to see the hidden logic of everything from a waiter's smile to the movement of stars and planets.

Scholars in all fields think in models. To understand relativity, Albert Einstein visualized the theory of relativity when he watched lightening striking two trains as they passed each other at a station platform. By visualizing those events, he could imagine a complex abstract theory.

The danger comes when we see the model as reality itself—as when, for example, free-market enthusiasts refuse to acknowledge irrational behavior because they assume that people always act in their self-interest. As the Polish philosopher Alfred Korzybski famously remarked, "The map is not the territory." Used the right way, though, a model helps you explore the territory.

CASE STUDIES: SUPER MODELS FROM SOCIAL SCIENCE

Social scientists have developed a number of models to analyze the worlds of politics, economics, and social relationships.

The most powerful model is the marketplace. The idea that buyers and sellers, acting in their own self interest, can produce a stable but also dynamic system of economic progress is almost magical in its appeal. Adam Smith's account of a pin factory, which shows the powers of specialization and the division of labor, offers a vivid model of factory efficiency.

Beyond the model of the marketplace, the social sciences have produced a number of compelling models that inspire the analysis of just about any political, social, or economic problem. Let's take a look at the most powerful models of our time.

The Prisoner's Dilemma

What happens when two partners in crime get arrested? Can they uphold their promises not to "rat" on each other when police interrogate them? What happens when one of them rats on the other?

That's the starting point of the Prisoner's Dilemma. When criminal suspects get caught, they are questioned separately. Their interrogators offer them a special deal: *If you rat on your partner, you'll get off with a reduced penalty. But if you don't rat, we'll go after you with a vengeance.*

Each crook operates with incomplete information; neither one knows whether the other will rat. Each crook also faces the possibility of a heavy penalty for staying mum, if his partner rats.

Consider this simple chart of choices and consequences:

	Crook B stays mum	Crook B rats
Crook A stays mum	Each gets 6 months in jail	A gets 10 years; B goes free
Crook A rats	A goes free; B gets 10 years	Each serves 5 years

The prisoner's dilemma model highlights tensions between individual and group interests. Every day, we need to decide whether to cooperate with others or act selfishly. Social order depends on how we answer these questions: Do I exceed the speed limit? Do I cheat on taxes? Do I let others do the hard work at the office?

How we decide depends on the stakes of the game, the information we have, and our beliefs about what others will do. Consider some of the puzzles that you can analyze with the prisoner's dilemma:

- **Court cases**: What are the motivations of the prosecution and defendant? How much do the two sides know about each other's thinking? How much do they have to gain or lose by cooperating with the judicial process? How much do they have to gain or lose by refusing to cooperate?
- **Diplomacy**: How do secrets affect international relations? How do covert treaties and behind-the-scenes relationships affect bilateral and multilateral relations? How much do nations need to know about enemies—say, whether an adversary is developing "weapons of mass destruction"— before making important decisions? How useful is "intelligence"—information gathered by spies and other clandestine means—in forging an effective foreign policy?
- **Environmental issues**: What gives companies incentives to pollute? How do companies keep their polluting secret? What if another company learns about it? Or a government agency? Or a watchdog group? How does public knowledge affect a company's decision to pollute? How does that knowledge affect the company's decision to be follow

environmental standards, even without the danger of formal sanction?

People make decisions with limited information. The prisoner's dilemma model offers a simple way to analyze those decisions. A recent Google search for "prisoner's dilemma" yielded 398,000 results. Another search for "game theory"—the sprawling field of research inspired by the prisoner's dilemma—produced 2.6 million results.

The Scope of Conflict

Contests of all kinds—from schoolyard brawls to presidential elections to global warfare—turn on the "scope of conflict." The key question is: What people or issues get brought into a conflict? Who and what get left out?

In his classic *The Semisovereign People*, E.E. Schattschneider describes how an ordinary fight degenerated into a riot:

> On a hot afternoon in August 1943, in the Harlem section of New York City, a Negro soldier and a white policeman got into a fight in the lobby of a hotel. News of the fight spread rapidly throughout the area. In a few minutes angry crowds gathered in front of the hotel, at the police station, and at the hospital to which the injured policeman was taken.

What can this incident suggest about conflict in politics and other realms, like business, community life, and even churches and families? Schattschneider offers this tidy model:

> Every fight consists of two parts: (1) the few individuals who are actively involved at the center and (2) the audience that is irresistibly attracted to the scene. ... The outcome of every conflict is determined by the extent to which the audience becomes involved in it.

We can depict Schattschneider's argument like this:

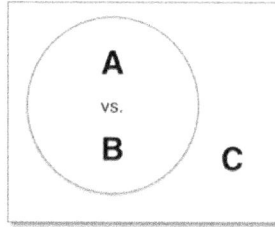

In this situation, A and B stand for the immediate participants in any conflict: the cop and the veteran, in Schattschneider's story. C stands for the onlookers who could determine the outcome by entering or staying out.

You can apply this scheme to lots of political conflicts. For each example, ask yourself: Which players are directly involved in the arena of conflict (A and B), and which ones outside the arena (C) could possibly join the conflict?

- **Vietnam War**: Hi Chi Minh, French, people of Vietnam, the U.S., the United Nations, corporate investors, the Soviet Union, Communist China.
- **Corporate politics**: CEO, COO, board members, shareholders, customers, divisions in the company, parts of the supply chain.
- **University affairs**: President, board of trustees, faculty, staff, students, alumni, athletic department, fundraisers, local government, competing universities.

Different groups, of course, will compete in the arena on different issues. The question is which actors and issues get brought into the scope of conflict.

The Games People Play

Eric Berne argues that three basic roles—Parent, Adult, and Child—shape how we think and interact with others.

- **Parent**: Tells the child what to do and how to feel. Teaches children the "scripts" that they need to succeed in the world.

Sometimes denies the child's desires, telling them they are "not OK" unless they follow the parent's rules and dictates.
- **Child**: Learns how to behave and what to value based on the parent's instructions and example—and rewards and sanctions. Cannot feel "OK" unless pleasing parental figures.
- **Adult**: Decides, on the basic of their own thinking and feeling, how to act. Feels a sense of control and efficacy—a sense that they are to be respected for who they are, not according to others' standards. Attains a sense of mastery and completeness.

Our lives begin with the Parent-Child relationship. To protect and teach, the Parent shows the Child how to behave, think, and feel. The Parent teaches the Child what is "OK" and what's "Not OK." Within a few years, the Child learns and internalizes a complete set of do's and don'ts—not just how to act, but also how to *feel*. Too often, the Child learns that she needs to earn love by pleasing the Parent; in other words, the Child is "Not OK" unless someone older and wiser says so.

Ideally, the Child eventually gains enough confidence and knowledge so that she ceases to depend on the Parent for assurances that she is "OK." In other words, she grows to be an Adult, with the capacity to explore, learn, and act according to her own standards and values. The more experiences and encouragement a person has, the greater her sense of power and confidence.

Unfortunately, the "scripts" of childhood often stunt passage into full adulthood. Too often, we follow our parents' "scripts" about money, work, discipline, school, friendship, religion, love, sex, race, class, neighborhoods, and more. We adopt the truisms and narratives we learned from parents, even when they are false or incomplete. We suffer because we fail to gain enough confidence to claim autonomy over our lives.

We become full Adults when we master a variety of life skills and learn to respect ourselves and others as equals. That mastery requires conscious effort to detach from our parents and their scripts.

Exit, Voice, and Loyalty

When dissatisfied, people have three possible choices. They can *exit* (leave the company, move to a different place, buy another product, vote for a different party), *voice* their concerns (speak out in letters, public forums, websites, and meetings), or express *loyalty* (stand by the organization, offering the support it needs to revive itself).

That's how Albert O. Hirschman describes the process of feedback and response in his classic work *Exit, Voice, and Loyalty*. So which approach works best? It depends. Let's consider the options in turn:

- **Exit**: In situations with lots of viable options, exit works well. Consumers regularly exit from one product when they become dissatisfied or when a rival offers a better deal. If I don't like my Mazda, I can switch to a Subaru or Volvo next time I buy a car. If AT&T drops my cell calls, I can switch to Verizon or T-Mobile.
- **Voice**: In some matters—like politics—the opportunity to exit is rare. You only vote every two years for Congress and four years for president. The voice is also muffled in a sea of other voices, with little known impact on policy preferences. What do you do the rest of the time? You raise your voice to reason, prod, complain, argue, threaten, and cajole.
- **Loyalty**: Sometimes, expressions of loyalty can offer the leeway organizations need to create change and reform. It sounds counterintuitive; if you support someone strongly, why would they want to change? But loyalty often prompts others to work hard to *deserve* that loyalty.

Effective action requires at least two of the three options. Voice works better with a credible exit threat. Loyalty works better when it could contribute to exit or voice. And so on.

Whatever you want to analyze—politics, economics, evolution, customers, sports, psychology, computer systems, even biology and medicine and physics—consider how exit, voice, and loyalty works.

Group Formation and Social Cooperation

How is collective action possible? How can organizations recruit members?

The "free rider problem" describes the greatest barrier for people to work together on a common problem. People often refuse to contribute to group efforts out a fear that non-contributors will still reap the rewards of the group action. No one wants to be a sucker.

In his classic *The Logic of Collective Action*, Mancur Olson offers two ways to overcome the free-rider problem.

- **Coercion**: Organizations may coerce members to contribute. The government, for example, assesses mandatory taxes—a legal way to force people to become part of the community. In many states of the U.S., unions may impose mandatory membership and dues to workers.
- **Benefits**: Organizations offer special benefits—known as "selective inducements"—to get people to participate. Unions and buying groups, for example, offer members cut-rate deals on everything from appliances to vacations. With these special deals, otherwise unmotivated people join the cause.

Without these strategies, organizations cannot survive. Even groups of committed, zealous activists fall apart without coercion or benefits. Without these organizational imperatives, free riders take advantage of the efforts of contributors.

The Power of Consent—and Withdrawal

We often think of power as a set of resources that some people use to control others. The president controls the federal bureaucracy. The media control information. The army controls arms and soldiers. Banks control money. And so on.

But power is really a process. Power goes to anyone who can get others to cooperate with them. Any time someone follows someone else's lead, they *consent* to their power. Every time we pay taxes, abide by business regulations, meet professional and educational standards —any time we accept someone else's rules, in fact—we consent to their power.

That suggests a powerful way to fight entrenched power, as Gene Sharp shows in his three-volume *The Politics of Nonviolent Action*. When we refuse to follow a rule, we *withdraw consent* from the system. As more people withdraw their consent, the government loses its ability to assert power. To challenge people in power, the best strategy is to organize people to withdraw their consent from the regime.

Even tyrannical regimes, like Nazi Germany or the Soviet Union, depended on the willingness of ordinary people to follow the system's rules. How can people withdraw their consent? Refusing to pay taxes. Violating unjust laws. Refusing to sign up for the military draft. Boycotting products. Subverting elections. Conducting strikes. Holding protest rallies. Occupying restaurants, churches, parks, and offices.

To understand the power of withdrawing consent, consider the period from 1989 to 1991, when the old Soviet bloc overturned their political systems. Activists in Poland, Hungary, Czechoslovakia, East Germany, Bulgaria, and finally the Soviet Union and 15 of its republics refused to follow the orders of the Communist leaders. For other examples of withdrawing consent, think of the Gandhi's battle for India's struggle for independence, the American civil rights movement, the antiwar movement, the anti-apartheid struggle in South Africa, and the Arab Spring.

In each of these events, activists told people in power: *We refuse to consent to current systems of power. We withdraw our consent.* When the government could not depend on people to consent to its power, revolutionary change took place.

———

AND ANOTHER THING . . .

Let us close with a word of caution about the power of models and analysis. No matter how smart their models and analysis, experts often fail to predict events or see the underlying causes of complex phenomena.

For a case study of the limits of expertise, consider the Simon-Ehrlich wager.

Paul Ehrlich ignited a global debate about overpopulation with the publication of *The Population Bomb* in 1968. The world's population had doubled, from 2 billion to 4 billion, from 1930 to 1968. Without a global effort to reduce the birth rate, Ehrlich warned, the human race was doomed. The world, he warned, faced catastrophic shortages of food and natural resources. He predicted that the global crisis would cause the U.S. population to fall to 23 million by 2000.

Erhlich was using a static model. He assumed that humans could only mine and drill for the amount of resources then known to exist, with current technology and methods.

All this irked a California business professor named Julian Simon. Humans, Simon reasoned, still occupied just a small portion of the planet. And as the population exploded, so did human ingenuity. Surely, Simon reasoned, we would find the resources we needed to sustain ourselves—and improve our standards of living—for centuries to come.

Simon's model was dynamic. Simon called human beings "the ultimate resource" because they were capable of making so many other resources possible. If oil deposits are exhausted in Texas or Saudi Arabia, surely we could find new deposits elsewhere—or drill deeper to get at the deposits that now seem impossible to extract.

In 1980, Simon challenged Ehrlich to a $10,000 bet. Contrary to Ehrlich's prophesy of global shortages, Simon said, the prices of raw materials would not increase over the long term. Pick any set of raw materials, he challenged Ehrlich, and put your money on the line. If prices rose over ten years, Simon would pay Ehrlich the difference.

By 1990, the prices fell for all five of the five metals that Ehrlich bet would rise. Ehrlich conceded the bet and sent Simon a check for $576.07.

Julian Simon offered one last prediction before his death in 1998. "The material conditions of life will continue to get better for most people, in most countries, most of the time, indefinitely," he said. "Within a century or two, most of humanity would approach the highest living standards of today's western nations."

Wryly, he added: "I also speculate that many people will continue to *think and say* that the conditions of life are getting *worse*."

CHAPTER 15
COMPOSITION

You compose because you want to somehow summarize in some permanent form your most basic feelings about being alive, to set down ... some sort of permanent statement about the way it feels to live now, today.

AARON COPLAND

BEHOLD A GREAT WRITER AT WORK. Watch John McPhee, the Pulitzer Prize-winning writer for *The New Yorker* who has authored books on nuclear proliferation, geology, oranges, trucking, Alaska, education, basketball, tennis, and writing.

Working in his office in Princeton, New Jersey, where he also teaches, McPhee assembles three-by-five cards to organize his book. He moves the cards around on his wall, pondering the right sequence. For his book *Encounters with the Archdruid*, McPhee used 36 cards, each coded with a category. After figuring out how he wanted to start, McPhee studied the cards until key themes and moments stood out. Eventually, he figured out how he wanted to end. Then, from his strong start to his strong finish, he organized them into the structure he wanted for his story.

The structure determines the reader's experience—emotional and intellectual—as much as the content.

Within the basic structure—beginning, middle, and end—two basic approaches present themselves. McPhee could use a simple chronology, with topical asides. Or he could explore a series of topics, with historical asides. Which approach works best depends on the audience, the subject, the narrative, and more. The best structure often takes time to find. McPhee explains:

> Chronology usually dominates. As themes prove inconvenient, you find some way to tuck them in. Through flashbacks and flash-forwards, you can move around in time, of course, but such a structure remains under chronological control and can't do much about items that are scattered thematically. There's nothing wrong with a chronological structure. On tablets in Babylonia, most pieces were written that way, and nearly all pieces are written that way now.

When you figure out your blueprint, devise a plan to follow it. Some writers, like the biographer Robert Caro and the novelist John Irving, decide how they want to end the book and devote all their work to reaching that end. Others believe more in the power of a strong beginning. The novelist Jennifer Haigh once told me that if her opening passage faltered, the whole book would vector off course.

Like McPhee, start by collecting the pieces of your story and organizing them. You can draw a map on a big piece of paper. Or like McPhee, you can pin them on a wall or lay them on a table. Move them around, like puzzle pieces. Pay attention to the beginnings and endings—not just for the whole piece, but for each of the sections as well.

———

ELEMENT 57: MAKE EVERY PIECE A JOURNEY

Every piece of writing offers an opportunity to take the reader on a journey. No matter how ordinary or extraordinary the topic, take the reader on a tour. In every piece—every email, memo, report; every story, essay, or analysis; every article or book—takes the reader from one place to another, different place.

Nothing excites the human imagination as much as change. In our everyday lives, we carry out predictable routines, doing the same basic activities at home, work, school, and around town. So we come alive when something changes. The same applies to the reader. So for every journey you give the reader, show change at every step—positive or negative change—to keep the reader's interest.

As the writer, think yourself as a tour guide. Start by knowing your point of departure. Point out the sights along the journey. Get off the bus once in a while, if a side trip could give the journey greater meaning—but don't stray too far. In every tour, start strong and finish strong.

Here's one way to make sure you create a journey for every piece: Write the first and last paragraphs first. Only after writing the start and finish should you write the middle paragraphs. Give yourself a roadmap. Make sure the map indicates the starting and ending points. Before you do anything else—taking as long as necessary—write your opening and closing paragraphs.

I discovered the magic of this approach while working on *Nobody Turn Me Around*, an account of the 1963 March on Washington. I had conducted more than a hundred interviews and explored thousands of pages of archival material before I started writing. One day, I panicked about my progress. So I decided to write the first and last paragraphs of about a dozen chapters. Here's how I started the preface:

> On a pitch-black night, a crescent moon barely visible in the sky, three teenaged boys walked along the gentle slopes of Highland Avenue on the edge of Lookout Mountain, then to U.S. Highway 11, north of their hometown of Gadsden, Alabama.

Here's how I finished that preface:

> On August 28, 1963, hundreds of thousands of demonstrators would carry those signs down Constitution and Independence avenues in what Martin Luther King called the greatest demonstration for freedom in the nation's history.

As soon as I had my opening and closing lines, it was easy to compose and organize the middle material. My goal was to take the reader from three teenagers hitchhiking to Washington for the march to marchers beginning the event with signs made by the teenagers.

On a pitch-black night, a crescent moon barely visible in the sky, three teenaged boys walked along the gentle slopes on the edge of Lookout Mountain, then to U.S. Highway 11, north of their hometown of Gadsden, Alabama.

On August 28, 1963, hundreds of thousands of demonstrators would carry those signs down Constitution and Independence avenues in what Martin Luther King Called the greatest demonstration for freedom in the nation's history.

Once I had the beginning and the end, the middle paragraphs lined up. Without a clear destination, I would have veered off course. But I always knew where I was going—and I knew what paragraphs would get me there, step by step. Just remember this format: *First, … Then, … Then, … Then, … Finally, …*

Pull one of your favorite books or stories off the shelf. Do the chapters have clear, definite starting points? Do they take the reader from one place to another, resolving the issues of the piece? Do the sentences and paragraphs unfold ideas, one by one? Do they move toward a conclusion? Does the piece feel whole and complete when you finish?

CASE STUDY: L.A. KAUFFMAN, *DIRECT ACTION*

How does a political movement gain public attention? How does a movement expand? Some glimpses come in L.A. Kauffman's account of the early stages of the anti-apartheid movement in the U.S.:

> One day in late 1984, three prominent critics of South African apartheid —Randall Robinson, Mary Frances Berry, and Walter Fauntroy—met with the South African ambassador to present a list of demands. They vowed to stay at the embassy until the demands were met, and the ambassador promptly had them arrested. Robinson later said they they hadn't expected to be arrested that day, and certainly had not at that point planned on mounting a sustained campaign of civil disobedience, but they quickly pulled together a response. More apartheid critics slowed up at the embassy the next weekday afternoon, and were

arrested. The same thing happened the next day, and the day after that, with organizers vowing that the protests would become a daily occurrence. The campaign, now called the Free South Africa Movement, rapidly gathered momentum. Celebrities like Harry Belafonte and Stevie Wonder came and were arrested; so did veteran civil rights leaders like Coretta Scott King and the Rev. Jesse Jackson. Almost two dozen members of Congress took part, and large numbers of ordinary people, as the actions continued month after month.

In one paragraph, Kaufmann gives the reader a complete journey, from one place to another different place:

One day in late 1984, three prominent critics of South African apartheid met with the South African ambassador to present a list of demands.

Almost two dozen members of Congress took part, and large numbers of ordinary people, as the actions continued month after month.

The paragraph moves through all the stages of Aristotle's narrative arc.

- **World of the story**: Establishing the setting (embassy), characters (prominent citizens), and goal (protest apartheid).
- **Rising action**: The protest spreads, as more people put their bodies on the line.
- **Resolution**: A full-fledged movement is poised to expand in cities and campuses across the country.

If you can create that simple 1-2-3 format in your paragraphs, sections, and whole pieces, everything you write will offer both clarity and drama.

———

ELEMENT 58: FIND THE RIGHT SHAPE

"The great book of Nature," Galileo once said, "is written in mathe-matical language and the characters are triangles, circles, and other geometric figures."

The shape of your writing—straight line, circle, or triangle—imitates Nature. The shape you give your writing affects what you say. Content follows form.

The straight line moves the piece in a clear direction—forward. Classic biographers begin with the hero's birth or background infor-mation about his family, then move, step by step, through his life. Consider the opening lines of this biography of Bonaparte:

> Napoleon Buonaparte was born at Ajaccio on the 15th of August, 1769. The family had been of some distinction, during the middle ages, in Italy; whence his branch of it removed to Corsica, in the troubled times of the Guelphs and Gibellines. They were always considered as belonging to the gentry of the island. Charles, the father of Napoleon, an advocate of considerable reputation . . .

And so on.

The circle structures the piece as a series of recurring patterns. In each cycle, the character moves through the familiar cycle of challenge, struggle, and discovery; when one circle ends, another begins. With each new circle, we confirm the familiar patterns but also gain deeper understandings and watch the hero advance to greater and greater challenges.

Milan Kundera's classic *The Unbearable Lightness of Being* works this way. He introduces three main characters—Tomas, Tereza, and Sabina—and follows their lives again and again. With each telling of their story, he reveals new conflicts and depth. He signals this scheme in the beginning when he talks about Nietzsche's concept of the "eternal recurrence," the idea that we relive our experiences, over and over.

Historians have long noted the recurring patterns of history. Arthur Schlesinger noted cycles of activism and conservatism in American history. Economic cycles regularly move from boom to bust and back again. Why? We pursue different approaches to extremes, then experi-ence a backlash; then that new approach goes to extremes, inviting another backlash. It was ever thus. Almost 500 years ago, Machiavelli wrote: "All cities and all peoples are and ever have been animated by the same desires and the same passions," he writes. The cyrcles of life repeat, again and again.

Finally, consider the triangle, which shows dynamic relationships among sets of threes. In one moment, the hero interacts with a villain and a sidekick; in the next, she interacts with a mentor and tempter; and so on. Just consider the most common relationship in all drama: the lover's triangle. The relationship is always subject to change because of the existence of a third party.

In philosophy, dialectics captures the same dynamic. Ideas move through three stages: *thesis*, *antithesis*, and *synthesis*. The thesis represents an idea that somehow dominates some sphere of life. The antithesis represents its opposite. When two ideas clash, they create a synthesis—a higher development of those two opposing ideas. The tech entrepreneur Jon Lonsdale explains this process, common in business: "Deep truths exist at both extremes of a dialectic, and the wisest stance on an issue will incorporate both of the opposites within itself." Nothing is absolute; nothing is forever; meaning is never fixed. Truth can only be found in change.

Politics and philosophy are full of threes. In politics we see battles between executive, legislative, and judicial branches; the U.S., Soviet Union, and Third World; and federal, state, and local governments. In philosophy, we talk about the body, mind, and soul; id, ego, and super-ego; and past, present, and future.

CASE STUDY: THE BILL CLINTON STORY

Let's use the life of Bill Clinton, the former U.S. president, to illustrate the different shapes of composition.

Beginning in Hot Springs, Arkansas, Clinton strives to become a popular band kid and falls in love with politics. As a representative of Boys Nation, he even gets to go to the White House and meet his hero, President John F. Kennedy. Then Clinton leaves home to attend Georgetown University, Oxford University, and Yale Law School. As an adult, Clinton plunges into politics, losing a race for Congress before getting elected attorney general and governor. Then, what Clinton has aimed for his whole life: the 1992 presidential campaign and two terms as president. The story ends with his ambitious career as a philanthropist and support for his wife Hillary's political career.

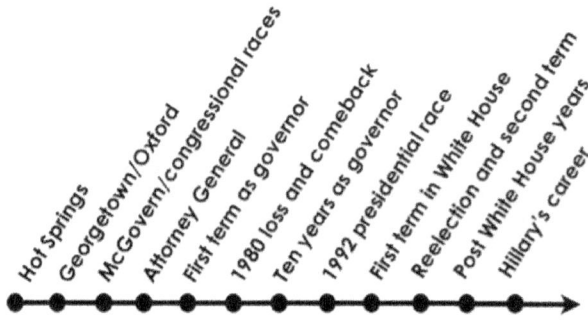

Hot Springs · Georgetown/Oxford · McGovern/congressional races · Attorney General · First term as governor · 1980 loss and comeback · Ten years as governor · 1992 presidential race · First term in White House · Reelection and second term · Post White House years · Hillary's career

With the straight line, the story takes on momentum. Every event is a setup for a later event. Other than that, life has no predictable shares or cycles. Things just happen, one after another. As the historian Arnold Toynbee notes, it's "just one damned thing after another."

A cyclical approach shows Clinton repeating the same patterns, again and again. In each stage, Clinton identifies a goal, finds friends and allies, fights battles, and then succeeds. Every success begins a new cycle.

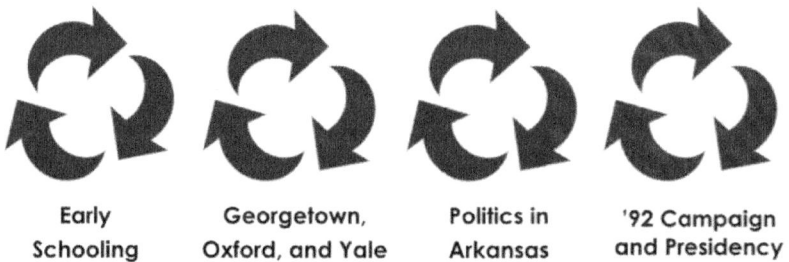

| Early Schooling | Georgetown, Oxford, and Yale | Politics in Arkansas | '92 Campaign and Presidency |

In the first cycle, Clinton as a boy, we see the future president's ambition as he works hard at school, joins a band, takes part in Boys Nation, and gets into Georgetown University. In the second cycle, young adulthood, Clinton excels as a student at Georgetown, makes new friends, and gets involved in campus politics. Then he spends a year at Oxford as a Rhodes Scholar and goes to Yale Law School, where he once again immerses himself in politics. In the third cycle, Clinton throws himself into politics; he works as a volunteer for the 1972 McGovern campaign, loses a race for Congress, and wins races for attorney general and governor. In the fourth cycle, Clinton builds a political record as governor, becomes a champion of education reform and a national spokesman for a "third way" in politics. Cycle after cycle, Clinton begins with a new ambition, develops a strategy, builds networks, works to win—and then starts the cycle all over, at a higher level of ambition.

The triangle tells a different story. Over his career, Clinton positioned himself against the two major camps in American politics—liberals and conservatives. With a strategy of "triangulation," Clinton put himself above unpopular congressional Democrats and Republicans. He took middle-of-the-road positions on crime, welfare, abortion, taxes, and military and foreign policy.

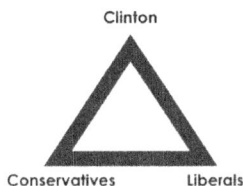

Sometimes Clinton sided with liberals; other times he sided with conservatives. Neither side felt completely comfortable with Clinton—but each, at different times, allied with him. At his best, Clinton took charge, encouraging the two sides to vie for his favor. Dick Morris, Clinton's political advisor, explains the strategy:

> Well, we were locked into a very sterile conflict between the left agenda and the right agenda. ... [W]hat you should do is take the best from each party's agenda, and come to a solution somewhere above the positions of each party. So from the left, take the idea that we need day care and food supplements for people on welfare. From the right, take the idea that they have to work for a living, and that there are time limits. ... Get rid of the garbage of each position, that the people didn't believe in; take the best from each position; and move up to a third way. And that became a triangle, which was triangulation.

How we assess Bill Clinton's life depends on what shapes we use to tell the tale. Is he a striver always looking for the next challenge? Does his character lead to a series of recurring cycles? Does he stand apart from other characters, charting a third way? The shape tells the tale.

––––––

ELEMENT 59: SLOT YOUR PARAGRAPHS

With the basic shapes of composition—straight lines, circles, and triangles, in addition to Aristotle's narrative arc—let's explore how to organize information within those shapes.

The key unit of all pieces is the paragraph. So let's begin with a quick review of the skills you need to write a good paragraph.

- Make every paragraph a journey, taking the reader from one place to another, different place.
- State and develop just one idea in every paragraph.
- Give each paragraph a three- to five-word label. Cut anything in that paragraph that does not support the idea expressed in that label. Write one label for each paragraph, as if you were writing a headline for a tabloid newspaper.

Now we need to arrange those paragraphs, put them in the right order. I call this process "slotting." Think of the way you put files in slots on desk organizers.

To slot paragraphs, first decide where you want to start and finish your piece. Then look at all your paragraph labels—the tabloid headlines. You might have dozens of these labels. So what is the best sequence for them? What is the best road to travel from the beginning to the end? You might be surprised how easy it is to arrange these paragraphs, if you have labeled them all and know where to start and finish.

Work from the outside in. Figure out what ideas best support the opening and which ones best support the conclusion. Gather a cluster of opening and closing paragraphs. Once you know the beginnings and endings, you can easily arrange the paragraphs in the middle.

Some years ago, I wrote a mess of a book draft. "There's a lot of great stuff in here," my editor, Hillel Black, told me, "but I don't see where you're going." So I made a stack of three-by-five-inch cards that identified the book's main ideas. Hillel ordered lunch and then we spent an hour or so moving the cards around on a table. Finally, we arranged the cards into a workable plan for the book.

That's what you can do with paragraphs. When you give them punchy labels, you can survey all your ideas at a glance. Then you can determine the order that works best.

CASE STUDY: MALCOLM GLADWELL, 'THE TERRAZZO JUNGLE'

To illustrate this idea, look at the work of Malcolm Gladwell, America's most successful nonfiction writer.

Gladwell's article "The Terrazzo Jungle" describes the evolution of shopping malls in America, focusing on the career of a developer named Victor Gruen. The story jumps around in time, moving from sweeping historical statements to comments about the characters' appearances and temperaments. Another major developer, Alfred Taubman, also plays a major role. But the story always comes back to Gruen's tragic journey.

As a young man, Victor Gruen revolutionized retailing with his creation of the modern mall. This innovation won him fortune and fame. Gruen—and, later, another developed named Al Taubman—paid close attention to every detail of mall designs and operations. By making the mall a destination—safe and clean and exciting—Gruen and Taubman made the mall a financial powerhouse. But in the end, Gruen was dismayed by the destruction and ugliness that his innovation caused.

What's Gladwell's secret? Partly, it's his structure. Each paragraph offers a coherent mini-essay. Because he writes such tight paragraphs—just one idea per paragraph—Gladwell never loses the reader. Even when he takes a detour, he makes sure to return quickly to the main road. Then he arranges his pieces well.

Now here's a list of the 26 paragraphs in this piece. I have given each paragraph a brief label, in the style of a tabloid headline. Think of each paragraph as a container for a single idea—an "idea bucket." See how the buckets line up in a sequence.

> 1. **Victor Gruen's story**: His life, from Austrian immigrant to mall mogul.
> 2. **Gruen's Southdale model**: The design of the modern mall.

3. **A media sensation**: How Gruen's work excited journalists and others.

4. **Southdales everywhere**: Developers copy the Southdale model thousands of times.

5. **Al Taubman**: A Michigan developer takes the model to the next level.

6. **Short Hills Mall**: A description of Taubman's signature mall.

7. **Details matter**: Taubman's attention to details—flooring, handrails, and visibility—to overcome "threshold resistance."

8. **Details matter, continued**: The design of corridors in malls.

9. **The power of anchors**: Exploring the case of Nieman Marcus.

10. **Other details**: Why malls have two stories, use ring roads and multiple entrances, and provide more parking at the second level.

11. **Control**: How developers manage mall environments.

12. **Old-style control**: The limited control of old-style downtowns.

13. **Vienna backstory**: How Gruen hoped to remake old Vienna.

14. **Suburban chaos**: Gruen's attack on unplanned communities and his plans for a community with apartment buildings, houses, schools, parks, a medical center.

15. **Lonely critique**: Developers and others ignore Frank Lloyd Wright's critique of Gruen.

16. **No mall community**: Gruen's mistake in assuming that he could impose Viennese mass planning on suburbia.

17. **A failed mall**: The failure of Framingham's Shoppers World.

18. **Tax breaks**: Depreciation transforms the economics of malls and strip development.

19. **Tax break impact**: Why building now trumps the stock market for investing.

20. **Logic turned on its head**: How malls transform regional economies.
21. **Gotham vision**: Gruen's vision for a Corbusian city in New York.
22. **Gotham vision, continued**: Gruen's vision, continued.
23. **Malls transform America**: Postwar America's embrace of the mall as a social as well as economic place, depopulating public spaces and older communities.
24. **Private versus public good**: The belief that merchants can produce something good for all.
25. **Too big**: Taubman's critique of Gruen.
26. **Malls maul**: Once an advocate of European urbanism, Gruen is shocked by the ugliness of malls and the destruction of small town America.

Gladwell takes us on a journey from Gruen's youthful idealism to his late-life disillusionment. The story moves from creativity to success to destruction.

By giving each paragraph a label, you can slot the whole story, from beginning to end, with short tabloid-style labels. Then you can review the whole piece at a glance—and decide whether passages need to be moved or removed from the piece.

———

ELEMENT 60: MAKE TRANSITIONS LIGHTLY

Imagine taking a train trip for a couple hundred miles. As the train glides and bumps on the tracks, you peer out the window. Along the way you notice farm houses, suburban tracts, storage sheds, manufacturing buildings, warehouses, parking lots, and city centers. Watching the changing landscape, your attention easily jumps from scene to scene.

Making transitions in a piece of writing is not much different. Readers easily jump from idea to idea, without much guidance. As a writer, we don't need to announce that we're about to shift to a new idea tor time or place. Usually, we just need to make the move. Just change the subject. One or two words usually offer enough information for the reader to understand the shift in focus.

Here are some other simple maneuvers to make transitions:

- **Continue the discussion**: Use words like *also, again, as well, another, in addition, furthermore,* and *likewise.*
- **Show location**: Use words like *above, below, by, near, under, over, alongside, in front of, behind,* and *in the back.*
- **Show time**: Use words like *when, then, before, after, suddenly, during, finally, later, lastly, meanwhile, until, then,* and *when.*
- **Pivot words**: Use words like *however, but, after, before, more than, less than, likewise, also, likewise, even though,* and *despite.*
- **Clarify**: Use expressions like *so, for example, consider, put another way,* and *to clarify.*
- **Question**: Use words like *so why ...? How ...?* and *When ...?*
- **Emphasize**: Use expressions like *again, because, on the other hand, again, frequently, in fact, surprisingly, often overlooked,* and *seriously.*
- **Conclude**: Use expressions like *finally, lastly, and so,* and *as a result.*

Your high school English teacher probably taught you to use wordy transitions, like this: *The second major cause of the French Revolution was ...* Or: *As we have seen in this paper ...* That's fine for high school, when you are learning how to connect separate fragments into one piece. But to write fluid prose—and to invite the reader to join the discussion—use minimal transitions.

Our brains naturally jump, quickly and easily, from one idea to another. In our video age, we jump countless times a day without noticing. Moviemakers call it "quick cutting." When a movie shifts from an establishing shot to an interior, from a bar scene to a scene on a city street, the audience easily understands the shift. Why? Because once you've completed one idea or scene, you are ready for a new one. We are always ready to jump.

CASE STUDY: KIM WEHLE, *HOW TO READ THE CONSTITUTION—AND WHY*

Nothing matters more in American politics than the Constitution. So let's give two cheers for Kim Wehle and her sprightly guide to the nation's legal system.

Wehle never rushes. Too often, writers try to pack too many ideas into a paragraph. Because you cannot understand Topic X without also understanding definition y and history z, authors pack it all together. Wehle, smartly, describes one idea at a time; she uses simple transitions to connect the points.

Wehle begins by asserting, correctly, that the Constitution faces grave dangers and tests. Then she elaborates, paragraph by paragraph. Here's how she makes transitions in subsequent paragraphs:

> *But mostly, the Constitution's structure is being tested by…*
> *But these days, rules are being broken…*
> *In thinking about constitutional structure, …*
> *Meanwhile, as everyone is busy arguing …*
> *But one day, the stresses…*
> *You see, it doesn't matter …*

With just a few words, Wehle guides the reader to each new aspect of her discussion.

Wehle breaks her chapters into sections, separated by spaces. Each section delivers a stand-alone treatment of an issue—and, as such, breaks from the previous section. Here's how she starts the sections in Chapter 1:

> *I talk to people about the Constitution a lot. …*
> *The Supreme Court's decisions regarding the structural*
>   *Constitution seek to ensure…*
> *Once again, the term* checks and balances *is not in the*
>   *Constitution. …*
> *Last, let's talk about executive power…*
> *By this point, we have walked through the first three topics…*
> *If a generation of Americans comes along…*

Kim Wehle makes sure we never get lost along the journey. Like every good tour guide, she directs us, with just a few words, to pay attention to each new sight along the tour.

———

AND ANOTHER THING ...

Man is a pattern-seeking animal. To understand anything—from brewing coffee in the morning to understanding Samantha Bee's jokes on late-night TV—we need to identify patterns. When we "get" the pattern, we can address complications.

The catchier the pattern, the easier the reader can follow—and get invested emotionally.

Consider Beethoven's Fifth Symphony, the most famous piece of music in the western world. The piece has been imitated everywhere, from the Beatles' song "Because" to the disco classic "A Fifth of Beethoven." The Allied forces in World War II used the piece as its victory march, since the opening motif spells out V (for victory) in Morse code. Everyone knows the opening, the foreboding four notes that announce, as Beethoven said, "death knocking upon the door."

Go anywhere in the world, whistle or hum those four bars, and you will get an instant look of recognition. Why?

It's not just that Beethoven makes such a bold statement. Think about how he does it.

We might see it as a simple progression, from beginning to end. The music moves in a straight line, with clear movement in one direction.

Or we could see the piece as an endlessly repeated cycle, with the same themes varying only in details. The piece moves back and forth, from heaviness to lightness. We experience power, energy, excitement, and dread from the pounding notes; then we experience lightness, sweetness, and hopefulness from the light notes.

Finally, most powerfully, Beethoven gives us a series of triangles: DA da da *DUM*. That three-part structure looks and feels like Aristotle's narrative arc. We experience a clear beginning, middle, and end.

You see this pattern in all great pieces of writing. Writes move forward, one moment after another ... with a recurring cycle, shifting back and forth, from heaviness to lightness, from specificity to generality ... three steps at a time, like a triangle or an arc.

An interesting thought, anyway: Beethoven's Universal Theory of Composition.

WRITING TECHNIQUES
FOR PART FIVE

CHAPTER 16
RHYTHM AND BEATS

How can we know the dancer from the dance?

WILLIAM BUTLER YEATS

EVERY PART of our world moves with tempo. We follow the pace of the seasons, months, weeks, and days. We follow the circadian cycles of light and darkness, the monthly cycles of the tides, and the annual changes of seasons. We synchronize our actions to our rates of breathing and the tick-tock of the clock. We feel our pulse quicken in moments of stress or exertion.

"The art of living is based on rhythm—on give and take, ebb and flow, light and dark, life and death," Henry Miller said. "By acceptance of all aspects of life, good and bad, right and wrong, yours and mine, the static, defensive life, which is what most people are cursed with, is converted into a dance, 'the dance of life,' metamorphosis."

The arts reflect the rhythmic nature of life. To give writing flow, we mimic the regularity of waves lapping on the shore. And then, to break through the monotony of such regular flows, we interrupt the rhythm.

Music offers a perfect example of creative rhythms. Music's tempo pulls us into a flow. Then the tempo changes and we are surprised—and more alert. "Our brains are keeping track of how many times particular notes are sounded, where they appear in terms of strong versus weak beats, and how long they last," Dan Levitan writes in *This*

Is Your Brain on Music. Listeners "take delight when a skillful musician violates the expectation in an interesting way—a sort of musical joke that we're all in on."

Other forms of expression follow music's rhythms and beats. Dance creates patterns of bodily movement in space. Visual art deploys patterns of color, shape, and solids and voids over surfaces. Language deploys patterns of sound and pacing in the spoken and written word. Stories have their own patterns, from the Aristotelian arc to the moment-by-moment beats of speech and action.

———

ELEMENT 61: USE BEATS TO MOVE STORIES FORWARD

A beat is, the Hollywood script doctor Robert McKee tells us, "the smallest element" of all stories.

A beat is a moment of change. Each beat changes the trajectory of the story. Each beat—every essential piece of dialogue, action, gesture, description, and detail—demands a response. I do this, you do that; I advance, you retreat; I ask a question, you answer; I make an offer, you counter; I make a gesture, you respond.

To give a scene movement, intrigue, and verve, depict a series of beats. When one character does something, get another to respond. Move back and forth—with a series of actions and responses—throughout the scene. In a well-constructed scene, every action raises a question; every answer, in turn, raises a new question.

Every beat offers new information and new possibilities. In a well-constructed story, every beat matters. If a beat does not somehow advance the story, we should cut it from the story.

If you could remove an action, response, detail, or thought from a passage without changing the trajectory of the passage, do so. If it does not contribute to the story's progress, delete it.

When you use details that do not advance the story, explanation, or argument, you confuse the audience. The reader expects that you have reasons for what you put into a piece. "If you say in the first chapter that there is a rifle hanging on the wall, in the second or third chapter it absolutely must go off," the Russian playwright Anton Chekhov once said. "If it's not going to be fired, it shouldn't be hanging there." Use beats that matter and delete the ones that don't.

You might wonder how to *pace* beats. How fast should this exchange take? How quickly should the characters act and respond? How briskly should the story move from scene to scene? The answer is simple: As fast as necessary to move the story forward, maintaining the wholeness of the scene, without leaving the audience behind.

Writers in all genres—stories, speeches and sermons, journalism, even corporate reports and analyses—would benefit from the use of beats. Just remember: *Keep things moving with brisk exchanges—and make every moment matter.* If you do that, you will always hold the reader's attention.

CASE STUDY: THE CUBAN MISSILE CRISIS

For 13 days in the fall of 1962, the U.S. and Soviet Union stood at the brink of nuclear annihilation. When American reconnaissance flights discovered that the Soviets were installing nuclear warheads on Cuba, putting 80 million Americans within reach of nuclear attacks, the Kennedy Administration took action to force the Russians to remove the missiles. The Russians—and their satellite state of Cuba—resisted. At one point, the U.S. and U.S.S.R. stood within hours of nuclear war.

Throughout the crisis, the two sides acted on incomplete information. Neither side knew how the other would respond to its moves. If the U.S. demanded the removal of the missiles, how would the Soviets respond? If the Soviets said no, would the U.S. attack Cuba? American President John Kennedy and Soviet Premier Nikita Khrushchev were both determined to avoid nuclear war, but also they had to defend their own reputations and fend off hawks in their own government.

Here's how the story moved, back and forth, as the two sides acted and reacted to each other:

> (–) Angry about the placement of American missiles in
>   Turkey, within 150 miles of the Soviet Union,
>   Khrushchev considers placing nukes in Cuba, within
>   range of the U.S.
> (+) Khrushchev hesitates, asking Cuban leader Fidel
>   Castro what he thinks.
> (–) Castro agrees to take the missiles. For Castro, the
>   missiles are a matter of personal and patriotic pride.

Castro is eager to take the missiles even though U.S. might then attack Cuba and wipe it off the map.

(+) Concerned, Kennedy seeks assurances that the Soviets will not place nukes in Cuba. Khrushchev assures him that they will not.

(–) American planes produce images that prove that the Soviets are, without a doubt, installing nuclear missiles in Cuba.

(+) Kennedy's inner circle of military advisors meet, establishing a process that will consider a variety of points of view.

(–) Military hawks in both the U.S. and U.S.S.R. push for military action, despite the knowledge that tens of millions would perish in a war.

(+) Kennedy's advisors embrace an alternative to an attack: a "quarantine" of Cuba, in which U.S. ships would intercept Russian ships until the Soviets pull out of Cuba. Quarantine is a fancy word for blockade, which would be considered an act of war.

(–) Angry, Khrushchev considers the quarantine to be an act of war. Hawks in the Kremlin advise him to defy the quarantine.

(+) Approached by U.S. ships, ten Russian ships halt their movement toward Cuba or turn around to return to the U.S.S.R.

(–) Soviets continue to build nuclear sites in Cuba and prepare for an American invasion. In the event of an attack, Cuba would rely on the Soviets' "conventional" nuclear warheads for its defense.

(+) The U.S. seeks ways to force the Soviets to remove its missiles from Cuba while allowing them to save face. Khrushchev proposes removing missiles in Cuba in exchange for the U.S. removing missiles in Turkey.

(–) The drumbeat for war continues. The Soviets have delivered 42 warheads; each has one megaton of power, the equivalent of six Hiroshima bombs.

(+) Khrushchev writes two letters to Kennedy, one pleading and the other threatening. Kennedy responds to the pleading letter and ignores the threatening one.

(–) Cubans fire on American spy flights over the island, ratcheting up the danger of war. The American military prepares for an all-out invasion.

(+) Khrushchev agrees to remove missiles from Cuba and promises never to put them back; in return, the U.S. pledges not to invade Cuba. Secretly, the U.S. also agrees to withdraw missiles from Turkey—later. Kennedy also demands withdrawal of bombers from Cuba; that process takes another 22 days.

Note this: Each of these beats changed the trajectory of the story. If any of these beats did not occur, the story could have turned in a dramatically different direction. Note also that positive and negative events alternate with each other.

The Cuban Missile Crisis was a complex event that has prompted thousands of detailed studies and analyses. The drama shifted back and forth, beat by beat. Even one change could have led to nuclear annihilation.

ELEMENT 62: USE BEATS FOR DESCRIPTIONS

The concept of beats, in theater, refers to action. Whenever someone does something, the story changes in some way. But beats not only pace action. Beats also pace *description*. To explore any topic, break it into pieces and describe it, beat by beat.

Think of your description as a kind of dialogue. One detail raises a question and a second detail answers the question. That second detail raises another question, which a third detail answers. On and on, the parts of the scene engage in a kind of silent dialogue.

In this way, we can create drama out of mere description. As we move through a description, each detail—*each beat*—takes the description to new levels of detail and meaning. Every moment adds information and increases tension, bringing us closer to a resolution.

Try this exercise. Make a list of the qualities of a person, place, or thing, moving from one part to another. Record everything you can see

—along with your thoughts about these observations. As I look out my window to a neighbor's house, I see:

- Packages sit in a pile in front of the house.
- A toddler stands in the plate-glass window, looking out.
- An extra sits car in the driveway; someone is visiting.
- The house's owner and his father, working by the side of the house, using power tools to customize a countertop for the kitchen.
- The next-door neighbor weeding her garden, on the border of the two lawns.
- Kids ride their bicycles along the sidewalk.
- A parent walks a child to a nearby park.
- And ice cream truck rolls by, with a carillon playing to attract customers.

Once you know what is in a scene, you can create an interplay of the parts. Using beats, you can create a rhythm: One observation leads to the next … and the next … and the next.

Allie was expecting an important package, but her husband Chris and his dad were working outside so she had to watch her son Owen as he looked outside from the living room window. Allie was so focused on Owen that she did not notice the package's delivery. She and Owen watched the kids bicycling outside; she thought nostalgically about riding her bike as a kid, while Owen wondered about the strange two-wheeled vehicles. The neighbor, working in the garden, called out to the kids: "Interested in making money on yard work?" They looked at each other, trapped, until the ice cream truck rolled by. They took advantage of the distraction, calling out to a woman walking her child: "Hey, Mrs. T, can we get you an ice cream bar?" The gardener returned to her work.

The details of this scene get energy from how they seem to interact with each other. The details are not just there. They are part of something active, something bigger. One by one, the details give the story forward movement.

You can do use beats also to explore abstract topics. The topics could be from any field—science, politics, psychology, economics, sports, the arts, or any other field. Pick a concept, like the impact of global warming on coastal communities, the causes of terrorism, or the effects of technology on human relations. List the issues that might help you to understand the issue. Move back and forth from one aspect of the idea to its opposite—and then on to the next logical idea and its opposite, and so on. Create a kind of double helix of ideas and their opposites.

When you do that, you'll be using beats for description. As we will see later, you can follow the same process to make an argument.

CASE STUDY: MALCOLM GLADWELL, *TALKING TO STRANGERS*

What happens when officers of the law see something suspicious happening in a neighborhood, at an airport, or in a car? How should they respond? How should they assess the situation? What clues should they look for?

Take a look at this passage, which describes the kinds of clues that a police officer observes when he pulls someone over:

> When he approached the stopped car, the new breed of officer had to be alert to the tiniest clues. Drug couriers often use air fresheners—particularly the kind shaped like little fir trees—to cover up the smell of drugs. (Tree air fresheners are known as the "felony forest.") If there are remains of fast food in the car, that suggests the driver is in a hurry and reluctant to leave his vehicle (and its valuable cargo) unattended. If drugs or guns are hidden in secret compartments, there might be tools on the back seat. What's the mileage on the car? Unusually high for a car of that model year? New tires on an old car? A bunch of keys in the ignition, which would be normal—or just one, as if the car was prepared just for the driver? Is there too much luggage for what seems like a short journey? Or too little luggage for what the motorist says is a long journey? ...

Gladwell gives us the officer's point of view as he peers in the window, perhaps scanning with a flashlight. Our eyes dart from clue to clue: air fresheners, fast-food bags, tools, odometer, tires, keys, luggage. Each clue could change the whole encounter.

A great scene involves not just great action and dialogue, but also a setting rich with cues. So get your reader actively involved exploring the scene, detail by detail. Each detail should make sense on its own and guide the reader on a voyage of discovery.

———

ELEMENT 63: YO-YO SCENE AND SUMMARY

Think about a typical day in your life, about what happens in your home, school, or workplace. Think about how you interact with family and friends, workmates and peers.

Your day alternates between action and repose. You quietly eat breakfast and get ready for work, then put yourself in a different frame of mind for the morning commute. You greet friends as you arrive, then retreat to review email or meet with a colleague. You huddle with colleagues to debate the best strategies for a common challenge, then work quietly at your desk. You have a lively dinner with your kids, then everyone scatters to do chores or homework.

Physiologically, we all need action, to experience what it feels like to move, to interact with the world, and to change. We need excitement. But we cannot experience movement and excitement all the time. We also need time to recover, sit back, ponder, and get background information. And then, after those moments of pause, we need action again.

I use the term "yo-yo" to describe this shift, back and forth, from action to repose. Your writing should offer the same kind of movement.

In one moment, describe action. Show your characters as they move around, interact with others, dealing with conflicts and challenges. Zoom into the action at critical moments. Place obstacles in front of them. Show how they act and react. Describe conflict. Get sensual. Excite readers with sounds and sights and physical sensations. Take the reader on a journey. Show change.

Then, in the next passage, take a break from the action. Offer background information about the characters and the story, about the issues, about the community and place and time. Give the reader enough to appreciate the action—not just what happened, but also what lies ahead.

Yo-yo back and forth. Depict action ... then offer summary or background information ... then show action again ... then summary. Yo-yo back and forth, from scene to summary.

To use the yo-yo format in drafts, give scenes and summaries distinctive markers. Note the scenes and summaries with headers. Or simply place a symbol at the beginning of each section. You might mark scenes with a hashtag and summaries with asterisks. Whatever you do, make it easy to see whether you are yo-yoing. Then, as you prepare your final draft, delete the markers.

CASE STUDY: CHARLES EUCHNER, *THE LAST GREAT DEBATE*

In September 1919, President Woodrow Wilson embarked on a 10,000-mile "Western Tour" to promote the League of Nations. For Wilson, the League was the lynchpin of the Paris Peace Treaty that ended World War I. But the Senate, under control of the opposition Republican Party, was reluctant to ratify the treaty. Majority Leader Henry Cabot Lodge believed the treaty undermined American sovereignty and could involve the U.S. in future European wars.

To tell this story, I follow Wilson as he traveled, by train, from the Midwest out to the Pacific Northwest and down the Pacific Coast and then, finally, inland to Colorado. In this "swing around the circle," Wilson rediscovered America's restless communities; at the same time, he struggled to explain the arcane details of the peace settlement. What better way to tell this story than to yo-yo, back and forth, from scene to summary?

Here's one scene, showing Wilson parading through the streets of Seattle:

> Amid the cheers, something ominous hung in the thick salt air. The Wobblies had been planning a protest; the president's men didn't know what form it would take. Probably just a lot of sign-waving and shouting, they thought. But would it turn violent?
>
> The president stood, smiling broadly and waving to the crowds, as the motorcade passed through the packed streets. But as his car advanced, the crowd's sounds grew strangely uneven.
>
> Then the presidential parade hit a wall of silence. For six blocks, members of the I.W.W. stood in stony silence along the road. The Wobblies packed the spaces between the buildings and the curbs. They folded their arms against their barrel chests. Most of the protesters

wore denim overalls. The veterans wore their service uniforms and stood along the curb, in front, so the president could see them as the car passed by.

The protesters did not speak but carried signs and wore hatbands bearing the words: "Release Political Prisoners." The demands referred to Eugene Debs, the former Socialist presidential candidate now sitting in jail under the Espionage Act for speaking out against the war and the military draft. ...

Wilson looked confused. The smile fell from his face. He stood for several moments, then his body collapsed on itself. His face turned ashen. His hand, holding his hat, fell to his side. He then looked straight ahead. After a few blocks of silence, he sat down. He put his top hat on again.

After six blocks the cheers resumed. The familiar friendly cheers returned. But the president remained seated. He waved but his exuberance was gone.

To make sense of this situation, I provide background information:

Since the announcement of the Western Tour, Seattle's politicians and police worked hard to contain any labor unrest that might disturb the president's visit. The eyes of the nation were on Seattle, a growing naval port. When in Seattle, the president would visit the Pacific fleet at Puget Sound. Nothing should mar those festivities.

Spies from both government agencies and private companies swarmed about the city. Scared at the prospect of a Bolshevik-style revolution in the U.S., the G-men infiltrated unions and churches for days to learn what protests were being planned. Union members began to regard each other with suspicion. Who was a spy in this meeting? No one knew.

Labor unrest continued to put the city on edge. Days before Wilson's arrival in town, printers, stereotypers, pressmen, and mailroom workers ended strikes at the *Ledger* and *News Tribune*. The workers had demanded daily wages of $10 to $12, a raise from their existing rate of $7 to $8 a day. But they came back to work when management extended their contract, which had expired on September 1, at the old wage rate.

By shifting back and forth, from scene to summary, we get both the immediacy of the story and the essential background information.

————

AND ANOTHER THING . . .

Like the beats in a movie or song, every phrase or sentence should respond to what happened before and set up what follows. Every passage should offer something new, even surprising.

Beats create tempo and move the journey forward. You nudge the reader toward X, and then surprise him with an assertion of Y. You look at Y in a new light, then surprise him with Z.

Beats also offer a useful way to test writing. A beat belongs if it advances a story in useful ways. If it doesn't, cut it. Apply this beat test to all aspects of your writing. Does the quotation add to the piece —*change* it—in a useful way? Does a statistic? A piece of historic background? A detail about a character's appearance or mannerisms?

If a beat adds useful insight, keep it; if it doesn't, let it go.

CHAPTER 17
NUMBERS

Throughout recorded time, there have been three kinds of people in the world, the High, the Middle, and the Low. They have been subdivided in many ways, they have borne countless different names ... but the essential structure of society has never altered.

GEORGE ORWELL

IN THE AGE OF MULTITASKING, consider this question: How many things can you pay attention to at the same time?

How about seven? For years, the "rule of seven" dominated thinking in education and business. The idea originated with experiments in the 1940s, which found that people can hold seven numbers in their shorterm memory. But other studies find out short-term memory much smaller. Some say we can focus on only two or three things at a time. Still others say we can focus on just *one* thing at a time.

With the rise of the Internet, we are inundated with information. As writers, our job is to sort that information for the reader. Rather than just dumping mountains of statistics and observations and logical arguments, we need to pick out and focus on essential images and ideas.

Just as a computer crashes when overloaded with data-heavy programs, so the human brain crashes when overloaded with too many demands for memory or action.

Consider the "Jam Test," an experiment at an upscale grocery store in Menlo Park, California. Researchers from Stanford and Columbia set up two displays. One offered customers a choice of six varieties of jams; the other offered a choice of 24 varieties. Customers at the small display bought a jar of jam 30 percent of the time; customers at the larger display bought a jar just 3 percent of the time.

Overwhelmed by choice, people stop trying to figure things out. They forget what they want, lose focus, and wander away.

Because readers can picture small numbers, it's easier to remember them. Take a moment to visualize the numbers one, two, and three. Close your eyes. Try to visualize what those numbers look like. The number one may look like an isolated object in the middle of a vast open space. The number two probably shows two things, side by side, close enough for comparison but far enough to be separate. The number three probably displays objects arranged in the shape of a triangle.

We organize our lives with these numbers every day, using simple shapes and configurations to manage our thinking. Whatever you write, then, offer these basic groupings. Avoid overwhelming readers with too many categories and choices, details and evidence.

―――――

ELEMENT 64: USE ONES TO HIGHLIGHT PEOPLE, PLACES, AND ISSUES

One may be the loneliest number, as Three Dog Night says in its hit song of 1969, but it's also the most powerful. When you focus on one thing, everything disappears.

Oneness suggests, above all, wholeness and unity. When something is singular and complete, it does not need outsiders. One is simple; in fact, the Latin root of simple, *semel*, means "a single time" and "for the first time." Oneness also stands for integrity. You could do worse, for example, than to organize your life around the Golden Rule or a commitment to service.

History books overflow with stories of singular characters: Christ, Cleopatra, Napoleon, Lincoln, Keller, and Gandhi, to note a random half-dozen. Singular events also punctuate history: the Declaration of Independence, Gettysburg, the murder of Archduke Ferdinand, the

Great Crash, Pearl Harbor, Hiroshima, JFK's assassination, and 9/11. Nothing focuses or organizes the mind like oneness.

In a sense, history has been a long march toward oneness. Religion has shifted from polytheism to monotheism. Government has shifted from congeries of small city-states to unified nation-states. In modern times, dreamers from Woodrow Wilson to Bill Gates have aspired to create a singular global community.

Oneness appeals to people because it sweeps away the confusion and clutter of manyness. When Thomas Hobbes wrote the *Leviathan*, in the aftermath of the English Civil War, he could see no other way to create order—and, ironically, liberty too—than to install a single Sovereign with absolute power. Two centuries later, John Stuart Mill's *On Liberty* outlines "one very simple principle"—the idea that people ought not interfere with other people's affairs—as the essential rule of human communities.

We use the number one to make sweeping claims about people, events, ideas, everything. Consider these passages:

- Alone among the revolutionaries, Washington could bring order out of chaos.
- Since Villa was the one man who could raise an army large enough to defeat the *federales*, Obregon had him assassinated in 1923.
- "I alone can fix it," Donald Trump told the Republican Convention in 2016.

Talking about "the one" focuses attention. But it always—*always*—oversimplifies. So follow a statement of oneness with a deeper explanation of how things work.

But that's only the beginning. Around that top dog, rivals rise up. Then things start to get interesting.

CASE STUDY: JOSEPH NYE, *THE PARADOX OF AMERICAN POWER*

What happens when a great rivalry ends—when one side prevails?

At the end of the Cold War, the United States emerged as the world's only superpower. After generations battling foes across the globe—Germany and the Central Powers in World War I; Germany, Japan, and Italy in World War II; and the Soviet Bloc in the Cold War—

the U.S. asserted total supremacy over the world. Or at least it looked that way.

America dominated global trade, higher education, medicine, entertainment, Internet and technology, finance, and R&D and star-tups. The U.S. spent more on arms than the next eight nations combined. American hegemony extended, seemingly, to all endeavors. "U.S. supremacy today extends to the economy, currency, military areas, lifestyle, language and the products of mass culture that inun-date the world, forming thought and fascinating even the enemies of the United States," a French diplomat said in the early 2000s. The German magazine *Der Spiegel* proclaimed: "Globalization wears a 'Made in U.S.A.' label."

So what does that mean? What does it mean to be No. 1 in a complex, interconnected, global world?

On one level, it means that the U.S. could assert itself in world poli-tics like no other power. The U.S. could set the global agenda for free markets, human rights, terrorism, global warming, and nuclear prolif-eration. Neoconservative analysts like Charles Krauthammer pushed for American presidents to "reassert American freedom of action." If you're going to be the only superpower, Krauthammer says, act like it: *Dominate the world, without apology.*

On another level, America's solo superpower status was just a holding pattern. Soon, another nation would emerge to compete with the U.S. Who? Most said China will dominate politics and the economy in the 21st century.

In his study of America's global power, Joseph Nye explores China's ambitions. He quotes experts to buttress his points. The Sinologist Arthur Waldron, for example, predicts that China's rise will lead to a major war in Asia: "China today is actively seeking to scare the United States away from East Asia rather as Germany sought to frighten Britain before World War I," he said. Partly out of insecurity, China is actively working to restructure the global system to put them at the top. The longtime foreign policy guru Robert Kagan suggests that China has no choice but to assert its power: "Chinese leaders … worry that they must change the rules of the international system before the international system changes them."

Others envision a bloc of American rivals, similar to the Warsaw Pact during the Cold War. One popular idea, in the early 2000s, was that the BRICS countries—Brazil, Russia, India, China, and South Africa—would pose a powerful economic counterpart to the U.S.

So what's the reality? Is the U.S. the undisputed master of world affairs? And if so, how does it matter?

Dominance is always just the beginning of the story. Even in a unipolar world, rivals emerge to take on the top power. That happened with *Pax Romana, Pax Britannica,* and *Pax Americana.* Oneness inevitable leads to twoness.

————

ELEMENT 65. USE TWOS FOR OPPOSITIONS AND COMPLEMENTS

When Noah filled the ark with pairs of animals, he had a specific purpose: Allow the reproduction of species. Writers use pairs for two different reasons—to show oppositions and complements.

First, using pairs sets up an opposition. When you put two characters in a scene, the two often battle each other. When you set up two ideas—like capitalism and socialism, men and women, science and the humanities—they reveal themselves by showing, clearly, what they are not. The author Christopher Vogler lists these oppositions:

Sloppy *vs.* Neat
Brave *vs.* Cowardly
Feminine *vs.* Masculine
Open *vs.* Closed
Suspicious *vs.* Trusting
Optimistic *vs.* Pessimistic
Planned *vs.* Spontaneous
Passive *vs.* Active
Low key *vs.* Dramatic
Talkative *vs.* Taciturn
Living in the past *vs.* Forward-looking
Conservative *vs.* Liberal
Underhanded *vs.* Principled
Honest *vs.* Dishonest
Literal *vs.* Poetic
Clumsy *vs.* Graceful
Lucky *vs.* Unlucky

Calculated *vs.* Intuitive
Introverted *vs.* Extraverted
Happy *vs.* Sad
Materialistic *vs.* Spiritual
Polite *vs.* Rude
Controlling *vs.* Impulsive
Sacred *vs.* Profane
Nature *vs.* Nurture

People often define themselves by contrast with some "other." The Crips and Bloods gangs get their identity as much from what they *aren't* as from what they *are*. So do residents of city neighborhoods, schools, cities and regions, and whole nations. Racial, ethnic, and religious tensions arise from this same kind of negative identity. Bigots fear intermarriage because it undermines their identity as a negation of the other.

But pairs don't just oppose each other; they also *reinforce* and *complete* each other. According to the ancient Chinese idea of yin and yang, opposites come from the same world and need each other. Examples of yin and yang include male and female, emotion and reason, power and finesse, work and ease, and art and science.

Think of some examples from American history. Muhammad Ali and Joe Frazier, while fighting for the heavyweight championship of the world, also battled for each other's respect. Bill and Hillary Clinton, partners in life and power, clashed behind the scenes over policy and personal affairs, but defied all the tabloid predictions of divorce. And don't forget the great rivalries of sports, like the Yankees and Red Sox, the Celtics and Lakers, and Notre Dame and Michigan.

Twos give stories energy. Nobody doesn't enjoy a love story: Romeo and Juliet, Anthony and Cleopatra, Tristan and Isolde, and Odysseus and Penelope. And don't forget Rhett and Scarlett in *Gone*

With the Wind, Jeff and Lisa in *Rear Window*, Nick and Amy in *Gone Girl*, or Philip and Elizabeth in *The Americans*.

As long as the tug-of-war continues—or as long as the characters' differences reveal interesting things—pairs work fine.

CASE STUDY: THE TWO-PARTY SYSTEM IN AMERICA

The founders of the American republic were wary of political parties, which they called "factions." Little good could come from dividing people into self-interested gangs of partisans, they said. Alexander Hamilton called political parties "the most fatal disease" of popular governments. James Madison hoped that the young nation would "break and control the violence of faction."

Still, partisan divisions appeared right away. After George Washington's unanimous election as president, his Federalist Party and the Republican-Democrats, led by Thomas Jefferson, battled for three decades. Then the Whig Party emerged to battle the Democrats. Since the Republicans replaced the Whigs in 1856, the Republicans and Democrats have battled for the political soul of the nation.

Over the years, the two parties have evolved. The Republicans have always been the party of big business, while the Democrats have been the party of laborers and the "common man." Immigrants generally ally with Democrats. The farm vote has passed back and forth, as has small business and specific industries like tech and health care. Blacks are now the Democrats' most reliable constituency but they favored Republicans after Lincoln freed the slaves.

Whatever the particular platforms, the two parties define themselves against each other. When one side takes a position, the other often takes the opposite position. It's almost like a game: *If I say up, you say down.*

Consider:

- As scientists concluded that global warming threatens the world's ecosystem—and human habitations—conservative think-tankers devised a market-based strategy to address the crisis. The idea of trading carbon credits, these neo-Smithians hoped, could nudge businesses and public and nonprofit agencies to reduce their carbon footprint. But as Democrats embraced the strategy, the GOP recoiled. Leading

Republicans, including Donald Trump, now declare the crisis to be a "hoax."

- Led by the work of conservative think tanks, Republicans embraced a model of health care that combined private insurance with public subsidies. Governor Mitt Romney of Massachusetts enacted this approach in Massachusetts. When Democrats embraced the strategy, Republicans turned against it. Under President Barack Obama, the Affordable Care Act passed with no Republican votes.

- During the 2012 presidential campaign, Republican Mitt Romney criticized Barack Obama for arguing the al Quada was the globe's greatest threat, sounding alarms about the Russian dictator Vladimir Putin. Obama retorted: "The 1980s are now calling to ask for their foreign policy back, because the Cold War's been over for 20 years." But when Republican Donald Trump colluded with Russia to influence the 2016 election, the Democrats saw Russia as America's prime threat—and the GOP dismissed it as a trifle.

- The two sides react to sex scandals depending on the letter at the end of the name ("D" or "R"). When Bill Clinton was caught in scandals, Republicans bemoaned the lack of personal integrity and impeached Clinton; Democrats dismissed the scandal as a meaningless side show. When the scandals involved Republicans, like Donald Trump and Jim Jordan, the Democrats argued for the importance of character and Republicans dismissed their concerns.

For a variety of reasons, the two parties have become more polarized in the last generation. The Republicans have become the party for big business, low taxes, and the evangelical right and against immigration, free trade, and global engagement. The Democrats have become the party of small business, social equity, civil rights, American leadership in the world, and scientific approaches to issues.

Joseph Biden, a product of an era when Republicans and Democrats often collaborated on policy issues, came to office in 2021 hoping to overcome partisan divisions. But in today's toxic environment of big money in politics and the bubble realities of cable news and social media, he struggled to change the tone of American politics. Whatever happens, the two parties will continue their tit-for-tat fight for control of American politics.

––––––

ELEMENT 66: USE THREES TO REVEAL DYNAMIC RELATIONS

The filmmaker Martin Scorsese was once asked for advice on how to write a good scene. His answer: *Put three people in a room.*

As architects and builders attest, triangles offer the sturdiest shape for construction. Unlike rectangles, which collapse under pressure, triangles maintain their shape and strength. Builders use triangles in skyscrapers, bridges, tunnels, and infrastructure. For this reason, one design expert has called for changing the shape of bricks from rectangles to triangles.

Trios also offer the most dynamic grouping for a story or analysis. Everything two characters do affects a third; that third force, in turn, shifts the balance of power among all three. Any time one of the parties shifts, the other two must respond. The alignment of power changes constantly; every shift offers new dynamics and insights.

Ancient peoples found holy mystery in earth, wind, and fire. The Bible teaches us about the Father, Son, and Holy Ghost. Photographic reproduction uses three basic colors: red, green, and blue. Traffic lights have three colors. Urban economist Edward Glaeser explains successful cities with a different triad: sun, sprawl, and skills.

Andrew Hodges points out the centrality of three in conflict:

> Three is the number of dividing and ruling. Three is the number of fighting an ally over how best to oppose an enemy. Three is the number of triangulation, which seems to mean doing what your enemies want, while leaving your friends with nowhere else to go."

Power struggles organize in threes, with two main contenders often hostage to the demands of a third contender who can make or break them. In the two-party system of American politics, the Democrats and Republicans win or lose depending on how well they appeal to the third force—the great mass of independents and undecideds.

How important are threes to drama? A literary theorist named James Stiller once examined the structures of ten Shakespeare plays and ten classic films. Almost always, three characters play the active role in the scenes. Stiller's findings make sense. Most of our everyday conversations and interactions involve three people. Even when bigger groups get together—when teenagers hang out at a pizza joint or when their parents host sprawling dinner parties—people cluster in smaller groups.

Literature offers countless triangles. Consider this partial list: Oedipus, Laius, and Jocasta (Sophocles's *Oedipus Rex*); the three daughters vying for Lear's legacy (Shakespeare's *King Lear*); Daisy, Tom, and Gatsby (F. Scott Fitzgerald's *The Great Gatsby*); and Santiago, the boy, and the townspeople (Ernest Hemingway's *The Old Man and the Sea*).

In fact, triangles give such power that we might consider using triangles to structure every key moment of our stories and analyses. So Aristotle's narrative arc might look like this:

By using triangles to advance a story—or analysis, as we'll discuss later—you create dynamism in every scene. But you don't overwhelm the reader with complexity. And you set up the next scene by leaving some issues unresolved.

CASE STUDY: THEODORE CAPLOW, *TWO AGAINST ONE*

Durable relationships require at least three parties. Pairs are always subject to breakup; trios can survive changes over long periods.

How do triads operate? Theodore Caplow has identified eight different kinds of triads. The dynamics of these triads depend on the interactions and resources of each corner of the triangle. Sometimes two corners overpower a third; sometimes one corner dominates the other two.

To illustrate these dynamic and ever-changing relationships,

Caplow recounts a controversy over public housing in Chicago in the late 1940s and early 1950s. This kind of skirmish remains common in today's cities and towns.

The controversy began when the housing authority proposed building seven new public housing complexes in the city. The authority attempted to gain the mayor's support; the authority's chairman gave the mayor seven possible sites for the projects and asked the mayor to endorse some of those sites. The authority was, in effect, seeking a two-against-one alliance that looked like this:

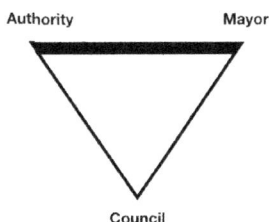

Authority   Mayor

Council

Three weeks later the mayor had not even read the authority proposal. He feared alienating council members from the districts where the projects were proposed.

Seeking to gain leverage in the battle, staff members from the housing authority leaked the proposed sites to a friendly newspaper. These staffers hoped to arouse the public to support their proposals. With a loud public outcry, they thought, the mayor and council would go along with the plan. They hoped for a triangle like this:

Authority   Public

Mayor and Council

But this move only angered council members, who held hearings but otherwise stalled the whole process. In response, the authority then took its case to the mayor, then to the party boss who controlled the mayor, then to leading figures in the council. Each effort failed to advance the authority's cause.

Opponents packed city council hearings to denounce the proposals. Public opposition prompted the mayor to oppose any project that council members opposed in their districts. Now the political situation looked like this:

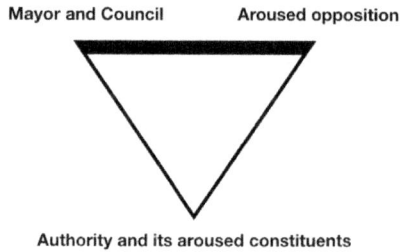

On and on, the conflict moved through a series of triads. The parties to the conflict—authority, specific factions in the authority, mayor, council, various coalitions of council members, newspapers, pro-housing activists, anti-housing activists—sought to gain the upper hand by creating powerful alliances and isolating their opponents.

One last point. The above examples may suggest that the only way to prevail in a triangular battle is to join with another power bloc to create a two-against-one advantage. But often, a single power can overwhelm the other forces. In cities with strong political machines—which control elections, patronage, media, real estate, and various local institutions—the mayor can dominate other powers with relative ease.

Always, triangles are dynamic. One day's dominant alliance could be the next day's fragmented foes.

ELEMENT 67: USE LISTS TO SHOW COMPLEXITY

Lists reveal a wide range of experiences and ideas. With a list, you offer the reader a survey of people, places, events, or ideas. The tour might not offer much focus. But that's OK. Sometimes we need to survey a long list before we can isolate the two or three key elements.

We usually make lists as memory aids. Lists for chores, shopping, meetings, and procedures help us to avoid taxing our memory. In a busy world, trying to remember too much often results in mistakes. Atul Gawande, a doctor at Brigham and Women's Hospital in Boston, has found that simple checklists of procedures save lives in the operating room. Any good doctor, in the midst of a tense and complex workday, might forget one or two actions he needs to take. Even one mistake can be fatal. Gawande explains:

> The checklists provided two main benefits... First, they helped with memory recall, especially with mundane matters that are easily overlooked in patients undergoing more drastic events. (When you're worrying about what treatment to give a woman who won't stop seizing, it's hard to remember to make sure that the head of her bed is in the right position.) A second effect was to make explicit the minimum, expected steps in complex processes.

Writers don't face such life-and-death situations. But lists offer a great way to summarize the essential parts of any complex situation, which you can then break down and explore in more detail. Long lists can be unruly—but not as unruly as scattered, easily forgotten ideas.

CASE STUDY: TIMOTHY SNYDER, *ON TYRANNY*

Can a stable, prosperous, and diverse democracy take a dark turn toward totalitarianism? What signs indicate the erosion of democratic norms and values? How do we know when elites have consolidated enough power to endanger human and civil rights?

Timothy Snyder considers these questions in his short book *On Tyranny*. A longtime student of nationalism and authoritarianism in Europe—from Hitler to Putin—Snyder offers twenty simple imperatives for societies facing a drift toward authoritarianism. Here's the list:

1. Do not obey in advance.
2. Defend institutions.
3. Beware of the one party state.
4. Take responsibility for the face of the world.
5. Remember professional ethics.
6. Be wary of paramilitaries.
7. The reflective if you must be armed.
8. Stand out.
9. Be kind to her language.
10. Believe in truth.
11. Investigate.
12. Make eye contact and small talk.
13. Practice corporeal politics.
14. Establish a private life.
15. Contribute to good causes.
16. Learn from peers in other countries.
17. Listen for dangerous words.
18. Be calm when the unthinkable arrives.
19. Be a patriot.
20. Be as courageous as you can.

Could Synder have organized these twenty ideas into, say, three major categories? Probably. He could have said, for example:

- Strengthen your connections to friends, family, colleagues, and neighbors.
- Resist unfair or oppressive practices, by government or its allies, wherever it arises.
- Do not let Orwellian language distort reality. Make sure you know what's going on and speak bluntly and honestly about it.

That about sums it up, right? But sometimes we need to know specific actions to take, rather than simply understand general principles of action. If a hurricane is coming, we need to look for specific signs—rain, winds, dark skies, cirrus clouds, rising sea levels, white capped waves, and so on—not general indicators like "blustery wet weather." Likewise, to fight authoritarianism, we need to know how to act in a number of different circumstances. If we're too general in our understanding, we might not be ready to act decisively.

Complex issues and crisis, especially, require close attention to details. That's why Snyder's list is so useful.

———

AND ANOTHER THING . . .

All writing, ultimately, isolates one or two or three subjects from the complex world. Why? Research on attention offers an important insight on how we pay attention.

In a psychology experiment at Harvard University, subjects watched a video of basketball players passing a ball; the subjects were told to count the number of times players wearing white pass the ball. Half of the viewers do not notice a student dressed in a gorilla costume who walks into the middle of the scene, stops, and beats his chest for the camera.

So what's the action in that scene—the players or the gorilla? It depends. Are you looking at the just the ball? Or just the one team in white shirts? Or both teams? Or are you tracking the whole scene? In the end, what you see depends on what you pay attention to.

When we organize ideas into ones, twos, and threes, we focus on different aspects of the picture. If I tell you to pay attention to one thing, you won't pay close attention to the other things. If I tell you to pay attention to two or three things, you will note the way those things *relate* to each other but probably not certain details about either one. If I tell you to pay attention to all of the elements of the scene—the ball, the two sets of players, and the student in the gorilla costume—you will get the gist of the scene but miss many details about them.

How you cluster your ideas depends on how you direct your attention. By putting the spotlight in one place, you remove the spotlight from other places.

PART SIX
ANALYZING AN ISSUE

When I first started teaching college classes, I confronted a stubborn problem with my students' papers.

Whatever the topic—understanding American political culture, the powers of the presidency, how the legislative process works, the most appropriate approach to reading the Constitution—student papers seemed vague and unclear, with no real point. In class, the students seemed to understand the ideas we were discussing. But they didn't express those ideas well on paper.

In their papers, these students talked about the "best" strategies for presidents, the "best" ways to businesses to market their products, the "best" diets for fighting disease, and so on. But this phrasing misses the essential part of analysis: "Best *for what?*"

One day, I wrote the following on the blackboard:

$$X \rightarrow Y$$

Something, I said, always causes *something else*.

The problem with papers about "the best" this or that, I explained, is that they focus on one side of the equation but miss the other side.

You can't understand X without understanding Y; you can't understand Y without understanding X.

From then on, I required my students to go through a rigorous process to identify a *causal argument*. Before writing a word, students had to identify the variables that might explain outcomes. Then they had to sort and operationalize these variables. Then they could gather evidence. Finally, they could identify which variables actually caused which outcomes.

In other words, they had to figure out which variables were "the best" explanations for what effects.

Most outcomes, of course, depend on several causes. So X is not one cause, but several variables. Think of it as X_1, X_2, X_3, and so on. Therefore:

$$X_1 + X_2 + X_3 \rightarrow Y$$

When you think about it, each of our essays explores some kind of causality:

- *Portraying a person*: What makes people act the way they do? How, in turn, do their behaviors affect other people?
- *Depiction of a place*: What specific qualities of a physical setting—city or country, inside or outside, modern or traditional, big or small, elaborate or plain, homey or cold, and so on—shape the people of a community?
- *Description of action*: What specific movements are necessary to cause an action? What needs to happen first? Then what? What sequence of movements and moments create an action? Explain this sequence like this: *First, … Then, … And then, … Finally, …*
- *Explanation of a complex process*: How do different processes come together to create a complex outcome?

Now we move to analysis. Analysis is really all of these things, but with a twist.

Previously, we focused on *one-and-only* subjects. We want to know about specific people, places, actions, and processes. Now we want to know about *patterns*—how certain kinds of things happen, over and over. We are moving from an *n* of 1 to an *n* of many.

THE PLAN OF ATTACK

In this section, we will focus on three essential skills of analysis:

- Chapter 18: Questions and brainstorming
- Chapter 19: Storytelling for analysis
- Chapter 20: Making a case

Look at the ground we have traveled in our work.

In the first two sections (people and place) we talked only about one-and-only phenomena. In the next two sections (action and process) we talked about things that could be one-and-only phenomena or things that happen over and over.

Now we are talking about things that happen over and over, predictably and reliably, as if dictated by an invisible law. Analysis explores how things work, not just once but again and again. This is the realm of science, where we discover recurring patterns that help us to understand how the world works.

CHAPTER 18
STORYTELLING FOR ANALYSIS

Here's the Law of Universal Specificity: You can't write about every-where or everyone, only about one person or one place. If you want to write about everybody, start with one person, in one place, doing one real thing.

THOMAS FOSTER

TO EXPLAIN his life and work as a scientist, Rodolfo Llinas tells stories of his youth, rich with metaphors.

As a boy, he visited his grandfather, who was a psychiatrist. Once he witnessed one of his grandfather's patients have a seizure. "I thought he was going to die," Llinas says. His grandfather explained that the patient didn't want to do what he did, but "there's something wrong with his brain."

That incident posed questions that Llinas has pursued for his whole career: What is the relationship between a person and his brain? Is the brain separate from our being? Or is the brain, in essence, the whole self? How do we understand—and shape—how the brain operates?

As a child, Llinas tinkered with a Victrola, taking it apart and putting it together again. "All of these [parts] by themselves had no property," he recalled. "But as a whole, they would make music." When he rebuilt the record player, he understood the elegance of the machine. Simple outside, it was complicated inside. "Once you understand something at that level, it's yours."

The Victrola gave Llinas, a neuroscientist at New York University's School of Medicine, a metaphor to understand the brain. The whole, he understood, is greater than the parts. But to understand that whole, you need to understand each of the parts and how they interact. To understand any subject—a brain, code, machines, businesses, politics, economics—the researcher has to shift back and forth from the parts to the whole.

What is the best way to understand the interactions of the parts and the whole? The most creative scientists look to stories to make sense of their work.

"At the end of the day, the scientist is a storyteller," says Gordon Fishell, a cell biologist at NYU. "Back in prehistoric times, we had a group of cave dwellers, and they didn't have a hell of a lot to do other than tell stories. Whoever holds the big stick gets to talk. You get to hold it as long as you hold the audience."

Scientific investigations often create the suspense of a great mystery. Researchers ask tough questions and develop a collection of answers—some right and some wrong. In their labs, conferences, and writing, researchers "iterate" those stories. They test one possibility, then another, then another. They gather data to see which storyline merits support. The wrong answers are just as important as the right ones, for the same reason that false clues lend drama to a good book or movie—they force people to think harder and find alternative explanations.

"Whether you're Spike Lee or Ingmar Bergman or a scientist, it's all the same thing," Fishell says. "Creative people create. Why did I want to do science rather than fiction or being a lawyer? In science, there's *truth* there." But it's still storytelling.

The lesson for writers: Analysis is just another variety of imagination and storytelling. You cannot analyze any issue—no matter how abstract it seems—unless you can picture it and make it part of a narrative. So whatever problem you want to analyze—the challenge of regional sprawl, the debate about global warming, the process of Darwinian evolution, the effects of music on the brain, or the causes of organizational failure—start with stories.

———

ELEMENT 68: NARRATE COMPLEX ISSUES

In my work with business groups, we use stories and characters to analyze the challenges of designing products and services, finding talent and financing, and marketing and sales. Whatever issue you face, good analysis begins with stories.

Still, many sober-minded business people and scientists, resist storytelling. It seems so ... *soft*. In one seminar of Fortune 500 executives, I noticed one COO squirm in his seat as we talked about character types in *The Wizard of Oz*. "We're not telling stories in my business," he said with exasperation. "That's fun, but we're trying to solve *problems*."

Another one called out: "Can we talk about grammar and emails?"

I never thought I'd hear anyone make that plea. But I could see the point. These executives wanted to write better emails and memos, not tell stories. Still, I wanted them to see how stories could help to analyze their business problems. So I asked them what challenges they face in their work and lives. They describe these scenarios like this:

- An executive at a manufacturing supply company considers strategies for growth. To make smart decisions, he needs to understand labor costs, equipment and other capital investments, advertising and marketing strategy, strengths of competitors, earnings-to-debt ratios, new product launches, and so on.
- A housing developer debates whether to build an apartment building near a commuter station or outside the city. To make the decision, he needs to understand the interplay of land and building costs, local wage levels, vacancy rates, interest rates, and the like.
- A health care provider creates fitness programs for major corporations. Her goal is to cut the company's rising insurance costs. To create the best program, she wants to understand the effects of exercise, nutrition, medications, emotional wellbeing, and age.

To understand these problems, we need to begin with storytelling. Once we explore some scenarios and narratives, we can begin to analyze the challenges. Inevitably, as we explore narratives involved in their work, these Type A executives begin to see themselves as actors in a larger drama, not just number-crunching problem solvers.

In that meeting with Fortune 500 executives, I asked seminar participants to identify people in their companies who fit the eight character types: hero and villain, sidekick and skeptic, mentor and tempter, heart and mind. After scribbling for a few minutes, the mood in the room changed. Then one executive said something like this:

> I've been thinking about my company battling for market share, struggling to keep prices low, keep the workers happy, all that. And all that *is* important.
>
> But you need to see the situation as a story too. We're the heroes of the story. Our competitors—actually, just a couple of them—are the villains. In our company we have both rational and emotional types. They always seem to line up against each other, and too often I try to please them both. And we have our mentor, the founder of the company, and these new investors who are trying to get us away from our traditional business. It just goes on and on.
>
> I *get* it. My job is to figure out: *What's the story?* What are we meant to become—as a company and as workers and creators? And how can I line up all these types to be on my side, or at least help me when I need them? And when they're against me, how can I deal with that? I knew that before. But now I see the patterns underneath the spreadsheet numbers and product strategies.

When you understand the narrative arc of your story—with all the complications of competing ideas and interests—you can understand your challenges. All analysis, after all, is just storytelling at a higher level of abstraction.

CASE STUDY: BARBARA EHRENREICH'S *NICKEL AND DIMED* AND ADAM SHEPARD'S *SCRATCH BEGINNINGS*

Does inequality prevent people from pursuing their dreams. Or is a good life open to all, but just require more commitment and resolve from the poor and working class?

Researchers have worked for years to answer this question. Thomas Piketty's *Capital in the Twenty-First Century,* which tracks inequality in the U.S. and Europe since the 1700s, argues that inequality poses a threat to society. People stuck at the bottom, too often, have no chance to rise. Conservatives disagree, saying that poor and working class people can thrive with hard work and sacrifice.

To explore the effect of low wages on poor and working class people in America, the journalist Barbara Ehrenreich decided to live with poverty-level wages. Educated and resourceful, she should be able to survive on low wages as well as anyone. A few passages reveal the difficulties:

> I can afford to spend $500 on rent or maybe, with severe economies, $600, and still have $400 or $500 left over for food and gas. In the Key West area, this pretty much confines me to flophouses or trailer homes —like the one, a pleasing 15-minute drive from town, that has no air-conditioning, no screens, no fans, no television, and, by way of diversion, only the challenge of evading the landlord's Doberman pinscher. …
>
> From the first day on [in a job waiting tables], I find that of all the things that I have left behind, such as home and identity, what I miss the most is my competence. I am beset by requests as if by bees: more iced tea here, ketchup over there, a to-go box for table 14, and where are the high chairs, anyway? Of the 27 tables, up to six are usually mine at any time, though on slow afternoons or if Gail is off, I sometimes have the whole place to myself. …
>
> You might imagine, from a comfortable distance, that people who live, year in and year out, on $6 to $10 an hour have discovered some survival stratagems unknown to the middle class. But no. … There are no secret economies that nourish the poor; on the contrary, there are a host of special costs. If you can't put up the two months' rent you need to secure an apartment, you end up paying through the nose for a room by the week. If you have only a room, with a hotplate at best, you can't save by cooking up huge lentil stews that can be frozen for the week ahead. You eat fast food or the hot dogs and plastic-foam cups of soup that can be microwaved in a convenience store. …
>
> I start tossing back drugstore-brand ibuprofens as if they were vitamin C, four before each shift, because an old computer-mouse-related repetitive-stress injury in my upper back has come back to full-spasm strength, thanks to the tray carrying. In my ordinary life, this level of disability might justify a day of ice packs and stretching. …

Her narrative makes a simple argument: When we pay workers a pittance, we force them to make sacrifices that undermine their health and security. At the very least, we need to offer everyone a living wage, as well as access to health care and opportunities for lifelong training.

Not so fast, said a conservative young man named Adam Shepard. He set out to test Ehrenreich's narrative by doing his own participatory study of life on the economy's low rungs. With $25 in his pocket, he took a bus to Charleston, South Carolina, to see if he could do any better than Ehrenreich. He did.

Shepard lived in a homeless shelter for a month while lining up a $9-an-hour job with a moving company. Over ten months, he saved $5,200, bought a used car, and found (he believes) the secret to surviving on low wages.

The secret, Shepard says, is a positive, upbeat attitude. To illustrate the point, he introduces us to Derrick, one of his coworkers. A high school dropout who was married with one child, Derrick worked hard and set an example for others while saving money to build a better life. Others—even young, able-bodied young men—lacked that discipline. They didn't commit themselves to their work. On pay day, they blew their wages on partying.

> There was a huge contrast, in attitude and otherwise, that separated guys like Derrick (who took their job seriously, wanted to excel, and wanted to be proud of what they had accomplished) from the guys who you could tell were coming to work just to make a few bucks to pay their rent. Moving furniture was so much more than that to guys like Derrick and Mike. They were professionals, seasoned veterans who had made sacrifices to put themselves in a position to do things that no one else could do. They were average guys performing above average feats. …

To pull himself out of poverty, Derrick refused to complain about his circumstances. Instead, he worked hard every day to improve his skills and his value. Shepard followed Derrick's example. Even when he was shoveling hundreds of pounds of dog waste from a courtyard, he found he could be upbeat:

As far as jobs go, it doesn't get much worse. There's no way to add glitz or glamour to it. … But as much as I really, really, really did not want to spend my Sunday picking up piles of poop, I never once thought about dropping the bag and leaving. Who would? Ten dollars an hour, cash! It was baffling to me that none of the other guys had showed up to claim their piece of the action. So I shoveled. And shoveled. Dodging one mound to pick up another, I realized that there was no secret to this job, no way to conceive a more efficient system that would get the job done quicker. I just had to drudge through it. Scoop and toss, scoop and toss. …

On one question, Shepard agrees with Ehrenreich. Most low-wage workers get little respect or support. The problem with low-wage work, he concluded, is not the low pay as much as low status.

Not many people that I met during my tenure at Fast Company [the moving company] complained about what they were getting paid. They were just mad at the lack of hands-on leadership. They didn't feel like they belonged to anything. They felt abused. They were robots, sent out to make money for the big boss man, go home, and return and repeat the next day. It was a vicious, destructive cycle, and it hurt the overall morale.

Most low-wage workers, alas, get treated poorly. It doesn't need to be that way. Research by MIT's Zeynep Ton and others shows that low-wage jobs can be turned into "good jobs" if companies invest in their workers and reorganized their work flows. But that does not happen in most low-wage industries. Supervisors rarely honor and support their employees' aspirations. They chew 'em up and spit 'em out, as evidenced by turnover rates as high as 90 percent.

Each of these narratives reveals something important about research: *Stories offer powerful starting points to explore the complexities of issues*. But to understand a problem more thoroughly, we need more. We need to gather data of whole groups of people. We need to identify all of the possible factors that produce all the possible outcomes. Then we need to gather evidence for each. We need to move from storytelling to analysis.

_____

ELEMENT 69: USE BEATS TO MAKE ARGUMENTS

A beat is a distinct moment—a small or large physical action, piece of dialogue, or any change in a scene. Every beat creates change. Every beat invites a response. With every beat, you push the story forward.

Plato and other Greek philosophers called the process of exchanging beats *dialectics*. One person would make a statement ("thesis") and a second person would counter ("antithesis"); after some consideration, they'd combine the best of both sides ("synthesis"). They moved from positive to negative and back again. In the process, they advanced, steadily, toward the truth.

Consider one of the most famous exchanges in philosophy. In Plato's *Republic*, Socrates and Thrasymachus debate justice. Thrasymachus declares justice to be "the interest of the stronger." Looking for a crack in his logic, Socrates asks whether bullies ever make mistakes about their best interests. Yes, Thrasymachus admits. Then Socrates asks: Since bullies don't always act in their own best interests, how can we say that the actions of the stronger party are always just? Here's how the debate concludes:

> Socrates: *Have we not admitted that the rulers may be mistaken about their own interest in what they command, and also that to obey them is justice? Has not that been admitted?*
> Thrasymachus: *Yes.*
> Socrates: *Then you must also have acknowledged justice not to be for the interest of the stronger, when the rulers unintentionally command things to be done which are to their own injury. For if, as you say, justice is the obedience which the subject renders to their commands, in that case, O wisest of men, is there any escape from the conclusion that the weaker are commanded to do, not what is for the interest, but what is for the injury of the stronger?*

Beat by beat, the argument proceeds. One positive beat prompts a negative beat, which prompts a positive beat, and so on. Every argument produces a counterargument. I say X, you say not-X, and we adjust. You say Y, I say not-Y, and we adjust.

To advance toward the truth on an issue, raise a question and offer an answer. Then look for the flaws in logic and evidence. Then look for a way to respond to those flaws. Then consider an alternative approach. On and on, Socratic analysts look at issues from all perspectives. They move back and forth, considering both positive to negative aspects of the question.

Beat by beat, you move toward some kind of truth.

CASE STUDY: ON THE ELECTORAL COLLEGE SYSTEM

You can use beats for any argument—in science, technology, politics, policy, art, music, education, business, you name it. Look at this op-ed article in the *St. Petersburg Times* about the Electoral College system. The article appeared after the contested 2000 election, George W. Bush won the presidency despite losing the popular vote to Al Gore.

As you read this excerpt, notice the shift back and forth from negative to positive statements.

(–) The Electoral College, adopted as part of a compromise during the Constitutional Convention in 1787, is an anachronism.

(+) But it is one of the more useful anachronisms in the American political system.

(–) The closeness of this presidential election—and the fact that Democrat Al Gore got a majority of the popular vote but lost the electoral vote—has caused critics to call for the Electoral College's abolition.

(+) But the election actually shows the system's merits.

(+) The Electoral College forces candidates to pay attention to the whole country. Without state-by-state tallies, candidates might simply "run up the score" in states where they are strong, rather than compete in close state contests.

(–) What about the people that the Electoral College ignores? After all, candidates that win a plurality of a state's votes capture all of that state's electoral votes. So in a close state, a big chunk of voters get no real electoral representation.

(+) In fact, the Electoral College gives minority voices a greater chance of being heard. A minority bloc has a greater chance to build support at the state level than at the national level.

(–) Still, you have to admit that democracy should follow the will of the majority.

(+) But a popular vote could endanger not only the interests of minorities, but the will of the majority as well. Fragmenting the vote into many parties could prevent the emergence of a viable majority coalition.

(–) Florida's recount controversy—an orgy of lawsuits and disputes over hanging chads—shows the havoc caused by America's federal system of voting. If we just gave the election to the popular-vote winner, Al Gore, we would not even need a recount.

(+) Actually, Florida recount underscores another merit of the Electoral College. Dividing the American electorate into 50 pieces makes it possible to identify voting irregularities. Imagine the chaos of a national recount. Voter irregularities in a national popular vote would get dismissed as "rounding errors." Under the current system, we can identify the source of the problems at the level of state, county, town, or even condominium development.

(+) Democratic vitality does not come from a simple popularity contest. It comes from a system that creates the possibility of consensus—and votes that truly matter.

The assertion that the Electoral College is an anachronism sounds like a condemnation. But the author quickly shifts to praise. Later points make surprising assertions about how the Electoral College influences candidates' behavior, how it makes accountability easier, and how it helps foster consensus through a two-party system. Each point offers a minor surprise.

Beats in arguments show a process of exploration. *Consider this … now consider that … now this … now that.*

———

ELEMENT 70: USE CLIFFHANGERS TO DRIVE ANALYSIS

If you can turn an analysis into a suspense story, you'll *own* the reader. And you'll be able to offer a balanced and powerful critique. In mysteries or suspense stories, the cliffhanger comes at the ends of chapters or episodes. A character finds herself in a perilous situation. Can she survive? Will she? How?

When you leave the resolution of an issue hanging, you invite the reader to play a guessing game. David Rock, a business consultant, explains: "Think of the brain as a *prediction machine.* Massive neuronal resources are devoted to predicting what will happen each moment." Cliffhangers mobilize these neuronal resources, getting the reader actively involved in the story.

To keep readers involved—whether you're penning a murder mystery, a biography, a sports story, or a technical or political analysis—create cliffhangers. Create situations where the reader frantically tries to predict the outcome.

Think of arguments as intellectual stripteases. Ad you make a case, reveal enough information to pique the audience's interest. Raise a question, then tease readers with possible answers, and get them guessing. When you conclude one point, tease your readers with the next puzzle.

Sales people have an expression: "Don't spill all your candy in the lobby." Too often, in their eagerness to win contracts, sales people rush into explaining, in detail, all the costs and benefits of their product. Before even hearing about the needs of their prospect, they offer detailed explanations of why their vacuum cleaner or car or heating system—or whatever—works better than the competition's. In the process, the salesman alienates his prospect. Feeling invisible and unheard, the prospect tunes out.

As a writer, it's better to explore ideas deliberately, piece by piece. It's more effective to tease the reader, creating a guessing game. If you keep the reader intrigued, you will get her to participate in your story or analysis.

When you use suspense to make an argument, you not only keep the reader engaged. You also have a chance to explore all sides of an issue. By lining up a number of possibilities, you can give each possibility its due. If you treat each possibility fairly—showing how much it contributes to the outcome—you will earn the reader's respect and engagement.

CASE STUDY: BARRY BLUESTONE'S 'THE INEQUALITY EXPRESS'

In his study of "deindustrialization" of America, Barry Bluestone explores the decline of the "social contract" between workers and companies. In the years after World War II, big business could count on steady growth and workers could count on decent wages and benefits. But in the 1970s and 1980s, manufacturing declined in the U.S. Wages flatlined. The middle class began to shrink. So Bluestone wonders: *Whodunit?*

Who or what caused this economic transformation? Why did manufacturers lose their competitive edge? Why did they pick up stakes and leave their communities? Why did workers lose their collective voice in labor unions?

One by one, Bluestone explores the possibilities as if they are suspects in a murder mystery. Suspect by suspect, he examines the possible explanations for the decline of American manufacturing:

- **Technology**: "Most businesses are not introducing technology that requires vastly improved skill."
- **The service economy**: "All of the employment growth during the 1980s came in the services sector, where wages were polarizing between high school dropouts and college."
- **Deregulation**: "Intense competition … forced existing firms to extract large wage concessions from their employees."
- **The decline of unions**: "Unions have made only modest inroads into the service economy."
- **Downsizing**: "Firms rely more heavily on part-time, temporary, and leased employees [and create] a 'segmented' labor force."
- **Winner-take-all labor markets**: "Inequality is not only rising across education groups but within them, very likely reflecting such winner-take-all dynamics."
- **Trade**: "Freer trade will ultimately reduce the wages of less-skilled U.S. workers by about a thousand dollars a year, partly as a result of NAFTA."

- **Capital mobility**: "Freer trade generally provides for the unrestricted movement of investment capital across borders."
- **Immigration**: "Central American, Caribbean, and Southeast Asians seeking refuge in this country [have boosted] the supply of low-skill workers seeking jobs."
- **Trade deficits**: "The trade gap … boosts the effective supply of workers at the bottom of the education-to-earnings distribution."

"What do these results suggest?" Bluestone asks. "[T]he answer to our mystery is the same denouement as Agatha Christie's in *Murder on the Orient Express*. They all did it."

That might not be the most satisfying response—you always want to point a finger at one villain—but Bluestone's writing creates suspense while educating us about a complex issue.

To make an argument, parcel out details and evidence slowly. Don't reveal your whole argument at once. Trick the reader sometimes. Make a strong case for an argument, then reveal its flaws. Do the same for other arguments, until you have sorted all ideas and come to a convincing conclusion.

This hide-and-reveal strategy allows you to break complex questions into manageable pieces. Rather than explore the factors behind deindustrialization all at once, Bluestone explores each of those factors, one at a time. With this slow, deliberate exploration of the problem, the reader carefully considers each possible answer before moving to the next.

By moving deliberately, point by point, you can explain terminology, lay out the evidence, and offer caveats carefully. That way, the reader gets what he needs, when we needs it.

———

ELEMENT 71: USE THE SENSES IN ARGUMENTS AND RHETORIC

Can you *see* justice or fairness? Can you *see* economic growth, productivity, or inflation? Can you *hear* relativity? Can you *feel* a normal distribution or a margin of error?

You might see little room for sensory experience in the abstract ideas of philosophy or scientific inquiry. But, in fact, we struggle to understand important concepts without appealing to the senses.

To understand the concept of fairness, for example, we might visualize equal portions of things ... or people taking turns ... or people bargaining with a mediator. To understand power, we might visualize something physical, like muscles or machinery. To understand leadership, we might envision a president in the Oval Office, a manager at a meeting, or a football coach or symphony conductor running a practice.

The more we use real-life images to understand abstract concepts, the better we can understand and explain those concepts.

And so we enter the realm of rhetoric, where reason and emotion join together. Politics often gives rhetoric a bad name. When demagogues twist facts and manipulate emotions, the worst kind of misinformation results. When used honestly, though, rhetoric offers the best way to appeal to both hearts and minds.

But we need emotions to think well. Emotions tap into our experiences—what felt good and bad in the past. They also tap into our capacity for empathy. When we imagine how our actions might affect other people, we think more rigorously. People who lack emotions, like people on the Asperger spectrum, often lack the ability to make hard decisions. Lacking emotional affect, people struggle to sort through information and make a "gut" call.

"Reduction in emotion," the brain researcher Antonio Damasio concludes, "may constitute an important source of irrational behavior."

Think of it this way. Emotions are whole-body distillations of our experience. They give us ways to analyze things, instantly. When a toddler touches a hot stove or an electrical outlet, the reaction is physical and emotional. That toddler knows, immediately and forevermore, that he does not want to repeat that experience. So when he approaches a similar situation, he knows—instantly—what to not to do.

The longer we live, the more experiences we have. We remember those experiences—and make sense of them—because of their physical or emotional elements. The more we can connect emotions to ideas, the quicker and more fully we can make decisions.

The bottom line is that writers need to use sensual language to analyze and convey ideas.

CASE STUDY: MARTIN LUTHER KING'S 'I HAVE A DREAM' ORATION

In the summer of 1963, the civil rights movement reached its moment of truth. The spring campaign in Birmingham, Alabama, broke the back of segregation in the South's most racist and violent big city. Thousands of demonstrations broke out all over the U.S. Long centered in the South, the movement moved into northern cities like New York, Philadelphia, and Chicago. Many activists lost patience with Martin Luther King's emphasis on nonviolence and integration. Meanwhile, President John F. Kennedy introduced the most comprehensive civil rights legislation in American history.

In August, upwards of 400,000 people gathered in the nation's capital for the March on Washington for Jobs and Justice. At that march, Martin Luther King Jr. delivered his "I Have a Dream" oration. King's hoped to hold the many factions of the movement together. Only a united movement could push Congress to enact Kennedy's legislation.

This oration was mesmerizing—but why? What makes King's oration the greatest of modern times?

Was it his urgent demand that America finally—after centuries of enslaving and oppressing blacks—finally grant them basic civil rights?

Was it King's evocation of American mythology and Biblical scripture?

Was it his ominous warning that blacks would no longer settle for half-measures and delay—and that danger lurked in an America without basic rights for all?

Was it King's inspiring image of America's next generation, sitting together at a table of brotherhood, black and white together?

Was it King's brutal honesty to the assembled that, when they returned home, they would face brutality and even death when they continued to agitate for their rights?

All of the above. But the brilliance of the speech goes beyond all that. To see how, go online and listen to the speech (bit.do/kings-dream). Pay attention to how King deploys sensual language to make his case:

- **Kinesthetic**: Crippled ... chains ... languished in the corners ... cooling off ... tranquilizing drug ... quicksands ... solid rock ... whirlwinds ... drinking from the cup of bitterness ...

meeting physical force with soul force ... engulfed ... tied up ... inextricably bound ... cannot turn back ... bodies, heavy with the fatigue ... stripped of their self-hood ... rolls down like waters ... like a mighty stream ... sweltering with the heat of injustice, sweltering with the heat of oppression ... fresh from narrow jail cells ... storms of persecution ... staggered by the winds ...

- **Visual**: A great beacon light ... a joyous daybreak ... long night ... dark and desolate valley ... sunlit path ... the red hills ... the color of their skin ... lips dripping ... every valley shall be exalted, and every hill and mountain shall be made low, the rough places will be made plain, and the crooked places will be made straight ... hew out of the mountain ...
- **Auditory**: The jangling discords ... a beautiful symphony ... able to sing ... let freedom ring ... sing in the words of the old Negro spiritual ...

King could not have touched his audience—or even made his reasoned, logical case—without appealing to the senses and emotions. People *need* emotions to think and act rationally. King used sensory language to tap into people's deepest emotions, in order to explain abstract ideals about the dilemmas of racism and discrimination.

———

ELEMENT 72: ALLOW IDEAS TO UNFOLD, ONE BY ONE

A good writer works like a tour guide. The guide does not point out everything on the tour. He selects a few telling sights and avoids irrelevant details.

When giving your reader a tour of a topic, remember to focus on just one or two things at a time. The more complicated your topic, the simpler your explanation should be. So let ideas unfold, one by one, so the reader follows every step of the process.

Too often, writers pack lots of background information into a paragraph or two, tight as a tin of sardines. But too much information, too soon, overwhelms readers. Your job is to *unpack* the many complex aspects of an issue and explain them, one by one. Use simple, familiar terms.

Remember Louis Malle's film *My Dinner With Andre*? Andre Gregory holds forth at a restaurant, with Wallace Shawn as his rapt audience of one. He talks about his adventures in Tibet, England, the Sahara. For most of the film, Shawn just asks questions: "What do you mean, exactly?" and "What would you actually do?" and "Well, tell me about it" and "You *did*?" That's how explaining works.

Think of your explanation as a list of ideas. You can structure your piece like this: *First, … Then, … Then, … Then, … Finally, …* This format forces you to focus on only one piece of the process at a time. That way you will avoid tripping over yourself, discussing too many issues at a time. Remember: Easy does it.

Recipes offer a useful model for explaining complex ideas. Cooks must perform their tasks one at a time, in the right order. To make a dish, you must move deliberately, step by step. To make cookies, for example, you might start by preheating the oven to 350 degrees. Then you gather eggs, flour, vanilla extract, sugar, chocolate chips, and so on. You whisk the flour and baking soda. Then you beat the butter and sugar. Then you add the eggs, salt, and vanilla. Then …

Preheat oven to 350 degrees.
In a small bowl, whisk together the flour and baking soda; set aside.
In the bowl of an electric mixer, combine the butter with both sugars.
Beat on medium speed until light and fluffy.
Reduce speed to low.
Add the salt, vanilla, and eggs.
Beat until well mixed, about 1 minute.
Add flour mixture; mix until just combined.
Stir in the chocolate chips.
Drop heaping tablespoon-size balls of dough about 2 inches apart on baking sheets lined with parchment paper.
Bake until cookies are golden around the edges, but still soft in the center, 8 to 10 minutes.
Remove from oven, and let cool on baking sheet 1 to 2 minutes.
Transfer to a wire rack, and let cool completely.
Store cookies in an airtight container at room temperature up to 1 week.

Take one step at a time.

To demonstrate the power of recipes as a model for writing, I once brought my Yale writing class to a kitchen, where we made an apple pie. The students narrated the process into a digital recorder. As students sifted and whipped and rolled, they stated what they were doing and how. They also offered their own thoughts about cooking. They talked about family traditions, special kitchen tricks, and likes and dislikes. Afterwards, I transcribed the conversation. The result was a good first draft of an essay on cooking.

Writing requires the same process as cooking or writing recipies: Take your time, do one thing at a time, in the right order, illustrating and explaining as you go.

CASE STUDY: JAMES ALTUCHER'S 'EVERYTHING YOU NEED TO KNOW ABOUT CYBER-HACKING AND THE RUSSIAN ELECTION HACKS'

We still don't know everything about Russia's attack on the U.S. election system in the 2016 election. We probably never will. Decades from now, historians will still debate the Russians' role in Donald Trump's rise to the presidency in 2016—just as, more than a half century later, historians still debate the real story of the Kennedy assassination.

But with the help of experts like James Altucher, we can get a sense of what happened in 2015 and 2016.

A longtime computer hacker, Altucher explains the vulnerabilities to computer networks: the easily guessed passwords, the armies of bots, the phishing expeditions, the use of spear phishing, the pervasiveness of malware, the distortions of electronic polling, and more. Vladimir Putin's invisible army not only overwhelmed social media sites like Facebook and Twitter; it also breached the electronic voting systems in all 50 states. Here are a few examples from Altucher's step-by-step analysis:

> An "open port" sends messages back and forth, like someone waving from a cruise ship as it pulls away. Most ports are simply closed. But some are open in order to receive various special messages. For instance, there is a port that listens for requests for web pages. ...
>
> There are other ports open to listen to other computers on the local network: requests for files to be transferred in non-HTTP protocols (like FTP), and most importantly, requests for email. Some software will OPEN unassigned ports for their own nefarious purposes. Malicious software that keeps track of every letter typed on the keyboard might open and use such a port. VERY common. ...
>
> A "bot" is a small piece of software that sits on your computer and sits on most of the other computers in your company's network. A bot is malicious. It has some code that is ready to do something bad to your network. ... Millions of bots exist on computers around the US. Maybe

70 or 80 percent of companies are infected with "bot armies." They are like sleeper cells waiting for a message to act. ...

I once visited a company manned by about 100 Ph.D.'s trying to figure out how to fight bot armies. They told me something that stuck with me: "No matter how smart we are, the people creating these bots are smarter." ... Bad things are happening and there's nothing we can do about it.

But since networks and security are constantly being updated in various unknown ways each year, it's often hard for the bots to stay updated. This is probably the best defense. ... If your computer is logged onto the Internet for about ten minutes without any security, then there's a decent chance a bot has infected it.

Altucher has two great advantages as an analyst of complex topics. First, he has insider knowledge. As a kid, he hacked for fun and he's been doing it ever since. Second, he takes his time explaining. Idea by idea, he explains how things work. He uses this simple formula:

First, ... Then, ... Then, ... Then, ... Finally, ...

Any time you need to explain something complex, return to that formula. Don't rush. You'll be amazed how well it works.

———

AND ANOTHER THING . . .

Progress in all fields—medicine, technology, machinery, transportation, space travel, psychology—comes from scientific inquiry.

We first learn the scientific method in school. We learn how to identify "variables" that may (or may not) be responsible for different phenomena. Do germs cause disease? Do chemical imbalances cause depression? Do standardized tests improve or impede learning?

But brain research shows us that we need to hear stories before we can explore abstract ideas and relationships. We cannot understand anything logically until we can engage it emotionally and see how the pieces fit into a sequence.

Try this. Consider how you would respond to the following scenarios:

- A vacation in Hawaii.
- Finding a new BMW in your driveway.
- Meeting a childhood hero.
- Finding your soulmate.
- The sudden death of a friend.
- Becoming the target of identity theft.
- Losing a job.
- Getting a cancer diagnosis.

These possibilities, positive and negative, arouse all kinds of emotions—and stories. The moment you read these items, you started to constrict a story about them. Just as we are constructing that story, we begin to analyze it. We step back, consider what kinds of people and issues might be involved in the scenario. If you find that BMW, you might jump for joy. I would immediately research out how to sell it, pay the taxes, and put the proceeds into my retirement accounts. If I am the target of identity theft, I will research different spyware blockers for my computer, reach out to banks and insurance companies, and reconsider how I use my electronic devices. (Actually I should do all that before the identity theft, right?)

Whatever you want to understand or explain a topic, start with a story that arouses the emotions. Then, deliberately and thoroughly, identify the aspects of the story you need to explore in m ore depth. That's the work of analysis.

CHAPTER 19
QUESTIONS AND BRAINSTORMING

WHEREVER WE GO, we ask questions. We spend all our days in dialogue, talking to ourselves and others about family and friends, community and cohorts, coworkers and merchants, and, especially, ourselves. We ask both profound and trivial questions. Teachers, research shows, spend 30 percent of the time in class asking questions —about 100 every hour.

Even when silent, we ask questions. We have 50,000 to 70,000 thoughts a day—many of them questions and answers to ourselves. We have a hard time shutting down our restless minds. "I have a notion," Socrates said, "that when the mind is thinking, it is simply talking to itself, asking questions and answering them."

The best questions explore how people live their lives. What motivates people? How do we deal with the challenges of family and career, struggle and overcoming, life and death? Each of us is a news maven, exploring the topics of the day. How do we create a good health care system? How does the Internet affect the news business? What makes a successful baseball team? How can children be motivated to learn? How can addicts overcome their need for alcohol or drugs or the Internet or food?

Even more important than any question is the string of followup questions. I might ask: What qualities make a person an expert? You might answer intelligence and hard work. So far, so good. But what do we mean by intelligence? Do we mean logic? Knowledge? Skills? How do we measure intelligence? What other qualities strengthen intelligence? Disposition? Interest? And what does "hard work" mean? Can we work hard and fail to gain expertise? Can we work more casually and get the skills we need? Can we quantify how many hours we need to practice to become an expert?

The sharper your question, the more information you'll find. With a focused topic, you know what information to look for—and that information is easy to spot. Looking for information about a broad topic is harder, because piles of information overwhelm us. With a broad topic, we're searching for a needle in a haystack; with a focused topic, we're looking for a needle in a sewing kit.

So how do you come up with a good question? The best way, in my experience, is to write down everything you know about your topic. Put it all on one piece of paper. That's critical. If you need a big piece of paper, that's fine. You can get an 11-by-17 piece of paper at Staples or Kinko's. Just be sure to put everything on one sheet, so you can see every idea that comes to mind.

How do you arrange these ideas on the sheet? Any way you like. Some writers cluster ideas by category. Others show relationships, like cause and effect. Others list sequences of events. Others create hierarchies of ideas. Others list data in one part of the sheet and general ideas or principles in another. Whatever you do, try to make your ideas visual. Draw diagrams and lines and timelines that show connections among the ideas and data.

Thinking begins with questions. Our job, as analysts, is to ask the right questions and screen out distractions. To write well, then, aspire to become a modern-day Socrates.

————

ELEMENT 72: TO GET STARTED, SPILL YOUR MIND

To explore a topic, do lots of research. Activate both your conscious mind and your subconscious mind.

Your conscious mind includes every idea that you can access with a little prompting. If you want to understand a topic, think about people, events, ideas, and events. Make observations and get your hands on data. Pull your files and highlight the key information. Find interview transcripts and material from archives and mark 'em up. Cull your PowerPoint files and look through old emails and memos. Call colleagues to get their perspectives.

All of this "top of the mind" work will produce a good overview of your topic. It might even offer enough information and ideas to write a great piece. But you should also tap into your lifetime of knowledge and insight, think imaginatively. Try to see the patterns that are not immediately obvious. Dig below the obvious information. Burrow into your subconscious to think through your topic.

The subconscious is a complex web of memories, associations, fears, and desires. Many of these thoughts we repress—that's why they're *sub*-conscious—so they often feel illicit or dangerous. We tend to press these thoughts under the surface. So be inquisitive. Even if you think you know the answers, pretend you don't. Turn every issue into a question. Don't believe the answers that occur to you right away. Instead, be curious. Explore the topic as if you don't know much. Be like a scientist: Seek to *disprove* rather than to *prove* your ideas.

Follow these nine practices steps to brainstorm ideas:

1. Prime yourself: Before brainstorming, do as much research as possible. When you read a book or article, write down a label for each major idea in the margins. That way, when you go back to brainstorm, you can review all the key concepts in a few minutes.

2. Keep a notebook: Bring a notebook wherever you go. Whenever you have an insight—especially about the topic of your writing—jot it down. Some people like an old-fashioned paper notebook. Others prefer to use their electronic devices. If you go electronic, try Evernote. This free app helps you jot down ideas wherever you are—on your phone, tablet, or computer. When you write in one place, it syncs automatically.

3. See everything at once: Too often we think serially. We have one thought, then another, then another, and so on. But you need to see all your ideas at once. So grab a big sheet of paper to hold all your ideas. Or spread out your notebook and record all your ideas on a topic on a two-page spread.

4. Ask lots of questions: The brain loves questions. When you ask yourself a question, the brain shifts into search mode. It comes up with all kinds of possibilities, rather than resistance.

Use the "divergence" strategy to generate as many creative ideas as possible. Businesses use "divergence tests" in hiring to find the most creative candidates. Here's how these tests work. Interviewers ask job candidates to list all the ways to understand a word or phrase. Narrow, literal-minded candidates list only obvious ideas; creative candidates list a number of surprising ideas.

Here's an example: *Name all the possible uses of a book.* You could say books offer reading materials, cutout pictures for posters, and goods to barter and sell. A more creative list goes far beyond the book's literary qualities. You might use a book for a doorstops, kindling, a weapon, a writing surface, a cutting board, a straight edge, a fan, a noisemaker, a blotter, coasters, a Rorschach test, and a symbol. How many more uses could you find for a book?

Divergence tests challenge you to leap beyond the obvious. That's a useful model for brainstorming. The more ideas you scribble on your page, the more creatively you can explore a topic.

5. Rush: Too often we suppress our good ideas before they have a chance to flower. We self-edit; we reject incomplete ideas before they have a chance to fully reveal themselves. So let the ideas just flow. Don't worry if they're good or bad. You can sort out them later.

If you rush your brainstorming—scribbling down ideas as fast as possible—we increase the chances that we will make creative associations. Innovation occurs when we connect ideas that no one connected before. As Einstein noted, "combinatory play seems to be the essential feature in productive thought." We cannot combine unlike things if we don't think of them first. So release all restrictions on your mind, at first anyway.

6. Move from sloppy to ordered to sloppy: Once you have filled your sheet with a mass of divergent ideas, see if you can spot patterns. Arrange ideas into categories. Draw lines to indicate connections between ideas.

Don't worry if all the ideas do not fit under your categories or groupings. That's a good sign. It means you have room to grow. So start to brainstorm again, with abandon. Try to squeeze new ideas out of the ideas that don't seem to matter. Then look for ideas to eliminate, either because they are redundant or just uninteresting.

7. Use prompts: To discover ideas, sometimes we need a gentle push. We need the beginning of a thought, with the implicit challenge to complete the thought. Prompts provide those nudges.

Prompts put you right in the middle of a problem, like this:

- Your company's energy costs significantly higher than your competitor's—so how can we remain competitive?
- Your hospital just cut its budget for critical diagnostic equipment—so how can we serve patients just as well?
- Commuters can't take the main highway for a year during reconstruction—so how can we accommodate the region's growing traffic?

You can think of prompts for every field that you might want to write about. Some actually come prepackaged. Consider two of them.

- A handy little book called *Plotto*, published in 1928, lists ideas for three sets of story possibilities—protagonists, possible actions, and possible conclusions. Mixing and matching the possibilities produces a set of 1,462 possible plots.
- A set of prompts called "TRIZ," a Russian acronym for "Theory of Inventive Problem Solving," identifies contradictions in design to guide the inventor to solve problems. Step by step, TRIZ suggests possible ways to mix and match different qualities of materials, energy, size, shape, and more.

Devise your own list of prompts. Write down all the kinds of issues that you would like to explore, even if finding that information seems impossible. If you stick with problems, thinking opening, your subconscious might make connections for you. The key is to tell our subconscious that we need answers. When we set a clear intention, the world opens possibilities for realizing that intention.

8. Mix Words and Images: Whenever possible, draw charts and pictures. Show how ideas relate to each other. When you scribble images, you excite your mind. You move away from linear thinking. You see a whole bunch of ideas, and how they relate to each other, at a glance.

Even if you think you're a terrible artist, draw. Simple stick figures work fine. Use them to illustrate the relations among characters (who), their passions and activities (what), the timing of actions (when), the location of activities (where), the reasoning behind activities (why), and their methods (how).

Try storyboarding. For every scene or section of your story or essay, draw a simple picture that expresses what's going on. Use 3x5 cards. Make a card for every idea. When you have all your ideas—or most of them—start arranging them into different formats. With this process, you will discover new ideas.

9. Chunk and Sort Your Ideas: Once you display your ideas, you need to arrange them. Grab another sheet of paper and create a schematic drawing of all your ideas. Try to identify the three or four major themes. Give each theme a memorable "tabloid headline." Create a hierarchy. Use arrows to show causality. Use big letters to show the fundamental ideas, smaller letters to show lesser ideas. Use bullets to indicate evidence.

After brainstorming, you will have a messy piece of paper with all you need to figure out complex problems. Think of the ideas on that brainstorming sheet as raw materials. With those raw materials, you can now design and build something of value.

CASE STUDY: BRAINSTORMING NONVIOLENCE

Suppose you want to analyze nonviolence as a strategy of political protest.

Start by priming your mind. Read the classics on nonviolence, works by Socrates, Tolstoy, Thoreau, Gandhi, and King. Also read the academic literature, starting with Gene Sharp's three-volume *The Politics of Nonviolent Action*. Explore histories of the American civil rights movement, India's independence movement, the Velvet Revolution, the anti-apartheid struggle, Arab Spring, and more.

Keep a notebook nearby to record ideas as they occur to you. That notebook will come in handy later.

When you brainstorm, *rush*. Let the ideas spill out, regardless of whether they seem to make sense. You can clean up your ideas—organize them, adjust them, add new ideas and images, show new relationships—later.

To explore nonviolence, our brainstorming sheet might look like this:

- **Nonviolence:** moral ("soul force")—Gandhi, Thoreau, Tolstoy, King, Gene Sharp—appealing to public opinion—strategy and tactics—the power of "withdrawing consent" from the system (boycotts, strikes, etc.)—
- **Violence:** escalation of conflict—government has superior resources—
- **Power:** who holds it—who wants it—power's rewards—power's tradeoffs—
- **Paradox:** when nonviolence depends on violence—
- **Examples in history**—India's independence movement, civil rights in U.S., Soviet Bloc countries in 1989, Russian Revolution of 1905—1991 Soviet coup attempt—spring of 1968—Burma?—Tibet?—Egypt 2011—1979 Iran Revolution?
- **Against nonviolence:** need for self defense—"any means necessary" (Malcolm X—what if moral appeals fall on deaf ears?—
- **Advocates of violence (forceful response):** Deacons for the Defense—Negroes With Guns—Black Panthers—Nation of Islam
- **Psychology of violence and nonviolence:** fear—courage—"cleansing" effect—phenomenology—ratcheting effect—escalation—breaking the cycle—Axelrod—
- **Kinds of nonviolent protest:** demonstrations, strikes, boycotts, sit-ins and other "-ins," alternative institutions, monkey-wrenching—
- **Can violence and nonviolence work together?** debate between King versus Malcolm X—combustibility of rallies with "open carry laws" (e.g., Charlottesville)—difficulty controlling rogue elements

Write down as many ideas as possible. Then sort the ideas. Finally, ask a question and begin gathering evidence.

———

ELEMENT 74: ASK THIS-OR-THAT AND W QUESTIONS

We can ask two kinds of questions, This-or-That and W questions.

This-or-That questions offer specific alternatives. For example: *Was*

Hemingway or Fitzgerald the better writer? Do you eat Corn Flakes or Wheaties for breakfast? Are we going to have dinner before or after the movie?

W questions begin with the words *who, what, when, where,* or *why.* While they focus on certain aspects of issues, they can be open-ended. You can answer these questions in countless ways.

Ask questions as if you are interviewing someone. When an answer doesn't satisfy you, ask another question. Push. Probe. Prod. Look for surprises.

For tips on asking great questions, let's turn to one of the great interviewers of the twentieth century. Here's how Studs Terkel, a master of oral history, describes his interviewing technique:

> I keep it simple: "What do you do? What is your day like?" Here's a good example: a gas meter [reader]. I ask: "What's the day of a gas-meter reader like? He says, "Well, it's dogs and women." And I say, "Dogs and women?" And then I realize the first is the reality, the second is the fantasy. You've got to know that. "Well, let's talk about the dogs first."

Terkel starts with the simplest questions, then goes deeper.

The best questions explore *how and why things happen.* What motivates a character? What incentives and arrangements produce a good health care system? What are the limits of free speech in a democracy? How will the Internet shape the news business? What makes a successful baseball team? How can addicts overcome cravings for alcohol or drugs?

If fact, you could combine This-or-That and W questions. Let's work through an example. Start by doing some basic reporting. Ask basic W questions, combined with This-or-That options.

- **Who** succeeds more—natively brilliant people or hard workers?
- **What** matters more—logical analysis or "big picture" thinking?
- **When** do we learn best? Reading? Studying notes and problems? Playing with different intellectual puzzles? Using our hands? Working with others?
- **Where** do we learn best? In the workplace? In school? In a quiet library or a bustling cafe?

- **What** does hard work mean—grinding for hours or organizing work into efficient, doable pieces?
- **How** does failure affect the learner—by discouraging or inspiring more work?

Good questions only begins the process. More important are the follow-up questions: *How come? When? What if ... ? But suppose ... ? I don't get it; can you explain, step by step? If that's true, then why ... ?* And so on.

When you combine This-or-That and W questions, you uncover a wide range of issues for your analysis. For example:

- Who gains the most from raw intelligence—and who gains the most from hard work? Stereotypes suggest that academics, lawyers, and other "white collar" professionals benefit most from raw intelligence, while "blue collar" workers like factory and service workers people benefit the most from hard work. But is that true?
- What do we mean by intelligence? Is Howard Gardner right that there are "multiple intelligences" (e.g., logical-mathematical, spatial, linguistic, bodily-kinesthetic, musical, interpersonal, intrapersonal, naturalistic, existential)? What do we mean by hard work? Does it mean working hard without thinking—or working smart?
- When might we deploy different kinds of intelligence and hard work? Are there circumstances when intelligence matters more—and other circumstances when hard work matters more?
- Where do these qualities matter most? Where do analytic skills work best and where do more practical skills work best? Does intelligence matter more in affluent or poor communities? How about hard work and discipline? In bureaucratic institutions or intimate communities? In work life or family life?
- Why does intelligence sometimes trump hard work—but not always? Why do we think of intelligence and hard work as different qualities, when they are related?

One caveat: As you unfurl a series of questions, keep your eye on a

North Star—the major issue you are exploring in the analysis. When your perspective changes, the North Star keeps you from wandering off course.

CASE STUDY: BRIAN LAMB'S INTERVIEWING STYLE

My favorite TV interviewer is Brian Lamb, the founder of C-SPAN and the host of "Book Notes" for 25 years. His secret? He follows the advice of his high school teacher, who taught him to "stay out of the way."

"I start out with the premise that everyone has a fascinating story to tell," Lamb says. "My job is to get that story and get out of the way." To explain Lamb's appeal, think of his opposite: the voluble TV reporters and commentators of cable TV. *Blah blah blah.* In an age of celebrity journalists, Lamb reminds us of the power of simple questions. In his interviews, Lamb's interview subjects spoke *ten times* as many words as he did. Be like Brian Lamb: Ask a question and then sit up and let your subject talk.

Here are some of the questions Lamb asks Dorothy Herrmann, the author of a biography of Helen Keller:

> *Who was she?*
> *When did she live?*
> *And you say she was deaf and blind. Could she speak?*
> *What about Polly Thompson?*
> *How many books have been written about Helen Keller?*
> *Let me just stop you to ask you who Anagnos was.*
> *Helen Keller wrote "The Frost King" in what year?*
> *And how long was it before that people thought it was a fraud?*
> *Anne Sullivan lived to what year?*
> *What year did you start the Helen Keller research?*

In this passage, Lamb asks one This-or-That question: "Could she speak?" The rest of the time, he asks simple W questions.

Follow Lamb's example. Ask as many brisk questions as you can. Let your interviewee do most of the talking. Let the answers pile up. Then you will have a rich trove of information and insights for your piece.

_____

ELEMENT 75. ALWAYS ASK: WHAT CAUSES WHAT?

People are impatient. When we tackle a complex problem, we want to leap to a conclusion. We want to know what's "best" or "fastest" or "smartest." The problem is that the concept of the "best" does not frame issues clearly. This binary way of thinking—is it X or Y?—narrows our thinking.

Let me explain. Consider the following questions:

- What's the best form of government?
- What's the best business startup strategy?
- What's the best strategy for assembling a good baseball team?
- What's the best approach to acting?

Those questions are important, no doubt. Who wouldn't want to get simple, clear-cut answers to problems, as fast as an answer on a quiz show? But what does "best" mean? When we say something is "best," we are begging the question: *Best for what?* So let's amend those questions to clarify matters:

- What's the best form of government … *for engaging citizens*?
- What's the best business startup strategy … *for identifying a market niche*?
- What's the best strategy for assembling a good baseball team … *for creating and preventing runs*?
- What's the best approach to acting … *for tapping into the character's deepest desires*?

Now we're getting to the nub of the matter. Look closely at these revised questions. Each question is really a search for *causality*. Each seeks to identify which factors *cause* what result.

I would venture to say that all analyses—and all stories too—make a causal argument. That statement can be stated simply:

X → Y

To understand any relationship or issue, we need to understand what factors cause what outcomes. Once we sharpen our thinking about cause and effect, we can get to work. Once we know the specific question we want to answer, we can look for evidence. Once we know what outcome we want to explain, we can explore all the behaviors and variables that might produce that outcome.

CASE STUDY: THE 'BEST' FORM OF GOVERNMENT ... *FOR WHAT?*

Consider this question: *What's the best form of government?* Before we can begin to answer that question, we have to ask: Best for what? Let's consider the possibilities.

What's the best form of government *for economic growth?* Maybe China wins the prize for this category. Here's how the nonpartisan Congressional Research Service describes this remarkable story:

> Since opening up to foreign trade and investment and implementing free-market reforms in 1979, China has been among the world's fastest-growing economies, with real annual gross domestic product (GDP) growth averaging 9.5 percent through 2018, a pace described by the World Bank as "the fastest sustained expansion by a major economy in history." Such growth has enabled China, on average, to double its GDP every eight years and helped raise an estimated 800 million people out of poverty.

The next obvious question is what has caused such a high rate of growth in China? The answer is heavy government involvement in the economy. China's ruling Communist Party directs the economy, boosting some companies and undermining others. The government actively steals intellectual property from foreign companies. The government invests vast sums in major projects, like the Belt and Road Initiative. Government-favored businesses enjoy extraordinary growth; others struggle for survival. Ordinary citizens are subject to surveillance everywhere through their smartphones and computers and public cameras. Still, if you want economic growth, China offers a model.

Next, ask what's the best form of government *for public safety?* In this category, Singapore triumphs. The Overseas Security Advisory

Council, a joint venture of the U.S. State Department and private partners, reports:

> Singapore remains one of the safest cities in the world. According to
> the Economist Intelligence Unit 2019 Safe Cities Index, Singapore
> topped the list as the world's safest city in the categories of Personal
> and Infrastructure security. The "Lion City" also ranked first in the
> 2019 Gallup Global Law and Order report. Crime is generally non-
> confrontational and non-violent in nature, and incidents are typically
> crimes of opportunity (e.g. purse snatching, pickpocketing, theft of
> unattended property). Violent crime is rare. If a weapon is involved, it
> is likely an edged weapon (e.g. knife, box cutter), as authorities strictly
> control firearms, and the punishment for possessing them is severe.

What factors account for such a low rate of crime? Singapore's anti-
crime measures are draconian. The government restricts freedom of
expression, association, and assembly. Violations are punishable by
long prison terms. The government has absolute right to remove
content it deems harmful from the Internet. Littering can bring fines of
$1,000. People convicted of drug offenses can be executed.

What's the best form of government *for educating young people*? Give
that award to South Korea. Here's how the Asia Society describes
Seoul's approach to schooling:

> A typical day finds high schoolers studying before school begins at
> about 8 a.m. Classes run for 50 minutes each, with a morning break and
> a 50-minute lunch period. The afternoon session resumes at about 1
> p.m., and classes continue until about 4:00 or 4:30, followed by the
> cleaning of the classroom. Students may then take a short dinner break
> at home, or they may eat at school. Teachers typically move from room
> to room, while students stay in one place. Students return to the school
> library to study or attend private schools or tutoring sessions until
> between 10 p.m. and midnight.

Now ask: What does this approach to education cause in South Korea?
To start, it has enabled South Korea to transform itself from a Third World
to a First World economy. What else? Critics, though, wonder whether
students enjoy the freedom needed to think and live creatively.

Now ponder this. Suppose you want to make a case that America has the best form of government. Get specific. Ask yourself: *For what?*

————

AND ANOTHER THING . . .

We need the idea of causality to make sense of a complex world. We need to identify what variables can help us to understand the world's complexity. But it's not always easy to tell what's the cause and what's the effect. As the philosopher Frederick Nietzsche writes: "Cause and effect: such a duality probably never exists; in truth we are confronted by a continuum out of which we isolate a couple of pieces."

When we search for cause and effect—and bring preconceived notions to the process—we sometimes mistake one for the other. Consider the conventional wisdom that education causes economic growth:

Education —> Wealth and Economic Growth

So politicians promote new initiatives—new spending for specialized programs, experiments like charter schools, standardized testing for accountability—to improve education. But in *Antifragile,* Nassim Nicholas Taleb argues that the causality goes the opposite way:

Wealth and Economic Growth —> Education

The experience of boom economies in Taiwan and Korea, Taleb argues, suggest that we misunderstand the dynamics of education and economic growth. Formal education did not boost growth there; in fact, Taleb suggests, formal education often *undermines* economic growth. Growth came first, then education. Here's how Taleb describes the issue:

> It's good to have a class of people who are educated. But education is the enemy of entrepreneurship. If you start having a high level of education, you start hiring people based on school success. School success is predictive of future school success. You hire an "A" student if you want them to take an exam, but you want other things like street

smarts [to promote entrepreneurship]. This gets repressed if you emphasize too-much education.

These questions are complex. We need to isolate the variables. But we need to be careful, also, not to choose the variables and measurements that confirm our preexisting point of view.

CHAPTER 20
MAKING A CASE

Put the argument into a concrete shape, into an image, some hard phrase, round and solid as a ball, which they can see and handle and carry home with them, and the cause is half won.

RALPH WALDO EMERSON

PEOPLE WRITE TO PERSUADE.

Academics seek to persuade when they write a history of ancient Rome or explore the connection between protein and cancer. Politicians seek to persuade when they write a piece of legislation. Pundits seek to persuade when they handicap elections. Artists also seek to persuade. In *The Unbearable Lightness of Being*, Milan Kundera makes an argument about tyranny, survival, love, and living in truth. In "Mississippi Goddamn," Nina Simone makes an argument about racism.

Some writers state their theses clearly, like the loud guy in the front pew of church shouting "Amen!" They say, directly, *X causes Y*. The best researchers—in both the hard sciences and social sciences—state their arguments clearly. Look at these examples from academic journals:

- Bacteria that attach to surfaces aggregate in a hydrated polymeric matrix of their own synthesis to form biofilms. Formation of these sessile communities and their inherent resistance to antimicrobial agents are at the root of many persistent and chronic bacterial infections.

- In this book I attempt to state and test a theory of delinquency. The theory I advocate sees in the delinquent a person relatively free of the intimate attachments, the aspirations, and the moral beliefs that bind most people to a life within the law.
- [O]ur analysis shows no apparent link between balance-of-payments and banking crises during the 1970s, when financial markets were highly regulated. In the 1980s, following the liberalization of financial markets across many parts of the world, banking and currency crises became closely entwined.

By stating their cases plainly, these scholars invite the reader to join ongoing debates. They stake their claim on a specific point of view, recognizing that other data or analyses might prove them wrong.

Analysis need not be so dry. Popularizers of scientific research—Malcolm Gladwell, David Rock, Susan Blackmore, Lauren Slater, and Lisa Genova, to name a handful—blend stories and academic analyses. They tell a real-life story, then step back and to provide scientific evidence about the subject. They yo-yo, back and forth, from scene to summary.

This yo-yoing gives readers the opportunity to experience ideas in both emotional and cerebral ways. It engages them in the process of analysis, rather than bulleting them with propositions and evidence. So here's the formula for engaging analysis: Explain the concepts and issues, provide scenes and evidence, and then step back to make sense of it all.

————

ELEMENT 76: CLIMB THE 'LADDER OF ABSTRACTION'

Imagine climbing a ladder that moves from the level of atoms all the way up to the most abstract thoughts. With every step, you reach ever more rarefied air, further from the rock-hard realities of ordinary life. Sometimes it gets disorienting at the top rungs. So then you move down a rung to get a clearer idea of the down-to-earth realities of life.

S.I. Hayakawa, a linguist who also served as a university president and U.S. senator, used this image to explain this range of ideas. At the lower rungs, we see lots of detailed information—specific people, places, actions, and results. At the higher rungs, we see abstract ideas —concepts like war, justice, fairness, and mind.

To think well, we need to up and down this ladder, from the specific to the general, then back down to the specific and up to the general again. Hayakawa argues:

> Interesting speech and writing, as well as clear thinking and psycho-logical well-being, require the constant interplay of higher-level and lower-level abstractions, and the constant interplay of the verbal levels with the nonverbal ("object") levels. ... The interesting writer, the infor-mative speaker, the accurate thinker, and the sane individual operate on all levels of the abstraction ladder, moving quickly and gracefully and in orderly fashion from higher to lower, from lower to higher, with minds as lithe and deft and beautiful as monkeys in a tree.

Whenever you struggle to understand a high-level concept, move down a rung or two. When you need to understand a basic concept, think of concrete examples at the ladder's lower rungs. Once you have a concrete idea of an issue, climb to higher rungs of the ladder to explore the idea in more general terms.

At the lower rungs of the ladder, we will find specific examples and data. One of my high school teachers, a genial and brilliant man named Robert Leonard, used to call the lowest rung the level of "for-instances." The point is to be as specific and concrete as possible. Get specific. Get concrete. Think of this as the "one and only" level of analysis.

As you climb to higher rungs of the ladder, we explore the topic in more general terms. At the second rung, we put that one-and-only thing into a group. At the next rung up, we consider a broader level of the thing; we might call this the set. Still higher is the category to which the set belongs. Finally, at the top, we find a broader universe of categories.

Here's what the ladder might look:

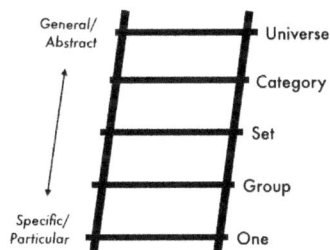

Here's how S.I. Hayakawa illustrated his concept with the example of a cow named Bessie:

- **Universe**: Assets that might be part of a farm or agricultural community, including buildings, infrastructure, systems, technical and business knowledge, professional networks, finance and insurance, and more
- **Category**: Farm asset; the larger group includes fields, harvesters and other equipment, harvested crops, and savings and government grants, to name a few
- **Set**: Farm livestock; the larger group would include chickens, sheep, pigs, goats, horses, donkeys, and mules
- **Group**: Cows of all kinds and places
- **One**: Bessie the cow, the one-and-only creature who lives in a particular time and place

Here's how we might develop the concept of a specific book:

- **Universe**: Communication of all kinds, including written communications, speech, and even databases and spreadsheets
- **Category**: Written communication of all kinds, including books, magazines, newspapers, blogs, reports, proposals, and even emails
- **Set**: Book, which these days could include ebooks as well as traditional pulp books
- **Group**: Novel, a particular kind of book. Others include nonfiction, analysis, poetry, and even picture books
- **One**: *All the King's Men*, by Robert Penn Warren

Here's how we might make sense of one child person teasing and taunting another in a particular time (during gym class, say) and place (at the playing field).

- **Universe**: Values and philosophy
- **Category**: Beliefs and feelings about how people ought to treat each other
- **Set**: Responses to a wide range of social interactions and arrangements
- **Group**: Anger at stronger people beating and taunting weaker people
- **One**: Sam defends Alex from a bullying classmate

Think of the rungs of the ladder this way: The lower the rung, the more concrete the topic, which enables you to visualize it; the higher the rung, the more abstract, symbolic, and general the topic. The bottom level is storytelling; the top level is theory.

To keep your mind nimble—and to explain even the most complex ideas to your reader—move up and down the ladder of abstraction.

CASE STUDY: MICHELE ROMMEL'S 'LOSING OBJECTIVITY'

In her analysis of *New York Times* coverage of two national emergencies —Japan's attack on Pearl Harbor in 1941 and al Qaeda's attacks on September 11, 2001—Michele Rommel examined the news coverage those events for one week each. She developed her own ladder of abstraction to assess the news coverage, ranging from Level 1 (statements of simple facts) to Level 5 (general statements).

Level	Identifying Characteristics	Example
1	Statement of action/being	"The bomb was dropped...," "The president spoke. . ."
2	Report, speaker identified	"The President said the troops rushed. . ."
3	Report, speaker anonymous	"Sources say the troops were ambushed..."
4	Evaluation of action/being	"The life-snatching bomb...," "An inspiring speech ended..."
5	Statement of opinion	"This horror should not be endured..."

She compares how *The Times* covered the two events:

Level	Pearl Harbor	Pct.	Sept. 11	Pct.
1	738	50	487	46
2	343	23	173	17
3	201	14	104	10
4	167	11	179	17
5	32	2	109	10

As you can see, the *Times* coverage in 2001 used twice as many general statements than it did in 1941. Evaluative and opinion statements (Levels 4 and 5) rose from 13 percent of all statements in 1941 to 27 percent in 2001.

"The results of this study suggest that news media, as represented by *The New York Times*, are losing objectivity in their reporting of surprise terrorist attacks on America," Rommel notes. "By reporting so much subjective emotion, the news media are not simply exposing popular sentiments—they are providing a construct in which to think and feel about the events." Put simply, media increasingly tell people what to think and feel rather than simply providing facts for audiences to assess on their own.

When people seek simple answers to complex issues, they often embrace general statements rather than taking the time to gather and analyze the issues in detail. A statement like "This horror should not be endured" may offer moral certainty. But such statements also short-circuit gathering of hard knowledge and critical thinking. Intelligent citizens need to think for themselves, not allow someone else tell them what to think.

All of the rungs on the ladder of abstraction serve important purposes. High levels of abstraction provide categories for thinking; more specific descriptions provide data and information for those categories.

Rommel's work models this principle. She carefully defines her terms, categorizes them, and then counts how many instances *Times* coverage fits those categories. Deftly, she moves up and down the ladder of abstraction.

S.I. Hayakawa would be proud.

———

ELEMENT 77: IDENTIFY AND OPERATIONALIZE VARIABLES

Analysis, as we noted before, is really a process of figuring out *what causes what.*

Scientists and mathematicians use the term *variables* to explain the many different factors involved in complex situations. For example, the Pythagorean theorem—

$$a^2 + b^2 = c^2$$

—has three variables, *a, b,* and *c.* When a variable on one side of the equal sign changes, a variable on the other side changes too.

To answer any complex question, you need to explore a wide range of possible explanations. Consider all the possible causes of the problem you seek to explain. What, for example, are the possible causes of wage stagnation? Of global warming? Of poverty? Of school performance? Make a list of all the possible factors that may explain the outcome you want to understand. Those are your variables.

To do their work, scientists usually talk about two kinds of variables:

- **Dependent variable**: The result, consequence, effect, or outcome. This is what you want to explain.
- **Independent variables**: All of the variables that might—or might not—explain the outcome. In other words, the factors that contribute to a particular result.

Consider the simple question: *What causes a student's performance to decline?* The dependent variable refers to the result we want to explain: student performance. The independent variables refer to the factors that cause the result: innate intelligence, social milieu, school quality, and more.

At assess a complex issue, we need some way to measure both dependent and independent variables. We need to gather evidence.

For the dependent variable of student performance, we might use data for grade-point average, class rank, or test scores.

For the independent variables, the factors that might contribute to an academic decline, we might consider class attendance, time spent on homework, teacher quality, family life, after-school activities, physical wellbeing (like sleep, nutrition, and exercise), faith, workload, pressures outside of class, among others.

How might we gather data--or put differently, how do we find things to count? Too start, we need to *operationalize* our variables. Some variables would be simple. We can easily count the number of minutes spent on homework and nightly hours of sleep. But we have to get clever to operationalize ideas like teacher quality, the quality of family life, and pressures outside class. To assess teacher quality, we might gather data from annual ratings or training. A family life score might require information about the presence of parents at home, the existence of home routines, the availability of books, and even whether the family eats meals together.

Let's explore operationalization in some detail. How can we find things to count? Consider just a few possibilities:

- **Existing data**: Organizations keep ungodly amounts of data on what they do. Business track labor costs, sales numbers, capital investment, productivity, debt, profits, stock prices, and more. Sports teams track player performances, fan bases, operating costs, and more. Schools track student grades, family backgrounds, faculty performance, teacher and administrator salaries, student demographics, and more. The government gathers data on every conceivable aspect of the population.
- **Surveys**: If you want to gather your own information, you could conduct a survey. Find a representative group of people and ask them questions. You can ask about behavior, possessions, experience, attitudes, you name it. As political pollsters discovered in the 2016 and 2020 campaigns, surveys falter when respondents do not give accurate information—either when they lack the awareness to answer accurately or they do not want to tell the truth. But well-worded questions can work around that problem.
- **Observation**: Watch what people do, recording each relevant piece of information. If you want to explore how people use space, set up a time-lapse camera to record people's actions. William Whyte does this in *City*, his study of urban life. If you want to assess people's shopping habits, go to stores and observe the way they move from display to display,

touch items, and gather goods in baskets. Paco Underhill does this in *Why We Buy*, his study of the retail industry.

- **Experimental data**: Set up experiments to see how people—or even lab rats—respond to different situations. Devise situations where experiment subjects face two or more choices. Or create a situation where subjects must respond to a change in circumstances. Or ask subjects to participate in an activity and ask them questions afterwards. Be sure to get a big enough sample size to detect patterns.
- **Auto-counts**: In the information age, we count things automatically as we work, buy, watch, and surf. Every time you get online, your computer tracks your actions. Google keeps tabs on your searches—and therefore, your interests and obsessions. Amazon gathers data on your searches and purchases—not just your obsessions, but what you're willing to pay for. No major company, in fact, doesn't gather and use these kinds of data. We now have so much data that we can measure virtually every aspect of human life.

Often, we create new statistics out of a set of smaller measures. Economists use the "Misery Index" (the sum of the unemployment rate and the inflation rate) to determine the strength of the economy. Baseball analysts use OPS (a combination of on-base percentage and slugging percentage) to determine the value of a hitter. Reading specialists use the Flesch Reading Ease Score (the average number of words per sentence and the average number of syllables per word) to measure reading ease.

After we identify and operationalize independent variables, we can analyze our data, one by one. This is what researchers mean by "isolating the variable." To see if one variable produces a significant impact on a process, we will see how changing that variable produces different results. To make sure that other variables don't distort the results, we will hold other variables "constant." In other words, we look at one variable at a time.

To assess what factors affect student performance, for example, we might start with data on how much students sleep. Then we might explore other possibilities. Maybe sleep doesn't matter as much as other variables, like alcohol use, kinds of classes, or peer influences.

Once you identify the variables, gather data on each one. Test the variables in different combinations. One by one, add variables to the equation. When one variable changes the equation more than another, we can conclude it's probably more important.

CASE STUDY: HOW DOES GOVERNMENT CREATE ORDER AND OPPORTUNITY?

How can a society prevent violence and promote happiness and prosperity? This is the fundamental question of politics and government.

In *Leviathan*, published in 1641, Thomas Hobbes offers a simple answer: strong authoritarian government. Hobbes argues that people are selfish and prone to violence; without some central authority, society will be ripped apart in a "war of all against all." Without a strong government, people would face "continual fear and danger of violent death" and their lives would be "solitary, poor, nasty, brutish, and short." But with a strong "sovereign," society can achieve a "commodious" level of material wellbeing and security.

In 1973, political scientists named John Orbell and Brent Rutherford decided to test his proposition. They started by operationalizing the key variables of the Hobbes hypothesis: Leviathan-like government control, violence in society, and the commodiousness of everyday life.

Too assess "Leviathanness," their catch-all term for government control over society, Orbell and Rutherford identified several factors: the political system's constitution, how much power any branch of government may wield, and the extent to which interest groups and political parties can influence policy.

To assess the level of violence—"war of all against all"—Orbell and Rutherford use statistical measures of civil strife (attacks on persons or property), conflict behavior (assassinations, general strikes, guerrilla warfare, purges, riots, demonstrations, people killed in domestic violence), and political violence (records on events in which physical force was used against other people).

Finally, to assess "commodiousness," Orbell and Rutherford tallied measures like mail per capital, income, literacy, movie attendance, and life expectancy.

The researchers then crunched the numbers and found that centralized, authoritarian systems actually produced greater levels of violence and lesser levels of material wellbeing. "Hobbes's predictions are wrong on both counts," they concluded. "It seems that social order is better maintained in politics without the concentration of governmental powers that Hobbes advocated."

The Orbell-Rutherford study, published in the *British Journal of Political Science* in 1973, produced a firestorm of criticism. To begin, the scholars misunderstood Hobbes. He did not advocate for any permanent totalitarian government; rather, he argued for a government strong enough to enforce a simple peace, which then allowed people freedom to pursue their own lives and pursuits.

In addition, the way Orbell and Rutherford operationalized their variables bordered on the absurd. Does the volume of mail, for example, really reveal a person's relationships with other people? Just think of all the junk mail you get every day and ask if it makes you feel connected to other people.

The lesson is simple. When you decide what to count, in order to measure variables, be careful. Avoid misstating the terms of the debate (like the idea that Hobbes would support authoritarian governments) and poor measures of key variables (like counting mail ton indicate sociability).

————

ELEMENT 78: CRUNCH THE NUMBERS

After identifying and operationalizing the variables, the next job is to gather and assess data on each one.

Researchers use a number of different statistics to analyze relationships. The statistical tools you choose depends on what you're trying to understand.

Test the variables in different combinations. One by one, add variables to the equation. When one variable changes the equation more than another, we can conclude it's probably more important. We can even assign numbers to measure how important.

Let's look at a few maneuvers you can do with numbers. Ask a hypothetical example, let's explore the test scores in a hypothetical class. Suppose the 15 students in the class earn the following grades: 67, 72, 72, 73, 74, 77, 78, 79, 79, 84, 94, 95, 96, 98, 98. What we learn about the class, the teacher, and the students? Here's a short list of statistical measures to analyze issues:

• **Minimum, Maximum, and Range**: To start, consider the

highest and lowest values and the distance between two. These figures tell you, without any hard labor, whether scores fit a short or long range.

The minimum score here is 67, the maximum 98, and the range 31 —a full distribution of faster and slower learners. With a low score had been 88, we might wonder if the material is too easy. With a low score of 52, we might wonder whether some students don't belong or if the teacher simply teaches poorly.

• **Mean**: The average of all cases. When you want a simple measure of what's "normal," find the mean. The mean helps us make sense of cases both near (close to average) and far (deviation).

The average score—calculated by adding all of the scores (1,235) and dividing by the number of cases (15)—would be 82.4.

• **Median**: The midpoint for all cases. In cases with extremes, the median offers a useful way to find out what's normal. In cases with lots of extremes, the average might not reflect the norm for the group. The midpoint sometimes does a better job showing what's "normal" in a group.

In a set of 15 scores, the midpoint is the eighth case. And that score is 79. So half of all students scored 78 or lower and half scored 78 or better. This class was split; some did very well and some did very poorly. That poses a different challenge for the teacher than if, say, all students got an 84 or 85.

• **Mode**: The value that occurs most frequently in a sample. The mode helps to identify common values that might exert greater influence on the mean or median.

In this case the mode scores are 72, 79, and 98. This statistic captures the split performances in the class.

• **Standard deviation**: How much a particular cases differ from the mean. A low S.D. tells you that the scores lie close to the average; a high S.D tells you that the scores are far from the average. The lower the S.D., the more homogenous and predictable the scores are.

The standard deviation in this case is 10.86, which indicates very high variety and unpredictability among grades.

• **Correlation**: How a change in one variable relates to a change in another variable. Correlation shows how related two factors are. A positive correlation occurs when two variables move in the same direction; a perfect correlation would have a score of 1. A negative correlation happens when the variables move in opposite directions; a perfect negative correlation would have a score of –1. Two variables with no correlation would have a score of 0.

Correlation does not mean that X *causes* Y, but it does suggest a relationship. Study time and test scores might be correlated but not causally related. That judgment requires further inquiry.

In our case study, additional data might reveal that time spent studying correlates well to exam grades. We might find that TV time correlates negatively to test scores.

• **T-Test**: Whether the means of two groups are substantially different from each other. T-Tests offers a way to assess whether two groups are comparable. They offer a way to see whether you're comparing apples with apples or apples with oranges.

Suppose we divided the class into two groups and the advanced students just happened to land in one group and the struggling students in the other. They would get a high T score. That would tell you that the two groups might need different approaches to teaching and learning.

Take care when using statistics. The nineteenth-century British Prime Minister Benjamin Disraeli warned against "lies, damned lies, and statistics." Bill James, the man who revolutionized baseball with exotic statistics, agrees. "Whenever we try to prove something by statistical analysis," James says, "we are at risk of going wrong in 6,000 ways."

CASE STUDY: EDWARD GLAESER ON URBAN VITALITY

To understand the role of cities in economic life, Harvard economist Edward Glaeser uses a wide range of variables. To explore economic vitality, for example, he looks at statistics for population, jobs, taxes, investment, and new firms. To explore housing markets, he looks at rents, new- and old-home sales prices, vacancy rates, permits, and construction costs and times

Then he gets clever. He compares regional economic data with the temperatures of different cities in winter months. Why temperatures? He wants to see whether a preference for warm weather communities gives the Sunbelt an advantage over the Frostbelt.

Let's look at one of those variables. Start by plotting the growth rates of 20 American cities from 1950 to 2000 against the average temperature for the cities in February.

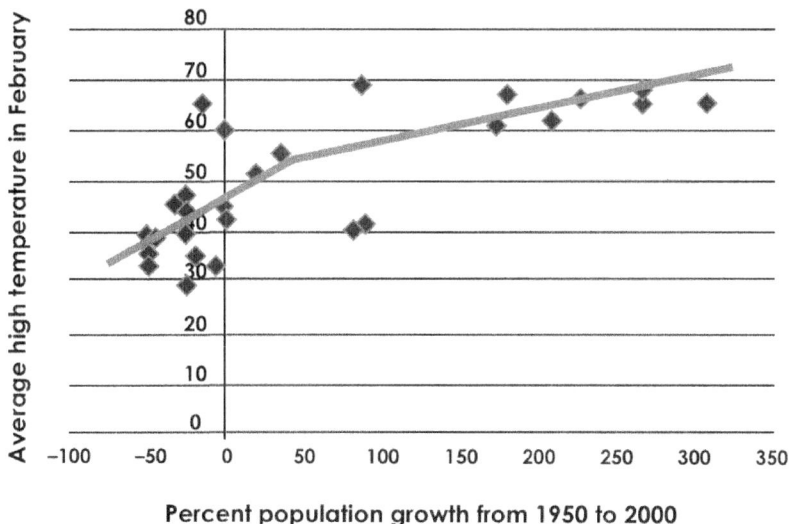

Percent population growth from 1950 to 2000

Then organize the cities into groups. Let's put all the cities with average February temperatures in the 20s and 30s, 40s, 50s, and 60s. What population trends do we see for all of the cities in those groups?

Cold-weather cities, we see clearly, lost population in this period; warm weather cities gained population. The upshot? To compete, cities in frigid climes need to mobilize other resources.

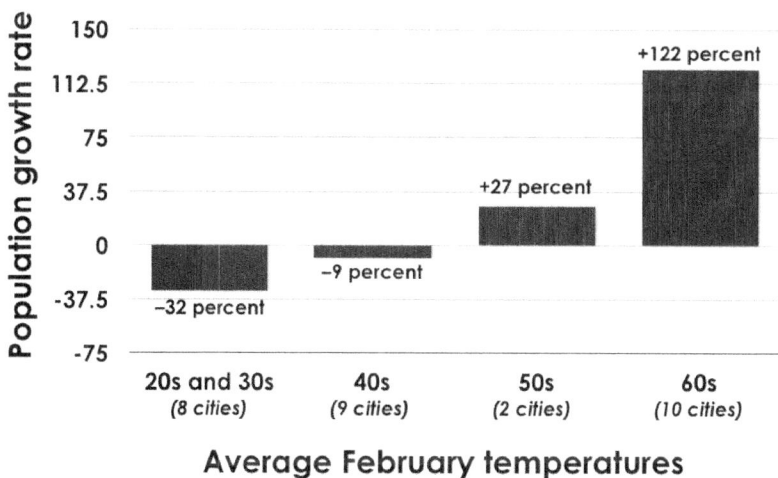

Average February temperatures

Like what? To figure it out, Glaeser offers two other clever measurements—statistics on car ownership and college degrees. Car ownership offers a proxy measure for regional sprawl since people need cars more in spread-out communities. And college degrees offer a good proxy measure for the education levels of the workforce. After crunching the numbers, Glaeser identifies "sun, sprawl, and skills" as the three leading variables for metropolitan economic growth.

At their best, statistics identify not just what variables *contribute* to an outcome, but *how much*. So Glaeser, through his statistical analysis, shows the importance of three variables to economic vitality. In this example, Glaeser can provide measures of simple correlation to make his point. To go deeper, he could determine the standard deviation to show just how much, say, growth rates varied in warm-weather cities than in cold-weather cities. He could also do a T-test to compare the averages in different groups.

So if we're creating an economic development strategy for a city, we can set priorities. If we're in a warm-weather area, we can emphasize the comfort of living there. If we live in a cold-weather region, like Boston or Minneapolis, we need to emphasize education at all levels. Whatever the location, we might consider how to provide affordable housing throughout the area.

Often the simplest numbers do the job. Consider use of real-time data to drive management and policymaking during Martin O'Malley's tenures as mayor of Baltimore and governor of Maryland. Rather than using all kinds of exotic measures, the "stat" process often began and ended with simple counting. Matthew Gallagher, a top policy advisor to O'Malley, once told me:

> I think you can get pretty far with addition, subtraction, multiplication, and division. And the vast majority of the analysis that we did fell into eighth-grade math skills. ... In one meeting I said something along the lines of, 'You know, we ought to do a regression analysis on these five data series.' And there were probably 50 people in the room and it just went way over everybody's head. Honestly, there wasn't like a huge appetite for that level of analysis.

Like all aspects of life, sometimes getting the simple things right goes a long way toward understanding complex challenges.

―――――

ELEMENT 79: PLAY THE GAME OF HALVES

A music director was talking about the tricks he uses to find the right voices for his community choir—and how to eliminate the off-key voices.

"I give them a simple song that they all know, like 'Twinkle Twinkle, Little Star.' I tell them to sing with gusto. And then I listen."

When he hears a discordant voice, he cannot always tell who is responsible. But he knows, roughly, the location of the off-key sound. So he cuts the group in half. "OK, just the tenors now!" he says. Or: "Everyone on the right side of the room, sing out!"

Halving the voices might not be enough to spot the wayward warbler. So he breaks the group in half again—and again, if necessary. Quickly, though, he identifies the problem.

As the director proceeds, he double-checks and triple-checks his assumptions. "The last thing I want to do is lose a good voice," he says. "I like to be wrong when I think I had found a bad voice. Maybe the bad-sounding singer was affected by someone nearby. Maybe he wasn't breathing right. Maybe he grew up in a family of bad singers. With some coaching, he might help the choir. So I want to prove my suspicions wrong."

Doing analysis works like that. You start with a big "universe" of possibilities, then deliberately isolate the possibilities. Eventually you identify the two or three factors that might answer your question. Then you test them.

The Greek philosopher Democritus called this approach the "game of halves." What would happen, Democritus wondered, if he could break a piece of matter in half, again and again? How long would it take to get to the smallest piece? Would the makeup of the pieces change when taken apart? What about when they're put together in different combinations?

When isolating variables, to separate "the signal from the noise," scientists look for ways they might be wrong. They seek to "disprove the hypothesis." Good scientists are actually happy when they discover flaws in their argument. They know that if they don't catch their flaws, someone else will. They also know that discovering flaws can point the way to other possibilities and, eventually, the truth of the matter.

Scientists take a deliberate, step-by-step process to move from information to insight. I suggest a simple process that moves through the following stages: *steep, spill, show and tell, cluster, cut, test, scale,* and *close.*

- **Steep**: Start by investigating your subject by reading books and articles, exploring archives and data, and interviewing people. Find out what experts say about the subject. Stand on the shoulders of others.
- **Spill**: This is brainstorming. Using all your resources— research materials, prior knowledge, logical leaps, educated guesses, wild speculation—spill all kinds of information in one space. In our discussion of brainstorming, I suggested getting a tabloid-size sheet (11 inches by 17 inches) for your purposes. Onto that sheet, spill everything you know, think, guess, or wonder.
- **Show and Tell**: Now take a stab at a story. Find some aspect of your subject and describe it in a narrative. Identify the "characters" and how they interact. Use your imagination. Be speculative. Find stories that suggest possibilities. If you think economic interests cause war, tell a story that makes that argument. Then tell a different story that focuses on something else, like ideology, religious values, greed, or fear.
- **Cluster**: Once you express your ideas, get another 11x17 sheet and cluster those ideas into different categories. Don't force it. If an idea doesn't fit under any categories, create a new category—or let it go. Lots of ideas won't fit anywhere; they're "outliers." But hold on to them. Keep them close by. You might need them later.
- **Test**: You are almost there! Now you need to test your variables. Operationalize your variables. Find something to count. Then test the variables, one by one.
- **Scale**: Expand and contract the "universe" of possible explanations. A computer analyst, for example, needs to zoom out to explore all the possible coding options—or zoom in to find the algorithm that works best for a particular need. A social scientist needs explore topics like war, peace,

wealth, poverty, or group formation as broadly as possible—
then zoom into the aspects of those issues that hold the
greatest explanatory value.

- **Close**: Now decide what the evidence shows you. Boldly,
but also modestly, state your conclusion. Remember to make
it causal: X, combined with certain other variables but not
others, causes Y.

Throughout the process, you are playing the game of halves. You expand and contract your questions, possible answers, variables, measures for variables, and answers. Like the back of the shampoo bottle says, you need to "rinse and repeat," over and over.

CASE STUDY: EXPLORING THE CAUSES OF WAR

If we wanted to come up with the biggest, hairiest, most audacious question imaginable, it might be something like this: *What causes war?* That question explores all of the elements of the human experience—psychology, economics, politics, geography, religion, language, wealth and poverty, technology, communications, historic rivalries, arms wars, power, and more.

So to illustrate the game of halves—and all the stages you need to take to do an analysis—lets's see what we can say about armed conflict.

- **Steep**: To gain a basic understanding of the causes of war, we might read a number of studies—both popular and academic, nonfiction and fiction. To get academic grounding, start with *An Introduction to the Causes of War*, by Greg Cashman and Leonard Robinson or Chris Coyne's *Handbook on the Political Economy of War*. For theoretical insight, read Sun Tzu's *The Art of War*, Carl von Clauswitz's *On War*, or Hannah Arendt's *On Revolution*. For notable accounts of American wars, see James McPherson's *For Cause and Comrades* (Civil War), Winston Churchill's *The Gathering Storm* (World War I), and David Halberstam's *The Best and the Brightest* (Vietnam), to name just a few.

- **Spill**: Now that we have explored the issues involved in war, we can brainstorm a number of variables (with prominent examples from history in parentheses):

Territory (the enduring battles of France and Germany
over Alsace and Lorraine)

Economic resources (proxy wars for access to oil)

Transitions in power (the fall of Soviet-bloc regimes)

Social movements (the anti-apartheid movement in South
Africa)

Religion (the holy wars of Islamic regimes)

Race and ethnicity (Yugoslavia, Rwanda)

Systems of government ("democracies never fight other
democracies")

Government instability (Depression-era regimes)

The use of war as a political diversion ("bread and
circuses")

Arms proliferation (Europe before World War I)

Trafficking in illicit drugs and prostitution (the influence
of the Medellin cartel)

Unstable international alliances (post-Bismarck Europe)

Entangling alliances (the secret ententes before World
War I)

Enduring rivalries (NATO and the Soviet bloc)

Discourse ("fighting words" of politicians, journalists,
and others)

Misunderstandings and miscommunications (the XYZ
Affair, escalation after the murder of Franz
Ferdinand)

Mercy. That's not even a complete list. Still want to do this? Let's go
. . .

• **Cluster**: Now organize these ideas into categories. Let's start with
the standard categories of economics, politics, and culture. So:

Economic factors

- Struggles over geography, especially transportation routes
- Economic strength
- Access to resources like oil and minerals
- The demands of the arms industry
- Wars over tariffs and trade rules
- Trafficking in illicit drugs and prostitution

Political factors

- Struggles over geography, especially transportation routes
- Transitions in power
- Social movements
- Systems of government
- Government instability
- The use of war as a political diversion
- Unstable international alliances
- Entangling alliances
- Internal instability and demagoguery
- Enduring rivalries
- Misunderstandings and miscommunications

Cultural factors

- *Religion*
- *Race and ethnicity*
- *Internal instability and demagoguery*
- *Mass media and propaganda*
- *Discourse*

Now comes the hard part. We have a question: *What causes war?* Now we need to identify variables, operationalize the variables, and gather and assess evidence.

• **Show and Tell**: Now we might explore a few examples of wars to explore the dynamics of armed conflict. Consider, for example, the tragedy of the American Civil War.

Historians have debated the causes of the war since Confederate soldiers attacked Fort Sumter, South Carolina, in the spring of 1861. The primary school story tells us that Abraham Lincoln fought the Confederacy to free the slaves. Most accounts agree that Lincoln fought to keep the Union whole. Now, shift perspective. Why did the South leave? Was it to maintain slavery? To protect plantation interests? To protect the prerogative to expand slavery into western territories? Protect global trade, which was threatened by high tariffs imposed periodically by Northern interests? Prevent the North from gaining control over Congress?

So let's try a story:

After the Panic of 1857, the long-simmering debate about tariffs—which had split North and South since the beginning of the Republic—burst into the open again.

The South, which favored low import taxes on goods, seemed to win the tariff battle with the passage of the Walker Tariff of 1846. But with the economic meltdown, northern interests agitated for a higher tax on imports.

The wily John Sherman took advantage of new House Speaker William Pennington's inexperience in 1859. When Pennington asked advice on committee assignments, Sherman pushed high-tariff allies. Sherman himself headed the Ways and Means Committee—and with it, the authority to promote the high tariff.

The House passed the Morrill tariff in 1860 in the midst of the presidential election campaign. That year, Abraham Lincoln made two issues the center of his presidential campaign—holding the union together and enacting a high tariff. Both enraged the South. The following spring, as Southern states announced their secession from the union, the Senate passed the Morrill tariff.

As Lincoln vowed war to preserve the Union, the tariff took effect. The tariff advanced the cause of Northern urban industrialists at the expense of Southern agrarian interests. Despite last-minute efforts to negotiate a compromise between North and South, the guns of war sounded at Fort Sumter on April 12, 1861.

If you accept this narrative, you might accept the argument that economic factors cause war. So maybe economic conflicts also caused the Peloponnesian War, the Seven Years War, the Napoleonic wars, the two world wars, the proxy battles of the Cold War, and the wars in Iraq and Afghanistan? Maybe; that's a debatable, testable thesis.

• **Scale**: The story of the American Civil War, of course, highlights a number of issues (not just economics, but also geography and ideology) but excludes others (like language, religion, and past enmities). To understand which factors may influence other conflicts, we need to expand our pool of wars.

Here's where the debate gets tricky. On what scale do we operate? If we stay with the big, hairy, audacious goal of explaining what causes *all wars*, we need to develop a data set that spans centuries. We need to identify a wide range of variables for the causes of those wars, then figure out how to assess them.

Or we could stay with a case study of a single war, as we have done so far with the U.S. Civil War. But that would not tell us about civil wars in other places. If we care about current history, we might care more about civil wars in Latin America or Asia than we care about the American civil war. If so, we need to expand our search to include all civil wars in a particular period.

So, for the sake of our illustration, let's look into civil wars in modern history. Civil wars play an increasingly important role in modern conflict. In fact, 94 percent of all armed conflict in the post-Cold War era (1989-2003) were internal conflicts. So how do we define a civil war? Let's start with this definition: *A civil war is an internal conflict with at least 1,000 combat-related deaths a year.* Only with such a clear-cut definition can we gather data.

• **Test**: We have surveyed the topic, brainstormed for ideas, told a story, and then decided what scope to give our analysis. Now it's time to gather data and test different variables. For an exemplary example, take a look at a detailed study of civil wars by Paul Collier and Anke Hoeffler, "Greed and Grievance in Civil War," published by the *Oxford Economic Papers* in 2004.

Like police detectives investigating a murder, Collier and Hoeffler look for motive and opportunity. What makes people want to break away from an established country? Using a sample covering 79 civil wars, Collier identifies a number of variables, along with measures for those variables. Under the category of "motive," or the grievances that rebels might have, the authors focus on four possible causes:

Possible causes	Example of operationalized variable
Ethnic and religious hatreds	Polarization measure developed by Joan-Maria Esteban and Debraj Ray
Political repression	Gastil Democracy Index, a measure of political openness developed by the Freedom House
Political exclusion	Countries in which the largest ethnic group constitutes 45 to 90 percent of the total population
Economic inequality	Ratio of the top to the bottom quintiles of income

Under the category of "opportunity," which assesses how well rebels could attract resources, the authors identify four more basic categories:

Possible causes	Example of operationalized variable
Dependence on natural resources	Ratio of primary commodity exports to GDP
Donations of diasporas	Size of emigrant group living in the U.S.
Funding from hostile governments	Position of the country in the Cold War
Low costs of rebellion	Mean income per capita, male secondary education, and growth rate of the economy

Using these and other measures, Collier and Hoeffler conduct regression analyses to determine which variables played significant roles on the breakout of civil wars. The most important factors, they conclude, are:

- The number of months since previous conflicts
- Level of democracy
- Social fractionalization
- The size of the country's diaspora
- Ethnic dominance
- Commodity exports
- Oil exports

Surprisingly, ethnic and religious tension, income inequality, and land inequality play insignificant roles in causing civil war.

So what matters more—motive or opportunity? "We cannot reject one model in favor of the other," the authors say. The best they can do is to identify the variables that make a significant difference. That gives us valuable information, as policymakers and ordinary citizens, about how to avoid a civil war.

———

AND ANOTHER THING . . .

The word analysis comes from the Greek *analusis*, from *ana* (meaning "up" or "throughout") and *lysis* (meaning "a loosening"). Analysis, in other words, is about breaking things up to see how they fit together.

Whatever we study, we want to figure out what causes things to come together and break apart.

What makes the elements of a larger entity work—separately and together? What causes bonding, connection, commonality? What creates splits, dissonances, tensions? How are these connecting and separating influences change over time?

How do relationships work? What are their basic elements? What about businesses? Nations? Political alliances? Schools? Neighborhoods? And what about less tangible things, like patriotism and prejudice, tolerance and manners, determination and patience?

How do health epidemics occur? What are their elements? How do they come together and break apart? What kinds of public health policies can contain these epidemics? What mistakes do governments make in their approach to epidemics? Why?

As the coronavirus pandemic of 2020-21 showed, societies thrive when they analyze these problems intelligently—and they suffer when they don't.

POSTSCRIPT: WRITING IS LIFE

At the beginning of our journey, I offered the Golden Rule of Writing. If you follow this simple imperative, I promised, you will write well every time—every sentence, paragraph, story, chapter, essay, report, book, you name it. It's so simple, and it yields powerful results instantly, but it takes real effort to make it automatic.

Then we explored how to write five specific kinds of essays—a profile of a person, a description of a place, a depiction of action, a breakdown of a complex process, and an analysis of a complex issue.

This sequence offers an ideal way to learn, because we move from the most concrete to the most general. As we explore these writing topics, we also learn about the mechanics of writing.

I think of this process as a modern form of apprenticeship.

Throughout history, novices learned skills by working as apprentices. The apprentice worked side by side with a master craftsman. The master talked the apprentice through the process, demonstrated how to use tools, and then invited the apprentice to try his hand. The apprentice tried and failed until he mastered the skills. Over time, he came to understand the logic and theory behind the work.

So I have tried to work with you, side by side. I have shown you the flow of the process, from beginning to middle to end. I have shown you how to take the pieces apart and put them back together again. And I have shown you how to step back and make sense of a complex, abstract issue.

As you embark on your journey, I want you to celebrate your work. Writing, you see, is not just an intellectual or emotional enterprise. Writing touches the deepest aspects of human life.

Writing is teaching. Writing is learning.
Writing is showing. Writing is telling.
Writing is disclosure. Writing is concealment.
Writing is raw. Writing is polished.
Writing is wild. Writing is disciplined.
Writing is intimate. Writing is universal.
Writing is intellectual. Writing is spiritual.
Writing is struggle. Writing is triumph.
Writing is power. Writing is humility.
Writing is a royal pain. Writing is a joy.
Writing is complex. Writing is simple.
Writing is everything we can think of. Writing is life itself.

Writing is, of course, ultimately a journey. We don't always know where we're going, or what we need to do to get there. The destination may change. Our feelings might change along the way. We always find surprises. And at the end of the process, if we do all the little things right, we're better for the experience.

In these times of change—when journalism, publishing, schools, work, and everything, in fact, involving the production and consumption of words, has changed—one truth remains. That truth is that writing matters, and always will.

Our job is to seize the dizzying new opportunities of writing. If we do that, we can all create great gifts, wherever we are, whatever we do.

A FAVOR

Thanks for reading. I appreciate the time you have given to reading this book.

Can I ask a favor?

Log on to your social media sites right now:

- LinkedIn
- Facebook
- Instagram
- Pinterest

If you're inclined, consider posting a review on Amazon.com. Give potential readers honest feedback about what you have learned by reading this book?

If you belong to an organization that cares about writing—a school, a business, a community group—consider setting up a seminar. If you organize an event of 10 or more people, you qualify for a tuition waiver.

Finally, drop me a line. Write to charleseuchner AT gmail DOT com. Tell me what you think.

Thanks again. I really appreciate it.

CHARLIE EUCHNER

SEMINARS AND CONSULTING

The core concept behind *Writing about Politics and Society* is WAC—Writing Across the Curriculum.

The best way to learn any subject, research shows, is to write about that subject. Only when we can explain a topic do we really understand it, inside out. The theoretical physicist Richard Feynman was not just famous for his breakthroughs in quantum electrodynamics. He was also revered for his dynamic style of teaching—explaining complex topics. Here is his formula for learning about any subject:

(1) Choose a topic that you want to master.
(2) Pretend you are teaching that topic to sixth-grade students.
(3) Find the gaps in your lesson. Review your notes. Rephrase the ideas so they are more accurate, complete, and understandable.
(4) Review and simplify your explanation.

Teachers do this verbally all the time. But an even greater challenge is putting these ideas on paper.

To transform learning in your organization, you might consider holding special seminars on writing across the curriculum. Invite Charles Euchner to deliver a one- or two-day seminar on writing in politics and society.

Euchner's Writing Seminars for Writing and Society show students at all levels how to write to explore.

Also consider using Euchner's consulting services to make writing the centerpiece of learning throughout the department or school. With a wealth of experience in higher education—as a professor, researcher, and administrator—Euchner can help you devise the plan to make writing a core learning tool across the curriculum.

ACKNOWLEDGMENTS

This book is the product of hundreds of conversations with fellow writers and teachers, students, people in business and government, and friends and family. I would like to thank a handful of the most important of those people.

Students in my writing classes at Columbia and Yale joined me in a bunch of terrific conversations about writing. I would make suggestions, the students would try them out, and then we would explore what worked and what did not. For the insights of this book, I owe them more than anyone else. I would also like to acknowledge Fred Strebeigh and my other colleagues at Yale, who offered potent advice about both writing and teaching in our many meetings over the years.

A number of people read drafts of this book. Marsha Rabe gave an early draft a careful proofreading and improved it immeasurably. So did Laura Meyerovich, Donna Baer Stein, and Isabel Chenoweth. Myra Brown, Katie Hafner, and Aaron Ritzenberg also offered invaluable advice.

I presented early versions of this book in seminars at Vanderbilt University, The Graduate Institute, the Met School of Providence, the National Education Association of New Hampshire, the New Haven Free Public Library, the Utah Humanities Book Festival, the International Book Fair, the State University of New York at Purchase, Hamden Hall Country Day School, Gen Re, the Eli Whitney Museum, Christian Community Action of New Haven, Codman Square Health Center in Boston, Richmond Events, NetCom Learning, Amneal Pharmaceuticals, Sandler Training, Oxford University Press, and a number of smaller groups.

Finally, Isabel Chenoweth and her children, Walker and Leila, offered their love and support throughout the process of writing this book. I cannot imagine life without the three of them.

ABOUT THE AUTHOR

Charles Euchner, a longtime college teacher and author, is the creator of The Elements of Writing, the only comprehensive system for mastering writing in all fields.

Euchner (pronounced *Ike*-ner) has taught and directed research institutes at a number of premier universities, including Harvard, Yale, Columbia, Penn, Holy Cross, Northeastern, and St. Mary's. He was educated at Vanderbilt and Johns Hopkins.

He is the author or editor of ten books. Critics have praised *Nobody Turn Me Around: A People's History of the 1963 March on Washington* (Beacon Press, 2010) as a dramatic reinterpretation of the civil rights movement. *Kirkus Reviews* calls it "dynamic ... sharp, riveting." Juan Williams, author of *Eyes on the Prize*, calls it "compelling and dramatic." Curtis Wilkie, a longtime chronicler of civil rights, says the book provides "a panorama of vivid characters." Roger Wilkins, a former White House aide in the civil rights era, said it "brings it all back in vivid detail." A short documentary based on the book, written by Euchner, won the award for best writing and editing at the 2011 Re-Image Film Festival and has aired on PBS stations.

Euchner's other books include works on the state of sports in modern America (*Playing the Field, The Last Nine Innings,* and *Little League, Big Dreams*), grassroots politics (*Urban Policy Reconsidered* and *Extraordinary Politics*), presidential politics (*Selecting the President* and *The President and the Public*), and regional politics (the two-part *Governing Greater Boston* project).

Euchner delivers writing seminars and keynote addresses all over the United States. His topics include writing, civil rights, sports, and urban politics and planning. To learn more, email charleseuchner@gmail.com.

In addition to his career in academe, Euchner has also been a reporter for *Education Week* and the coordinator of Boston's citywide master planning process. He has contributed to major newspapers and magazines including *The New York Times, The Boston Globe, The American,* and *Commonwealth,* and has been interviewed for hundreds of media outlets including "Nightline," "All Things Considered," "The Diane Rehm Show," "Talk of the Nation," "NBC Nightly News," and more.

For information about Writing Code seminars, call (203) 645-6112 or email charlie@theelementsofwriting.com.

———

www.theelementsofwriting.com
www.writeacrossthecurriculum

PRAISE FOR THE ELEMENTS OF WRITING

The Elements Of Writing—from, which *Writing the Essay* is drawn —has won praise from teachers and writers alike:

The Elements of Writing is an essential reference for writers and storytellers. I use it myself and recommend it to my students. The classic literary examples are extremely helpful. I feel smarter just having this book by my bedside, and I discover new insights every time I pick it up.

> – *Lee-Sean Huang, cofounder and creative director, Foosa*

The rare writer's handbook that is both useful and a pleasure to read. The book's structure is original and smart; aspiring writers can read the book cover to cover or can look up specific issues. Besides articulating his own "tricks of the trade," Euchner offers a huge, wonderful array of examples. In clear, lucid terms, Charlie Euchner explains and shows what makes for strong prose.

> — *Aaron Ritzenberg, Department of English, Yale University*

This book offers a great way to get everybody from students to practicing professionals excited about the skills, knowledge, and work habits that go into the composition of clear, solid prose. Too often, this information gets presented in a way that turns people off or triggers anxiety, making the challenge of writing well seem far more daunting than it really is. Charlie Euchner's approach gets the job done with just the right blend of rigor, encouragement, and fun.

— *Alex Heard, Editorial Director,* Outside *magazine and author of* The Eyes of Willie McGee

Charles Euchner is the rare talent who can both write and teach. As I struggled to write my first book, he pulled me back to reality and explained the tricks of the trade. With brilliant simplicity, he explained all the big—and little—things that lead to a successful book. Remember what you are trying to say. Open each story with a strong lead. Use stories to explain your analysis and concepts. Help the reader see, feel, and smell the situation. Within a month, I had learned what I needed to write a book. Euchner has now codified his wisdom. This book which teaches all the skills you need to become a strong writer. Trust me, it works.

— *Former Ambassador Nancy E. Soderberg, author,* The Superpower Myth

Writer and educator Charles Euchner provides a simple, intuitive, skill—based approach to writing in all genres. I've incorporated the approach in my classroom to help my students write their autobiographies. It is difficult to write about one's life, but this book helps students to find the right words, in the right order, to construct their personal narrative. It's a must read for all educators who are serious about guiding the young authors to unlock their unique voices and develop as both writers and thinkers.

— *David Cass, Teacher/Advisor, The Met School, Providence, R.I.*

Lots of people, especially writers in business, know what they want to say but are not sure how to get it down in a comprehensible and simple fashion. Euchner has a dead simple tool that will help in composing and editing any written work.

—*Gerry Lantz, President, Stories That Work*

FOR MORE INFORMATION

You can transform writing in your organization—your business, school, agency, or other group—with just one seminar.

Books are great. You can immerse yourself for hours in a book, and you can go back to check facts or do exercise.

But seminars offer a more dynamic setting. As questions arise, you can ask them. You can work on projects as a group—creating stories, developing characters, showing action, building sentences, editing drafts, making arguments. Students not only learn from the seminar leader, but also reform each other. The sparks from one student creates new learning possibilities for others. In a seminar, you engage all the senses. You encounter surprises.

Consider bringing Charles Euchner, the author of *The Elements Of Writing,* to your organization. Euchner will not only teach you the simple, intuitive skills of writing—in his breakthrough story-to-construction-to-analysis sequence—but will give you strategies to put your new skills to work right away.

The payoff—faster, better writing, with more opportunity for creative and rigorous thought—comes right away.

Charles Euchner's seminars have been praised for their fast-paced but relaxed style and the breadth and depth of information. Participants in seminars get workbooks and other supplemental materials to master all the skills of writing on the spot.

Email charlie@theelementsofwriting.com or call (203) 645-6112.

Printed in Great Britain
by Amazon

36304103R00243